GENDERED LIVES IN THE WESTERN INDIAN OCEAN

Indian Ocean Studies Series

Richard B. Allen, series editor

Richard B. Allen, *European Slave Trading in the Indian Ocean, 1500–1850*

Erin E. Stiles and Katrina Daly Thompson, eds., *Gendered Lives in the Western Indian Ocean: Islam, Marriage, and Sexuality on the Swahili Coast*

Gendered Lives in the Western Indian Ocean

*Islam, Marriage, and Sexuality
on the Swahili Coast*

EDITED BY

Erin E. Stiles and
Katrina Daly Thompson

OHIO UNIVERSITY PRESS
ATHENS, OHIO

Ohio University Press, Athens, Ohio 45701
ohioswallow.com
© 2015 by Ohio University Press

Printed in the United States of America
Ohio University Press books are printed on acid-free paper ∞ ™

25 24 23 22 21 20 19 18 17 16 15   5 4 3 2 1

Cover image: Typical henna decorations prior to Islamic wedding.
(Wikimedia Commons)

Cover design by Beth Pratt

Library of Congress Cataloging-in-Publication Data
Gendered lives in the western Indian Ocean : Islam, marriage, and sexuality on
the Swahili Coast / edited by Erin E. Stiles, Katrina Daly Thompson.
   pages cm. — (Indian Ocean studies series)
 Summary: "Muslim communities throughout the Indian Ocean have long
questioned what it means to be a "good Muslim." Much recent scholarship on
Islam in the Indian Ocean considers debates among Muslims about authenticity,
authority, and propriety. Despite the centrality of this topic within studies of
Indian Ocean, African, and other Muslim communities, little of the existing
scholarship has addressed such debates in relation to women, gender, or sexuality.
Yet women are deeply involved with ideas about what it means to be a "good
Muslim." In Gendered Lives in the Western Indian Ocean, anthropologists,
historians, linguists, and gender studies scholars examine Islam, sexuality, gender,
and marriage on the Swahili coast and elsewhere in the Indian Ocean. The book
examines diverse sites of empowerment, contradiction, and resistance affecting
cultural norms, Islam and ideas of Islamic authenticity, gender expectations,
ideologies of modernity, and British education. The book's attention to both
masculinity and femininity, broad examination of the transnational space of
the Swahili coast, and inclusion of research on non-Swahili groups on the East
African coast makes it a unique and indispensable resource"— Provided by
publisher.
 Includes bibliographical references and index.
 ISBN 978-0-8214-2186-4 (hardback) — ISBN 978-0-8214-2187-1 (pb) — ISBN 978-
0-8214-4543-3 (pdf)
 1. Women—Tanzania—Zanzibar—Social conditions. 2. Muslim women—
Tanzania—Zanzibar—Social conditions. 3. Sex—Religious aspects—Islam. [1.
Family life—Tanzania—Zanzibar. 2. Tanzania—Social conditions.] I. Stiles, Erin
E. II. Thompson, Katrina Daly, 1975–
 HQ1798.5.Z8Z3635 2015
 305.409678'1—dc23

2015026449

Contents

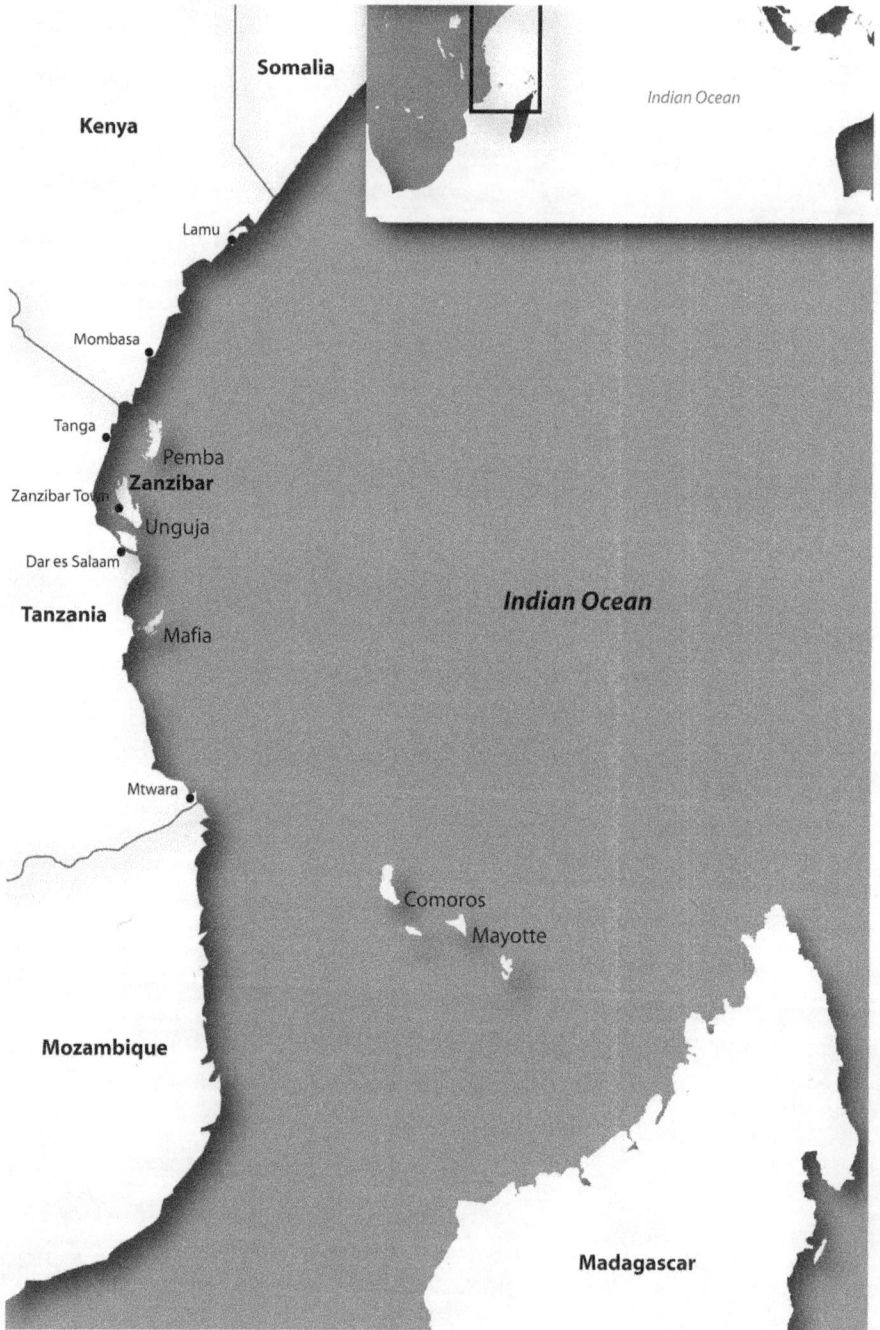

Somalia

Kenya

Lamu

Mombasa

Tanga

Pemba

Zanzibar

Zanzibar Town

Unguja

Dar es Salaam

Tanzania

Mafia

Mtwara

Mozambique

Comoros

Mayotte

Indian Ocean

Indian Ocean

Madagascar

Introducing Gender, Sexuality, and Marriage into the Study of Islam in the Western Indian Ocean

KATRINA DALY THOMPSON AND ERIN E. STILES

MUSLIM COMMUNITIES THROUGHOUT the Indian Ocean and beyond have long debated what it means to be a good Muslim. A great deal of recent scholarship on Islam in the Indian Ocean considers debates among Muslims about authenticity, authority, and propriety vis-à-vis the influence of Islamic reformism and reformers, "those groups whose ideology pushes for social re-instatement of what they regard as 'pure Islam,' as it was practiced by the Prophet and his followers, and who are publicly visible in their activism against undue innovative practices (bid'a)."[1] Notable among them is anthropologist John R. Bowen's now classic work *Muslims through Discourse,* which examines Islamic belief and practice in the eastern Indian Ocean through debates in the highlands of Aceh, Indonesia.[2] In the western Indian Ocean, anthropologists Michael Lambek and Kai Kresse have each similarly examined Muslim debates about knowledge, authority, and ritual practice in Mayotte and the Kenyan coast, respectively.[3] In the introduction to *Struggling with History: Islam and Cosmopolitanism in the Western Indian Ocean,* Edward Simpson and Kai Kresse argue that although "Islam underpins many of the social networks that span the Indian Ocean," we should question how much "unity" a general adherence to Islam gives to the region. They write that despite the "importance of an imagined Muslim community . . . it will have to be conceded by insiders and outsider observers alike that, especially among Muslims who share apparently similar beliefs, factionalism and creative rivalries often exist."[4] In fact, they argue that "the most fundamental of social equivalences" for Muslims is not a shared experience of Islam but rather "a general tendency in society to exist between reformers and those they seek to oppose."[5] Debates about authenticity and appropriate piety are thus central features in Muslim communities the world over. Despite the centrality of this topic within studies of Indian Ocean, African, and other Muslim communities, little of the existing scholarship has addressed such debates in relation to women, gender, or sexuality.[6] Yet women are deeply involved and impacted by debates about what it means to be a "good Muslim"—a label that often hinges on notions of normative gender performance and understandings of appropriate Islamic sexuality that affect both men and women.

Bridging some of these gaps in existing scholarship, the key question this volume asks is how ideologies of normative sexuality and gender are discursively constructed, performed, negotiated, or rejected within and outside marriage. We address this question by considering the gendered experiences and practices of Islam on the westernmost edge of the Indian Ocean, examining debates and changing understandings of what is "Islamic" with reference to marriage, sexuality, and normative understandings of masculinity and femininity. In this way, we build on a growing body of scholarship in the study of Islam in the Indian Ocean and beyond that considers debates about authenticity, authority, and proper Islamic practice, over time and in response to historical and global forces. In particular, we extend the body of work that considers how these debates play out in the gendered lives of Muslim women and men in other parts of the world through our focus on the Swahili coast.[7]

The Swahili coast includes the coast and islands of East Africa that border the Indian Ocean, from southern Somalia to northern Mozambique. It is called the Swahili coast because it is the home to people who speak various dialects of Swahili as their first language, and the name "Swahili" itself comes from the Arabic word *sawāhil* (sing., *sāhil*), meaning "coast." Most first-language speakers of Swahili are Muslims.

The Arabic-derived names for Swahili people (Waswahili), Swahili culture (Uswahili), and the Swahili language (Kiswahili) index the long history of interaction between coastal East Africans and other Indian Ocean peoples, including not only Arabs but also Persians, Indians, and other Asians from as far away as China. All these peoples, as well as Europeans who colonized Kenya, mainland Tanzania (then Tanganyika), and eventually Zanzibar, interacted with coastal Swahili speakers and in some cases intermarried with them, creating long-lasting influences not only on the Swahili language but also on the practice of Islam, local systems of governance, law, and education, architecture, food, clothing, and more. Contemporary coastal East Africans continue to interact with the Indian Ocean region through annual trips to Mecca for the *haji* (hajj; <Ar. *hajj*), travel to visit friends and family in Oman, through the import of clothing and other goods from the Persian Gulf, especially Oman, Saudi Arabia, and the United Arab Emirates, and the export of goods such as cloves to India and Indonesia and mangoes to the Gulf States.[8]

The Indian Ocean region is increasingly understood as an important part of the study of Africa.[9] Historian Gwyn Campbell, for example, proposes the term *Indian Ocean Africa* to describe the entire eastern portion of the continent.[10] Such an approach brings a necessary focus on the relationships between people along the Indian Ocean littoral, relationships between ordinary people and relationships that preceded not only European hegemony in Africa and India but also the concept of the nation-state.[11] Scholars of the Swahili coast, in particular, have argued that we can better understand cosmopolitanism and globalization within East Africa by contextualizing it within the Indian Ocean region.[12]

In this book, we focus on diverse local sites along the western Indian Ocean, including Mombasa and Lamu Town in Kenya and Zanzibar Town, rural northern Unguja, Mafia, "Peponi" (a pseudonym for a village near Tanga), Pemba, and Mtwara in Tanzania. While we encouraged the contributing authors to focus on local sites along the Swahili coast rather than to conceive of an abstract and essentialized Swahili culture, it is important to remember anthropologist Michael Lambek's words: "It is difficult to imagine any society that is simply traditional, simply local."[13] Thinking about local sites on the Swahili coast not only as local but also as part of the Indian Ocean region allows us to see how, despite their uniqueness, they are interconnected, not only as societies in which various aspects of "Swahili culture" are created and lived out and where Swahili is spoken but also as sites with shared histories of trade and interaction with other Indian Ocean societies. Anthropologists Edward Simpson and Kai Kresse have argued that the "impression of unity" in the Indian Ocean region is in fact "derived from particular kinds of social diversity which are recognizable to people within the region."[14] Such unity-in-diversity is evident in the various places you will encounter in this book, where Swahili cultures draw on diverse cultural practices that derive from Africa, the Middle East, Asia, and beyond. In particular, they share a religion (Islam), similar trading practices, experiences of colonialism, and ongoing—even increasing—globalization. We touch on each of these briefly before moving on to a closer examination of this book's contribution to the scholarship on gender and sexuality within changing conceptions of Islamic authenticity.

Many Indian Ocean studies scholars have argued that Islam is the common thread that unites the region as a cohesive area. Zanzibari historian Abdul Sheriff, for example, argues that three prominent cultural themes in Indian Ocean Studies are Islam, slavery, and mobility.[15] Similarly, cultural studies scholar Isabel Hofmeyer delineates three of the major themes in Indian Ocean studies as Islam, creolization, and the transoceanic passages of people.[16] Indeed, in proposing that we think about eastern Africa as "Indian Ocean Africa," Gwyn Campbell suggests that we cannot study Islam in eastern Africa without considering the region's relationship to the rest of the Indian Ocean world. David Parkin similarly observes a consistency across the Indian Ocean that comes from a shared Islamic tradition.[17]

Scholarship on Islam in the Indian Ocean has focused on some key issues. A number of scholars have considered Islam in the Indian Ocean through the work and efforts of traveling scholars and have argued for recognizing something akin to an Indian Ocean public sphere that is rooted in Islam and sustained by religious intellectuals in port cities.[18] Hofmeyr, for example, writes, "Islam provided the dominant idiom of public life in most coastal cities and promoted new categories of travelers, most notably pilgrims, administrators and scholars using Arabic as an international language."[19] With regard to the Swahili coast, anthropologist John Middleton has similarly argued that an "important area of exchange is educational and religious services and duties, as Islamic scholars move from one town to another, establishing schools and religious beliefs and opinions."[20]

Many studies of Islam and Muslim networks in the Indian Ocean have thus considered how people and ideas move about the region. An excellent example of this is Anne K. Bang's *Sufis and Scholars of the Sea* (2003), in which she traces the physical movement and intellectual impact of the scholar Ibn Sumayt between Hadhramaut (southern Yemen), Comoros, and the eastern coast of Africa. Bang writes that "the Indian Ocean was to a large extent crowded with 'middle men' like Ibn Sumayt, trading in different goods, but leaving behind a piece of their baggage—be it material, religious or intellectual."[21] Bang's focus is thus on the impact of scholarly exchange with Hadhramaut on Islamic thought and practice in eastern Africa. In particular, she suggests the impact of the 'Alawiyya (a Sufi order based in Hadhramaut) on the rise of a "new Islam" in nineteenth-century Africa. She notes, for example, that the popular practice of *maulidi* (<Ar. *maulid*; a celebration of the Prophet Muhammad's birthday) was instrumental as a "vehicle of Islamization" in Lamu and Zanzibar.[22]

THE SITES you will encounter in this book are all places where Islam is practiced by the majority of the community. Using several sites on the Swahili coast as examples, historian Edward Alpers points out that while "what one knows about Lamu or Baga-moyo may not hold true for Pemba at any point in time," Swahili societies are nevertheless "characterized by local variations on a general theme of Afro-Islamic culture."[23] Many scholars use Islam as indexical of an early Swahili identity, such as Middleton, who writes, "The population of the coast may be said to have be-come 'Swahili' by the eleventh century, with a general acceptance of Islam and the appearance of modern forms of the Swahili lan-guage."[24] Some have even gone so far as to argue that one cannot be Swahili without being Muslim, although of course there are some people who are culturally Swahili but practice Christianity or who have lapsed in their practice of Islam. Islam is so much a part of Swahili identity that some in the region believe that one can "become Swahili through the adoption of Islam and Swahili culture,"[25] although Janet McIntosh shows that, at least in the case of the Giriama in Malindi (Kenya), "profound differences of 'blood' or [other] deep constitutional differences" prevent them from being recognized as Swahili even after adopting Islam.[26] It is important to emphasize that Islam is an essential part of Swahili culture rather than essential to the identity of every individual within Swahili societies. Recently, Kjersti Larsen has argued that as Swahili communities are experiencing decline in economic, po-litical, and social conditions in recent decades, "Islam is re-invoked as a source of knowledge that not only explains the current state of life and living, but also gives directions on how to cope with and to change the situation for the better. Islam is both what reinforces Swahili identity and a particular way of life, and at the same time, given the current international climate, further marginalizes Swahili society in the eyes of the 'other.'"[27]

If Islam is an important part of Swahili identity, so is cosmo-politanism—what historian Laura Fair calls "a discursive and performative practice" that reflects "a sophisticated appreciation for international mixing and appropriation of cultural styles and symbols from multiple, geographically dispersed sites."[28] The Indian Ocean world is an arena in which numerous European countries, as well as the United States, came into contact with Africa, the Middle East, and Asia.[29] Many of these regions made their mark on the Swahili coast through both colonialism and the slave trade. Arabs arrived on the coast as early as the seventh century, introducing Islam and playing an important role in the slave trade, through which Africans from the interior were captured and exported to the Arab world. Kilwa Island, a port city just off the coast of what is today southern Tanzania, became the leading trading center for the region. The earliest Europeans to reach the region were the Portuguese, in the late fifteenth century,[30] conquering Mombasa, Kilwa, and the other islands. By the late sixteenth century, coastal people had begun to resist the Portuguese through alliance with Omanis who had settled along the coast. Throughout the seventeenth century there were military struggles between the Portuguese and the Omanis, and the Portuguese were eventually pushed out. The eighteenth century saw an increased demand for slaves in southern Arabia, as well as in various European colonies, including the Mascarene Islands (east of Madagascar), which at the time were controlled by France. A number of treaties between the British and the Omanis signed in the nineteenth century eventually made the slave trade illegal, during which time Zanzibar—by then the headquarters of the Omani sultanate—had also become a British protectorate.[31] German colonists arrived in Tanganyika in the late nineteenth century, making it part of German East Africa, which also included present-day Rwanda and Burundi. They also controlled the Kenyan coast as part of the German protectorate, but lost these areas to Britain after just a few years. Present-day Kenya had become part of the British East Africa Protectorate in the late nineteenth century and a British colony in 1920. When Germany was defeated in World War I, the British took control of Tanganyika, ruling the country until its independence, in 1961. Britain remained in control of both Kenya and Zanzibar until 1963. The Omani sultan continued to rule Zanzibar until the following year, when the sultanate was overthrown during what came to be known as the Zanzibar Revolution.

German and British colonialism, in particular, strongly influenced the systems of government, law, and education along the Swahili coast, as they did in other parts of East Africa. Today we find "traditional" systems of education such as *unyago* (a puberty ritual for girls) alongside local Islamic schools (*vyuo* [sg.

chuo] or *madarasa* [lit., "classes"]) and government-run schools (*shule* or *skuli*) modeled after the British system. Legal systems in Zanzibar and Kenya combine elements of both Islamic law and British common law.

In light of the long history of coastal people's interactions with the Indian Ocean region, Europe, and, more recently, the United States, we can see that globalization is not a new phenomenon.[32] Indeed, historian Jeremy Prestholdt's recent work carefully argues this point by showing how consumer tastes in nineteenth-century East Africa both shaped and were influenced by the global economy.[33] What is new, perhaps, is the rate at which people, products, and cultures now spread around the globe, making their impact on the Swahili coast and causing rapid cultural changes. Since the influence of the Arab world and India has been going on for so many centuries, it tends to be the more recent influence of the West that coastal people notice and associate with globalization. Today, almost everyone in the region has some access to a cell phone, for example, and these are used not only to talk and send text messages to friends and family locally but also to communicate with extended family in Oman or those on hajj in Mecca, and, increasingly, to connect to the Internet and post photographs to Facebook. Globalization has long affected weddings (a central focus of this book), with most of the Swahili terms related to marriage and weddings borrowed from Arabic—such as *arusi* (wedding, also *harusi*), *nikaha* (legal marriage ceremony), *mahari* (dower; or bridal gift), and *hina* (henna). Wedding dresses and cosmetics are imported from the United States and other Western countries; henna designs are copied from Yemen, India, and the Gulf; flowers that originated in India are used to scent the bride and her marital bed; and expensive video cameras are brought from Dubai to document the many celebrations that constitute Swahili weddings.[34]

GENDER, MARRIAGE, AND SEXUALITY IN THE INDIAN OCEAN

All the chapters of this volume focus in some way on aspects of gender, sexuality, and marriage. In Indian Ocean studies, an emphasis on the public sphere has meant that these topics have often been overlooked. For example, Hofmeyr notes that "recurrent rubrics" or "unifying themes" in studies of the Indian Ocean are "trade, capital and labour; religion (often linked to trade); pilgrimage; travel; war, colonial rule and anti-colonial movements; and port towns. Other themes focus on particular groupings like Muslims, the Portuguese, British rule and so on."[35] Scholarship on the transoceanic passage of people has largely focused on male merchants and slaves, leaving women largely absent from the literature.

Only a handful of publications have looked at the role of women in relation to the Indian Ocean region, such as Mandana Limbert's focus on women who have moved from East Africa to Oman, Minou Fuglesang's examination of women's use of Hindi film videos in Lamu, and Sarah Mirza and Margaret Ann Strobel's demonstration that transnational cultural connections are part of the everyday lives of women in Mombasa.[36] These examples are part of a substantial literature on women's lives on the Swahili coast, which we bring into conversation with other Indian Ocean scholarship.

Throughout the Indian Ocean and elsewhere, travelers established sexual relationships with local women, who were often slaves.[37] For example, cultural anthropologist and historian Engseng Ho contrasts the way that "Hadramis and other non-Europeans" engaged with locals in the Indian Ocean with the way that Europeans colonized other parts of the world: "non-Europeans entered into relations with locals that were more *intimate,* sticky, and prolonged than the Europeans could countenance."[38] Ho's reference to intimacy euphemistically indexes all kinds of relationships between Arabs, Africans, Indians, and other non-Europeans: friendships, trading partnerships, slave ownership, concubinage, marriages, and more. Many scholars refer, in passing, to intimacy or marriage between Arabs and Africans as the basis for the "creolized" nature of Swahili culture. The notion of creolization speaks to both creolized, or mixed, cultural practices and the role of women in intermarriage and childbirth. Zanzibari historian Abdul Sheriff speaks to these intimacies on the Swahili coast in a passage typical of Swahili studies scholarship:

From the times of the *Periplus* [*of the Erythraean Sea*], many of the crew and passengers perforce liaised with or married local women to produce a rainbow population both racially and culturally. Some of them settled down and were absorbed, adopting the local language and much of the local culture; but in the process they also imparted to the host community elements of their own cultural heritage in language, literature and belief systems, laying the basis for a new synthesis that is uniquely Swahili.[39]

Given the frequency of references to "liaisons" between traveling men and local women and the creolization or cultural synthesis that characterizes the Indian Ocean region, it is surprising that marriage and sex have not been a more significant theme in Indian Ocean studies. The work of anthropologists Akbar Keshodkar and Mandana Limbert are notable exceptions: Keshodkar examines how Zanzibaris of Indian ancestry maintain a group identity and diasporic connections to India through endogamous marriages, and Limbert considers marriage between Omanis in East Africa and among those with Zanzibari heritage in Oman.[40]

Even when "liaisons" across ethnic groups are mentioned, the focus on mobile men and (presumably more stationary) local women tends to elide the question of women's agency in these intimate relationships. Sometimes, such elisions allow scholars to depict women as having more agency than they probably did. For example, historian Patricia Romero writes, "The Swahili are a mixed people," including "local Africans who intermarried with visiting Arabian sailors and merchants in the Indian Ocean trade."[41] Although she does not mention the sex of those involved in such intermarriages, we know that "sailors and merchants" were men and therefore "local Africans" were women. Not only does she neglect to mention women, but the grammatical subjecthood of the verb *intermarried* implies that local African women *chose* to marry Arab sailors and merchants, even though it is likely that most of these marriages were arranged by the fathers of these African women.

In other cases, a scholarly focus on male agents results in the depiction of women as lacking agency altogether. For example, Middleton writes, "Relations between Swahili merchants and their trading partners have been personal rather than market-oriented. Exchange has been on an individual basis and the relationships typically have been long-lasting, often based on the marriage of an overseas merchant to a daughter of his host Swahili family."[42] Notice Middleton's focus on relations between men—Swahili merchants and their trading partners—rather than on the relations between Swahili women and their "overseas" husbands. Women, he suggests, were treated as an object to be exchanged among men, understood only in relationship to men—their daughters or wives—rather than as individuals in their own right. While it is certainly true that women's rights and freedoms are often curtailed in relation to men's, a closer look at marriage and sexuality on the Swahili coast enables us to see that coastal women have more agency than previous historical scholarship has suggested.

GENDERING DEBATES ABOUT ISLAMIC AUTHENTICITY

Throughout the Indian Ocean and beyond, Muslims debate what it means to be a good Muslim, with understandings of appropriate beliefs and practices often changing over time. For example, historian Scott Reese examines the manifestation of translocal Islamic ideas in debates in 1930s Aden, Yemen. As a "translocal community," Aden was situated in the middle of various economic, political, and intellectual networks in the Indian Ocean. Reese surmises that "at the heart of these disputes was the desire of all parties to shape and define the identity and boundaries of their community. These 'petty squabbles' were, in part, disputes over who had the right to define what it meant to be a 'good' Muslim in Aden."[43] Mandana Limbert has considered generational differences in understandings of proper Islamic piety in the present day in Bahla, Oman. She discusses in particular the norms of social life exemplified in neighborly visiting; although the younger generation may view this sociality as a distraction from piety, older Omanis consider it a proper part of Muslim social life.[44]

The majority of scholarship on Islam in the Indian Ocean and Africa has looked at these debates and disputes as the domain of men, often focusing on the knowledge and authority of men.[45] Yet research has begun to show how Muslim women are involved in and impacted by such debates as well. For example, historian Jonathon Glassman shows how debates on the Swahili coast in the late nineteenth century about proper Islamic practice were in some ways a critique of women's participation in ritual activity.[46] More recently, Limbert shows that most debates in Oman about the "proper" way to perform traditional practices focused on gender,[47] and Francesca Declich has shown that women and men differently translate and understand devotional poetry in Somalia, arguing that these differential, "positional" understandings not only allow negotiation of meaning but also "possible different Muslim and gender identities."[48] In a similar vein, a major emphasis of this volume is Muslims' gendered lives along the western rim of the Indian Ocean. A popular hadith says, according to the Prophet Muhammad, "Marriage is half of religion": thus practices of and attitudes toward various aspects of marriage and sexual relationships tell us a great deal about local interpretations of Islam.

Examining marriage and divorce, sexuality, and gendered access to various forms of education and socialization, *Gendered Lives in the Western Indian Ocean* explores the tensions between different interpretations of Islam as they relate to gendered practices of religion.[49] In this way, we contribute to the growing literature on an Islamic public sphere and the impact and influence of reformist thought in the Indian Ocean, while also remedying the major omissions of the existing literature: a lack of consideration of Muslim women's lives and women's religious thought and practice; and Indian Ocean men as gendered individuals. The existing emphasis on knowledge and authority in studies of Islam in the western Indian Ocean is important, and we extend this focus by looking specifically at the authority that comes from knowledge about marriage, gender, and sexuality vis-à-vis Islam. We turn now to a consideration of how these themes play out in the chapters that follow.

The book is divided into three parts. The first, composed of three chapters, considers the historical transformation of gender expectations of girls and women both during the colonial period and in contemporary coastal East Africa. The four chapters in Part Two examine the way in which women perform gender norms in ritual practice and expressive culture. Part Three, composed of four chapters, turns to issues of masculinity in both ritual settings and everyday marital life in Indian Ocean Africa. Together, the authors consider both colonial and postcolonial and contemporary concerns and show both change and continuity over time. Methodologically, our approaches vary, and the chapters embrace an interdisciplinary approach to understand the lived experience of Islam among women and men in the western Indian Ocean.

Expectations in and of Muslim Marriages

Most of the chapters in this volume touch on Muslim marriages in some way. And while a great deal of previous research has addressed marriage on the Swahili coast,[50] we offer an emphasis on the way in which the *expectations* of marriage of both men and women are formed and manifest in practice. Even though there are important parallels across communities of the Swahili coast, expectations vary over time and across space and are shaped by historical forces and changing conceptions of proper Islamic practice; we explore variations in what it means to be a Swahili man or woman, and as Rebecca Gower and Stephen Salm emphasized two decades ago, we recognize that "Swahili women have not occupied a static identity in terms of spatial and temporal factors."[51]

As elsewhere in the Indian Ocean, a reformist or transcultural Islamic discourse is becoming increasingly prevalent and increasingly influential on the Swahili coast. In his look at Swahili intellectual life in late twentieth century, Kresse notes a shift from "internal" to "external" dominance, as young scholars were increasingly funded to study abroad in places like Saudi Arabia, Kuwait, Iran, and Pakistan.[52] Advocates of a "reformist" approach to Islam on this westernmost edge of the Indian Ocean argue that Islamic belief and practices should be transcultural and consistent from place to place, and that this consistency should extend to marriage practices. Kresse examines the writings of late-twentieth-century scholar Sheikh Muhammad Kasim

Mazrui, for example, who advised Swahili Muslims on "how to deal with controversial local practices from an Islamic point of view," including aspects of marriage and divorce.[53] Mohamed S. Mraja similarly considers how the reformist views of the influential Zanzibari scholar and *kadhi* Sheikh 'Abdullāh Sālih al-Farsī (1912–1982) influenced local marriage practice among Digo Muslims in Kenya; al-Farsī was critical of elder involvement in marriage and excessive mahari amounts as being contrary to normative Islamic practice.[54]

The influence of such discourses is apparent in local-level talk about and understandings of marriage and marriage practice throughout the region. In this volume, anthropologists Pat Caplan, Susi Krehbiel Keefe, Kjersti Larsen, and Erin Stiles and applied linguist Katrina Daly Thompson all touch on variations within discourses of marriage, considering how people in Swahili communities address their expectations of marriage vis-à-vis Islam, conceptions of *mila* (traditions or customs), and economic and other considerations. Some chapters, especially those by Caplan, Keefe, and Meghan Halley, a medical anthropologist, specifically consider how processes of globalization, particularly in terms of changing educational standards and, in some cases, the circulation of transnational discourses of a "universal" Islam, inform local ideals of marriage.

In a useful overview of Islamic reform in Africa, Roman Loimeier recognizes that reform movements "have been very outspoken with respect to spiritualistic interpretations of religion and condemned many different forms of alleged 'superstition' and popular rituals as unislamic innovations."[55] Hanni Nuotio has explored the impact of such critiques in the context of women's involvement in possession and maulidi in Zanzibar.[56] Several chapters in this volume consider how similar critiques play out with regard to marriage practices. Caplan, Thompson, anthropologist Nadine Beckmann, and historian Corrie Decker all address a decreasing emphasis on local rituals and practices to prepare young women for marriage, such as the initiation rite once common among Swahili women that is known as unyago. Reform-minded individuals often view rites like unyago as contrary to "universal" or transcultural standards of Islam. In her look at the rise of girls' schools in colonial Zanzibar, Decker shows that Islamic reformers and colonial officials agreed that practices like unyago were possibly harmful to young women. Muslim elites—most often of Omani descent—were suspicious of local marriage practices that they viewed as too "African." In her chapter, however, Larsen importantly points out that those who engage in such practices do not see any conflict between rites like unyago and Islam, and Thompson shows that some individuals will deny participation in such "traditional" practices, even as they take part in them.

In a comparative look at two different weddings on Mafia Island, one in the 1970s and another in 2002, Caplan takes up transformations both in marriage and in understandings of gender roles and sexuality. She situates these changes within new discourses on proper Islamic practice that people in Mafia attribute to influences from elsewhere in the Indian Ocean region—primarily Arabia and postrevolutionary Iran. Caplan describes the kinds of expectations women have of marriage and the changing constraints women face. In the 1990s she observed a waning emphasis on certain practices that were locally associated with mila, such as unyago, and an increasing emphasis on conforming to what was regarded locally as a more authentic, transcultural Islam. Caplan suggests that this increasing emphasis on a more universal Islam might have been a factor in lessening emphasis on mila, but she also notes other changes, like an increasing emphasis on education for girls, the spread of HIV/AIDS, and increasing poverty in the region.

In her chapter, historian Elisabeth McMahon shows that such changes are not new, dating back to (at least) the time of slavery. Focusing on slaves and ex-slaves on Pemba Island, she shows that with emancipation came new opportunities for ex-slaves to choose their own marriage partners. Moreover, although as Muslims, female ex-slaves could not themselves easily initiate divorce, some used conversion to Christianity as a way around this, taking advantage of the Christian missions that had been established on the islands. In other times and places, apostasy—leaving Islam—has resulted in severe sanctions and even death,[57] but McMahon's work demonstrates that in Pemba conversion from Islam to Christianity was an accepted practice and a useful strategy for women who sought greater control over their own lives. Such revelations highlight the variation in practices and interpretations of Islam in the lived experience of Muslims across time and in different local contexts.

Islam and Sexuality

Another area in which the chapters examine debates about Islam is with regard to sexuality; most chapters examine sexuality within the context of marriage, though some touch on premarital and extramarital sexuality. The chapters by Larsen, Caplan, Beckmann, Stiles, and Thompson emphasize the importance of a satisfying sexual relationship in a Muslim marriage, and some particularly note the importance of women's satisfaction. Larsen, for example, describes the importance of female sexuality in her analysis of songs Zanzibari women learn to prepare for marriage, and thus she extends the discussion in Swahili studies of knowledge and the authority it connotes to knowledge about sexuality; there is a similar emphasis on knowledge in Thompson's chapter.[58] In her chapter, Caplan observes that women on Mafia, particularly during her research in the 1960s and 1970s, frequently asserted their right to a satisfying sexual life both in and even outside of marriage. And in her analysis of recent court cases involving impotence from rural northern Unguja, Stiles shows that both women and judges emphasize the sexual dimension of an Islamic marriage in courtroom discourse. Although divorce suits involving claims of impotence are rare, the cases show that sexuality is an important dimension of marriage in its own right—not simply the means of procreation, similar to understandings of impotence elsewhere in the Indian Ocean region.[59]

Thompson's chapter analyzes a premarital sexual instruction ceremony known as *singo,* looking at it as a form of language socialization that aims to teach young women how to talk about sexuality in appropriate ways, through a discursive emphasis on the links between Islam and sexuality within marriage. She shows that sexuality is an important aspect of women's identity as Muslims, and part of the benefit of singo is to teach young women about the links between sexuality and Islam. She notes that the prevalence of singo in contemporary urban Zanzibar might be because of the Islamic elements it incorporates; some women described singo as more Islamic than unyago. Through initiation, women are taught to "transgress norms of embodied modesty" in their marital activities. By doing so, women are learning to be good Muslim wives as conceived in terms of a more transcultural view of Islam.

In her chapter, Beckmann discusses how people in Zanzibar Town talk about sexuality as potentially both dangerous and productive. She describes the ways in which people attempt to control and channel sexual desire, and argues that talk about sex is often linked to ideas about what makes someone a good Muslim—ideas of immorality are often linked to sexual impropriety. Like Caplan, Beckmann also examines how HIV/AIDS has changed the way Zanzibari Muslims discuss and understand sexuality, and she shows that many people in Zanzibar Town talk about AIDS in the context of what they view as a "moral decline." She argues that Islam is not monolithic, and illustrates this by looking at competing discussions of sexuality—she notices a difference in how those associated with reformism in Zanzibar exhibit a more "uncomfortable approach" to sexuality, while others, particularly of the older generation, critique this attitude as detrimental to the development of a positive sexuality in a marriage.

Education and Womanhood

Muslim communities the world over have seen an increasing emphasis on education in the twentieth century, particularly for girls and young women. Decker's chapter, for example, examines colonial educational policy and female authority in twentieth-century Zanzibar. British colonial policy sought to transform marriage and understandings of girlhood. Although increased education for girls did result in certain transformations, such as a later age of marriage for girls, Zanzibari women teachers also used colonial ideas about "normal age" to reinforce local norms of elder authority. Islamic reformers and British colonial officials had waged a campaign against local initiation rites (*ukungwi*) that trained girls for marriage—including the sexual dimensions of marriage. Decker shows that increasing education for girls often delayed age of first marriage but resulted in problems of older, initiated girls—and sometimes young married women—remaining in schools, which challenged the authority of teachers as "elders." Teachers employed the British conceptions of "normal age" to remove students from school who challenged their authority.

In Halley's chapter, we visit a Swahili-speaking Makonde community of southern coastal Tanzania in the present day. Halley examines changes resulting from expanding education in the region, and by extending the book's focus to a Makonde community, she demonstrates the importance of considering cultural variation among Swahili-speaking peoples as well as among Muslims. Like Decker, Halley considers girls' education, sexuality, and marriage and how Western-style educational systems are understood and used in local contexts. Following anthropologist Anna Tsing,[60] she examines the "friction" that results from the meeting of a Western educational system and local cultural norms and impacts adolescent sexuality and young women's reproductive health. Points of friction have resulted in high, and perhaps increasing, rates of pregnancy among girls, contrary to trends elsewhere in Africa and beyond. While marriage is delayed as a result of increased education for young women, sexual activity is not, in keeping with Makonde cultural norms whereby initiated young people engage in sexual relationships, regardless of marital status, but differing significantly from normative expectations for sexual relationships in most other Muslim communities. Halley draws connections to similar relationships between economics, gender, and sex roles elsewhere in Indian Ocean Africa and argues that due to a poor economy, increased educational opportunities do not lead Makonde girls to hopes of lucrative employment after schooling but rather to hopes of leveraging their sexual attractiveness as schoolgirls into marriage with prosperous men.

Normative and Subversive Masculinities vis-à-vis Islam

Despite an overwhelming focus on men's activities in both Indian Ocean studies and Swahili studies, scholarship has not adequately addressed the role of masculinity—that is, societal expectations for "appropriate" male behavior.[61] We consider notions of masculinity in ritual settings, in everyday marital life, and in marital disputes. By revealing how masculinity is performed, debated, and discussed in various arenas, we consider both normative and subversive notions of masculinity. There is an emphasis on common norms of masculinity in various parts of the Swahili coast—particularly of married Muslim men. A man is a good provider, the head of household, sexually robust, committed to Islam, and, in some cases, he has multiple wives.

Rebecca Gearhart, an anthropologist, considers ideas of Swahili manhood in the context of preparations for weddings in Lamu Town. Through wedding preparations, men are trained in the dominant norms associated with an idealized Swahili Muslim masculinity. In this context, an ideal Swahili man is a head of household, a good provider, dignified, and kind. Gearhart's chapter suggests that in Lamu Town male and female spaces are distinct and essentially autonomous, with men inhabiting public space and women inhabiting domestic space. Wedding rituals, she proposes, enhance and demarcate these separate spheres and train a man in the proper mode of behavior for the public sphere. In an important parallel to Thompson's chapter, Gearhart shows that wedding rituals do not simply socialize men into norms of married life and interaction with a wife but also into the world of adult men. Young men are now expected to contribute financially to the expenses of immediate and extended family and to assist with ritual preparations for weddings and funerals; they may now be consulted on financial and other matters deemed of grave importance and of the realm of adult men.

In her chapter, Linda Giles, also an anthropologist, makes an important contribution not only to the study of Swahili masculinity but also to literature on Islam and spirit possession in the western Indian Ocean. Giles challenges the findings of other scholars who have argued that it is low-status or homosexual men who are more likely involved in spirit possession guilds in the region[62] by showing that men who conform to normative notions of masculinity are also involved. Giles draws parallels between the possessive relationship and marriage: whereas the spirit is the dominant partner in a relationship with the possessed, a Muslim man is expected to be the dominant partner in the relationship with his wife; thus, she writes, it is difficult for men to submit to a relationship with a spirit. The initiate into a spirit guild is even referred to as a *mwari,* a term used in other settings to refer to a girl being initiated into womanhood during puberty. Although possession and initiation into spirit guilds can challenge masculinity because of these parallels, the men Giles worked with were able to leverage spirit possession into pursuing "masculine" work as Islamic ritual specialists.

Keefe, writing about polygyny in a coastal Tanzanian village, shows the gulf between idealized masculinity and reality. She proposes that men see marriage as a moral institution that reflects Muslim values, and thus men in Peponi hope to have multiple wives, seeing it as an essential aspect of their identities as Muslim men as well as a means of indexing their masculinity and economic success. However, the majority of them are thwarted from achieving this goal both because they are not as economically successful as they would like to be and because women use various tactics to prevent them from marrying multiple wives. Keefe also explores aspects of performed masculinity that show the influence of various global discourses on local understandings of masculinity. She describes how some men in the community claim an Arab identity as a way to show cosmopolitanism and connections to a world beyond the village and to a global Islam. At other times, the same men may perform cosmopolitanism by affecting an American accent or persona.

In her chapter, Stiles shows that both lay people and legal professionals view a sexual relationship as a legally essential dimension to an Islamic marriage, and that a man's impotence is grounds for divorce. Women's filing of divorce cases can be understood as a challenge to masculinity through a public airing of their husbands' impotence, and thus lack of masculinity. Women refer to situations of impotence both euphemistically and legalistically, such as by saying "Sipati sheria zangu" (I am not getting my legal due). In this sense, a sexual relationship is categorized as an essential, legal part of an Islamic marriage, and a husband who fails to provide his wife with a sexual relationship is failing as a man and particularly as a Muslim husband. Stiles also shows that women are possibly using accusations of impotence—a dire and serious challenge to masculinity—as a means of influencing husbands to divorce them.

Several other chapters also show how women are challenging norms and ideals of masculinity. In examinations of women's preparations for marital sexuality through unyago and singo, Larsen and Thompson show us both dominant and subversive notions of masculine sexuality. In an interesting parallel to court cases that focus on impotence, Larsen shows that unyago songs, performed in female-only settings, undermine dominant notions of masculinity by ridiculing husbands. In one song Larsen analyzes, a woman scolds her husband and his penis for being lazy and sleeping when she wants to make love. Thompson similarly writes about women's conversational subversion of masculinity in her chapter on marriage preparations and singo rites.

MORE REMAINS to be done in work on gender, sexuality, and Islam in the western Indian Ocean. A number of themes we explore in this book certainly deserve fuller consideration in future research. Chief among these is a "queering" of the question with which we began; we asked how ideologies of normative sexuality and gender are discursively constructed, performed, negotiated, or rejected within and outside marriage the role of gender transgression and homosexuality in relation to debates about being a good Muslim, but *negotiation* and *rejection* of such ideologies are only touched upon in this volume. In her chapter, Giles provides a brief review of research on male homosexuality on the Swahili coast and notes that the passive role in male homosexual relations bears a resemblance to the passivity inherent in men being possessed, which potentially threatens masculinity. In Stiles's chapter, a judge explains that a man's preference for other men would be grounds for a divorce, yet the judge does not discuss or moralize on homosexuality outside this legal ramification. This leads to questions about overlap or lack of it in the legal and moral understandings of same-sex sexuality. We know that Swahili men and women are expected to marry heterosexually, even if they are known "homosexuals," something Keefe briefly discusses with regard to men who prefer men.[63] How might homosexuality be silenced, condemned, or addressed in sex instruction ceremonies? How do queer men and women conceive of their heterosexual marriages in relation to their sexual preferences, sexual and gender identities, and Islam? How does a "good Muslim wife" relate to a husband known by the community to be having sex with men? How might attitudes toward same-sex practices be changing in light of the rise of reformist approaches to religion? How might the cosmopolitanism for which the Swahili coast is known affect local attitudes toward homosexuality?

Another avenue for future research is how ideologies of sexuality, gender, and marriage are similar or different across the communities who live on the Swahili coast but do not conceive of themselves as Swahili, such as the significant community of *Wahindi,* people of Indian origin. There is a great deal of research on Indians in East Africa,[64] but little of it addresses sex or gender.[65] What role do race, ethnicity, language, and heritage play in how non-Swahili speakers conceive of what it means to be a Muslim man or woman in this region? To what extent does intermarriage occur, and why or why not? We believe that interdisciplinary methodologies are ideally suited to addressing these questions.

TOWARD INTERDISCIPLINARY METHODOLOGIES

In addition to the broader goals of this volume, we seek to make more particular methodological contributions to academic study of the Swahili coast and the Indian Ocean region. We consider the positionality of researchers, primarily in terms of gender and religious identity, and how positionality influences research methods and analysis. In many parts of the Indian Ocean, nonliberal interpretations of Islam mean that men and women often inhabit separate social worlds. Such separation is relevant to many aspects of the research presented in this book, not least of which is the different ways women may speak in women-only environments versus in public, mixed-gender settings. For example, Joan Russell writes of her experience researching Swahili discourse in Mombasa, "although members of the Swahili-speaking community enjoy talking and engage it in a great deal of the time, one of my earliest observations was that women were more relaxed and more inclined to talk freely when together in a group—particularly of the same age—than when in a mixed group."[66] Similarly, in her chapter, Stiles shows how women spoke differently to her than to a male judge or his male assistant. The chapters of Beckmann, Thompson, and Larsen focus on female premarital instruction, a prime example of a genre of talk that only occurs in a gender-segregated environment.

The stark differences between women's speech in different settings speaks to the need for female researchers in this environment. Although we did not intend to restrict ourselves to research done by women, it is probably no coincidence that our call for chapters about gender, sexuality, and marriage yielded chapters only from female scholars. James Gregory questions the assumption that male ethnographers cannot do research on women, arguing that this assumption is an excuse for not collecting information about women.[67] But it remains the case that little work has been done on Swahili women by male researchers, the few exceptions being mostly historians working with archival materials.[68] As more women have entered the field of Indian Ocean studies we have seen a much more nuanced approached to women's lives—although more in anthropology than in other fields. This has led, for example, to a much better understanding of the role of Islam in women's lives.

Women doing research in Indian Ocean Africa may in fact have an advantage over our male counterparts in that we can not only enter female-only spaces, but also, in the case of foreign or non-Muslim women (or both), sometimes enter a liminal space between masculinity and femininity in which we are allowed to converse with men[69]—although not always without earning scorn from local women.[70] For example, Hirsch found that when she first arrived in Mombasa, her status as a researcher trumped her gender and she initially had more access to male than female talk—also a result, she notes, of local devaluations of women's speech, which people assumed would hold no interest for a researcher.[71] While such local assumptions can be frustrating, being treated as an honorary male can also be fruitful: Stiles, Halley, Gearhart, and Giles were sometimes able to interview men and boys, gaining valuable information about court procedure, attitudes toward the education of girls, men's experience of marriage ceremonies, and men's involvement in spirit possession. However, Thompson found that while her identity as a Muslim woman facilitated her work with women in Zanzibar Town, it hindered her ability to interview men. Local interpretations of both gendered and religious identities (not to mention age, marital status, and sexual preference) are important factors in research that involves conversational interaction, as almost all the work in this book does.

Mary Nooter reminds us that ethnographic research is premised on revealing what is concealed.[72] This book reveals a number of matters that Swahili Muslims normally keep secret and thus raises questions about research ethics. Does the use of pseudonyms, for example, do enough to conceal our research participants' secrets? While Swahili speakers often rely on euphemism and other forms of word play that conceal hidden meanings, our research reveals these hidden meanings for readers unfamiliar with Swahili. Writing and other mechanisms for recording, even when used with informed consent, have the potential to violate secrets. It is for this reason that the women Thompson describes in her chapter allowed only audio, but not video, recording, choosing to keep their physical appearances concealed from others' gaze. When Stiles did research in northern Unguja, she was never permitted to audio- or videotape courtroom discourse, but only to take notes. As the Swahili say, "Hakuna siri ya watu wawili" (There is no secret between two people), meaning that once a second person knows your secret, it is no longer a secret. The initiation of researchers into secret knowledge also means that such knowledge may be difficult for other researchers to verify. For example, Beckmann's, Larsen's, and Thompson's chapters offer slightly different views of contemporary unyago and singo, raising questions about the different secrets to which each was exposed. As Nooter writes, "Cultural representation is never an objective presentation of facts, but is filtered once through the perspectives of the members of the African society studied, again through the eyes of fieldworkers, and finally through the medium of publications."[73] Interpretations of the rituals in which Swahili girls take part as they become adult women and wives vary according to the age, status, level of formal education, and religiosity of those who share them with us; as well as across time and space. Merging anthropological, historical, and linguistic data from diverse locations with broader theoretical observations concerning boundaries, knowledge, and performance, this book offers new relationships among language, gender, and power.

NOTES

1. Edward Simpson and Kai Kresse, "Cosmopolitanism Contested: Anthropology and History in the Western Indian Ocean," in *Struggling with History: Islam and Cosmopolitanism in the Western Indian Ocean,* ed. Simpson and Kresse (New York: Columbia University Press, 2008), 13.

2. John Richard Bowen, *Muslims through Discourse: Religion and Ritual in Gayo Society* (Princeton: Princeton University Press, 1993).

3. Michael M. Lambek, "Certain Knowledge, Contestable Authority: Power and Practice on the Islamic Periphery," *American Ethnologist* 17, no. 1 (1990): 23–40; Lambek, *Knowledge and Practice in Mayotte: Local Discourses of Islam, Sorcery and Spirit Possession* (Toronto: University of Toronto Press, 1993); Kai Kresse, *Philosophising in Mombasa* (Edinburgh: Edinburgh University Press, 2007).

4. Simpson and Kresse, "Cosmopolitanism Contested," 23.

5. Ibid., 23–24.

6. Roman Loimeier surveys Islamic reform in sub-Saharan Africa, including East Africa, in "Patterns and Peculiarities of Islamic Reform in Africa," *Journal of Religion in Africa* 33, no. 3 (2003): 237–62.

7. For scholarship on similar debates in Egypt and Lebanon, for example, see Saba Mahmood, *Politics of Piety: The Islamic Revival and the Feminist Subject* (Princeton: Princeton University Press, 2005); Lara Deeb, *An Enchanted Modern: Gender and Public Piety in Shi'i Lebanon* (Princeton: Princeton University Press, 2006).

8. Peter J. Martin, "The Zanzibar Clove Industry," *Economic Botany* 45, no. 4 (October 1991): 450–59; E. I. Niyibigira, V. Y. Lada, and Z. S. Abdullay, "Mango Production and Marketing in Zanzibar: Potential, Issues and Constraints," in *XXVI International Horticultural Congress: Horticultural Science in Emerging Economies, Issues and Constraints* 621 (2002): 89–93.

9. Kate Kingsford, "Wider Worlds: The Indian Ocean and African Studies," *African Affairs* 111, no. 442 (2012): 145–51; Thomas Spear, "Early Swahili History Reconsidered," *International Journal of African Historical Studies* 33, no. 2 (2000): 257–90; Randall L. Pouwels, "Eastern Africa and the Indian Ocean to 1800: Reviewing Relations in Historical Perspective," *International Journal of African Historical Studies* 35, no. 203 (2002): 385–425.

10. Gwyn Campbell, "Islam in Indian Ocean Africa," in Simpson and Kresse, *Struggling with History,* 50.

11. John C. Hawley, *India in Africa, Africa in India: Indian Ocean Cosmopolitanisms* (Bloomington: Indiana University Press, 2008), 7–8.

12. Kjersti Larsen, introduction to *Knowledge, Renewal and Religion: Repositioning and Changing Ideological and Material Circumstances among the Swahili on the East African Coast,* ed. Larsen (Uppsala: Nordic Africa Institute, 2009), 15; Simpson and Kresse, "Cosmopolitanism Contested"; Abdul Sheriff, "Between Two Worlds: The Littoral Peoples of the Indian Ocean," in *The Global Worlds of the Swahili: Interfaces of Islam, Identity and Space in 19th- and 20th-Century East Africa,* ed. Roman Loimeier and Rüdiger Seesemann, Beiträge zur Afrikaforschung 26 (Berlin: LIT Verlag, 2006), 15–30.

13. Michael Lambek, "Choking on the Qur'an and Other Consuming Parables from the Western Indian Ocean Front," in *The Pursuit of Certainty: Religious and Cultural Formulations,* ed. Wendy James (London: Routledge, 1995), 263.

14. Simpson and Kresse, "Cosmopolitanism Contested," 13.

15. Abdul Sheriff, *Dhow Cultures and the Indian Ocean: Cosmopolitanism, Commerce, and Islam* (New York: Columbia University Press, 2010).

16. Isabel Hofmeyr, "The Black Atlantic Meets the Indian Ocean: Forging New Paradigms of Transnationalism for the Global South—Literary and Cultural Perspectives," *Social Dynamics: A Journal of African Studies* 33, no. 2 (2007): 3–32.

17. David Parkin, "Inside and Outside the Mosque: A Master Trope," in *Islamic Prayer across the Indian Ocean: Inside and Outside the Mosque,* ed. Parkin and Stephen C. Headley (London: Routledge, 2000), 1–22.

18. Mark Frost, "'Wider Opportunities': Religious Revival, Nationalist Awakening and the Global Dimension in Colombo, 1870–1920," *Modern Asian Studies* 36, no. 4 (2002): 937–67, cited in Hofmeyr, "Black Atlantic," 7–8. On public intellectuals in a Swahili context, see Kai Kresse, "'Swahili Enlightenment'? East African Reformist Discourse at the Turning Point: The Example of Sheikh Muhammad Kasim Mazrui," *Journal of Religion in Africa* 33, no. 3 (2003): 279–309; Kresse, "The Uses of History: Rhetorics of Muslim Unity and Difference on the Kenyan Swahili Coast," in Simpson and Kresse, *Struggling with History,* 223–60.

19. Hofmeyr, "Black Atlantic," 8.

20. John Middleton, *The World of the Swahili: An African Mercantile Civilization* (New Haven: Yale University Press, 1992), 58.

21. Anne K. Bang, *Sufis and Scholars of the Sea: Family Networks in East Africa, 1860–1925* (London: RoutledgeCurzon, 2003), 3.

22. Ibid., 23.

23. Edward A. E. Alpers, "'Ordinary Household Chores': Ritual and Power in a Nineteenth-Century Swahili Women's Spirit Possession Cult," *International Journal of African Historical Studies* 17, no. 4 (1984): 678.

24. Middleton, *World of the Swahili*, 37.

25. Susan Beckerleg, "Medical Pluralism and Islam in Swahili Communities in Kenya," *Medical Anthropology Quarterly*, n.s., 8, no. 3 (September 1994): 302.

26. Janet McIntosh, "Reluctant Muslims: Embodied Hegemony and Moral Resistance in a Giriama Spirit Possession Complex," *Journal of the Royal Anthropological Institute* 10, no. 1 (March 2004): 97.

27. Larsen, *Knowledge, Renewal*.

28. Laura Fair, "Remaking Fashion in the Paris of the Indian Ocean: Dress, Performance, and the Cultural Construction of a Cosmopolitan Zanzibari Identity," in *Fashioning Africa: Power and the Politics of Dress*, ed. Jean Allman, African Expressive Cultures (Bloomington: Indiana University Press, 2004), 13. See also Kelly M. Askew, "As Plato Duly Warned: Music, Politics, and Social Change in Coastal East Africa," *Anthropological Quarterly* 76, no. 4 (2003): 609–37; Adria LaViolette, "Swahili Cosmopolitanism in Africa and the Indian Ocean World, AD 600–1500," *Archaeologies* 4, no. 1 (2008): 24–49; Simpson and Kresse, "Cosmopolitanism Contested."

29. Hofmeyr, "Black Atlantic," 6; Loimeier and Seesemann, *Global Worlds*.

30. A. Y. Lodhi, "Muslims in Eastern Africa—Their Past and Present," *Nordic Journal of African Studies* 3, no. 1 (1994): 89; David Parkin and François Constantin, "Some Key Dates in Swahili History," *Africa: Journal of the International African Institute* 59, no. 2 (1989): 144.

31. Parkin and Constantin, "Key Dates."

32. See Loimeier and Seesemann, *Global Worlds*.

33. Jeremy Prestholdt, *Domesticating the World: African Consumerism and the Genealogies of Globalization* (Berkeley: University of California Press, 2008).

34. Amina A. Issa, "Wedding Ceremonies and Cultural Exchange in an Indian Ocean Port City: The Case of Zanzibar Town," *Social Dynamics* 38, no. 3 (2012): 467–78.

35. Hofmeyr, "Black Atlantic," 8.

36. Isabel Hofmeyr, Preben Kaarsholm, and Bodil Folke Frederiksen, "Introduction: Print Cultures, Nationalisms and Publics of the Indian Ocean," *Africa: The Journal of the International African Institute* 81, no. 1 (2011): 1–22; cf. Minou Fuglesang, *Veils and Videos: Female Youth Culture on the Kenyan Coast* (Stockholm: Almqvist and Wiksell International, 1994); Sarah Mirza and Margaret Strobel, eds., *Three Swahili Women: Life Histories from Mombasa, Kenya*, trans. Mirza and Strobel (Bloomington: Indiana University Press, 1989).

37. Fernando Rosa Ribeiro, "*Fornicatie* and *Hoerendom*; or, the Long Shadow of the Portuguese: Connected Histories, Languages and

Gender in the Indian Ocean and Beyond," *Social Dynamics* 33, no. 2 (2007): 33–60.

38. Engseng Ho, *The Graves of Tarim: Genealogy and Mobility across the Indian Ocean* (Berkeley: University of California Press, 2006), xxi, emphasis added.

39. Sheriff, *Dhow Cultures,* 276.

40. Akbar Keshodkar, "Marriage as the Means to Preserve 'Asian-Ness': The Post-Revolutionary Experience of the Asians of Zanzibar," *Journal of Asian and African Studies* 45, no. 2 (April 2010): 226–40; Mandana E. Limbert, *In the Time of Oil: Piety, Memory, and Social Life in an Omani Town* (Stanford: Stanford University Press, 2010).

41. Patricia W. Romero, "Mama Khadija: A Life History as Example of Family History," in *Life Histories of African Women,* ed. Romero (London: Ashfield Press, 1988), 140.

42. Middleton, *World of the Swahili,* 22.

43. Scott S. Reese, "The 'Respectable Citizens' of Shaykh Uthman: Religious Discourse, Trans-Locality and the Construction of Local Contexts in Colonial Aden," in Simpson and Kresse, *Struggling with History,* 210.

44. Limbert, *Time of Oil.*

45. For example, Bowen, *Muslims through Discourse;* Kresse, "'Swahili Enlightenment'?" For a critique, see Katrina Daly Thompson, "How to Be a Good Muslim Wife: Women's Performance of Islamic Authority during Swahili Weddings," *Journal of Religion in Africa* 41, no. 4 (2011): 427–48.

46. Jonathon Glassman, *Feasts and Riot: Revelry, Rebellion, and Popular Consciousness on the Swahili Coast, 1856–1888* (Portsmouth, NH: Heinemann, 1995).

47. Limbert, *Time of Oil.*

48. Francesca Declich, "Contested Interpretations of Muslim Poetries, Legitimacy and Daily Life Politics," in Larsen, *Knowledge, Renewal,* 123.

49. See Lara Deeb's work in Beirut and Saba Mahmood in Cairo: Deeb, *Enchanted Modern;* Mahmood, *Politics of Piety.*

50. Pat Caplan, "Gender, Ideology and Modes of Production on the Coast of East Africa," *Paideuma* 28 (1982): 29–43; Caplan, "Perceptions of Gender Stratification," *Africa: Journal of the International African Institute* 59, no. 2 (1989): 196–208; Marc J. Swartz, "The Isolation of Men and the Happiness of Women: Sources and Use of Power in Swahili Marital Relationships," *Journal of Anthropological Research* 38, no. 1 (1982): 26–44; Carol M. Eastman, "Women, Slaves, and Foreigners: African Cultural Influences and Group Processes in the Formation of Northern Swahili Coastal Society," *International Journal of African Historical Studies* 21, no. 1 (1988): 1–20; Middleton, *World of the Swahili;* Mirza and Strobel, *Three Swahili Women;* Glassman, *Feasts and Riot;* Susan F. Hirsch, *Pronouncing and Persevering: Gender and the Discourses of Disputing in an*

African Islamic Court, Language and Legal Discourse (Chicago: University of Chicago Press, 1998); Erin E. Stiles, "When Is a Divorce a Divorce? Determining Intention in Zanzibar's Islamic Courts," *Ethnology* 42, no. 4 (October 2003): 273–88; Stiles, "'There Is No Stranger to Marriage Here!': Muslim Women and Divorce in Rural Zanzibar," *Africa: Journal of the International African Institute* 75, no. 4 (2005): 582–98; Stiles, *An Islamic Court in Context: An Ethnographic Study of Judicial Reasoning* (New York: Palgrave Macmillan, 2009); Thompson, "Good Muslim Wife"; Katrina Daly Thompson, "Strategies for Taming a Swahili Husband: Zanzibari Women's Talk about Love in Islamic Marriages," *Agenda* 27, no. 2 (2013): 65–75.

51. Rebecca Gower, Steven Salm, and Toyin Falola, "Swahili Women since the Nineteenth Century: Theoretical and Empirical Considerations on Gender and Identity Construction," *Africa Today* 43, no. 3 (September 1996): 265.

52. Kresse, "'Swahili Enlightenment'?," 281.

53. Ibid., 279.

54. Mohamed S. Mraja, "The Reform Ideas of Shaykh 'Abdallāh Sālih al-Farsī and the Transformation of Marital Practices among Digo Muslims of Kenya," *Islamic Law and Society* 17, no. 2 (2010): 245–78.

55. Loimeier, "Patterns and Peculiarities," 241.

56. Hanni Nuotio, "Zanzibari Women in the Maulidi Ritual," in Loimeier and Seesemann, *Global Worlds,* 187–208. See also Kai Kresse, "Debating Maulidi: Ambiguities and Transformations of Muslim Identity along the Swahili Coast," in Loimeier and Seesemann, *Global Worlds,* 209–28.

57. Samuli Schielke, "Being a Nonbeliever in a Time of Islamic Revival: Trajectories of Doubt and Certainty in Contemporary Egypt," *International Journal of Middle East Studies* 44, no. 2 (2012): 301–20.

58. See also Thompson, "Good Muslim Wife."

59. Carolyn Fluehr-Lobban, *Islamic Law and Society in the Sudan* (London: Routledge, 1987); Essam Fawzy, "Muslim Personal Status Law in Egypt: The Current Situation and Possibilities of Reform through Internal Initiatives," in *Women's Rights and Islamic Family Law: Perspectives on Reform,* ed. Lynn Welchman (London: Zed Books, 2004), 14–91; Vardit Rispler-Chaim, *Disability in Islamic Law,* vol. 32 (Dordrecht: Springer, 2006).

60. Anna Lowenhaupt Tsing, *Friction: An Ethnography of Global Connection* (Princeton: Princeton University Press, 2005).

61. For an exception, see Laura Fair's discussion of sports and masculinity in Zanzibar, in *Pastimes and Politics: Culture, Community, and Identity in Post-abolition Urban Zanzibar, 1890–1945* (Athens: Ohio University Press, 2001).

62. See, for example, Kjersti Larsen, *Where Humans and Spirits Meet: The Politics of Rituals and Identified Spirits in Zanzibar,* Social Identities 5 (New York: Berghahn Books, 2008).

63. See also Katrina Daly Thompson, "Discreet Talk about Supernatural Sodomy, Transgressive Gender Performance, and Male Same-Sex Desire in Zanzibar Town," *GLQ: A Journal of Lesbian and Gay Studies* 21 (in press).

64. See, for example, James Brennan's history of Indians in Dar es Salaam: *Taifa: Making Nation and Race in Urban Tanzania* (Athens: Ohio University Press, 2012).

65. The work of anthropologist Akbar Keshodkar is an important exception: Keshodkar, "Marriage as the Means."

66. Joan Russell, *Communicative Competence in a Minority Group: A Sociolinguistic Study of the Swahili-Speaking Community in the Old Town, Mombasa* (Leiden: Brill, 1981), 180.

67. J. R. Gregory, "The Myth of the Male Ethnographer and the Woman's World," *American Anthropologist* 86, no. 2 (1984): 316–27.

68. See, for example, Alpers, "Ordinary Household Chores."

69. Jennifer Hunt, "The Development of Rapport through the Negotiation of Gender in Field Work among Police," *Human Organization* 43, no. 4 (December 1984): 283–96.

70. Janet Bujra, "Women and Fieldwork," in *Women Cross-Culturally: Change and Challenge,* ed. Ruby Rohrlich-Leavitt (The Hague: Mouton, 1975), 551–57, cited in Gregory, "Myth of the Male Ethnographer."

71. S. Hirsch, *Pronouncing and Persevering.*

72. Mary H. Nooter, "Secrecy: African Art That Conceals and Reveals," *African Arts* 26, no. 1 (January 1993): 55.

73. Ibid., 62.

PART ONE

Historical Transformations of Gender, Sexuality, and Marriage

ONE

Schoolgirls and Women Teachers

Colonial Education and the Shifting Boundaries between
Girls and Women in Zanzibar

CORRIE DECKER

ACROSS AFRICA, COLONIAL OFFICIALS promoted schooling
and other forms of intervention to protect girls from what they
considered oppressive African customs, such as female circumcision and "child marriage."[1] In Zanzibar, British colonial girls'
schools, which were established in 1927, served as the state's
primary weapon against *ukungwi*, an indigenous initiation ceremony that marked the transition from girlhood to womanhood.
Ukungwi did not include female circumcision, but colonial officials, as well as Zanzibar's male Islamic elites, believed that these
local initiation rites for girls were dangerous because of their
overt sexual overtones and encouragement of early marriage for
girls.[2] British officials worked to direct girls away from ukungwi
and toward the colonial education system, where they would
learn about hygiene, marriage, and motherhood.[3] The attack on
ukungwi was not simply a battle against local custom; it was also

part of a colonial campaign to inculcate Western understandings of age and childhood.

At the heart of Zanzibar's ukungwi were biocultural benchmarks (puberty, initiation, marriage, and motherhood) inherent to Swahili definitions of childhood and adulthood. In contrast, Western educators measured maturation in terms of numerical age and number of years in school. Colonial schools attempted to institutionalize quantifiable stages of childhood and redefine the boundaries between "girls" and "women" in Swahili society, but Swahili biocultural age-grade systems were resilient. During the first two decades of colonial girls' education in Zanzibar, these tactics began to work. An increasing number of girls entered the government schools and many of them delayed marriage for years after puberty. However, these schools—the very mechanism designed to replace indigenous beliefs about female age grades with Western concepts of age and childhood—became, in the 1950s and 1960s, the tool by which female Zanzibari teachers maintained a strict delineation between the "woman" teacher and the "girl" student and thereby reasserted their authority as elders. Rather than an institution of Western cultural imperialism, the colonial school, I argue, reinforced the fundamental principles of the indigenous age-grade system symbolized in the ukungwi custom.

Historically, *ukungwi* consisted of two main events: one-on-one instruction from a female initiation instructor (*kungwi* or *somo*) in hygiene, marriage, and sexuality at the onset of the girl's menses; and the communal initiation dances (*unyago*) that taught girls the mechanics of sex and how to have intercourse that is pleasurable to both partners. Not all girls attended the communal dances. Some instructors taught the girl only how to be a good, "respectable" wife (a wife with *heshima*), and some also introduced her to an array of sexual techniques. Often, the instructor, at times a family friend or relative, became the girl's confidante and adviser for many years to come. Critics rarely differentiated between these and other iterations of initiation, which varied widely depending on the ethnic, class, and cultural position of the family.

In the West, "modern" childhood was a by-product of capitalist industrialization, which led to greater distinction between children and adults in the home and workplace and brought about universal schooling.[4] The small but growing scholarship on the history of childhood in Africa also associates the emergence of "modern" childhood with the spread of colonial institutions and global trends.[5] Modernity sought to reform the African age-grade system, which Oyèrónkẹ́ Oyèwùmí argues was possibly the most important form of social distinction in precolonial African societies.[6] On the Swahili Coast the long history of Islam in the region meant that social and cultural distinctions were also strictly gendered, especially among elite and upwardly mobile urbanites. Nevertheless, the indigenous age-grade system and the initiation practices inherent to it, remained prevalent well into the twentieth century, and, as Meghan Halley's contribution to this volume indicates, are still pervasive among schoolgirls in East Africa today.[7] Zanzibar's colonial girls' schools came onto the scene at the same time that new "respectable" initiation dances became widely popular among the urban elite and middle-class women.[8] Both socialization systems claimed to prepare girls and young women for marriage and motherhood. Both were ultimately concerned about a pubescent, unmarried girl's access to information about sexuality and her ability to maintain heshima (respectability). The colonial system managed female socialization by carefully tracking schoolgirls' ages, grade levels, and physical development. The schools implemented a "normal-age" policy that grouped children according to numerical age and school grade and challenged indigenous biocultural measures of maturation.

Biocultural and numerical calculations of age, however, were not mutually exclusive. Neither was the age-grade system always under attack by colonial officials. In theory, British Indirect Rule relied on the codification of African custom, though modified by colonial officers and African chiefs.[9] These policies tended to favor male elders, chiefs, and others who claimed authority over women and youths. Colonial schools were ambiguous institutions. On the one hand, they gave young people access to status and income normally reserved for their parents and grandparents. On the other, they instituted a culture of discipline to keep young people and women in check.[10] Most colonial girls' schools in Africa claimed to prepare girls for marriage and motherhood.[11] Some schools in Africa even went so far as to incorporate a modified version of initiation.[12] Zanzibar schools, too, emphasized domesticity and ensured parents that marriage was the ultimate destination for schoolgirls. Education officials walked a fine line between reinforcing these gendered and generational customs and instilling new concepts of childhood socialization that would combat "bad" traditions such as initiation and early marriage.

Close examination of Department of Education reports, correspondence, newspaper articles, census reports, and other documents housed at the Zanzibar National Archives, along with oral histories that I conducted with former students and teachers between 2004 and 2012, reveals that Zanzibari teachers enforced the normal-age policy primarily because it allowed them to assert Swahili distinctions between the "girl" and the "woman."[13] Zanzibari teachers, products of colonial schools themselves, embraced colonial logic about age and childhood in order to convince their European superiors to expel older and married students, a tactic that ensured their authority as female elders in the classroom and in Swahili society.

EDUCATING GIRLS AGAINST INITIATION AND EARLY MARRIAGE

The Zanzibar Islands were the center of an Omani Empire that claimed control over long stretches of the Swahili Coast during the nineteenth century. After Britain declared a protectorate over the islands of Zanzibar (Unguja) and Pemba in 1890, the new government kept the Omani sultanate in place but took over most administrative tasks. Given that Zanzibar was a "protectorate," the colonial government had to employ the rhetoric of collaboration in implementing policy. Both British officials and male elites were on board with the plan to establish girls' schools as a tool to combat female initiation, particularly because initiation was an institution controlled by nonelite women. Furthermore, having already been exposed to Western education for at least a generation, many male elites were convinced of the need to institutionalize and standardize notions of age and childhood.

Yet colonial education in Zanzibar was never entirely Western. Zanzibaris attribute the establishment of "modern" schools not to British overseers but to Sultan Ali bin Hamoud, who in 1905 recruited a modernist teacher from Egypt to begin what would become the first government-run boys' school on the islands. One member of the Omani elite wrote that the sultan "saved Zanzibaris from being lured by the missionary schools."[14] Though most Zanzibaris remained wary of colonial education until well after World War II, colonial educators made an effort early on to address the demands of Muslim elites. This was especially true for government girls' schools, which were designed to reinforce elite ideologies of respectability (heshima) in the face of widespread initiation practices.

British Resident F. B. Pearce first suggested the establishment of girls' schools in 1917 as a means to combat child marriage, which he called a "bad custom" among Arabs and Swahilis. "At the age when [girls] should be attending school," Pearce wrote, "they have in many cases assumed the duties and cares of a household drudge."[15] "I realise the necessity of endeavouring to alter these old and pernicious customs," he continued, "and of course this consummation will not be arrived at by Government remaining supine." In Pearce's vision, the masculine intervention of the government stood up to these dangerous practices in order to "consummate" their goal of offering a "modern" Western alternative to early marriage. At the same time, he urged that the matter had to "be approached with caution," that colonial intervention had to be slow and methodical if they ever wanted to "lighten the lot of these Mahommedan girls." Pearce proposed a balance between aggressive intervention in the name of protection and gentle persuasion to convince the young Muslim virgins and their parents that girls should be educated.

When the first government girls' school opened, ten years after Pearce's memo, officials struggled to keep girls in school for more than a few years.[16] G. R. Johnson, the headmistress of the school, known as the Zanzibar Government Girls' School (ZGGS), reassured parents that the school strove "to make good Muhammadan wives and mothers."[17] She explained in a 1934 public speech, "our lasting work in this respect hardly begins before the girl reaches the age of thirteen," and urged that girls be kept on longer in order to "reap the benefits of the modern education offered in this school."[18] That year, the administration also took legal measures against early marriage for girls. The Penal Decree of 1934 prohibited a man from having sex with a wife "who has not attained both puberty and the age of thirteen (unless he had reasonable cause to believe she had)."[19] Similar prohibitions existed in Islamic law, though without the numerical age stipulation, as Muslim scholars dominating the discourse on child marriage in Zanzibar argued that puberty could begin as early as age nine, the age they claimed 'Aisha was when she reached puberty and married the Prophet.[20] The question of age was a subjective one, but British officials fixated on thirteen, presumably the standard age of puberty, when it came to policies aimed at protecting girls.

Among elite girls in Zanzibar, the initial target demographic for the schools, the age of puberty was a crucial turning point. It was the age at which a girl left Qur'anic school and adopted the *buibui,* a Muslim woman's covering that, at that time, was a symbol of elite respectability popular among urban nonelites as well. From that point on, the girl would enter seclusion and prepare for marriage. Puberty was the moment at which a girl began to learn about Islamic respectability as she stayed with her somo or kungwi for seven days for private instruction.[21] She also learned about menstruation, personal hygiene, sex, motherhood, and other lessons to prepare her for marriage. This initiation process and instruction preceding the girl's wedding made possible her transition into womanhood, which culminated in the wedding itself.[22] It was at this moment that the *mwari* (adolescent girl) was thereafter referred to as Bibi (Mrs., or a married woman). Even if a woman divorced, she retained the title Bibi, an indication that she had attained maturity.[23] It was perhaps no coincidence that colonial girls' schools came into existence amid the growing popularity of new initiation dances in the 1920s. The schools arose out of collaboration between Islamic reformers and colonial officials, those who agreed that certain cultural practices, like ukungwi, were potentially harmful to girls. However, many parents of students continued to remove their daughters at puberty for this very purpose.

The goal for the education officials was not only to keep girls in school longer but also to recruit them at the right age and ensure their regular progress so that the ages of the students correlated with the Department of Education's "normal-age" policy. The "normal age" for schoolchildren at each grade appears in table 1.1. Each grade correlated with a specific age: Standard I with age seven, Standard II with age eight, and so forth. "Sub-Standard" was equivalent to kindergarten, Standards I through VII roughly correspond with American grades 1 through 7, and Forms 1 through 6 with American junior high and high school grades 8 through 12. Later, Standard VIII was added and, in Zanzibar, the high school course was limited to Forms 1 through 4 (also called Standards IX through XII), roughly equivalent to American grades 9 through 12. At the time of Pearce's 1926 memo, these discrepancies were irrelevant because Zanzibar did not offer courses above Standard VI. It was only with the gradual expansion of education in the early 1940s that Standards VII and VIII (sometimes referred to as "upper primary" or "lower secondary") were added. The full secondary course for girls (Forms 1 through 4) was available starting in the early 1950s. By this time the addition of Standard VIII shifted the "normal" ages so that a girl would be about six at the time she began Standard I and around seventeen or eighteen by the time she finished Form 4 (Standard XII) if she completed the full primary and secondary courses. Girls' schools in Zanzibar did not offer Forms 5 and 6 during the colonial period.

TABLE 1.1. Normal-age chart reproduced from a 1926 Colonial Office circular

Normal Age	Below 6	6, 7	8, 9	10, 11, 12	13, 14	15, 16, 17, 18
Standards and Forms	Sub-standard	I, II	III, IV	V, VI, VII	1, 2	3, 4, 5, 6

Source: ZNA, AB 1/33, Advisory Committee for Education in the Colonies, Colonial Office Circular, 1926.

The first girls' school, which opened in 1927, welcomed girls between the ages of five and eight to register. When only nineteen girls showed up for the first class, school officials extended the age limit to twelve years in order to accept siblings of these girls.[24] Likewise, the first class of schoolgirls on Pemba Island in 1930, at the Chake Chake Girls' School, consisted of "fairly old girls," between the ages of the nine and twelve.[25] The normal-age policy was not off to a good start in Zanzibari girls' schools.

One of the obstacles to this policy was the fact that many parents did not know the exact ages of their children. Though the government required the registration of births in town from 1908, and hospital births became increasingly popular beginning in the 1930s, many parents in town and rural areas did not keep records of children's exact ages.[26] The colonial administration used the census to promote a culture of age calculation and demographic labeling more generally. The 1924 census differentiated between "male and female adults" (people twelve years of age and older) and "male and female children" (those under twelve). However, the report gives no indication of how the ages of individuals were determined. Reporting of ages was "one of the census items most liable to error, even in a developed community," seemingly defined as a community with a bureaucratic paper trail and a custom of categorization.[27] In "Eastern communities" like Zanzibar, the census report noted, "many persons do not know their real age and are very satisfied with rough approximations which sometimes are totally misleading." Numerical records of age were (and are still) less important than relative age, that is, one's position vis-à-vis one's elders and juniors. This was truer for Zanzibari girls than for boys. Many more boys than girls attended colonial schools, came before the juvenile courts, and registered with the state as laborers when they came of age. Most Zanzibari girls, on the other hand, remained beyond the reach of formal colonial structures. It was only when they came into direct contact with the state, as when they registered for school, that girls would be expected to provide such information. For this reason, census enumerators were instructed to make their own estimates when in doubt.[28]

Delineating between "children" and "adults," especially among females, continued to be the biggest challenge to census workers. The 1948 census stated that the "model marriage age group" was between twenty and twenty-four years, but it referred to "women" of child-bearing age as those between the ages of 15 and 44.[29] "Children" were those who were under fifteen, three years later than the boundary between "children" and "adults" specified in the 1924 census (twelve) and two years later than the legal minimum for consummation of marriage in the 1934 penal decree (thirteen). Married girls between ten and fourteen appeared in the census as simply "females."[30] Census takers were reluctant to refer to ten-year-olds as "women," but Zanzibaris would have not considered them "children" if they were married. Whether at the age of twelve, thirteen, fourteen, or fifteen, colonial reports struggled to draw the line between "girls" and "women." At the same time, they could not accept the unpredictable and varied age of puberty and marriage as standard markers of maturation.

The school was the primary institution through which the state inculcated its own standardized notion of childhood. For example, school medical inspections, which were introduced into Zanzibari schools in the early twentieth century, helped officials determine schoolgirls' ages and stages of physical development.[31] In addition to her height, weight, and other characteristics, medical history cards recorded a girl's "age of puberty." These exams normalized physical measurements of children and formed a scientific body of knowledge from which to correlate schoolgirl ages and school grades.[32] In addition to the schools' normal-age policies, medical inspections regulated the academic progress of children and created cohorts defined by the educational institution rather than indigenous age grades and biocultural stages of development. The colonial administration used the schools to educate the public about Western practices of calculating age numerically and determining levels of childhood maturation in terms of school grades. Scientific discourse, backed by colonial officials' moral claim to protect young girls from early marriage and premature exposure to sex, was the basis on which the state asserted its right to replace parents and initiation instructors as the authority guiding girls through maturation and toward marriage and motherhood.

For all the hype around establishing standardized measurements of childhood development and organizing groups of children according to numerical ages, the normal-age policies were never fully implemented in Zanzibar, at least not before World War II. The education department had to remain flexible as to the age at which students could enter the schools, the time it took students to complete the primary standards, and the age at which they left the schools in order to encourage parents to send their children to school and keep them there beyond puberty. *Normal age* was a rhetorical term that did not reflect the actual demographics of school grades.

Despite growing support for the girls' schools, many parents withdrew their daughters from school before they finished the primary course, regardless of their ages. The reasons given for withdrawal include "puberty," "marriage," and moving outside the town or area the school serviced, most likely for marriage.[33] In the early 1940s education officials stepped up their campaign to enroll girls early and keep them there after they reached puberty. The director of education asked newspaper editors to publish the following mock Q and A as a message to parents:

Government Girls' School

The life of this school has, so far, been a short one, only 15 years.

Question: Why has it taken so long to reach the present standard [Full Primary]?

Answer: Because you have not supported girls' education with enthusiasm.

Question: Why do some of our girls not even reach the top of the Primary School?

Answer: Because you delay sending them to school until they are above the normal age of entry, and take them away for marriage before they have reached the top class. Some of course are below average, as in every country.

Question: When should we send them to school?

Answer: Between the ages of 5 and 6.

Question: When would they reach the top of the Primary
   School if we entered them at 5 years?

Answer: Between 12 and 13.

Question: They would then be able to go on to Secondary Classes?

Answer: Yes of course, when these are established.

Question: When could a clever girl complete her secondary
   course?

Answer: Between 17 and 18 years old.

Question: What do our girls learn at school at present?

Answer: They learn first to "hitimu" in religion. [*Hitimu,* to
   graduate, referred to memorization of the first thirty chapters
   of the Qur'an.] . . . They learn to read and to write and to
   do arithmetic. They learn Arabic, Swahili, and English. They
   learn Geography and some history, and how to sow [*sic*]
   by hand and with a sewing machine. Cooking, housecraft,
   hygiene, and child-welfare, and many things besides.

Question: Isn't that rather a lot? Why do you teach so much in
   so short a time?

Answer: Because we have to teach them as much as possible
   in the short time you leave them with us, in order to equip
   them for life as well as we are able.

Question: If we brought them earlier and left them longer,
   would they learn differently?

Answer: They would have more time to devote to the above
   studies. Some of the studies would not be taken so early in
   their school career. They would also learn more.[34]

It was only after completion of the primary and secondary courses,
and at the "normal age" that corresponded to those grades,
that, according to the director, girls were ready for marriage and
motherhood. This approach was somewhat illogical: what were
they to do with girls over the age of thirteen who had completed
the primary course in the years before secondary courses were

introduced? Fortunately, the government began to resolve this issue when they appointed secondary-school teachers to work at the ZGGS in 1943. Three years later, the secondary courses were held at a separate Government Girls' Secondary School.[35]

Colonial efforts to attract girls to the schools and to keep them there beyond the age of thirteen gradually came to fruition. Though in the 1930s it was very common for parents to withdraw their daughters at puberty or earlier for marriage, after World War II more girls stayed on to complete the primary course. Some even continued their education after marrying and having children.[36] Others delayed marriage while they advanced to secondary school, the teacher-training program, or university.[37] By the 1950s and 1960s the schools had become crowded and entry into higher grades more difficult and competitive. The supply could not meet the demand. In rural areas, many girls even attended boys' schools where girls' schools were not available.[38]

DEFINING THE BOUNDARY BETWEEN "GIRLS" AND "WOMEN"

The success of colonial efforts to educate Zanzibari girls brought mixed results. As officials boasted about the growing numbers of girls attending government schools, they began to enforce the normal-age policy in order to manage the new problem of overcrowding. The secondary school embraced this tactic in the mid-1950s. One former student reported that only eleven of the forty girls in her Standard VIII course who took the entrance exam were admitted to Form 1 in 1957. When she finished Form 2, two years later, only half of the total sixty girls in her class were given the opportunity to complete the secondary course.[39] The Government Girls' Secondary School, renamed the Seyyida Matuka Girls' Secondary School, had moved into a larger building in 1958, but space was still limited. Less than 20 percent of the total number of boys *and* girls who took the secondary-school entrance examination entered Form 1. The 1959 report of the Committee on Education explained that there was "no fixed pass mark" for the secondary-school entrance examination. Rather, students with the highest scores were admitted on a first-come, first-served basis until the spaces were filled. In fact, the funding situation had become so dire in 1959 that expansion of primary and secondary schools was "at a halt" despite increasing demand and the inevitable "corresponding increase in public dissatisfaction and social unrest."[40]

By the late 1950s, the aims of the Department of Education had changed. No longer were colonial educators desperate to educate any and all girls, regardless of age. Now normal-age stipulations could be used to exclude those for whom space was not available, those deemed "too old" for school. The Department of Education's report for the three-year period between 1955 and 1957 stated that the Zanzibar Education Advisory Committee and the Pemba committee discussed, among other things, "age limits for admittance to secondary schools" and "the age of admission to primary schools."[41] Secondary students who underperformed or progressed too slowly for their grade and age were asked to leave. This was the case with Farida, a Form 3 student who at "nearly twenty" was, according to the secondary-school principal, "3 years beyond the most responsive age for her Education."[42] Likewise, sixteen-and-a-half-year-old Khadija was "two years over the most responsive age for the stage she has reached."[43] As students who were older than their peers, they were easy targets for the enforcement of the normal-age policies. Their mothers had heeded the government's call to keep their daughters in school as long possible. And now the teachers, themselves Zanzibari women, were using the same logic about the normal age of schoolchildren to expel them. Were these teachers so committed to perpetuating colonial rules about age and school grade levels that they would interrupt a girl's final years of education simply because her numerical age did not correlate exactly with that of her peers? Perhaps Western understandings of age and childhood development had finally begun to take hold in Zanzibar.

A closer look at the cases in which older girls were expelled from school suggests otherwise. Khadija was not only beyond the "most responsive age" for her cohort, she was also an "undesirable influence in the school." The principal notified her father that her "desk often contains lurid magazines and she has more than once been caught reading them during lessons."[44] It was not uncommon for teachers to read women's magazines, which might have piqued student interest in them.[45] We do not know what constituted "lurid" in Khadija's case, but the magazine likely included images of partially uncovered women in suggestive poses, such as the global "modern girl" image popular in African newspapers at the time.[46] The content of the magazine was perhaps less problematic than the fact that it was in the hands of a schoolgirl. The real question was whether or not Khadija had earned the social right to access the adult material. In early colonial Zanzibar, female literacy itself had been suspect. Many elders worried that if girls learned to write, they would write secret love letters to boys.[47] The right to possess and peruse a magazine, especially one that contained suggestive material, was the right of the adult woman, not the "girl." Even though the "girl" in this instance (Khadija) had likely reached puberty, gone through initiation, and may even have been married, as long as she was a student in the school she was not allowed to act like a woman.

Farida, too, was considered a problem student. She received failing marks on her exams. More troublesome, she did "not take her work seriously and [was] considered an unsettling influence on the rest of the class."[48] Farida had "been seen several times leaving school at break, meeting 2 young men beyond the D.S. [Domestic Science] School and going off down past Victoria gardens." The superintendent of education for women and girls, J. C. M. Bowen, wrote to the girl's father that she had hoped Farida would develop "a more mature attitude" toward her studies. Yet it was her sexual behavior that made her "irresponsible" and "a very bad example" for other students.[49] As with Khadija, Farida's sexual maturity and associated transgressions, rather than her age per se, made her a difficult student. Teachers framed the issue in terms of the normal-age discourse that colonial officials could understand, though they were primarily concerned with the girls' sexual development. "Bad behaviour" was a euphemism for subversive sexuality—meeting boys and reading magazines—and highlighted elder women's anxieties about pubescent, unmarried, and literate girls in Swahili society.[50]

In addition to sexual maturity, a girl's refusal to obey teachers was also grounds for her expulsion, apparent in the story of Fatma. Fatma was expelled for being "defiant and idle" and "resentful of correction."[51] She had been warned and "was asked to see that her work and behaviour improved." One of her teachers wrote that she "is quite intelligent and could do well but she rarely applies this intelligence and usually wastes her time, my time and the time of the whole class." Other teachers echoed these concerns. Bibi Samira Seif, the most educated Zanzibari woman on the education staff, reported that Fatma "is not interested" in her studies and "does not make any effort to learn." According to another teacher, Bibi Shukla, Fatma was "very lazy, inattentive in class, sometimes disobedient, untidy and irregular in her work." Although she could "speak English quite fluently," she failed all her courses.[52] Fatma was expelled because she challenged the authority of teachers. She thought she could outsmart them, a characteristic that undermined their control over the class. The lack of obedience in the classroom, which demonstrated that she had little respect for traditional age-based authority, also had dangerous connotations in the heightened tensions of the nationalist era, when youth became more engaged in politics.[53]

For many older girls, school was a source of fun, a path toward personal independence, and, as colonial officials hoped decades earlier, a way to delay marriage. As teachers worried about the presence of older girls in school, parents fretted about what their daughters might do if they remained at home. One mother pondered that if her daughter left school, she would "idle her time at home and get into mischief."[54] Farida's father visited the school and begged the teachers to take her back the first time they expelled her. He told the school authorities that she "got everything she wanted—long holidays on the mainland, her own car, which she [drove] around town and now she was asking to go to U.K. etc." He wanted her to go back to school so that she would not stay at home "doing nothing." Farida's father was not able to convince school officials. Her teachers expelled her permanently because though the girl "enjoyed school she took nothing very seriously."[55] Clearly she also took liberties not traditionally granted to "girls" in Swahili society. Girls who had bought into the notion that school could be an escape from marriage became a nuisance to parents and teachers alike. Parents hoped keeping their daughters in school meant keeping them out of trouble, but teachers were threatened by the presence of such girls in the classroom.

Fed up with Farida, Principal Banoum of the secondary girls' school wrote to Miss Bowen, the superintendent of education for women and girls,

> Is there any point in retaining this girl? I deplore the policy of letting them drift on into Standard XII [Form 4]. They are confident they can do this and a few just stay on to "complete Standard XII" as it ensures them a better job subsequently. Some expect to get admission to T.T.C. [teacher training college] or to a higher grade in the hospital or in government service on the ground that they have completed Standard XII. The fact that they have never done a stroke of work in 4 years seems to make little difference. This girl is on reduced fees; but does not seem to value the opportunity she has had.

> Keeping her back in St[d]. XI would not do any good. She has been warned and reprieved before. It would also make it impossible for me to admit the girl . . . about whom you spoke to me recently and who seems worth helping.[56]

The high competition for places in the higher standards of the girls' schools made girls such as Farida unworthy of the educational opportunity. Overt sexuality, discipline problems, and even poor grades gave teachers reason to enforce the normal-age policy.[57]

Principal Banoum, a British woman, was not only frustrated with Farida, she was concerned about the tendency of girls to stay in school just to brag that they had completed the highest grade. She wrote to Bowen, "This exploitation of 'completed St. XII' was brought to my notice some months ago by Bibi Samira: she laughed about it. Bibi Shariffa boasts of it. I feel it needs investigation by responsible authorities who are, virtually, being held to ridicule if they accept 'completed Standard XII.'"[58] Bibi Samira and Bibi Shariffa were two of the top Zanzibar female teachers working for the government. Principal Banoum's comment highlights a point of divergence between British and Zanzibari teachers. Zanzibari teachers were not disturbed by the fact that many girls do not take seriously the department's academic standards. At the same time, British officials were unable to understand how completion of Standard XII might be viewed as a rite of passage as much as an indication of an academic ability. Regardless of a student's marks and academic abilities, completion of Standard XII earned her the right to seek employment and make claims to a new status as an adult.

A look at the shifting demographics of female students and teachers provides some insight into the significance of this claim to status. Before 1940 girls became teachers after finishing Standard VII or VIII, and at the average age of 14.4. This increased to 17.3 in the 1940s, 19.9 in the 1950s, and 20.6 in the early 1960s as secondary courses became available.[59] The addition of higher grades to primary and secondary schools and the tendency of girls to stay in school longer account for this increase. The ages of students and teachers did not necessarily increase proportionally; students were not always of the "normal age." There remained some ambiguity around the distinction between older students and younger teachers. The problem of distinguishing between students and teachers was one reason that teacher training was moved from the Zanzibar Government Girls' School to the Ng'ambo Girls' School across town in the 1940s. The Department of Education's 1944 annual report stated, "The Teacher Training Centre for women is inadequately housed in the same building as the Girls School. . . . As a result of this there is also an unfortunate tendency, difficult to avoid in the circumstances, for the students to be regarded, and to regard themselves, as school pupils rather than as members of the larger community who are being trained to assume responsibility."[60] The move did not solve the problem. Schoolgirls attending the Ng'ambo school viewed the teachers-in-training as "girls of sixteen or eighteen," and as potential friends.[61] Teachers-in-training were in limbo. As school leavers they were no longer children, but as "students" they were not quite adults. Their immature status is apparent in the fact that the teacher-training contract required a signature from a "parent or guardian," though "guardian" could sometimes refer to the student's husband.

Parents would allow their daughters to become teachers only if the profession was a respectable one, that is, one that upheld the student's good reputation and did not conflict with her ability to marry. Knowing this, colonial officials encouraged female teachers-in-training to marry their male counterparts upon completion of the program in order to form "double-harness teams" working for the government.[62] Though "girls" upon entering training, certified female teachers would become married "women" by the time they took charge of a class. The education department made certain concessions, such as generous maternity leave for married female staff, to ensure the respectability of the teachers.[63] Most female teachers working for the government were indeed married and highly respected by the community.[64]

By the end of the colonial period, the department increased their demands on their female employees, demands that often came into conflict with the women's domestic duties.[65] As more female students completed the higher standards and desired to become teachers, officials worked less to convince parents that the profession was a reputable one for women. When faced with a threat to their status, female teachers began to expel older and disobedient students. If they could not rely on the government to ensure their respectability as elders, they would demand respect from their students. And doing so required hardening the boundary between them and their "girls."

In 1960, the same year that Farida, Khadija, Fatma, and others were forced to leave school, teachers and school administrators launched a formal campaign to ban married and pregnant girls from the secondary school. Here, too, frequent absence from class and bad grades were cited as reasons, but the girls' "poor influence" on their classmates was the crux of the issue. One student, Rukia, was married, divorced, remarried, and pregnant with her second child. Principal Banoum suggested Rukia be expelled because, as the teacher wrote, "She has been absent for nearly three weeks this term although the child is not yet born and she deliberately absented herself from the School Certificate trial exam last July. Since 1958 she has been regarded as a poor influence because of her very slack attitude."[66] Firyal, a student who got married only after becoming pregnant had "an attitude of inattentiveness in class and a decline in the standard of her work." A girl whose respectability was in question, she was deemed "unsuitable for Secondary Education." Unlike Farida and Khadija, numerical age was never cited as an issue here. Neither Rukia's nor Firyal's age mattered as much as their social status as wives and mothers and, in Firyal's case, her immoral conduct.

In a memorandum for the Zanzibar Education Advisory Committee, the staff of the new Seyyida Matuka Girls' Secondary School reported that the five married students attending the school had missed classes, underperformed, or were in some other way a negative influence on their classmates.[67] In the past, girls had been allowed to continue their education after marriage in order to encourage all Muslim girls to attend school. Now, female officials urged that this concession should be allowed only in primary schools in the villages, where girls' education was still a novelty and where early marriage was still rampant. They urged that "teacher-training colleges and other post-primary institutions" also limit admission to "unmarried girls." The Education Advisory Committee concluded that married students "did not derive the full benefit of the education provided and very often found it impossible to continue with their studies."[68]

The final decision was put on hold until the newly elected Zanzibari's education officials could consider the issue, and a law banning married and pregnant girls was not in place until after independence. In the meantime, the education department staff implemented the policy at their discretion. For example, when an unmarried student in the Pemban primary boarding school became pregnant in 1963, Bibi Samira suggested she be given "another chance" because she was "too young to be expelled."[69] The director of education agreed that the headmistress should keep her in school unless she had some reason to question the girl's "moral character."[70] It is surprising that the headmistress of the school did not automatically read the pregnancy as a sign of the pupil's immorality. The fact that the girl was a boarder meant that she was under the care of the education department at the time she became pregnant. If anyone was to blame for her indiscretion, it was the teachers themselves. Furthermore, officials were more lenient with students in primary schools outside Zanzibar Town. In the more crowded secondary school in town, the rule remained in effect. Some students even lied about their marital status and tried to hide a pregnancy in order to avoid expulsion.[71]

Throughout these debates, education officials referred to both married and unmarried students as "girls" in English or the gender-neutral term *watoto* (children) in Swahili, even though indigenous cultural paradigms dictated that a "girl" (mwari) earned the title of a "woman" (Bibi, or Mrs.) at the time of marriage. In the government schools, the title Bibi ("Mrs.") was reserved for teachers.[72] Regardless of marital status, all female Zanzibari teachers were called Bibi followed by their first names, the custom with married women in Zanzibar. Rather than a symbol of one's marital status, within the education system, Bibi was a title earned upon completion of the teacher-training program. Students were always "girls" and teachers were always "women." Courses at the Domestic Science School reinforced this practice. The school offered a "brides' course" for girls who finished Standard VIII and who could not or did not want to enter secondary school. The course taught students "to improve their English language, their way of living" and taught them "useful crafts which we are sure will be great help to them when they leave this School."[73] Though the class was open to students of various ages, some of whom were already married, it continued to be called a "brides' course" instead of a "wives' course" to encourage girls to take it before getting married and to emphasize the social distinction between teachers and students.

Students who had married, become pregnant, or like Farida and Khadija demonstrated other markers of sexual maturity, challenged this structural distinction between the "girl" student and the "woman" teacher. As girls passed the age of puberty and acted like adult women by flirting with boys, marrying, or having children, they no longer fit the description of the innocent "girl" that colonial education would save from initiation and child marriage. Instead of replacing these customs, Zanzibari teachers used the colonial schools to redefine them. When students challenged the authority of female staff as both teachers and community elders, female teachers fought back with the normal-age policy and the threat of expulsion. The government schools thus failed to fully transform local notions of age and childhood. In fact, in the early 1960s female teachers made sure they reinforced the indigenous age-grade system by policing the boundary between the prepubescent and the sexually mature, unmarried and married, "girls" and "women."

FROM THE perspective of British education officials, the girls' schools were a success. They offered an alternative to initiation and delayed marriage for many Zanzibari children. By the end of the colonial era, few girls left school at the age of twelve or thirteen for initiation and marriage. Many more stayed in school until the age of sixteen, seventeen, or, in rare cases, twenty. They waited until finishing primary, secondary, or teacher-training programs before they got married, and some even studied at the university level before marrying.[74] But marriage could not be avoided forever. Girls who used the schools to do so became a social problem. Their sexual maturity, and the sexual knowledge that they presumably obtained through ukungwi, was dangerous as long as it existed outside matrimony, an issue that, as we see in Meghan Halley's chapter in this volume, still influences school-girls' sexuality on the Swahili Coast today. As schools added higher grades to the curriculum, they risked exposing younger girls to the taboo sexuality of their more mature classmates.

Even more worrisome was the intimate knowledge from experience that married and pregnant students brought to their peers. If understanding of sexuality was what separated "girls" from "women," then the schools would have to do what initiation rites had done in the past: divide prepubescent girls from wives and brides-to-be. This became even more imperative when sexually mature students threatened the authority of Zanzibari teachers by acting out in class. Colonial officials promoted an ideology of childhood based on numerical age and school grades, but female teachers reified indigenous concepts of relative age and biocul-tural maturation by imposing their authority as "elders" over schoolgirls. Neither system existed without the other: a student was perpetually a "girl" and a teacher could be none other than a woman with the title Bibi. An aberrant student who defied these divisions was problematic, but not because she challenged colonial authority; rather, it was because she dared to challenge the authority of those whom the colonial education system had codified as female elders. The system of female authority that the colonial state and male elites hoped to eradicate resurfaced under the control of female government teachers and the lines that initiation drew between "girls" and "women" became the boundaries that defined colonial childhood itself.

NOTES

Abbreviations

KNA	Kenya National Archives
UKNA	The National Archives, Kew, UK
ZEDAR	Zanzibar, Education Department, Annual Report
ZGGS	Zanzibar Government Girls' School
ZNA	Zanzibar National Archives

Unless otherwise noted, all interviews were conducted by the author.

1. Heather Bell, "Midwifery Training and Female Circumcision in the Inter-war Anglo-Egyptian Sudan," *Journal of African History* 39, no. 2 (1998): 293–312; Peter Kazenga Tibenderana, "The Beginnings of Girls' Education in the Native Administration Schools in Northern Nigeria, 1930–1945," *Journal of African History* 26, no. 1 (1985): 93–109; Elke Stockreiter, "Child Marriage and Domestic Violence: Colonial Discourses on Gender and Female Status in Zanzibar, 1900–1950s," in *Domestic Violence and the Law in Colonial and Postcolonial Africa,* ed. Emily S. Burrill, Richard L. Roberts, and Elizabeth Thornberry (Athens: Ohio University Press, 2010), 138–58; Lynn M. Thomas, *Politics of the Womb: Women, Reproduction, and the State in Kenya* (Berkeley: University of California Press, 2003); Brett Lindsay Shadle, *Girl Cases: Marriage and Colonialism in Gusiland, Kenya, 1890–1970* (Portsmouth, NH: Heinemann, 2006).

2. Laura Fair, "Identity, Difference, and Dance: Female Initiation in Zanzibar, 1890 to 1930," *Frontiers: A Journal of Women Studies* 17, no. 3 (1996): 146–72; Corrie R. Decker, "Biology, Islam and the Science of Sex Education in Colonial Zanzibar," *Past and Present* 222, no. 1 (February 2014): 215–47. See also Karl Weule, *Native Life in East Africa: The Results of an Ethnological Research Expedition,* trans. Alice Werner (London: Sir Isaac Pitman and Sons, 1909).

3. For more on girls' education in Zanzibar, see Corrie R. Decker, *Mobilizing Zanzibari Women: The Struggle for Respectability and Self-Reliance in Colonial East Africa* (New York: Palgrave Macmillan, 2014).

4. Jackie C. Horne, *History and the Construction of the Child in Early British Children's Literature* (Farnham, UK: Ashgate Publishing, 2011);

Hugh Cunningham, *Children and Childhood in Western Society since 1500* (Harlow, UK: Pearson Longman, 2005); Cunningham, *The Invention of Childhood* (London: BBC Books, 2006).

5. Lynn M. Thomas, "The Modern Girl and Racial Respectability in 1930s South Africa," *Journal of African History* 47, no. 3 (2006): 461–90; Abosede A. George, *Making Modern Girls: A History of Girlhood, Labor, and Social Development in Colonial Lagos* (Athens: Ohio University Press, 2014); G. Thomas Burgess and Andrew Burton, introduction to *Generations Past: Youth in East African History,* ed. Burton and Hélène Charton-Bigot (Athens: Ohio University Press, 2010), 1–24.

6. Oyèrónké̩ Oyèwùmí, *The Invention of Women: Making an African Sense of Western Gender Discourses* (Minneapolis: University of Minnesota Press, 1997), 31.

7. Fatma Baraka, interview, Zanzibar Town, December 20, 2008; documentary: "As Old as My Tongue: The Myth and Life of Bi Kidude," directed by Andy Jones, ScreenStation Productions and Busara Productions, 2009; Meghan Halley, "Sex and School on the Southern Swahili Coast: Adolescent Sexuality in the Context of Expanding Education in Rural Mtwara, Tanzania," chap. 5, this volume.

8. Fair, "Identity, Difference," 158.

9. Thomas Spear, "Neo-traditionalism and the Limits of Invention in British Colonial Africa," *Journal of African History* 44, no. 1 (2003): 3–27.

10. Richard Waller, "Rebellious Youth in Colonial Africa," *Journal of African History* 47, no. 1 (2006): 77–92.

11. See, for example, Kathleen Sheldon, "'I Studied with the Nuns, Learning to Make Blouses': Gender Ideology and Colonial Education in Mozambique," *International Journal of African Historical Studies* 31, no. 3 (1998): 595–625; Carol Summers, "'If You Can Educate the Native Woman . . . ': Debates over the Schooling and Education of Girls and Women in Southern Rhodesia, 1900–1934," *History of Education Quarterly* 36, no. 4 (December 1996): 449–71.

12. Sean Morrow, "'No Girl Leaves the School Unmarried': Mabel Shaw and the Education of Girls at Mbereshi, Northern Rhodesia, 1915–1940," *International Journal of African Historical Studies* 19, no. 4 (1986): 620.

13. Archival and oral research for this project was generously supported by the Fulbright Institute of International Education; the University of California, Berkeley, Department of History; and the University of California, Davis, Department of History.

14. Ali Muhsin al-Barwani, *Conflicts and Harmony in Zanzibar: Memoirs* (Dubai: Ali Muhsin al-Barwani, 1997), 30.

15. Zanzibar National Archives (hereafter ZNA) AB 1/224 F. B. Pearce, British Resident, to Walter H. Long, Secretary of State for the Colonies, October 1, 1917, p. 9.

16. Zanzibar Protectorate, Department of Education, *Annual Report, 1927,* 14 (hereafter ZEDAR).

17. ZEDAR, 1934, 29.

18. Ibid.

19. J. N. D. Anderson, *Islamic Law in Africa* (Oxford: Frank Cass, 2013), 62.

20. ZNA, AD 1–171, pamphlet produced by *kadhi*s (Islamic judges) in Zanzibar on the issue of child marriage, 1959. See also Decker, "Biology, Islam"; Stockreiter, "Child Marriage."

21. Some people distinguish between the somo, a friend of the family who becomes a long-term companion and guide for the girl, and the kungwi, a person hired to prepare the bride for marriage.

22. Fair, "Identity, Difference," 152; Katrina Daly Thompson, "How to Be a Good Muslim Wife: Women's Performance of Islamic Authority during Swahili Weddings," *Journal of Religion in Africa* 41, no. 4 (2011): 427–48. See also the chapter by Thompson in this volume.

23. Fatma Baraka, interview, Zanzibar Town, December 20, 2008. If a woman never married, she continued to be called a mwari regardless of her age. The formal title *Bibi* (Mrs.) was technically reserved for women who had been married.

24. ZEDAR, 1927, 21.

25. ZEDAR, 1930, 22.

26. Amina Ameir Issa, "From Stinkibar to Zanzibar: Disease, Medicine and Public Health in Colonial Urban Zanzibar, 1870–1963." (University of KwaZulu-Natal, 2010), 141, 178; "Jamila" (pseud.), interview, Zanzibar Town, January 29, 2005; "Salama" (pseud.), interview, Zanzibar Town, January 27, 2005. Jamila was from Pemba and Salama from Zanzibar Town. Neither woman knew their exact ages. During the early twentieth century, when children's birthdates were recorded they were often dated according to the Islamic calendar rather than the Christian one. Al-Barwani, *Conflicts and Harmony,* 1.

27. Zanzibar, Census, 1948, chap. 3, "Analysis by Age and Sex," sec. A.

28. Zanzibar, Census, 1924, p. 8; Zanzibar Census, 1948, chap. 1, "Introduction and Definitions," sec. C, "Possible Sources of Error."

29. Zanzibar, Census, 1948, chap. 3, sec. D

30. Zanzibar, Census, 1948, chap. 4, "Analysis of Marital Condition," sec. B, "Analysis of Arab Persons over 14 Years of Age," Section C: Analysis of African Persons over 14 Years of Age: nearly 100 percent of women were married by the age of 20, 89 percent of "women" in the age group 15–19 were married, and more than 13 percent of "females" in the age group 10–14 were married.

31. Issa, "From Stinkibar to Zanzibar," 175.

32. An example of a British colonial medical history card appears in Kenya National Archives (hereafter KNA), CA/3/27, Government Indian

Girls' School Mombasa Inspection Report, July 1944. Girls who attended schools on the coast and the islands in the 1930s, 1940s, and 1950s were subject to regular health inspections by teachers, nurses, doctors, and dentists. "Asha" (pseud.), interview, Zanzibar Town, December 6, 13, 2004; "Muna" (pseud.), interview, Zanzibar Town, January 27, 2005; Inaya Yahya, interview, Zanzibar Town, February 8, 2005.

33. ZEDAR, 1932, app. 5, Report on the Zanzibar Girls' School, 1932, 37; ZEDAR, 1935, app. 3, Report of the Superintendent of Female Education on the Government Girls' School, 24; ZNA, AD 21/2 Chake Chake School Inspection Report, August 1937. In the 1935 report the headmistress wrote regarding those withdrawn from the school that "in the remaining seven cases no reason was given but all were probably withdrawn on account of age."

34. ZNA, AD 21/3, Foster, Director of Education, to newspaper editors, July 31, 1942.

35. The National Archives, Kew, UK (hereafter UKNA), CO 618/80/4, Zanzibar Education Department, Boarding School for Girls at Pemba, 1944–45; ZNA, AB 1/42, Director of Education to Acting Development Secretary, November 21, 1947.

36. "Asha," interview, Zanzibar Town, December 6, 2004.

37. "Muna," interview, Zanzibar Town, January 27, 2005; Inaya H. Yahya, interview, Zanzibar Town, February 8, 2005.

38. Zanzibar Protectorate, *Report of the Committee on Education, 1959* (Zanzibar: Government Printer, 1959), 4. In 1960 the Department of Education estimated that almost two thousand girls attended "mixed primary schools" in the villages. *Department of Education Report for the Triennium*, 1958–60, p. 13.

39. Nasra Mohamed Hilal, interview, Zanzibar Town, July 16, 2012.

40. Zanzibar Protectorate, *Report of the Committee on Education, 1959*, 13.

41. Zanzibar Protectorate, Department of Education, *Report for the Triennium 1955–1957*, 8.

42. ZNA, AD 21/8, Secondary School Pupils, Principal, Seyyida Matuka School, Zanzibar, to Sheikh Salim M. Barwani (Farida's father), December 3, 1960.

43. ZNA, AD 21/8, Secondary School Pupils; Principal, Seyyida Matuka School, Zanzibar, to Sheikh Masoud Borafin (father), November 24, 1959; copy of letter forwarded to Superintendent of Education for Women and Girls, November 23, 1960. See also Banoum to Sheikh Masoud Borafin, November 24, 1960.

44. ZNA, AD 21/8, Banoum to Sh. Masoud Borafin, November 24, 1959.

45. "Muna," interview, Zanzibar Town, January 27, 2005.

46. Thomas, "Modern Girl." The modern girl aesthetic appeared in African newspapers in the 1930s, but can be seen in Zanzibari newspapers

well into the 1950s. One example is in the Bagban Perfume advertisement in *Afrika Kwetu,* September 22, 1955.

47. "Muna," interview, Zanzibar Town, January 27, 2005; "Asha," interview, Zanzibar Town, December 6, 2004; Inaya H. Yahya, interview, Zanzibar Town, February 8, 2005.

48. ZNA, AD 21/8, Secondary School Pupils, Principal, Seyyida Matuka School, to Miss Bowen, Superintendent of Education for Women and Girls, November 25, 1960.

49. ZNA, AD 21/8, Joan Bowen, Superintendent of Education for Women and Girls, for the Acting Director of Education, to Farida's father (Sheikh Salim M. Barwani), December 6, 1960.

50. Corrie R. Decker, "Reading, Writing and Respectability: How Schoolgirls Developed Modern Literacies in Colonial Zanzibar," *International Journal of African Historical Studies* 43, no. 1 (2010): 89–114.

51. ZNA, AD 21/8, Bowen, for Director of Education, to Bibi Binti Shariff, November 23, 1960.

52. ZNA, AD 21/8, Banoum, Principal, Seyyida Matuka School, to Bowen, Superintendent of Education for Women and Girls, November 19, 1960.

53. Thomas Burgess, "Cinema, Bell Bottoms, and Miniskirts: Struggles over Youth and Citizenship in Revolutionary Zanzibar," *International Journal of African Historical Studies* 35, nos. 2–3 (2002): 287–314.

54. ZNA, AD 21/8, Banoum, Principal, Seyyida Maatuka School, to Superintendent of Education for Women and Girls, December 12, 1960.

55. ZNA, AD 21/8, Banoum, Principal, Seyyida Matuka School, to Superintendent of Education for Women and Girls, November 25, 1960; Banoum to Sheikh Salim M. Barwani (Farida's father), December 3, 1960; Joan Bowen, Superintendent of Education for Women and Girls, for the Acting Director of Education, to Farida's father (Sh. Salim M. Barwani), December 6, 1960.

56. ZNA, AD 21/8, Banoum, Principal, to J. C. M. Bowen, Superintendent of Education for Women and Girls, December 1960.

57. ZNA, AD 21/8, Banoum to Superintendent of Education for Women and Girls, November 25, 1960.

58. ZNA, AD 21/8, Banoum, Principal, Seyyida Matuka Girls' Secondary School to Miss Bowen, Superintendent of Education for Women and Girls, November 25, 1960.

59. ZNA, AD 24/7, List of Female Teachers and Dates of and Ages at Appointment, attached to Samira S. Seif, Superintendent Woman Education Officer, to Director of Education, February 16, 1962.

60. ZEDAR, 1944, 3.

61. "Muna," interview, Zanzibar Town, January 27, 2005.

62. ZEDAR, 1935, 17.

63. ZNA, AD 1/186, Senior Medical Officer to Chief Secretary, May 27, 1946. See also Elisabeth McMahon and Corrie Decker, "Wives or

Workers? Negotiating the Social Contract between Female Teachers and the Colonial State in Zanzibar," *Journal of Women's History* 21, no. 2 (2009): 39–61.

64. ZNA, AD 1/186 Female Teachers 1944–61; "Muna," interview, Zanzibar Town, January 27, 2005; "Asha," interview, Zanzibar Town, December 6, 2004; Inaya H. Yahya, interview, Zanzibar Town, February 8, 2005. For more on the history of female teachers, see Decker, *Mobilizing Zanzibari Women.*

65. McMahon and Decker, "Wives or Workers?"

66. ZNA, AD 21/8, Principal, Seyyida Matuka School, to Superintendent of Education for Women and Girls, September 16, 1960.

67. ZNA, AD 21/8, Memorandum for Zanzibar Education Advisory Committee.

68. ZNA, AD 21/8, Extract from Minutes of the 52nd Meeting of the Education Advisory Council, October 11, 1960. The matter was put on hold until the newly elected administration could address the issue. Married and pregnant girls were not allowed in the schools after independence, in 1964.

69. ZNA, AD 2/5, Wete Girls' Boarding School, Samira Seif to Director of Education, July 10, 1963.

70. ZNA, AD 2/5, Director of Education to District Education Officer, Pemba, July 13, 1963.

71. ZNA, AD 21/8, Banoum to Superintendent of Education of Women and Girls, August 18, 1960.

72. British teachers were called either "Miss" or "Mrs." depending on their marital status, but there is no equivalent to "Miss" in Swahili.

73. ZNA, AD 2/9, A Short Talk by Mrs. Saada Barwani, November 1962.

74. One example was Inaya H. Yahya. Yahya, interview, Zanzibar Town, February 8, 2005.

TWO

The Value of a Marriage

*Missionaries, Ex-slaves, and the Legal Debates over
Marriage in Colonial Pemba Island*

ELISABETH MCMAHON

THIS CHAPTER EXPLORES THE history of marriage among slaves
and ex-slaves on Pemba Island and the different approaches men
and women took to marriage over time. I look at Pemba, the rural
sister to Zanzibar Island (Unguja), because most of the enslaved
population there had at least a nominal conversion to Islam yet
they were not necessarily born in the Zanzibar Islands. The vast
majority of slaves in the islands were originally brought from
the mainland territories of modern-day Tanzania, Malawi, and
Kenya. Slaves usually converted to Islam after their enslavement,
although little research has been done to show exactly what
the impetus for conversion was, whether by force of the slave
owner or by the choice of the enslaved. At the moment of emancipation most slaves on Pemba at least nominally defined themselves as Muslim; however, it is difficult to estimate the depth of
their religious conviction. Slaves born in the islands were called
wazalia (lit., those born there; sing., *mzalia*) and were often

incorporated into their owners' families at emancipation, which gave them some economic and social security at emancipation. Without this connection, "freedom" left most slaves on Pemba socially and economically vulnerable. This vulnerability led former slaves, especially women, on Pemba to use a serial-marriage pattern in order to secure their daily existence. Serial-marriage patterns were commonly found in Muslim communities, where women were not expected to work outside of the home. Adult women were reliant for economic support on a husband, who provided housing, food, and clothing; thus if she was widowed or divorced she remarried after the required three-month waiting period. Another aspect of the vulnerability of slaves on Pemba was their willingness to use the help of Christian missionaries. At least 15 percent of all slaves who applied for their emancipation on Pemba used the help of the British Quaker missionaries.[1] Very little work has been done on the role Christian missionaries played in the emancipation process of the islands, even though three different mission organizations had stations on both Zanzibar and Pemba. This chapter focuses on the ways in which enslaved women and men negotiated marriage and used Christian missions for their own ends in the marketplace of marriage.

Emancipation began in 1897 in the Zanzibar Islands with an abolition order that required slaves to seek their emancipation from a government official and ended in 1909, when all slaves were declared "free" in the islands and on the mainland Swahili coast, controlled by the British. While marriage during enslavement was often arranged by owners, marriage after emancipation offered men and women new opportunities to choose their partners. Formerly enslaved men were excited about the freedom of choice emancipation brought in marriage partners. It appears former slave men hoped to recreate the patriarchal households of their former owners, in which the heads of the household had the respect and obedience of all members, were able to create new lineages of their own, and in some cases could make marital matches for love. Many former slave women, on the other hand, viewed marriage as a temporary endeavor that allowed them to gain material and sometimes social capital. Women on both Unguja and Pemba had little compunction about leaving husbands if they found a suitor whom they liked better or who could better fill their needs.[2] Enslaved women on Pemba were generally not wazalia, thus they were of lower status in the community and had little control over their bodies and sexual relationships.[3] The moment of emancipation offered these women a new freedom to control their sexuality through marital partners. This is not to suggest that formerly enslaved women were not sexually or economically vulnerable—they definitely were—but emancipation did offer many women a new choice, one that they regularly exercised.

Marriage on Pemba Island in the late nineteenth and early twentieth centuries generally followed Islamic practices. To marry in an Islamic ceremony, two people had to come before the *kadhi* (Islamic judge, *qadi*), the imam (religious leader), or the wali (government official) and declare their intentions. They had to state that *mahari* (dower) was being paid, how much was being paid at that time, and how much was deferred. The couple needed to bring several witnesses with them who could declare that the woman was not currently married to any other man. Polygyny was allowed for men, although no more than four wives were allowed at any given time. However, very few slave men in the records from Pemba had concurrent wives. Much as Susi Krehbiel Keefe (this volume) notes for the present, men in the past wanted multiple wives and viewed polygyny as a means to demonstrate their social status. Yet, because of the cost of maintaining wives equally (as required by the Qur'an), polygyny was an ideal unattainable for enslaved men and most ex-slaves.

Although choice in marriage partner was an exciting option for newly emancipated women, they still encountered the problem faced by all Muslim women: the legal inability to initiate a divorce outside a courtroom. Divorce for men simply required that a husband declare in front of witnesses that he divorced his wife. Wives could not similarly divorce their husbands, though they could request a divorce from a judge as long as they could prove one of several complaints against their husbands. Acceptable reasons for divorce included desertion, lack of maintenance (the provision of housing, clothing, and food), or inability to consummate the marriage (for further discussion of this point see

Stiles, this volume).[4] The requirement that women go to court for a divorce limited women's ability to get divorces; thus they used a variety of ways such as a woman "buying a divorce" from her husband by returning the mahari, absconding from the island, and in the earlier years of the emancipation order, using conversion to Christianity to allow her to divorce a Muslim husband. Although judges tried to keep marriages together, it was quite common for marriages to end in divorce.[5] While divorce was common on the island, most women and men practiced serial marriage, if a divorce occurred. Building families was a central reason for marriage: when interviewed by Quaker missionaries, slaves and ex-slaves expressed a real desire to have children to rebuild the families lost through enslavement.[6]

When scholars discuss marriage among slaves and ex-slaves, it is usually as a sidenote to their focus on family history. For most enslaved populations, marriage is about creating and legitimating families. In Cape Town, an area with a significant level of research on marriage among slaves and ex-slaves, scholars have argued that family structures were matrifocal because of the instability (and illegality, before 1834) of slave marriages.[7] The apprenticeship period of 1834–38 across the British Empire created a crisis in constructing marriage and families among ex-slaves, a pattern that would be repeated seventy years later along the Swahili coast and in the larger Indian Ocean world.

Abdul Sheriff notes for slaves in the Persian Gulf that the men despaired of being able to ever marry or have children.[8] Only around 35 percent of men were able to marry and then it was not until they reached their thirties and forties. Then enslaved men were married to "slave girls"; thus it appears female slaves were able to marry at younger ages. However, Sheriff argues that slave marriages were used by owners for the purpose of reproducing the enslaved population and not for slaves to create families. Jonathan Miran's work on the Red Sea coast offers another problem faced by Muslim communities around the Indian Ocean: ex-slave women could marry both freeborn and ex-slave men, while ex-slave men could not marry free-born women.[9] Because of the principle of *kufu* (suitability or compatibility in marriage, <Ar. *kafa'a*), ex-slave men were limited in whom they could marry.[10]

Little has been written about marriage among slaves in coastal East Africa in the nineteenth and early twentieth centuries.[11] Scholars have written about the sexual relationships between enslaved women and free men; however, very little research has been published about the marital (or sexual) relationships between enslaved men and women on the Swahili coast.[12] Colonial officials often implied that slave women used their sexuality to ally themselves to men when useful. However, these relationships were never discussed in terms of commitment or marriage but rather as short-term sexual alliances. How did slaves feel about these relationships? Did they see them as a commitment equivalent to a marriage? Could slaves leave these relationships? These questions encouraged me to explore the relationships of enslaved men and women and how these shifted in the emancipatory period (1897–1909) on Pemba Island. I found that with abolition many ex-slave women and men revisited their marriage choices, either divorcing their partners or finding a partner for the first time if they had not been able to marry while enslaved.

MISSIONS AND SOURCES

Missionary activity began in earnest on Pemba in 1897, when three different missions began on the island, the largest and most prominent being the Friends Industrial Mission (Quakers).[13] The Quakers came to the island in order to agitate for abolition of slavery in the islands, which came within months of the beginning of the mission. After the abolition order began the process of emancipation, the Quakers bought a large plantation on the island in order to offer ex-slaves a "new life" where they would both learn the skills of independent peasants and be protected from their former owners. Each ex-slave family that came to the mission was assigned a plot of land for their own benefit and hired as wage laborers to help the missionaries produce cash crops in order to pay for the mission. Men and women who worked on the mission did not have to convert to Christianity, although they were certainly proselytized at every opportunity by the missionaries.

The most "promising" of the men were given jobs as interpreters, "boat boys," cooks, and eventually teachers. These employees were paid monthly wages rather than piecework wages and earned considerably more than the day laborers living on the plantation. All these positions were held exclusively by men. Women were hired as construction laborers and farmers but were otherwise exempted from the "professional" positions on the plantation. This eventually created a "female problem" for the missionaries, who offered little benefit to women to convert to Christianity. The mission meeting noted in 1902 concern over a male convert who wanted to get married but no suitable wife was available to him. The missionaries discussed the problem of their adult converts:

> Up to the present time our boys have been educated with more care than our girls and we have more boys than girls under our care. This would seem to be a disadvantage only it has been unavoidable. We have been especially thoughtful lately about the prospects of the youth and fear it will be long before they will be the virtuous happiness in married life which we so much desire, but our teaching and training now will surely make it easier for the next generation to do right.[14]

However much the missionaries hoped to convert more females in the future, their policies toward marriage and divorce made conversion unappealing to women.

The Friends missionaries left a large collection of documents held at the Friends House in the UK which help illuminate the daily lives and relationships of laborers (who were almost entirely ex-slaves) on their mission. The Friends held monthly meetings beginning in 1897, when they opened their mission, that detailed the concerns of the missionaries, their interactions with laborers on their plantation, any converts, the salaries of their employees, the feasts they held, the progress of building up a plantation and a mission, and especially their activism in trying to end the legal status of slavery on the island. Several of the missionaries remained on the island for more than thirty years, bringing an incredible level of consistency in their reports, including in-depth knowledge of their laborers and their lives. Moreover, they kept what they called the "sacred book" of all slaves who sought help from them in getting their emancipation. This book contains approximately one thousand names of slaves seeking emancipation, as well as the names of their owners, any kinship relations among the slaves, their ethnicities, and various other occasional notes. Wedged into the monthly meeting notes were brief life histories of slaves and the daily dealings of ex-slaves when their personal lives, especially in relation to marital issues, came into the purview of the missionaries.

Theodore Burtt, one of the first Friends missionaries, who stayed from 1897 to 1932, also kept his personal letters that give details of individual slaves' complaints. Burtt interviewed twenty-nine slaves during his time in Pemba, writing down their life histories in a notebook. These histories were clearly answering specific questions: How were people enslaved? Did they like their owners? Why did they leave? Whom did they leave with? Did they have any children during their lifetimes? How many times had they married? None of the answers were formulaic, and Burtt took the time to write down such details as whether or not they loved their spouses. However, all the interview data was written down in English and not Swahili. Thus Burtt's interpretation of the intentions of the ex-slaves he interviewed are all that researchers have to determine how the slaves and ex-slaves constructed their relationships with one another.

As noted above, missionary documents generally have biases, just as does any other form of document, that we must read against in order to draw useful information. Since the population of Pemba was primarily Muslim, people who associated with the Christian missionaries were of lower status in local society. Perhaps for this reason, the missionaries on Pemba were spectacularly ineffective at converting ex-slaves. Until the 1930s, with the influx of mainland laborers to the island, the Friends had no more than a handful of confirmed converts at any given time. The Friends missionaries generally interacted with ex-slaves of the lowest status, not those who were either wazalia or chose to remain enslaved.[15] The silence on those who remained enslaved is deafening in their documents, so I focus my discussion of marriage among slaves and ex-slaves on those ex-slaves who did not have strong connections within the freeborn Muslim society on Pemba.

The creation of families during enslavement was not always by choice. At times owners assigned female slaves to their male slaves as "wives."[16] Most women interviewed by Friends missionaries spoke of these marriages matter-of-factly, indicating they may not have had much choice in marriage in their home communities before enslavement. Many young women spent their early years as concubines to their owners (or their owners' sons) but eventually were married off to other slaves.[17] Some slaves were given choices in their marriage partners and reported marrying "for love." Marriage partners were generally found among the slaves living on the same land, although slaves could at times marry slaves who belonged to other owners.[18] Regardless of how marriage partners were chosen, if they were enslaved divorce was rare because of the lack of potential marital partners. Generally, when enslaved people on Pemba married it was for life, or at least the life of the partner who died first.[19]

Loyalty and love among enslaved partners was not unusual, and the relationship clearly held importance to the slaves. During enslavement the bonds of marriage had practical value both because of the limits in slaves' movements and access to marriageable partners and also because marriage partners supported one another in their condition as slaves. One enslaved man, named Mamba, reported that he had fled several owners in his lifetime, although he was always reenslaved. When his last owner allowed Mamba to marry, he remained extremely loyal and did not try to flee his situation because he finally had the opportunity to marry.[20] Mamba remembered his last owner as being a brutal man who beat him for no reason, yet Mamba stayed because his loved his wife. While Mamba had repeatedly attempted to subvert the power of his owners over his person by running away, the emotional satisfaction offered to him through his love for his wife allowed him a new level of tolerance for being enslaved. Mamba's case demonstrates the value of marriage between slaves, who found their partners helpful in surviving the brutality and indignities of enslavement.

Marriage partners offered each other the possibility of creating family ties, of which they had been stripped in their enslavement.

Among slave and ex-slave parents, their children offered them a family. But more than that, children offered them social value within the community. While slave owners saw the children as additions to the labor force, enslaved parents clung to their children as a means to assert their value as human beings. Enslaved parents made choices for their children that were often not best for the parents but that allowed them to remain connected to their children physically or emotionally.[21] The story of Swema, brought to light by historian Edward Alpers, serves to show the emotional ties that parents had with their children.[22] Alpers recounts the slow descent of Swema into slavery and how Swema's mother attempted to stave off separation from her daughter at all costs. The dramatic account describes the terrible separation of Swema from her mother along a caravan route to Zanzibar, where Swema's mother was left to die and Swema was badly beaten in order to physically part her from her mother. The tenacity of Swema and her mother in their attempt to stay together demonstrates the intense emotional bond the two had for one another and explains why slaves would try to replicate family bonds through marriage and having children.

Marriage was not always ideal for all partners, and some did run away from each other when they fled enslavement. From the histories collected by Burtt, it appears that regardless of marital status, an enslaved spouse was more likely to flee slavery if he or she had no children. In some cases, when a couple's first child died, one of the parents fled to the mainland.[23] These cases indicate the important bonds created between marital partners through parentage. The cases also demonstrate the devastating effect that a child's death could have on couples. Faida, a female ex-slave, recalled to Burtt that her first marriage was based on mutual desire between herself and her husband. However, after their first child died at age one, her husband fled the plantation they lived on, leaving both enslavement and Faida behind. Another slave named Feruzi claimed he married his wife for love but after the death of their first child, his wife fled to the mainland with her brother with whom she had been enslaved. Feruzi expressed great sadness because his wife was expecting their second child when she left.[24] These two cases from Pemba Island demonstrate the tie children could create between spouses and how marriages could break down with the death of slaves' children.

However, both men and women recognized the choices that emancipation offered them about marriage partners. After emancipation they could get divorced if they wished and they often did so, much to the dismay of the Friends missionaries on the island.[25] The example of Songoro Makonde demonstrates a typical marital pattern in the histories collected by Burtt. Songoro was enslaved as a teenage boy.[26] He marked his ascent into adulthood as the moment he got married to a fellow slave "by his own choice." They remained married until she died. Songoro then remarried another slave woman, who eventually died as well. After the death of his second wife, Songoro again remarried. The emancipation order came during his third marriage and so he and his wife sought their freedom and moved to the Friends mission.[27] However, according to Burtt, as soon as she received her freedom paper, Songoro's wife absconded with "all his clothes, plates, etc." and he never saw her again. Much as Pat Caplan argues in this volume, the expectations and rules of marriage change over time and in response to events outside the control of local populations. Thus, after emancipation ex-slave partners, especially women, no longer had to stay in marriages they found unsatisfying.

EX-SLAVE MARRIAGES

While colonial officials and missionaries fretted over what they referred to as the "lability" of marriage among ex-slaves, former slaves rejoiced at the new opportunity for choice in marital partner that was opened to them by the abolition order. Both men and women recognized the choices that emancipation offered them with regard to marriage partners. The dynamics of marriage changed rapidly after emancipation among the ex-slave community, a change that was visible in the years leading up to World War I as men and women negotiated their newfound right to choose their partners and choose whether to stay in a marriage. The desire to replicate families and have children remained a fixture of the lives of ex-slaves; however, men and women were no longer dependent on one another for survival in quite the same way as they were while enslaved. In the histories of slaves written down by Burtt and in court documents, former slave men clearly hoped to assert a form of patriarchy they had witnessed among slave owners. However, female ex-slaves could no longer be controlled as they had been during enslavement, and, coupled with the higher number of men on the island, this precipitated a marriage crisis because women refused to cooperate with the desires of ex-slave men.[28]

Colonial officials worried constantly about ex-slave women becoming prostitutes, and one even declared that Pemba was "a giant brothel" after abolition.[29] This concern belied colonial fears of women remaining unmarried and thus not under the control of a male "guardian." Yet it appears that most ex-slave women did marry, whether to a single partner or through serial marriages. However, once women reached their forties and fifties they were less likely to remarry after divorce or being widowed.[30] The age at which women stopped remarrying is telling of their reason for tying themselves to men: children. One of the most valuable aspects of marriage for individuals was the possibility of having children. For enslaved and emancipated people (as well as freeborn), children were highly prized. Some literature on the Swahili coast notes the infertility of women, especially enslaved women, along the coastal areas, which may have prompted complaints from colonial officials and missionaries that enslaved women used abortion to avoid motherhood, and although this may occasionally have been the case, it is unlikely given the emphasis placed on having children in East African societies.[31] In an investigation of ex-slave fertility done in 1908, one colonial official in Zanzibar contradicted other Europeans by noting that he had seen many "places prepared at which the women offer up prayers to God to give them children."[32] Despite some colonial statements that enslaved women rarely had children, the data from the Friends' records suggests enslaved women tried to have children. Out of ninety-six families who sought their freedom in 1898 via the Friends mission, forty-six included multiple generations of a family. Most of the families had only one child, and from the life histories recorded by the Friends it is clear that a number of these children did not live to adulthood. For example, one woman who had a family on the mainland before being enslaved never saw her preenslavement children again. Her new owner on Pemba married her to a slave husband and within a year she gave birth to a boy she named Juma. Now called Mama Juma, she fought to keep Juma after the abolition order.[33] At emancipation her owner offered to free Juma and raise him within the owner's family. Mama Juma refused her owner's request; she wanted to keep her only child with her so she fled with him to the Friends mission. Sadly, a year later Juma died, leaving his mother childless and bereft. Even without a living child, she insisted on keeping her name as Mama Juma, signifying to others the importance of motherhood to her. Likewise another ex-slave woman, Mama Radhie, gave birth to eight children; however, only two lived past childhood.[34] Clearly then the ability to procreate was an important aspect of marriage for both enslaved and ex-slave populations.

However, women did not need to have a spouse to have a child. A woman with a child was more likely to be able to remarry since she had proven her fertility. This begs the question of why women bothered to marry at all. Most women did marry or lived in households with a male head of household, whether or not they were married.[35] During enslavement women and men were equal producers in the household, and in fact woman often worked more than men because they both worked in the plantations and cooked for the household. But the general sustenance for the household came from the labor of both men and women. However, after being emancipated women had to find new ways to feed themselves, since men more easily found work as porters or *vibarua* (day laborers). Many women continued to work in the plantations, as vibarua or as prostitutes, but most situated themselves in relationships that allowed them to work for their household only (outside of the clove harvest season, when everyone worked in the fields), as was typical in freeborn peasant households.[36] This meant planting a plot of land for vegetables and cassava to eat, cooking, and maintaining the home, while a man brought in some regular income. Harold Ingrams, a colonial official on Pemba in the 1910s with a knowledge of Arabic, noted that ex-slaves "regard their marriage ties very loosely indeed; often no more than five or ten rupees is mahr [*mahari,* dower], and in other cases a sum is named as mahr but none paid at all. Divorce is frequent, and the women rarely observe their Iddet [*edda,* the three-month waiting period after divorce]."[37] Ingrams's statement offers several insights into why ex-slave women remarried after being divorced or widowed rather than staying unmarried. First, if women were not observing the edda, it was likely because they could not afford to do so.[38] If their mahari was nonexistent or only a few rupees, then the women probably needed to be married for their maintenance. Second, the statement makes the point that an acknowledgment of paying mahari was important to ex-slave men and women, and they thus viewed these marriages as more than temporary; just because the mahari was small did not nullify the value it held. Women wanted the legitimacy of marriage and thus required mahari no matter how small to make sure the relationship was recognized as a marriage.

The case of Fatahi wadi Juma, a Zaramo man, indicates the meaning that marriage held for ex-slave men and women. Fatahi fell in love with a woman named Hanzorani, whom he met after emancipation, but Hanzorani was already married so they remained only friends.[39] Fatahi lived with a woman named Andihalo during those years, but he never married her. When Hanzorani was widowed, Fatahi quickly proposed marriage. According to the Quakers, after their marriage Hanzorani and Fatahi remained together until her death, very much in love. Clearly, for Fatahi the act of marriage had real meaning, which explains why he did not marry Andihalo, whom he did not love. This also demonstrates that some ex-slave women chose to live with a man without actually marrying him. This allowed both partners the freedom to leave at any time. Fatahi may have been a particularly good partner and that is why Andihalo agreed to stay with him even without the security of a mahari.

Although both men and women could choose their partners, after emancipation women were more in demand as marital partners because only ex-slave women could marry both ex-slave and freeborn men. Men and women both remembered men aggressively intervening in marriages and luring married women to leave their husbands. Ndaniyenu, an ex-slave woman living on the Friends mission, recalled that she "was persuaded by another man . . . to leave her husband." Likewise Feruzi, who "married for love," had his "home broken" by Songoro Mnyasa, another ex-slave who convinced Feruzi's wife, Mtahawi, to leave her husband.[40] In 1910 a man was brought up on murder charges with the motive being jealousy over a woman.[41] The murdered man, Majaliwa, reputedly was having an affair with a woman named Tausi, whom the murderer Nasibu wanted to marry. Tausi declared that she had not had a relationship with Majaliwa, but that she was afraid of Nasibu, who had beaten her and tried to make her marry him. Tausi's refusal to marry Nasibu, even when afraid of him, indicates the difficulty men had in controlling women in the postemancipation era. Ex-slave men had a difficult time imitating the patriarchy of slave owners, who generally received respect from their female household members and could discipline their household members if disobeyed. An ex-slave man who tried to discipline his wife—such as by refusing to let her participate in community events or gossip with her friends, or by beating her—could find himself quickly deserted.

The case of Fatahi demonstrates the desire of men to replicate patriarchy when possible after emancipation. After Hanzorani's death, Fatahi married and divorced four women in quick succession. Fatahi could have married Andihalo while waiting for Hanzorani because, as a Muslim man, Fatahi only had to utter a pronouncement to divorce Andihalo, or he could have had two wives, although it is unlikely he could afford to maintain two wives given his social position.[42] We must ask then why did Fatahi not marry Andihalo when after Hanzorani's death he married four times? His multiple remarriages suggest a man who wanted to have a wife who would maintain a home for him, allowing him to act as a patriarch, even if only in his own mind. Andihalo was willing to go without a mahari, but perhaps the women Fatahi married after Hanzorani's death were not willing to do so, which would make sense given that Fatahi was likely much older and a less desirable spouse. The evidence suggests that while men may have tried to control women, in the period immediately after emancipation ex-slave women had considerable agency in their relationships with men.[43] The higher ratio of men to women on the island in the early emancipation era gave women some leverage in their refusal to put up with men who were too overbearing as spouses and explains why women sought to end unwanted marriages.

Just as women and men valued marriage ceremonies, women wanted a measure of freedom of choice. As mentioned above, some ex-slave husbands wanted to control their wives, replicating the power they perceived their owners as having. Ex-slave men beat their wives and punished them for infractions of male control.[44] Needless to say, in the early years after abolition ex-slave women who were in demand as marital partners had little tolerance for male misbehavior; however, married women could not easily initiate divorce. Some ex-slave women found a loophole in the divorce proceedings by using conversion to Christianity or Islam (depending on their current religious allegiance) in order to divorce their partner who was affiliated with the opposite religious faith. Muslim officials were happy to divorce newly reconverted Muslim women from Christian men, but this loophole created a marriage crisis among the mission communities, who were also trying to attract female converts but found to their dismay that female converts used the missions as a means to leave unwanted husbands.

THE MAKING OF A MARRIAGE CRISIS

The new missionaries who arrived in 1897 were determined to teach the ex-slaves living on their mission what they viewed as Christian morality. The Quakers in particular wanted to introduce a concept of Christian marriage based on the notion of helpmeets, a couple who were ostensibly equal partners in the marriage and household, who would marry for life. Within the first year of the mission, several people living on the mission asked to be married in a Christian ceremony, and the Quakers gladly granted this wish. However, in 1901 the Quakers faced a conundrum: did they have the right to perform marriages among their converts? A couple married by the Quakers sought a divorce and when the Quakers refused, the couple went to the wali court to seek a divorce. The British official attached to the wali court, Mr. Farler, explained that the Quakers had no right to perform marriages because only individuals designated by the government could do so and therefore the marriage was never legal in the first place.[45] This decision set off the first in a series of marriage crises among the missionaries and their converts.

The Quaker missionaries were disturbed by Mr. Farler's refusal to acknowledge marriages performed by them as valid. They wrote to the British consul, who responded in December 1901,

> His highness readily agreed to my suggestion and has instructed the Wali of Chake Chake [a town on Pemba Island] to recognize as valid marriages between two native Christians which are duly solemnized by any European member of your mission who is properly authorized to solemnize them. The head of the mission, should however communicate to the Wali the names of the members of the mission who are so authorized and should keep a register in which all such marriages are to be entered and which is open at all times to the inspection of the sultan's officials.[46]

Thus it was now acceptable and legal for the Quakers to marry their converts. But Mr. Farler threw another wrinkle into this debate when he declared that the Quakers could only marry ex-slave converts. This would have limited the missionaries from marrying any converts who were not ex-slaves. While this was mostly a moot point because in general few members of the nonenslaved population chose to convert to Christianity, it nonetheless became an issue of contention for the Friends. The missionaries *wanted* to convert both former slaves and freeborn people and were therefore upset by Mr. Farler's caveat. Eventually it was sorted out that the Quakers could marry any Christians as long as both the husband and wife declared themselves to be Christians. This seemed to settle things for the Quakers, until the first of these officially married couples sought a divorce.

Bakari and Faida were married by the Quakers after 1902 but soon began to quarrel. By 1903 they began asking the Quakers for a divorce, but the Quakers refused. They wanted the couple to work things out. Bakari and Faida were not the only couple married by the Quakers who sought a divorce. Juma Marufu and Bahati Yangu also requested a divorce. The Quakers suggested that Juma and Bahati live apart for a while, trusting in the old adage "separation makes the heart grow fonder."[47] It did not work. In the meantime Bakari and Faida went to the wali and asked him for a divorce. The wali granted it since both husband and wife wished for the divorce. Bakari and Faida remained living on the mission but were no longer married or living together, until Mr. Farler heard about the divorce, when he declared that only the Quakers could grant a divorce between two people they had married. In April 1905 he told the missionaries to inform Bakari and Faida that they were still married and could not remarry.[48] Another colonial official, Mr. Lister, suggested the Quakers contact the British consul again, who stated that Mr. Farler was wrong and that the wali was the *only* person who could divorce mission converts married as Christians.[49] The consul argued that Christians were still subjects of the sultan and therefore "subject to the same courts and the same laws as those who are Mohammedan [Muslim]." The consul also chastised the missionaries for refusing to conduct Christian marriages between people who had been legally divorced.

The consul's ruling, in early 1906, upset the missionaries because it meant that not only did Muslim officials have the right to divorce Christians from one another but that the Quakers lost the right to decide who could and could not be divorced among their converts. While the years 1903 to 1905 saw a wave of couples seeking divorce from the missionaries, after 1906 they could simply go to the wali. Couples such as Juma and Bahati, mentioned above, no longer had to wait and repeatedly request a divorce from the Quakers. In May 1905 the Quakers had again refused to allow Bahati and Juma a divorce, two years after they had first requested one. After the consul's ruling, Bahati and Juma were able to go to the wali and end their marriage. After 1906 the missionaries became more careful about vetting potential marriage partners. A new system was put into place that all converts requesting Christian marriage had to be interviewed individually by members of the mission. One of the early couples to go through this process, in 1908, Herbert Mtondoo and Sikpekeyangu, were refused a marriage permit when another woman suggested that Mtondoo had not been faithful to Sikpekeyangu.[50]

In late 1912 the Friends again felt the need to bring into public discussion the issue of who could divorce Christians. Instead of trying on their own to convince the British resident to change the ruling, the Friends sought the help of other missionaries on the island.[51] In discussions with the Catholic and Anglican missionaries on Pemba, the Friends found they had a common problem in divorce. However, a new wrinkle had developed: in the early cases of divorce among Christian converts, both wives and husbands wished for the divorce so the wali readily granted the divorces, but if one spouse did not want it, the wali refused to grant the divorce. This was often the case when the wives wanted a divorce but the husbands did not. The wali was guided by the principles of Islamic law: men could divorce their wives, but women could be divorced only by their husbands.[52] Thus as Christian women sought to divorce their husbands, they hit a snag. The wives quickly found a way around their problem by going to the wali and declaring that they were no longer Christians and were now Muslims. When that happened, the wali would accept their conversion and declare their marriage as null and void because legally a Muslim woman could not be married to a Christian man. Thus, not only were the converts divorcing but the missionaries were also losing converts and, in particular, female converts.

The year 1912 was a stressful one for the Friends. In February they instituted a new policy that if a couple was married in a Christian ceremony and one party to the marriage was later adulterous, then the adulterer was banished from the church (and thus divorced from their spouse) and forced to move away from the plantation. The missionaries exhorted church members "to be very earnestly advised not to choose as a wife any woman who is not desirous of receiving Christian teaching and willing to attend religious meetings."[53] The gendered language of this guideline speaks to the point that in 1912, fifteen years after the mission began, most of their converts were still men. When writing to the Anglican leadership in the United Kingdom, who was responsible for the Universities' Mission to Central Africa (UMCA) mission located on Pemba, in November 1912 the Friends were even more explicit: "our weaker Christian women are hereby ensnared by wily Moslems who desire them, and we have had some serious difficulty."[54] These comments from the Friends indicate both the very real threat marriage issues had to their ability to convert women and the leeway female ex-slaves had in negotiating marriage and divorce in the early emancipatory period. By 1920 the marriage crisis among convert women had ended; women could no longer use conversion between Islam and Christianity as a means to end unwanted marriages because the government came to treat Christian marriages like Muslim ones.

MARRIAGE AMONG slaves had been a source of strength for some but generally offered women little choice. When emancipation began, some ex-slave women rejoiced in their ability to leave unwanted spouses. Yet newly free Muslim ex-slave women did not have complete freedom in marriage either. In their second and later marriages, such women could choose their husbands, but it was still difficult to initiate a divorce. Historically, Muslim women along the Swahili coast had used a *khuluu* divorce as a means of "buying a divorce"; however, most ex-slave women did not have the economic resources to buy themselves out of a marriage.[55] Ex-slave women—regardless if they lived on a Christian mission or among the larger Muslim community of Pemba Island— sought choice in whom they married and sought to advocate for themselves if their husbands attempted to assert too much control over them. Although Christian missionaries were eager to have female converts, they had not planned for the difficulties they would encounter with ex-slave women who refused to remain tied to an unwanted partner.

Women and men continued to marry for a variety of reasons, but the hope of creating families was central to their relationships with one another. Men certainly hoped to become patriarchs, building lineages and respect from their households, as they had witnessed during their enslavement, yet women had little patience for patriarchy. Women needed spouses to create families, to build respectability within their communities, and at times to have access to land and an income. Yet women had significant opportunities to remarry and did so at will. The marriage crisis in the Christian communities attests to the ways in which some ex-slave women used every means at their disposal to keep the freedom of choice they received at emancipation to marry and divorce.

NOTES

Abbreviations

FIM   Friends Industrial Mission
NA   National Archives, United Kingdom
PNA   Zanzibar National Archives, Pemba branch
UMCA   Universities' Mission to Central Africa
ZNA   Zanzibar National Archives

1. Elisabeth McMahon, *Slavery and Emancipation in Islamic East Africa: From Honor to Respectability* (New York: Cambridge University Press, 2013).

2. Laura Fair, *Pastimes and Politics: Culture, Community, and Identity in Post-abolition Urban Zanzibar, 1890–1945* (Athens: Ohio University Press, 2001), 210.

3. Since comparatively fewer slaves (700 on Pemba to 6,000 on Unguja) were voluntarily manumitted, it appears few slaves on Pemba were wazalia. Wazalia were much more likely to be manumitted than recently enslaved Africans.

4. Harold Ingrams noted in the 1910s and 1920s that inability to complete sexual intercourse either through impotence or because a man's penis was too large constituted reasons for divorce. William Harold Ingrams, *Zanzibar, Its History and Its People* (London: H. F. and G. Witherby, 1931), 238.

5. For modern comparisons on divorce and the variety of ways women could achieve a divorce along the Swahili coast see Erin E. Stiles, *An Islamic Court in Context: An Ethnographic Study of Judicial Reasoning* (New York: Palgrave Macmillan, 2009); Susan F. Hirsch, *Pronouncing and Persevering: Gender and the Discourses of Disputing in an African Islamic Court,* Language and Legal Discourse (Chicago: University of Chicago Press, 1998). For a historical discussion of marriage and divorce among freeborn people in urban Unguja, see Elke E. Stockreiter, "Tying and Untying the Knot: Kadhi's Courts and the Negotiation of Social Status in Zanzibar Town, 1900–1963" (PhD diss., University of London, School of Oriental and African Studies, 2008).

6. Friends Industrial Mission (hereafter FIM), TEMP MSS 419/1–7, Theodore Burtt, Notebook, 1899.

7. For discussions of family among slaves and ex-slaves, see Pamela Scully, *Liberating the Family? Gender and British Slave Emancipation in the Rural Western Cape, South Africa, 1823–1853*, Social History of Africa (Portsmouth, NH : Heinemann, 1997); John Edwin Mason, "Fortunate Slaves and Artful Masters: Labor Relations in the Rural Cape Colony during the Era of Emancipation, ca. 1825 to 1838," in *Slavery in South Africa: Captive Labor on the Dutch Frontier*, ed. Elizabeth Eldredge and Fred Morton (Boulder: Westview, 1994), 67; Vertrees C. Malherbe, "Illegitimacy and Family Formation in Colonial Cape Town, to c. 1850," *Journal of Social History* 39, no. 4 (2006): 1153–76.

8. Abdul Sheriff, "The Slave Trade and Its Fallout in the Persian Gulf," in *Abolition and Its Aftermath in Asia and the Indian Ocean World*, ed. Gwyn Campbell (New York: Routledge, 2005), 113–14.

9. Jonathan Miran, "From Bondage to Freedom on the Red Sea Coast: Manumitted Slaves in Egyptian Massawa, 1873–1885," *Slavery and Abolition* 34, no. 1 (2013): 135–57.

10. Wael B. Hallaq, *Sharī'a: Theory, Practice, Transformations* (Cambridge: Cambridge University Press, 2009), 274–5.

11. Sarah Mirza and Margaret Strobel address marriage among slaves in *Three Swahili Women*, but the discussion is limited. Mirza and Strobel, eds., *Three Swahili Women: Life Histories from Mombasa, Kenya*, trans. Mirza and Strobel (Bloomington: Indiana University Press, 1989). Laura Fair mentions relationships between former slave women and men (but it is not always clear whether the men were also former slaves); most of her discussion is about lovers rather than spouses. Fair, *Pastimes and Politics*, chaps. 2, 4. Marc Swartz offers a discussion of power dynamics in Swahili marriages but does not address marriage among slaves in the nineteenth century. Swartz, "The Isolation of Men and the Happiness of Women: Sources and Use of Power in Swahili Marital Relationships," *Journal of Anthropological Research* 38, no. 1 (1982): 26–44. Elke Stockreiter has a wonderful work on marriage and marriage contracts in urban Zanzibar, yet in most cases she does not denote if the participants were ex-slaves. Stockreiter, "Tying and Untying."

12. For discussion of women as concubines see Patricia W. Romero, *Lamu: History, Society, and Family in an East African Port City* (Princeton: Markus Wiener, 1997), 123–24; Katrin Bromber, "Mjakazi, Mpambe, Mjoli, Suria: Female Slaves in Swahili Sources," in *Women and Slavery: Africa, the Indian Ocean World, and the Medieval North Atlantic*, ed. Gwyn Campbell, Suzanne Miers, and Joseph Calder Miller (Athens: Ohio University Press, 2007), 120; McMahon, *Slavery and Emancipation*, 209–18; Jan-Georg Deutsch, *Emancipation without Abolition in German East Africa, c. 1884–1914* (Athens: Ohio University Press, 2006), 69–78; Margaret Strobel, *Muslim*

Women in Mombasa, Kenya, 1890–1975 (New Haven: Yale University Press, 1979), 50–51; Fair, *Pastimes and Politics,* 101. The marriage of enslaved men to enslaved women has almost never been the subject of scholarly work because so few sources exist to document this history.

13. The other two missions were run by the Anglican Universities Mission to Central Africa and a French Catholic mission about which absolutely nothing has been written on the islands.

14. FIM, PZ(F)/3, meeting minute book, 1898–1902.

15. There is a large literature that discusses the choice of many slaves in the islands to remain enslaved to their owners rather than seek government manumission. This literature tends to focus on the social value slaves received from their owners (by becoming lower-status members of their owners' lineages); however, I have argued elsewhere that many slaves remained with owners out of economic desperation. For a discussion of slaves connections to their owners, see Romero, *Lamu;* Strobel, *Muslim Women;* Fair, *Pastimes and Politics;* Frederick Cooper, *Plantation Slavery on the East Coast of Africa,* Yale Historical Publications 113 (New Haven: Yale University Press, 1977); Cooper, *From Slaves to Squatters: Plantation Labor and Agriculture in Zanzibar and Coastal Kenya, 1890–1925* (New Haven: Yale University Press, 1980), among many others. For the case of economic desperation see McMahon, *Slavery and Emancipation,* chap. 6.

16. FIM, TEMP MSS 419/1–7, Theodore Burtt, Notebook, 1899, Mama Juma and Mariamu binti Msa; Cooper, *Plantation Slavery,* 223–24.

17. FIM, TEMP MSS 419/1–7, Theodore Burtt, Notebook, 1899, Hatusawa, Mame Taki, Sanura and Tufaa; Zanzibar National Archives, Pemba branch (hereafter PNA) AI1/44 HHSCZ, Civil Appeal no. 15 of 1934, Bahati binti Serenge vs. Mohamed bin Musa bin Burhan Shirazi.

18. FIM, TEMP MSS 419/1–7, Theodore Burtt, Notebook, 1899, Ndaniyenu; FIM Slave Register; PNA AI1/34 HBMCZ FCS Court, Chake Chake Civil Case no. 986 of 1928, Fatuma binti Ali bin Sababu vs. Hamadi Kheri and Juma Kheri.

19. A number of slaves reported multiple marriages during their enslavement; however, the cause of remarriage was always death of the first spouse, not divorce. FIM, TEMP MSS 419/1–7, Theodore Burtt, Notebook, 1899

20. FIM, TEMP MSS 419/1–7, Theodore Burtt, Notebook, 1899, Mamba.

21. See examples from FIM, PZ(F)/3, diary of boys home, 1902–6.

22. Edward A. Alpers, "The Story of Swema: Female Vulnerability in Nineteenth-Century East Africa," in *Women and Slavery in Africa,* ed. Martin A. Klein and Claire C. Robertson (Madison: University of Wisconsin Press, 1983), 185–219.

23. FIM, TEMP MSS 419/1–7, Theodore Burtt, Notebook, 1899, Faida.

24. FIM, TEMP MSS 419/1–7, Theodore Burtt, Notebook, 1899, Feruzi.

25. FIM, TEMP MSS 419, Private letters of Theodore Burtt, November 24, 1909.

26. FIM, TEMP MSS 419/1–7, Theodore Burtt, Notebook, 1899, Songoro Makonde.

27. The Friends mission offered slaves seeking emancipation help with the process and, if they desired, a plot of land in which to grow food and live. In exchange for the land, former slaves were asked to work as paid labor on the plantation and in picking during the clove harvests. Private plantations on the islands used the same system—former slaves received land in exchange for weeding help and paid labor during the harvests. The Friends did not require former slaves to weed in exchange for the land: however, they did make all their workers endure an hour-long, early- morning prayer service.

28. Women were more likely to seek their emancipation from the government, with 57 percent of applications coming from women. However, the 1924 census suggests that men marginally outnumbered women on the island. These sources suggest that women had more choice in finding marriage partners after emancipation. ZNA, AC5/5, Vice-Consul, Pemba, Letters for statistics on the gender breakdown of slaves seeking emancipation; ZNA, BA34/2, Report of the Native Census of Zanzibar, 1924. For examples of court cases, see Thomas Symonds Tomlinson and Gordon Kennet Knight-Bruce, *Law Reports Containing Cases Determined by the High Court for Zanzibar and on Appeal Therefrom by the Court of Appeal for Eastern Africa and by the Privy Council*, vol. 3, 1923–27 (London: Waterlow and Sons, 1928).

29. "Report of the Slavery Commissioner for Pemba Island," Africa no. 4 (1901), *Correspondence Respecting Slavery and the Slave Trade in East Africa and the Islands of Zanzibar and Pemba* (London: Printed for His Majesty's Stationery Office by Harrison and Sons, 1901).

30. A survey of probate records on Pemba Island from 1910 to 1940 shows that 41 percent of women died without a spouse. For examples, see PNA, AK1/82, Raia binti Salim Seif, 1910; PNA, AK1/323, Manashamba binti Hadidi Swahili, 1914; PNA, AK1/3310, Hashima binti Baraka, 1934; PNA, AK1/4197, Binti Hamis, 1941; FIM, TEMP MSS, 419/1–7, Theodore Burtt, Notebook, 1899.

31. "Report by Vice-Consul O'Sullivan on the Island of Pemba, 1899," Africa no. 8, *Correspondence Respecting Status of Slavery in East Africa and Islands of Zanzibar and Pemba* (London: Printed for His Majesty's Stationery Office by Harrison and Sons, 1899). Also note that officials never gave proof for this theory, only their opinion. Father Bale told O'Sullivan-Beare he believed jealous wives sterilized concubines. ZNA, AC8/5, February 28, 1903; D. F. Roberts and R. E. S. Tanner, "A Demographic Study in an Area of Low Fertility in North-east Tanganyika," *Population Studies* 13, no. 1 (1959): 61–80.

32. NA, FO 403/394, East African correspondence 1908, General Raikes to Mr. Cave, enclosure 1 in no. 7, p. 26. He was speaking specifically of enslaved or former slave women.

33. FIM, TEMP MSS 419/1–7, Theodore Burtt, Notebook, 1899, Mama Juma.

34. FIM, TEMP MSS 419/1–7, Theodore Burtt, Notebook, 1899, Mama Radhie.

35. ZNA, AC5/3, Vice-Consul Pemba, letter July 5, 1899; Africa, no. 6 (1902), *Correspondence Respecting Slavery and the Slave Trade in East Africa and the Islands of Zanzibar and Pemba* (London: Printed for His Majesty's Stationery Office by Harrison and Sons, 1902), 14.

36. Henry Stanley Newman, *Banani: The Transition from Slavery to Freedom in Zanzibar and Pemba* (New York: Negro Universities Press, 1969), 109–120; Africa, no. 4 (1901), *Correspondence Respecting Slavery*, 13; Cooper, *Slaves to Squatters*.

37. Ingrams, *Zanzibar*, 220–21. Edda is the three-month period of waiting that every Muslim woman is supposed to observe after a divorce before remarrying, according to the Qur'an.

38. For modern examples of men avoiding payment of edda maintenance, see Stiles, *Islamic Court*.

39. FIM, TEMP MSS 419/1–7, Theodore Burtt, Notebook, 1899.

40. Ibid., Ndaniyenu, Feruzi and Songoro Makonde.

41. *Zanzibar Gazette*, June 14, 1910.

42. Fatahi's residence on the Friends mission indicated that he was without a social support network or ownership of property, thus it is likely that he could not afford two wives.

43. Marcia Wright discusses how even during the colonial era, men on the mainland sought to control women and their labor. Marcia Wright, *Strategies of Slaves and Women: Life-Stories from East/Central Africa* (New York: Lilian Barber Press, 1993), 129–30.

44. For descriptions of violence against women, see *Zanzibar Gazette*, June 14, 1910; FIM, PZ(F)/3, 1898–1902, April 16, 1898.

45. Mr. Farler hated the Quakers and regularly feuded with them until his death, in 1907. He likely was being contrary with the Quakers when he made this decision. FIM, PZ(F)/3, meeting minute book, 1898–1902.

46. Ibid., December 7, 1901.

47. FIM, meeting minute book, 1903–15, July 30, 1903, April 4, September 7, 1904, March 8, May 28, 1905.

48. Ibid., April 1905.

49. Ibid., December 1905.

50. Ibid., August 5, September 8, 1908.

51. Rhodes House, Universities Mission to Central Africa SF 76I, Christian Marriage in Zanzibar, 1912–14.

52. An Islamic judge could declare that a wife was divorced from her husband if the wife could prove the husband was not maintaining her with housing, clothing, and food. For detailed discussions of marriage rules in

East African Islamic courts see S. Hirsch, *Pronouncing and Persevering;* Stiles, *Islamic Court;* Stockreiter, "Tying and Untying."

53. FIM, meeting minute book, 1903–15, February 1912.

54. Rhodes House, GB162 United Society for the Propagation of the Gospel UMCA SF 76 I, letter, November 11, 1912.

55. For discussion of modern divorce on the Swahili coast, see Stiles, *Islamic Court;* S. Hirsch, *Pronouncing and Persevering.*

THREE

Two Weddings in Northern Mafia
Changes in Women's Lives since the 1960s

PAT CAPLAN

IN THE 1960S AND 1970S several scholars, myself included, analyzed Swahili society in terms of *mila* (custom, tradition) and *sheria* (shari'a; law, Islamic law).[1] Although no scholar argued that these were bounded categories, they were often used in popular Swahili discourse and sometimes in opposition to each other. Here this distinction is used in accordance with local parlance where I have carried out anthropological fieldwork since 1965—including participant-observations, interviews, censuses, attendance at meetings and rituals, the taping and transcription of life histories, photography and filming—mostly but not entirely in the villages of northern Mafia. The sphere of activities locally called mila was often associated with women, who performed rituals such as *unyago* (girls' initiation), *siku ya mwaka* (the solar new year), and the mila activities associated with weddings (singing and dancing) and with male circumcision (*jando*). There were specific songs associated with each of these rituals, but in addition, part of the rejoicing (*sherehe*) was often the singing of impromptu *kalewa* songs, full of double entendre and frequently bawdy.

The first section of this chapter looks at findings from my field research in northern Mafia Island in 1965 through 1967, 1976, and 1985, drawing on a number of earlier writings in which I argued that women in this area had a high degree of control over their own sexuality, and that the mila aspects of initiation rituals and weddings constructed and maintained this ethos.[2] Yet I noted that at the same time there were powerful constraints on women's lives in terms of marriage, high fertility, heavy workloads, and the requirement to avoid shame, such as getting pregnant before marriage. Here I revisit and summarize these findings before contrasting them with a later period.

In the second section I consider the period since the beginning of the 1990s, by which time female initiation rituals were no longer performed, boys' circumcision was carried out in hospitals, and weddings had begun to be less exuberant. The diminution of the importance of mila was most obvious in new forms of clothing, especially of women. Part of the explanation for these changes could be the influence of the new globalized (and politicized) Islam upon Swahili culture.[3] However, there were many other factors at play: life had begun to get considerably harder for many in economic terms and HIV/AIDS was spreading even to relatively remote areas like Mafia Island. Yet there were also new educational opportunities and better health facilities, especially for children and pregnant women. In this chapter I explore some of the paradoxes and contradictions that have arisen for women in these uneven processes of change through a comparison of two weddings, one filmed in 1976 and the other in 2002.

WOMEN AND MILA: 1960S–80S
A Wedding in 1976

In 1976, as part of a project to film a village on Mafia for a television series and with my assistance as "consultant," a BBC crew shot footage of a wedding in Kanga village in northern Mafia, a region noted for its sexually explicit songs and dances of women.[4]

This wedding was typical of many I attended on Mafia during the 1960s, 1970s, and even 1980s.

The legal heart of a marriage was and remains the contract between the bride's family and the groom, in a ceremony (*nikaha*) conducted by the sheikh or imam that includes the payment (or promise to pay) by the groom of the Islamic legal requirement of *mahari*. This was the sheria aspect of weddings, without which a marriage would not be legal, but it lasted a very brief time, unlike the mila aspects that surrounded it. As was usual, the bride herself did not attend, and in the case of the wedding filmed, neither did the groom, whose place was taken by his younger brother acting as a proxy.

The mila aspects of the wedding included payments by the groom and his family of sums of money known as *mkaja* (belt) to the mother and *kilemba* (turban) to the father of the bride, a feast for many guests, and hours of singing and dancing by the women. This last began days before the actual wedding with a women's get-together for the *uanikaji* (drying—that is, the drying in the sun of the unhusked rice to be used in the wedding), then, on the day after the drying, its pounding (*utwanzi*) into husked rice with pestles and mortars. The night before the wedding there would be an overnight party (*kesha*) at the bride's house, when there would be singing and dancing, especially by women. On the day itself, there would be the arrival of the bride's trousseau, carried in a procession by the groom's female relatives, and the cooking and serving of the feast, followed by yet more singing and dancing. This might be performed only by women in the form of kalewa dances, or by women and men together in the form of *sonondo* and *mkwaju* dances. Sonondo was a form of dance primarily performed by younger people who formed a circle in which solo dancers took it in turn to exhibit their skills. Music was often provided by a *zumari* (a kind of clarinet). Mkwaju dances were performed with a small band consisting of drums and a rubbing board (serrated board over which a stick is drawn). The instrumentalists were also the singers, and the soloist would use both known and extempore songs, often bawdy. Females and males, both youngsters and adults, danced together in a circle.

Later in the day, after the legal wedding, the groom would enter the bride's chamber, which also involved payment by the groom to the bride's instructor (*mkunga*) and to the bride herself, before the consummation of the marriage. Finally, usually after a few days, the bride was moved to her husband's home, along with her trousseau—gifts from her husband and her parents.

Most of this Kanga wedding was captured on film, and it is not surprising that one TV critic wrote at the time, "Preparing for a village wedding in Chole [Mafia] intelligent and humorous people in brilliant clothes demonstrated far better than any superficial globetrotting the richness and vitality of the species."[5] Yet such exuberance has also to be seen against the many constraints on women's lives at the time, to which I now turn.

Constraints on Women's Lives in the 1960s to the 1980s

During this period women were supposed to avoid shame (*aibu*) by not contravening the rules about appearing in front of men in public. Women walking through the village went along a network of back paths; they entered shops, even the village medical clinic, through the back door, not the front, where men might be sitting; they wore a black cloak (*buibui*) when traveling outside the village. Most important, they were kept in seclusion after puberty and before marriage, so as to safeguard their virginity. The biggest shame of all would be for a daughter to bear a child out of wedlock, as happened in Baleni village just before I arrived there in 1966 when, according to both local gossip and district court records, an unmarried girl had borne an illegitimate child and it was killed by her relatives. Nonetheless, girls did of course sometimes get pregnant, and in my first visit I gradually was told of people who "had no father."

Most women married very young—sometimes even before puberty, as the following interview indicates. It was recorded in 1994, when an old woman called Mwaharusi remembered her first marriage:

Mwaharusi: My mother and father married me off to a husband.

Pat: Were you still small then?

Mwaharusi: Yes, I hadn't even reached puberty at that time.

Pat: Weren't you afraid?

Mwaharusi: How could I not be afraid? But what could I do about it?

Pat: You weren't asked, you were just sent?

Mwaharusi: Yes, that's right.

Pat: And was it a very big wedding?

Mwaharusi: Yes, it certainly was. They danced the *kidatu* [a dance performed mainly by young people] and they had flags.

Pat: And what about the trousseau?

Mwaharusi: Yes, there was a trousseau. It was over there near Kurugeni's place.

Pat: So what did you get in it?

Mwaharusi: Ah! What should I get? I got *kanga* [fabric wraps], a *buibui,* shoes, bras.

Pat: So after the wedding then it was the consummation [*kuingia ndani*]? Were you on your own at that time? So didn't it hurt?

Mwaharusi: Yes, it certainly did. Older people stay with you and the husband comes in and he greets you formally. A month after my marriage I began to menstruate.

In the 1960s, likewise, girls were married off, even being taken out of school as soon as they started menstruating or even before if a suitable match came up. Here a young woman called Bimkubwa, who was living in Kanga village in 1966, tells me feelingly about what had happened to her:

> As a child, I was sent to live with an aunt in Zanzibar and I went to school there. I loved it! I really wanted to continue my education. But when I started menstruating my relatives on Mafia sent for me and married me off to one of the schoolteachers. I got pregnant immediately, I

didn't even know how to carry a baby properly. So that was the end of my education. And here I am stuck in this village, with a baby and having to learn not only how to look after it but even how to cultivate.

Later I asked her mother's brother, who was a teacher at one of the Qur'anic schools and who had had a major role in arranging her marriage, why this girl's education had been so curtailed. He was vehement in his defense of what happened: "She was a big girl, she had to get married, otherwise one day the children she could have borne (by marrying early) would accuse her before God (of failing to give birth to them)!" In other words, his interpretation of Islam meant that women should marry early and bear many children.

By 1976 the educational situation had improved on Mafia, as in much of the rest of Tanzania, and there were more schools and more places for pupils. In addition, the government had campaigned hard for all children, whether boys or girls, to go to primary school and complete its seven years. In a field trip that year to northern Mafia I found most girls and boys were attending school and that girls were no longer always withdrawn at puberty, and thus tended to marry at a slightly later age than previously. Nonetheless, they still had little choice in whom they married. The following interview is with a woman called Mwajuma, who describes her daughter's forthcoming marriage. It was recorded during the BBC filming that same year and indicates that by that time, girls were supposed to be asked about their marriage partners, but that was essentially just a formality:

Pat: What about the girl herself—did you ask her, or will you just marry her off?

Mother: Oh no, the girls these days . . . now formerly, a young girl had no right to say, "I want this one" or "I don't want that one."

Pat: What about today?

Mother: These days, you ask them if they like him or they don't like him.

Pat: And what about Saidia—have you already asked her?

Mother: Oh, yes, Saidia has already been told [about her marriage to her cousin].

Pat: And what did she say?

Mother: She said, "I don't want him," but she just said it to be stupid—she doesn't really mean it. She herself wants to marry him—so her cousin will marry her.

Here the girl is "told" about her marriage and gives a negative reply, but this is discounted by her parents. Furthermore, a girl might be married off to a man who already had a wife—as I found as the interview proceeded:

Pat: But isn't he already married, and with children?

Mother: Yes, he's already married. He has four children, maybe three, I'm not sure. One was born just recently, this year. But his wife—the reason why he wants to marry again is that she is very reserved. She doesn't talk to him; she doesn't talk to anyone, least of all to her husband; she just stays at home. I don't know why; you'd never know whether or not anyone was there, because she is so reserved; she's not talkative at all.

Pat: You mean his present wife?

Mother: Yes, his wife. So that's why he wants another wife, someone to chat to and talk to, someone with a few ideas in her head, like Saidia.

Pat: But perhaps Saidia doesn't want to marry a man who is already married? Doesn't she have anything to say about that?

Mother: No, she doesn't. She asks, "Since my cousin wants to marry me, is he going to divorce his wife and abandon his children?" I said to her, "She'll get divorced because of her haughtiness. A man who likes to laugh wants a wife who's the same. If you're arrogant, who will want you?"

Pat: So if he marries Saidia he's going to divorce his other wife?

Mother: Yes, he wants to divorce that other wife, at least that's what he says. I don't know what will happen in the future. Even last year he wanted to divorce her.

A man marrying a second wife might use the quarrels with his first wife that usually followed to divorce the latter since, under Islamic law, men did not have to give a reason for repudiating their wives.

While women were keen to bear children and saw procreation as an important outcome of sexual activity and an intrinsic aspect of marriage, many admitted to "getting tired" of bearing many children and often asked me about how to stop pregnancy. Contraception was then difficult to obtain in northern Mafia, and furthermore during this period husbands had to give consent, which many refused to do. Women were under pressure to have many children and exercised little control over their fertility, a situation that sometimes led to tragedies such as the death of babies or mothers.[6]

Yet it was clear that women's sexuality was very important to them and that they thought they had a right to enjoyable sex, whether inside or outside marriage. This factor was seen in the girl's initiation ritual (*unyago*) that I attended in 1967.[7] The expert (*fundi or simba* [lion]) and her helpers not only taught the girl about sex and how to please her husband, but also how to please herself, including having extramarital affairs. This was a major theme not only in the unyago ceremony but also in the songs women sang at weddings and boys' circumcisions.

Kalewa Songs and Their Themes

For eighteen months between 1965 and 1967, I worked in several villages in northern and central Mafia, including Kanga, Bweni, Banja, and Baleni.[8] During that time, I recorded several hundred women's songs at weddings, ceremonies for girls' initiation or ear piercing, and boys' circumcisions either on my tape recorder or in my notebooks. Subsequently I would discuss their meanings with knowledgeable women. The songs and dances were frequently explicitly sexual. Women danced the kalewa, which involved using two pestles laid like a cross on the ground, with the dancer singing either a well-known or an extempore short song of only one or two lines. In addition, the singer, or other women, would often perform hip dancing (*kucheza kiuno*). In this section, I give examples of a number of such songs and identify some of the themes that preoccupied women. These included the pleasures of sex, the tensions and jealousies aroused by polygyny, marital relations, and the pleasures and problems of lovers and extramarital sex. The songs always involved double entendre, often referred obliquely to specific people, and were sometimes sung in the form of a competition or confrontation. I include the Swahili original, a literal translation, and then the figurative meaning (in brackets).

The Pleasures of Sex

Hakuna mchezo wa kipole, bado shingo na mkono.	There is no slow dance, only neck and arm. [In love making there are no slow movements.]
Fundi yule, kaomba sidiria, na neno limeingia.	The expert wanted a bra, and the word got out. [A man wanted a woman and everyone heard about it.]
Mimi sijapiga kilemba, na miye sijaenda.	I haven't yet put on a turban, and I haven't yet been there. [I haven't had that man yet.]
Itiwa chumvi, itiwa na bizari, ukoro una hatari.	If it has salt and spices put on it, the testicle is fantastic!
Haiiti chumvi, haitii sukari, utamu wake hatari.	You don't need salt, you don't need sugar; its sweetness is fantastic! [Reply to above.]
Tumbo limeniuma, linakatika uchungu.	My stomach is hurting me; it is cutting me up with bitterness. [Longing for sex is cutting me up.]

Jealousy

Sitaki dada ufanye kilele, kilemba changu mwenyewe.	I don't want you to make a fuss, Sister, this turban is mine. [Cowife, he's more my husband than yours.]

Kama unavyoona kwa magomvi na kilele, sitaki kusema naye.

As you can see from the quarreling and shouting, I don't want to speak to her [the woman who took her husband].

Nasema kaniweka hasara, mpaka kesho karibuni, wallahi nakuwapa amini, mume sinayo mimi

I say that she has caused me infinite loss [lit., until the day after tomorrow], by God, I swear that I do not have your husband. [A woman sings this to a jealous wife whom she suspects of seducing her husband.]

Ukiona udada na udugu sitawi, ujua pana hatari

If you see sisterhood and brotherhood flourishing, be aware of the danger! [It is likely to be your best friend who will steal your husband or your wife.]

Dada nakutuma, usitafute kilele, na yeye kaja mwenyewe.

Sister, I am sending you away on an errand; don't you make a fuss; he came [to me] of his own accord. [A woman tells her cowife, "You go off somewhere; don't make a fuss (or think it was I who called our husband); he came to me himself."]

Marital Relations

Under most interpretations of Islamic law, a husband is supposed to support his wife by giving her food and clothes. Yet on Mafia, where there is great poverty and where women do most of the agricultural work, such rules are interpreted in a relaxed way. Nonetheless, as an elderly woman told me when we were discussing what made for a good marriage, "Love comes from giving." A mean husband who does not buy clothes is often the subject of impromptu kalewa songs:

Hawi mtu ila aende ukindu, kakushinda, nitakurudisha mwenyewe.

She is not really a human being unless she goes to cut raffia. He has defeated you, I will get you to return [to your natal home] myself.
[The mother of a neglected wife

complains about her son-in-law's treatment of her daughter, who has to make her own living by cutting raffia and seeks to persuade her to leave him.]

Shuka yao ukuju, mbovu kofia pakacha, miye atanipa nini?

If his cloth is worn out, and his hat looks like a palm-leaf basket, what can he give me? [If the husband himself dresses so badly, what hope is there that he will ever give the neglected wife anything?]

Nifue nivai nini? Nguo yangu moja, ikauke nikavae

If I wash my clothes, what shall I wear? I have only one dress; let it dry so that I can wear it again. [The husband hasn't given his wife enough clothes.]

Kula, nakula, kulala na nalala, dhiki yangu kitambaa

As for eating, I eat; as for sleeping, I sleep. My problem is clothes [lit., a cloth]. [In this case a husband provides food and shelter, but not clothes.]

Wali nakula, chai nakunywa, dhiki yangu kitambaa

I eat rice, I drink tea; my problem is clothes. [Same meaning as previous verse.]

Nachoka kupikia Jaluo, hana kula, hana nguo

I am tired of cooking for the Luo; he has no food, he has no clothes. [A Luo is a man who gives his wife nothing. So what is the use of cooking for such a one?]

Adultery

Many songs openly describe extramarital relations:

Kinu changu kizima, nitwanga nitakavyo, medhali nitoke

My mortar is in good condition and I will pound it as and when I like, even if I go outside to do so. [My vagina is OK, so I will use it as I like.]

Nikila samaki, miiba nitatema, nipata nifaidi tena	If I eat fish, I will spit out the bones, so that I may get profit again. [If a woman commits adultery and keeps quiet about it, she can do it all over again.]

Women sometimes justified their outside affairs in terms of the gifts they got:

Kipini, nitanunua kipini, sahani nitanunua sahani, au ajabu neno gani?	A pin, I will buy a pin, a plate; I will buy a plate. What is surprising about that? [If I fornicate I will get jewelry and household utensils from my lover; that's what happens.]
Shilingi kumi ameumpa Yahaya, pita akisimulia	Yahaya [her lover] gave her TSh10 and she goes around telling everyone. [A woman has sex for money and spreads the word around.]

However, lovers do not always give presents:

Ulisema uzinzi kapata safari, unaona hukupata mali?	You said fornication would get you a trip; don't you see that you don't get any wealth for it? [A woman boasted that she would get some profit out of her affair, but she thought wrong.]

Singing Competitions (Kuimbana)

Women would often sing replies to the songs of their friends or, more often, their rivals or enemies, and here the meaning of a song depended on who was singing and the listeners' knowledge of the circumstances. In the three-song sequence below, women sang about a man who had recently moved to the village of Baleni:

Itoka barua Nduruni, ifike Kipandeni, Baleni kaja mgeni	A letter came from Nduruni [Utende], it reached Kipandeni, [it said that] a stranger had come. [A man who formerly worked in

Utende had come as a stranger to
Baleni.]

Kafika mgeni mbona, *nafuu yetu sote*	If a stranger has come, it is for the advantage of all of us. [This is the reply to the song above.]
Ameweka nadhiri, akinao *karani, nitachinja* *ng'ombe pangani*	She made a vow that if she "got" the clerk, "I will slaughter a cow at the spirit shrine." [A woman wanted to marry the newcomer and made a vow that if she got him she would sacrifice a cow to a spirit.]

Insulting Those in Power

Songs sometimes had a political meaning and were designed to
insult those holding power, usually through impugning their
sexual abilities, as in the following sequence about the current
local Tanzania African National Union (TANU)[9] secretary—the
second song answered the first:

Malimu Silima kajitia *kinuni, na yeye si* *mtwanzi*	Teacher Silima has put himself at the pestle, but he is no pounder. [The then TANU secretary was well known for chasing women but he was actually impotent].
Malim Silima kajitia *mtaani, la ajabu neno* *gani?*	Teacher Silima has put himself into the town (quarter); what is surprising about that? [Teacher Silima has made himself available in the town (quarter). There is nothing surprising in that.]

Discussion

During the first twenty years of my research on Mafia Island, I
could see that women had many problems in their lives, such as
lack of choice in marriage and bearing more children than they
wanted; I also saw that they were disadvantaged in relation to

men in terms of divorce, polygyny, and inheritance. Yet at the same time they also exercised a considerable degree of agency and were able to analyze themselves and their social relations, even make fun of them, through their songs. So women's situation—their gender and sexuality, their marriages and affairs—was complex. Unquestionably, however, those activities locally described as mila, coupled with the cognatic system of kinship and descent, which gave them rights to land, ensured that women had a high degree of autonomy. In the late 1980s and early 1990s that began to change.

THE WANING OF MILA? 1990S–2000S
A Wedding in 2002

In 2002 I filmed a wedding that took place in the same village as had the earlier one filmed a quarter of a century earlier by the BBC. It was very unlike the first. There were no songs or dances, and the women behaved and dressed very differently than they had in 1976. I was told that the lack of rejoicing (*furaha*) was because there had been several recent deaths in the village, but it turned out they were not so very recent and the explanation somehow sounded unconvincing. Rather, I suspected that either it was that the old songs and dances were no longer performed, which is what some people had told me, or else that, since this was the wedding of the daughter of the village imam, well known for his devotion to strict Islamic observance, mila aspects had been put aside on this occasion. I was particularly struck by the fact that a significant minority of men had beards and the groom wore an Arab headdress (a Palestinian-style kaffiyeh), but even had I not been aware of it, one of the male guests asked me if I had noticed this. I asked the reason why. "Because we are Muslims and nowadays we are following Arab things more," was the reply. The bride, too, wore different clothes than had the bride in the earlier film or others I had seen—she had on a long dress and the modern form of buibui (long coat) and jasmine flowers (used often in Zanzibar but not on Mafia) in her hair. But it was not only at such a wedding that clothes had changed.

Changes in Women's Clothing and the "New" Islam

When I first carried out fieldwork on Mafia in the 1960s, women mostly wore two kanga [fabric wrap]—one tucked around the chest, and another covering the shoulders and sometimes the head. Underneath they wore a petticoat (*gagulo)* with a drawstring, and sometimes a locally stitched bra (*sidiria*). On public occasions, they often substituted their kanga for the more expensive wraps known as *vitenge* but for work in the fields, many women wore black cloths known as *kaniki* until the government banned them on the grounds that they looked "dirty" and they became unavailable. On formal public occasions, particularly when traveling to other villages, women sometimes wore the black covering garment known as a buibui, but often it was left open at the front and hitched up to facilitate walking, so it actually covered very little. This mode of dress can be clearly seen in different contexts in the film series *Face Values* and *Other People's Lives,* made by the BBC in 1978 and 1982.

By 1994 things had begun to change. Even in the 1980s I had encountered a new form of clothing for women, a black headscarf with a tasseled border called *shangingi,* which some men complained they now had to supply as part of the bride's trousseau. Women by this time almost always wore dresses under their kanga wraps, especially when they attended events like weddings. On such occasions, I began to notice that guests coming from the south of the island even covered themselves with the new garments then termed *koti,* but now known commonly as buibui or sometimes by the Arabic term *jilbab.* These were thought to be the height of fashion, and I recall meeting one close friend in the district capital, divorced and reportedly looking for a new husband, who asked me to help her buy such a garment. The original form of buibui described earlier was now considered very old-fashioned and was worn only by older women or those too poor to be able to buy the modern garment.

In 2002, I returned to Mafia for another period of fieldwork, taking with me those sections of the *Face Values* film series that had been shot on the island so that I could screen them once again. This was my usual practice and it was one of the first things people would ask me about on arrival. This time, I found that in Kanga village a young man had set up a small "cinema" showing video films on a TV monitor, powered by a generator. Before the public showing, I tested the cassette at the cinema owner's house, and his young wife watched it. She was incredulous: "What was the matter with those women? Didn't they have any clothes to wear?" Her comment highlighted the big changes in women's clothing that had taken place between 1976 and 2002. My village brother[10] did not want me to screen the film, claiming that seeing people who had been deceased would be upsetting, but I pointed out that I had shown it many times before with no negative consequences and that many people had asked for it. I suspected that he, too, found the dress and comportment of the previous generation somewhat embarrassing.

By the time of this and later visits, in 2004 and 2010, all girls wore headscarves when attending school, and adult women took care to cover their heads with their kanga, even tying rather than draping them as before so that they stayed in place. Dresses had become everyday garments, even for working in the fields. In 2010, I found that all the girls, no matter how young, who attended Qur'anic school had to wear a particular new kind of *hijab* (a newly adopted term on Mafia) which covered not only their heads but even their shoulders. However, no women on Mafia had yet adopted the fashion that was spreading in Zanzibar, Dar es Salaam, and Lamu of the *nikabu,* or "ninja" face mask.[11]

ONE OF my village sisters had become meticulous in covering herself, even to the extent of offering me her hand only when wrapped in her kanga. Her son, my nephew, must have guessed at my discomfort because he later said to me, "Don't imagine that because people change their dress, their hearts have changed— they are still the same."

A simple explanation of these changes could be sought in a new version of Islam, globalized and militant, initially coming from Iran via glossy Swahili-language magazines after the Iranian Revolution, in 1969, and later from the Persian Gulf with funding for new mosques and *madarasa,* which was entering Tanzania and spreading even as far as Mafia. This version of Islam was very different from the relatively relaxed version I had known as Swahili Islam; it was rather more puritanical and fundamentalist. But it was attractive because it gave people the impression that they were turning to a version of Islam which was not only "purer" but also more modern and global.[12] Its preachers spoke against many mila aspects of culture—including the spirit possession cults, some of which were termed *bidaa* (innovations deemed unacceptable)—and also promulgated the new forms of clothing that covered the heads and often the arms of women.

However, to seek to understand such changes purely in religious terms would be oversimplistic. They also have to be analyzed in terms of new constraints and opportunities in people's lives.

Problems and Opportunities

In the mid-1980s, Tanzania abandoned its attempts to create African socialism and moved increasingly to a neoliberal economy. Structural adjustment, devaluation of currency, and other factors led to price rises for bought goods and lower prices for cash crops, all of which made life increasingly hard for many people, including most of those on Mafia. People talked of *maisha magumu* (difficult life) both in their letters and on my return to northern Mafia in 1994.[13] By this time, too, HIV/AIDS was becoming a threat, even on Mafia, where, although the rates were much lower than in many parts of the mainland, they were increasing.

At the same time, new opportunities had arisen. Mafia finally got a secondary school in 1994 and more were built later, and so children no longer had to go to the mainland if they were chosen to pursue studies beyond primary school; there were also more primary schools. However, paradoxically the previous policies of free education were revoked and school fees introduced. As a result, some children from families that could afford to support them continued their studies, while others from poorer families or ones where their labor was required did not go to school at all and literacy rates plummeted.

Some health facilities improved, assisted by foreign aid, particularly in terms of the vaccination of children, so that child mortality rates dropped and women got more medical help in giving birth, as Bimkubwa (the girl who had been taken out of her Zanzibar school in the 1960s, now a woman in her fifties) explained to me in 2002:

> Pat: If you compare life when you came back [from living for some years on the mainland] and now?
>
> Bimkubwa: It's much harder now!
>
> Pat: So has there been any development here at all?
>
> Bimkubwa: Not yet, unless perhaps in terms of children getting educated, especially girl children.
>
> Pat: What about health?
>
> Bimkubwa: That is better; pregnant women go to the clinic to have their babies, whereas previously they gave birth at home.

Furthermore, a determined woman could, with some familial assistance, make choices that would have been unthinkable until recently. Let us return to the 2002 wedding. The many indicators of the influence of the new Islam in the imam's daughter's wedding had in fact not precluded the bride from postponing her marriage until she had completed both secondary school and further vocational training—which meant that, very unusually on Mafia, she was in her mid-twenties when she finally married—nor had it kept her from choosing her own husband, a civil servant posted into the village, as she herself explained in an interview:

> Bride: I studied here in primary school, then did a year in Kitomondo Secondary School [on Mafia],[14] where the teaching and facilities are poor. I then moved to Kibaha [on the mainland], which has a much better school, and started secondary over again, doing four years to 1998. I was the only one there from Mafia and I only came home in vacations. But I did not get chosen to go further so I went to Dar and stayed with my elder brother and did my training as a lab assistant. When I finished, I worked for

nine months in the district hospital in Kilindoni without a salary, hoping I would get a proper job, but I did not, and I got fed up with working eight hours a day for nothing, so I came back here to the village.

Pat: What about getting work here?

Bride: Yes, I've asked to work here; they finally agreed I can work in the clinic, but they will not pay me a salary.

Pat: I hear you are getting married?

Bride: Yes, in two weeks, to the *mratibu* [village secretary].

She went on to tell me that she intended to continue her career and that her husband would support her choices: "We are planning our lives together"—they were clearly intent on being an upwardly mobile couple. I asked her whether she thought things were better now for girls than they used to be and she replied in the affirmative: "Yes, they can study and choose their own husbands." It seemed that even her father, the imam, had agreed to her choices (it was rumored somewhat reluctantly), which I found rather remarkable given the conversations I had had with him in earlier years about a woman's proper role.

This view that young women now had more freedom to continue their education and choose their own husbands was widespread, and it also applied to young men, as in this extract from an interview in 2002 with two youths:

Pat: What do you think about marriage?

Abdallah: The first time you came here, it [a wedding] was probably all organized for you and paid for [by parents and other relatives]. But now things have changed. You can choose your partner but you have to try and get the money for mahari [marriage payment] together yourself by fishing,[15] for example; that's why men delay marriage.

Pat: Why has mahari gone up so much?

Abdallah: Because it's actually used [by the parents] to pay for things like the beds and mattresses which the bride needs.

So that's why people delay marriage—they have to get the money together first.

Pat: What would you look for in a wife?

Abdallah: For those of us who are educated, we want someone who is educated, too, someone you can exchange ideas with.

Juma: You want someone who can understand things, help you in your business.

So by this time some men and women were looking for partners with whom they could "plan" their lives—a phrase I heard increasingly, whether it referred to the numbers of children they had, or the building of a house, or running a small-scale business. The current economic situation of the "hard life" meant that parents could no longer be relied on to support their adult children, but at the same time the former no longer made decisions for the latter, as had been the case previously.

Women also recognized the changed economic circumstances of the times, telling me that they now often bought their clothes themselves, even those of their children, because they realized how difficult it was for husbands to provide fully. I was often told that "women have to help these days." In order to do this some had set up women's groups (*vikundi*) and engaged in cooperative microenterprises to get some cash, like the following group, some of whose members I interviewed:

Woman: Our group started in 2000 and there are ten members. We do small businesses like sewing, plaiting raffia, and embroidering cloth.

Pat: Where do you sell?

Woman: Here we haven't yet got the means to send our stuff outside, and here there is no market.

Pat: Why did you start this group?

Woman: To improve our lives a bit [*kuendesha maisha kidogo*].

Pat: What do you do with the money? Do you have a bank account?

Woman: We divide it up at present—but we do want to open a proper bank account.

Pat: Would you be able to borrow if you did?

Woman: Yes.

Pat: How often do you meet?

Woman: We planned to meet every month, but it depends.

Pat: Who do you get advice from? Do you go to the village government or the mratibu?

Woman: No, we plan things ourselves.

Pat: So what are your needs at present?

Woman: We want a sewing machine and then we could learn to sew and make some money, but we have no capital—we need money also to buy things like pots and kanga from Dar es Salaam to sell here.

Pat: Are you all related?

Woman: No, we are neighbors; we decided to get together.

Pat: There didn't used to be such groups, did there?

Woman: No, but now life has become harder.

Pat: In what ways?

Woman: In respect of food, clothes, and money!

Here, then, the marital contract had changed as a result of the increase in poverty, and women found themselves needing to provide items previously supplied by their husbands. Some women had also got involved in health issues, especially around HIV/AIDS.

By 1994, the time of my fourth field trip to the island, AIDS was becoming a problem, and by 2002, although the morbidity rates on Mafia were still relatively low compared with, for example, Dar es Salaam, they were creeping up.[16] In subsequent years, women were becoming increasingly aware that the sexual double standard rendered them vulnerable, as the following interview, recorded in 2002 with the leader of one of the women's groups in the village, makes clear:

> Leader: In our group we sing songs at the clinic about AIDS. We want people to have only one wife, one husband; we want to stop polygyny.

> Pat: What about men with two wives?

> Leader: They should be tested [for HIV/AIDS]. Even if you stay faithful you don't know what your partner is doing. So we are confronting the men.

> Pat: Who do you discuss this topic with?

> Leader: We try to do so with the men but they say "Oh, you are just being jealous."

> Pat: Aren't they afraid of getting AIDS?

> Leader: No they don't seem to be.

> Pat: Does anyone else talk to them?

> Leader: Dr. Kombo [the village paramedic] does try.

> Pat: And do any men use condoms?

> Leader: No way!

> Pat: What about the schools and AIDS?

> Leader: I'm not sure what they do, but I think they should have special classes on the topic, because this desert [*jangwa*— she means a desert of ignorance] is not a small one. But lots of people don't want to listen. They should discuss it both in schools and in Qur'anic schools [*madarasa*]. The men go

off to Dar, to Lindi, wherever; they do their thing [*shughuli zao*, have sex outside marriage] and then come home [to their wives].

Pat: What about giving advice to young girls?

Leader: Yes, we talk to them and tell them what the situation is.

Another women who worked as a volunteer in the clinic also brought up the subject of HIV/AIDS in her interview in 2002:

Pat: What about AIDS—are you involved?

Volunteer: We try to spread the word about AIDS through songs and explanations, including to our own children. We do not have any modesty [*haya*] about this any more. There is no sense in it. Prevention is better than cure (*kinga kabla tiba*)!

Pat: How many people have died of AIDS in Kanga?

Volunteer: About five or six. We talk to everyone—we tell them they have to leave off sleeping around [*washarti*]. And not to share razors and needles, not to care for AIDS patients without wearing gloves, which, however, are not available.

Pat: What about condoms?

Volunteer: Only the young rascals [*wahuni*] use them, those who go off to town. Almighty God is still watching over us [here in the village], but in Kilindoni [district capital] and Utende [tourist center], where there is such a mixture of people, it's much worse.

That year I noticed posters not only at the clinic but also in the schools—one in a secondary school said "AIDS is something to talk about," a big change from the situation when it had first manifested and many people had said it should not be discussed with children, as it might give them wrong ideas (see also Nadine Beckmann's chapter in this volume). In short, the advent of AIDS had meant for women a new level of openness about sexuality and its consequences, even opposition to polygynous marriages, in spite of resistance from men.[17]

Women in Public Life—Religious and Political

By the new millennium, some of the old conventions, such as separate paths through the village or separate entrances to the clinic for women and men, were no longer observed. Perhaps because of their more modest dress, women would walk (some secondary schoolgirls even cycled) boldly along the main street. This situation is scarcely surprising and has been discussed in many societies where women take care to dress in a way that gives the message that they are "good."[18] This enables them to operate more comfortably in a variety of public arenas from which they had been excluded in the earlier period, as will be seen. I was particularly struck, on visiting a local Qur'anic school in 2004, to find a handful of women, all dressed in the "new" Islamic fashion, attending advanced Qur'anic classes, which had never been the case in the past. There was also talk of building a new mosque that would be large enough to have a (separate) space for women.

Such changing ideas about the role of women could be carried into the wider sphere, and by the time of the new millennium more women were active in public affairs in the village, ranging from the village council to the clinic. In the following extract, Mwajina talks about her work as a village councillor (*jumbe*).

Mwajina: There are five women and eleven men on the village council.

Pat: Do the women get heard?

Mwajina: They do listen to us! And we have the right to speak. Previously women did not go to meetings, but now they do.

Pat: So do you think women's lives are better today than they used to be?

Mwajina: Yes, they are, because they study and they travel—I myself have been to Dar es Salaam and Zanzibar, right up to Ras Nungwi—both in 1984 and again in 1999.

Mwajina also worked as a volunteer (*wavi*) in the clinic:

Pat: What work do the volunteers do?

Mwajina: They ensure that children are vaccinated and propagate better feeding. The other volunteers are another woman and two men. They give advice and also medicine for filariasis.

Pat: What about birth control?

Mwajina: We do give advice.

Pat: Do you still find women getting one pregnancy after another?

Mwajina: Not so much, since birth control is available and is being used.

Another female volunteer at the clinic also reported positively on developments in the lives of women and children:

Pat: What improvements do you see in children's health?

Volunteer Two: LOTS, not a little. We go around; we copy [what we see]. Now you see children well dressed; pregnant women even wear shoes these days and they dress properly.

Pat: How do you do your work?

Volunteer Two: We go from ward to ward in the village, from house to house, explaining things to people.

Her views were shared by the members of the woman's group already quoted:

Pat: What about the health of children? Is it better these days?

Woman: Yes, definitely; they get vaccinated now.

Pat: What about women in pregnancy?

Woman: Yes, that too. They get examined, and they mostly give birth in hospital. The only problem is if they have to go to Kilindoni [because of the lack of transport].

Pat: What about birth control?

Woman: You can get it easily now.

Pat: Do you still have to have the husband's permission?

Woman: No, some just go ahead and take a rest for a while.

Pat: So how many children do women want nowadays?

Woman: You tell us what you think!

Pat: No, I want hear your views first!

Woman: Four is good. [Most women present agreed with that.]

Both these extracts indicate that by the new millennium women were able to exercise much more control over their fertility, having gained access to contraception, even without the husband agreeing. Furthermore, the improvement in child health as a result of the vaccination program meant that most children survived infancy, and women did not have to bear so many children in order to ensure the survival of the desired number.

Nonetheless, there remained issues, such as sex preference for boys on the part of males. At the end of the interview with the women's group in 2002 above, I asked whether men still preferred male children.[19] The women replied that they did, but said, "We want ones who are like us" (*wenzetu*, girls). They said that "each side pulls" and that "next time I'll get what I want."

SOME OF the complexities of the historical changes on Mafia Island regarding gender, marriage, and sexuality have been influenced and shaped by economic and political circumstances, by changes in disease, health, and education and by ideologies including those of both old and new forms of Islam. I cannot help wondering what today's young women, viewing footage like the BBC film or reading some of my publications, would think of their mothers and grandmothers who used sex in so many ways: for pleasure, for children, for exchange with husbands and lovers, who would give material returns. I wonder how they would hear the bawdy songs and view the hip dancing. Would they understand what these were all about—the human, and particularly the female, condition—or would they condemn some of the earlier practices as un-Islamic, as possibly encouraging the spread of HIV and AIDS and ask, What was the matter with those people? Yet perhaps these are only surface manifestations and, as my village nephew suggested, "hearts remain the same."

NOTES

1. For examples, see Pat Caplan, "Gender, Ideology and Modes of Production on the Coast of East Africa," *Paideuma* 28 (1982): 29–43; Caplan, "Women's Property, Islamic Law and Cognatic Descent," in *Women and Property, Women as Property,* ed. Renée Hirschon (London: Croom Helm, 1983), 23–43; Kai Kresse, *Philosophising in Mombasa* (Edinburgh: Edinburgh University Press, 2007); Roman Loimeier and Rüdiger Seesemann, eds., *The Global Worlds of the Swahili: Interfaces of Islam, Identity and Space in 19th- and 20th-Century East Africa,* Beiträge zur Afrikaforschung 26 (Berlin: LIT Verlag, 2006); Mark Chatwin Horton and John Middleton, *The Swahili: The Social Landscape of a Mercantile Society* (Oxford: Blackwell, 2000); John Middleton, *The World of the Swahili: An African Mercantile Civilization* (New Haven: Yale University Press, 1992).

2. Pat Caplan, "Boys' Circumcision and Girls' Puberty Rites among the Swahili of Mafia Island, Tanzania," *Africa: Journal of the International African Institute* 46, no. 1 (1976): 21–33; Caplan, "The Swahili of Chole Island, Tanzania," in *Face Values: Some Anthropological Themes,* ed. A. Sutherland (London: British Broadcasting Corporation, 1978).

3. See Loimeier and Seesemann, *Global Worlds;* Gerard van der Bruinhorst, "Siku ya Arafa and the Idd el-Hajj: Knowledge, Ritual and Renewal in Tanzania," in *Knowledge, Renewal and Religion: Repositioning and Changing Ideological and Material Circumstances among the Swahili on the East African Coast,* ed. Kjersti Larsen (Uppsala: Nordiska Afrikainstitutet, 2009); Abdin Chande, "Radicalism and Reform in East Africa," in *History of Islam in Africa,* ed. Nehemia Levtzion and Randall L. Pouwels (Athens: Ohio University Press, 2012), 349–72.

4. This footage was eventually made into the BBC TV series *Face Values* (producer David Cordingley for the BBC and Royal Anthropological Institute, broadcast 1978). Later a further two short films that focused on Mafia Island were also made: *Chole—A Woman's Place* and *Chole—Circumcision,* part of another BBC series, *Other People's Lives* (producer Peter Ramsden for the BBC and the Royal Anthropological Institute, broadcast 1982).

5. Michael Ratcliffe, *Times,* April 14, 1978.

6. Pat Caplan, "'Law' and 'Custom': Marital Disputes on Northern Mafia Island, Tanzania," in *Understanding Disputes: The Politics of Argument,* ed. Pat Caplan (Oxford: Berg, 1995), 203–22; and Caplan, "Monogamy, Polygyny or the Single State? Changes in Marriage Patterns in a Tanzanian Coastal Village, 1965–94," in *Gender, Family and Work in Tanzania,* ed. Colin Creighton and Cuthbert K. Omari (Aldershot, UK: Ashgate, 1999), 44–66.

7. Caplan, "Boys' Circumcision and Girls' Puberty Rites."

8. See Pat Caplan, *Choice and Constraint in a Swahili Community: Property, Hierarchy, and Cognatic Descent on the East African Coast* (London: Oxford University Press, 1975).

9. TANU ruled Tanzania from its independence, in 1961 (as Tanganyika), until after the union of Tanganyika and Zanzibar, when TANU merged with the Zanzibari Afro-Shirazi Party (ASP) to form the CCM, or Chama cha Mapinduzi, which is still the ruling party in Tanzania.

10. There were two village families into which I was incorporated, and I called their members by appropriate kin terms.

11. See Minou Fuglesang, *Veils and Videos: Female Youth Culture on the Kenyan Coast* (Stockholm: Almqvist and Wiksell International, 1994); Allyson Purpura, "Knowledge and Agency: The Social Relations of Islamic Expertise in Zanzibar Town" (PhD diss., City University of New York, 1997).

12. See also Loimeier and Seesemann, *Global Worlds of the Swahili.*

13. Pat Caplan, *Local Understandings of Modernity: Food and Food Security on Mafia Island, Tanzania,* report presented to the Tanzania Commission for Science and Technology (COSTECH) on fieldwork carried out June–August 2002, Mafia Island, Tanzania, 33, http://www.gold.ac.uk /anthropology/staff/pat-caplan/project-tanzania-global/. P. Caplan, "'But the Coast, of Course, Is Quite Different': Academic and Local Ideas about the East African Littoral," *Journal of Eastern African Studies* 1, no. 2 (July 2007): 305–20.

14. Mafia was one of the last districts in Tanzania to have its own secondary school. Kitomondo was the first and was opened on Mafia in 1994.

15. By this time, young men could sometimes earn more than their fathers if they could fish or dive for lobsters, which fetched a good price.

16. In my report to the Tanzania Research Council (COSTECH) at the end of my 2002 fieldwork, I noted that "between 6% and 9% of the population is affected, but there seems little doubt that more people in the south, especially around Kilindoni, are likely to have AIDS." Caplan, *Local Understandings of Modernity,* 33.

17. Janet Bujra has similar findings for lack of condom use in marriage from her research in Lushoto. Bujra, "Risk and Trust: Unsafe Sex, Gender and AIDS in Tanzania," in *Risk Revisited,* ed. Pat Caplan, Anthropology, Culture, and Society series (London: Pluto Press, 2000), 59–84. See also

Carolyn L. Baylies and Janet M. Bujra, eds., *AIDS, Sexuality and Gender in Africa: Collective Strategies and Struggles in Tanzania and Zambia,* Social Aspects of AIDS (London: Routledge, 2000).

18. Veiling and its many meanings in Muslim societies are extensively discussed by the contributors to Lois Beck and Nikki R. Keddie, eds., *Women in the Muslim World* (Cambridge, MA: Harvard University Press, 1978). For information on veiling among the Swahili, see Fuglesang, *Veils and Videos;* Françoise Le Guennec-Coppens, "Social and Cultural Integration: A Case Study of the East African Hadramis," *Africa: Journal of the International African Institute* 59, no. 2 (January 1989): 185–95; Margaret Strobel, *Muslim Women in Mombasa, Kenya, 1890–1975* (New Haven: Yale University Press, 1979). See also Emma Tarlo, *Visibly Muslim: Fashion, Politics, Faith* (Oxford: Berg, 2010).

19. Pat Caplan, "Where Have All the Young Girls Gone? Gender and Sex Ratios on Mafia Island, Tanzania," in *Agrarian Economy, State and Society in Contemporary Tanzania,* ed. Peter G. Forster and Sam Maghimbi (Aldershot: Avebury Press, 1999).

PART TWO

Contemporary Expressions of Coastal
Femininity and Womanhood

FOUR

Pleasure and Danger
Muslim Views on Sex and Gender in Zanzibar

NADINE BECKMANN

AN EXAMINATION OF LOCALLY grounded interpretations of Islam helps dispel some of the overly simplified and essentialist tropes about Muslim sexuality that have emerged in Western public discourse in recent years and points to the fact that lived religion is far from monolithic and is open to a huge array of interpretation.[1] An analysis of the ways in which sexual relations are interpreted and negotiated in one specific locality, Zanzibar, provides a corrective to the simplistic portrayal of oppressive and male-centered sexual practices in Muslim communities and an insight into the ways Zanzibaris deliberate Islamic teachings in their attempts to define what constitutes a good Muslim. While gender relations are far from equal in Zanzibar, marital sexual pleasure is emphasized for both men and women, and extensive education on techniques to enhance the sexual experience for both partners is carried out for women in particular.

The chapter also reveals that these interpretations are neither static nor homogenously accepted—on the contrary, local moral worlds are constantly debated and redefined in everyday practice. The growing threat of HIV and AIDS in Zanzibar, and the increasing influence of essentialist strands of Islam very clearly show this ability to adapt and reassess. Convergences and divergences are explored between Muslim ideology, put forward by mosque leaders and reiterated in everyday discourses about sexual norms and values in Zanzibar, and actual practice by Zanzibaris, whose concerns center on ways to contain the powerful, ambivalent force of sexuality—on how to enhance its positive side and control its negative facets.

Starting with an analysis of views on marital and nonmarital sexuality and its management in Zanzibar, I discuss the positive and negative outcomes of sex and link them to the ambivalent qualities of the body fluids involved. I illustrate strategies used to control sexual desire and to negotiate sex by HIV-positive people, and conclude with a brief discussion on the influence of more essentialist trends in Zanzibari Islam.

Findings derive from fifteen months of ethnographic fieldwork in Zanzibar in 2004–5 and several follow-up visits in 2007 and 2008. Living with a local family in Zanzibar Town and working closely with a group of HIV-positive people, I participated in a range of sexual education sessions, from HIV- and AIDS-related information to premarital sex education by groups of women, and to individual sessions within my host family and with some of my closest informants. The latter often occurred ad hoc, when sitting together with individual members of my host family or close informants, where an unmarried girl or younger married woman would be instructed about marital life, including the often detailed description of sex positions and practices, by an older woman, even the mother, despite the fact that such information should not be passed from mother to daughter.[2] The majority of the observed sessions took place in urban Unguja, both in Stone Town and Ng'ambo, but I also attended education sessions and weddings in rural Unguja and in Pemba. Using participant-observation as a main method, I took part in numerous weddings, observed marital and nonmarital interactions between men and women, and discussed matters of sexual practice, marriageability, sexual attraction and desire, and ways to manage these with young men and women (both married and unmarried, abstinent and sexually active), countless women and men of the parental and grandparental generations, traditional midwives, and religious leaders.

GENDER RELATIONS AND THE AMBIVALENT FORCE OF SEXUALITY

In Zanzibar discourses about sex are closely bound up with ideas of what it means to be a morally good person and a good Muslim. Several local terms describe immorality, and most of them have some sexual connotations: *uasherati* literally means promiscuity, extramarital sex, and indecency; *uhuni* is translated as vagrancy and decadence; and *zinaa* (nonmarital sex) and *umalaya* (prostitution) explicitly refer to sexual immorality. Notions of moral behavior focus on premarital and extramarital abstinence, piety, and decency in dress and behavior, but they encompass much more: being a good person is connected to a range of behaviors, including friendliness and helpfulness, modesty, humbleness, and self-restraint in every sense—sexually, but also emotionally, by not submitting to anger, jealousy, or even overly excited expressions of joy.

Always being balanced, calm, and in control of one's emotions and actions are thus ideal character traits for men and women, young and old. It is acknowledged that these traits need constant work and become easier with growing age and piety. While boasting and womanizing is often condoned among young men (though frowned upon by elders), however, girls and young women are closely monitored and scolded for being gregarious. Shyness, respect and passivity are regarded as ideal female features and make for *tabia nzuri* (good character), which is highly desired in terms of marriageability. Men should also be modest and respectful but are expected to assume a more active role; since women's basic character is regarded as less emotionally stable and controlled, men assume the role of a guardian. Unmarried women in particular should have as little contact with men outside their family as possible and the traditional image of women not leaving the house unaccompanied is valued by husbands, especially during the first years of marriage. With time and the birth of children, however, women usually gain more autonomy, and older women's authority is widely respected.[3]

Sexuality is perceived as a powerful and highly ambivalent force, as both creative and enjoyable, but at the same time dangerous and corrupting. In his monograph on sexuality in Islam, Abdelwahab Bouhdiba argues that sexuality is central to Islam as a religion and that, unlike Christianity, Islam is inherently positive about sex, as long as it takes place within prescribed boundaries.[4] Sexuality and erotic pleasure are not only desirable but a sign of divine power and are thus integrated into the legitimate domain of the religious: sex entails the power of creation, "a mimicry of the act of God."[5] In practice, however, he maintains, the sexual ethics of Muslims have deteriorated from an ideal model embodied by the Prophet Muhammad—this view, quite typical of Muslim apologetics, is shared by many Zanzibaris.

The result is a stark contrast drawn up in Zanzibar between an idealized notion of marital sex as enjoyable and creative and the condemnation of extramarital sex as dangerous and destructive. Sex within marriage is described as a drawn-out process, pleasurable for both husband and wife. Unsanctioned sex, on the other hand, is portrayed as a quick, unfulfilling, and dangerous encounter that brings *aibu* (shame) to the whole family, corrupts people's minds and endangers their health. The presence of HIV and AIDS in the islands has added even more urgency to the need to channel the destructive force of sexuality; illicit sex has always been dangerous, but now it is fatal. *UKIMWI ni adhabu ya Mungu* (AIDS is God's punishment) is the dominant explanation for the new disease in Zanzibar, and a sense of moral decline is evoked whenever the topic is discussed. Young people in general, and women in particular, are often blamed for this decline, and gender and generational struggles are invoked: "The young don't listen to the elders anymore," explained Abdallah (a pseudonym), a man of about fifty years. He went on:

> *Wasichana siku hizi hawataki ndani, wanaongea na wanaume barabarani! Hamna haya wala heshima siku hizi.*

> Girls don't want to stay in the house; they talk to men in the streets! There is no shame or respect these days.

An emphasis on gender segregation and the restricted movement of women in the public sphere aims at limiting the opportunities for men and women to meet, but is often unsustainable in an economic climate that increasingly requires women to engage in paid work outside the house. Moreover, the "lures of modernity"[6] have arrived in Zanzibar, too, in the form of new goods, fashions, and lifestyles that emphasize *starehe* (enjoyment) and *uhuru* (freedom). Nevertheless, long-standing notions of modesty in behavior and dress, obedience of the young to the elders and of women to men, virginity at first marriage, and the selection of suitable marriage partners by parents are highly valued. Young people today have to negotiate a terrain that is characterized by a heightened sense of uncertainty about how gender relations, and especially sexual relationships, should be handled.

"AT LEAST KEEP IT SECRET": OUTCOMES OF ILLICIT DESIRE

Any sexual relation outside of marriage (*zinaa*) is considered *dhambi* (sin) and is socially and legally condemned and considered destructive and polluting, bringing misfortune, disease, and death. Opportunities for extramarital sex without being found out are rather limited in Zanzibar's close-knit community. Twenty-four-year-old Sele reflected on the rules of nonmarital dating practices: "You do the talking in the streets, so if you go inside you get to the action straight away." A slow progression over weeks or months from courting to kissing and fondling and finally penetration does not appear to be common. Nonmarital sex is therefore often portrayed as unenjoyable: "with your husband you take time," Assia, aged forty-nine years, explained, "but with a boyfriend you do it quickly, you may be disturbed any time—how can you fully enjoy?"

While still perceived as sinful and socially and physically detrimental, extramarital sex for married women is easier to conceal, since they enjoy more freedom of movement than do unmarried women; for married men it is morally condemned, but generally assumed. Premarital sexuality, however, can have grave social consequences in Zanzibar Town, especially for the woman involved. *Ameshaharibiwa* (she's been ruined) is a common comment about a girl who lost her virginity outside of marriage; her *heshima* (respect) is destroyed, and both men's and women's *tabia* (character) suffers, because this kind of sex is viewed as corrupting: once tried out, sex is said to dominate a person's thoughts with ever-increasing desire and to make it difficult to refrain from behavior that is classified as immoral, including disrespect of the elders or drug and alcohol abuse. Hence, illicit sex spoils a man's reputation—and thus chances of finding a suitable marriage partner—too, though to a far lesser extent than for the woman. Although most people get married eventually, premarital sex or even rumors about a woman being of loose character severely affect her position in the marriage and lower the amount of respect she can claim from her future husband. Young women, in particular, must therefore always guard their reputation, and best pretend not to be interested in sexual matters at all.

In order to be able to navigate illicit relationships in a socially more acceptable way, they need to be managed as secret encounters. Such behavior is still regarded as immoral but socially more acceptable, especially if the relationship eventually results in marriage, as the case of Sharifa, the twenty-year-old daughter of a well-respected family that identifies as Arab, demonstrates. While first-time brides are expected to be inexperienced in romantic matters and embarrassed when meeting their future husband, often taking long detours in order to avoid running into the groom, Sharifa had been in a relationship with her future husband before the wedding—he had been her "boyfriend," a neighbor whispered, using the English term. While this does not necessary imply a sexual relationship, the fact that she insisted on spending their wedding night in a hotel room aroused suspicion. She neither wanted a *somo* (instructor) to teach her about sex nor the family waiting for the result of the virginity test. This was criticized by wedding guests and her parents. But the rumors were forgotten quickly, as they had legitimated their relationship and had never publicly announced whether the bride had been a virgin. This, it was conceded, after all was a matter between husband and wife.

The dominant principle in the management of nonmarital relationships is *siri*, secrecy, the pervasive concern with concealment of private matters. It is generally accepted that thoughts, feelings, and conduct that violate the practice of social conformity should not be disclosed but should remain concealed at all times due to the fear of *aibu*.[7] In this situation, lying—or using *ujanja* (craftiness, cunning) as it is called locally—is permitted, in order to protect other's feelings: a weighing of different degrees of sin takes place, taking into consideration all members of one's social network who might be affected by the disclosure of an affair.

If a premarital relationship results in pregnancy the consequences are particularly severe. While the man might be praised for his masculinity and boast about it among his peers, nevertheless his reputation suffers profoundly, and secrecy is often preferred. The woman, on the other hand, invariably brings great shame to her whole family, and girls sometimes attempt to commit suicide or have an abortion. Abortion is illegal in Zanzibar, but it is accessible in the hospital in exchange for a bribe. Additionally, there is a range of substances (most notably the root of the henna plant and the pharmaceutical antibiotic tetracycline) used to induce abortion, prepared by traditional health practitioners and midwives, or self-administered at home. An alternative is to find the father of the unborn child and force him to marry the girl to contain the shame—if necessary by inducing a police investigation, since nonmarital sex is illegal in Zanzibar.

How a breach of sexual norms unfolds its consequences to a whole network of people is exemplified by the case of Usara, a fifteen-year-old housemaid and shop vendor working in Stone Town, who came from a poor family in rural Unguja. On New Year's Eve 2004, Usara did not come home from the shop in the evening. Her employer's family searched for her all over town, informing the police and worrying a great deal. On the next day she was found in another part of town, carrying a mobile phone and some money. After intense pressure to tell what had happened, she admitted, "I was with a man, celebrating the New Year." She was taken to the police station to confess the name of the man so that he could be forced to marry her and thus save her heshima, but she refused to say anything. Usara and her older sister were sent back to their village on the same day. "The sister would only be hassled for Usara's behavior, and, anyway, I don't want anyone of that family in my house again," the employer argued. She brought *aibu* not only to herself and her own family, but also to her employer's family, which could not tolerate such a display of immorality inside their house. While they acceded that the man should have restrained himself more, almost the entire blame was put on Usara.

At night, after Usara had gone back to her village, her lover called and her employer arranged a meeting. The lover turned out to be more than twice Usara's age and did not feel guilty at all. "We're humans, aren't we?" he said. "And she approached me and gave me her number." To teach him a lesson, Usara's employer claimed that the girl had AIDS. This story caused great amusement when recounted again and again. Nobody cared about Usara's feelings or that her reputation might suffer even more when she was falsely accused of being HIV positive; she seemed to have lost all claims to mercy and respect. "She had sex outside wedlock, so it's most likely that she actually has AIDS," her employer explained, "and now probably both have it." Asking what would happen to her now, I was told that she will probably still be able to get a husband, though not a respectable one. The proverb *mhuni anampata mhuni* (in this context: a bad girl gets a bad boy) reflects the message of the third verse of the Qur'anic sura "Light": "The adulterer is only [fit] to marry an adulteress or an idolatress."[8]

Usara's story exemplifies how strongly girls' sexuality is regulated and how the moral discourse that has incorporated AIDS as a powerful means to underline local Muslim norms concerning the management of sexuality serves to direct people's actions into socially acceptable forms of behavior. It also shows the social risks involved in engaging in unsanctioned sex, ranging from loss of respect for the whole social network, to decreased marriageability and loss of status within marriage, to the loss of job or abandonment by the marriage partner. As Jennifer Hirsch and colleagues found for rural Mexico,[9] secrecy and concealment serve to minimize such social risks, rather than viral risks (e.g., of HIV infection): the concern for secrecy leads to profound uncertainty about others' hidden actions and often mistrust between partners.

"Men are like lions," Zainab, a twenty-three-year-old woman said, emphasizing the dangerous nature of male sexuality, "you can never trust them." And a young man in search of a bride lamented, "There are no virgins these days; it's very hard to find someone you can trust." This evaluation contrasts with an ideology of marital faithfulness and trust that makes it nearly impossible for both men and women to act upon the viral risks that sex entails in times of HIV/AIDS. The use of condoms, for example, is problematic, since the acquisition of condoms in itself may indicate illegitimate sex: being seen to buy condoms is feared to lead to rumors, and for young unmarried people it is particularly difficult to access them. When I asked if she could buy condoms, twenty-five-year-old Ulfat responded, "The shop owner would say, 'What do you need condoms for? You don't even have a husband!'". Moreover, within the relationship, and especially within marriage, insisting on using condoms engenders mistrust, as it insinuates one of the partner's unfaithfulness, and women often face physical violence for even bringing up the topic. The effectiveness of condoms is also frequently questioned in Zanzibar: while the vast majority of Zanzibaris know that HIV is spread by bodily fluids, an explanation of AIDS as divine punishment addresses the question: Why did I get infected, at this particular point in time? The moral explanation used to supersede the mechanical one, although this situation has slowly been changing over the last years. Where HIV and AIDS are seen as direct punishments from God, it is the immorality and sinfulness of the act, rather than the mixing of body fluids, that explains the infection. In this logic, social and viral risks merge and become one.

LEARNING TO BE A GOOD LOVER

In stark contrast to the dangers of illicit sex, marital sexuality ideally should be characterized by complementarity and should give pleasure to both men and women. The view that women, too, should enjoy sexual intercourse is strongly emphasized in Zanzibar, and ways to enhance pleasure are part and parcel of premarital education sessions. These include the performance of different sex positions and teachings on how positioning and movement (especially the rolling of the hips) can enhance both male and female pleasure, as well as instruction on the use of *shanga* (bead chains worn around the belly used to indicate sexual availability and as sex toys) to stimulate erogenous zones, and on the oral stimulation of both partners. Sexuality is said to create a stronger bond between husband and wife, to bring joy and relaxation as well as spiritual exaltation. "When a woman has sex with her husband she changes," married women of all ages kept pointing out to soon-to-be brides; "Her face has *nuru* (radiance); it shines." While complementarity and harmony are emphasized as features of a good marriage, the relationship between husband and wife is envisaged as hierarchical: the husband's role should be that of a benevolent patriarch, guarding and caring for his family, while the wife should follow her husband's instructions and make sure that he is content, by running the household, raising the children, and looking after his needs.

Sex education constitutes an important part of preparations for first weddings in Zanzibar. These sessions are largely directed at women—aiming to turn the bride from an innocent virgin into a good lover—and reflect the gendered interpretations of sex in Zanzibar: while girls' sexual purity is expected at first marriage, it is generally assumed for men to have some sexual experience by the time they marry. The practice of *singo,* a cleansing body scrub usually accompanied by teachings on sexual practices, is an integral part for brides, as Katrina Daly Thompson's chapter in this volume illustrates, but is becoming rarer for grooms; many men now refuse this practice, performed by older women who strip the groom naked, ridicule him with sexually allusive insults, and try to arouse him to "measure his masculinity." Premarital education for men is thus usually much shorter, consisting of an older male relative telling the groom to treat his wife well, avoid conflict, and live together in harmony. The increasing awareness of AIDS in the islands, however, underlines the importance of avoiding illegitimate sex. Obligatory premarital HIV tests have thus been incorporated into wedding preparations and, arguably for the first time, also subject men's virginity at first marriage to some scrutiny.[10]

Sexual education for the bride takes place in the weeks before her first wedding by her *somo*, a married woman close to her (usually a grandmother, aunt, or neighbor) who acts as her confidante throughout her life and had instructed the girl at the time of menarche, explaining the changing processes her body goes through and the new roles and behaviors these changes require. On the day of the wedding the *somo* is joined by other women from the family and neighborhood. The following is an abbreviated account of such a session for Salma, an eighteen-year-old bride, just before she was fetched by her husband's family.

A group of older women gather in the back room, around the bride. Another young woman is called in, too—the women are concerned about her marriage and determined to teach her to be a "better" wife. They instruct the bride to respect the in-laws and live peacefully with her new family. Then they explain how a wife should prepare herself for her husband; they take turns throwing in topics, competing for the best advice, making sexually allusive jokes and demonstrating sexual dances and positions: "Have a shower and brush your teeth—chew some cloves to make your breath smell sweet." "Perfume yourself and your clothes with *udi* (incense of aloe wood); wear makeup, jewelry, negligees, and *shanga*!" "When your husband comes home, have his meal ready and massage his neck so that his muscles become soft. Don't argue with him, make him feel good first and then talk about problems calmly. Never talk to others about marital problems; this only concerns the couple." Examples are also provided of negative outcomes of wives' chitchat about family affairs.

Another woman takes over: "When you go to bed, dance for your husband like this [ties *kanga* around her hips and dances in the local style, *kukata kiuno* (lit. cut off the hips), moving only the bottom with the rest of the body staying still]. Give him everything a prostitute would give, so he has no reason to search elsewhere!" Another woman shouts: "But don't accept it if he just says, 'Come, I want you'—my husband used to do that and I said, 'You're like a child; you know nothing!' He must make you want to have sex." They acknowledge that sometimes a woman may just not feel like having sex: "If you are *baridi* [lit. cold] you can relieve him with your hands, your mouth, or your breasts. You rub him in oil, kiss behind his ears and suck on his earlobes—he'll come in a minute!" The other women scream with laughter as the scene is acted out by two of the bride's aunties. "After the first time, only wipe off the fluids—if you shower you'll take away all the *utamu* (sweetness) and cool down again. Only when you're finished for the night you must wash your hair and clean your vagina with hot salt-water until it's as dry and tight as a virgin, otherwise you'll get diseases." Food metaphors are constantly used to explain sex, and heat and moistness are associated with sexual desire. The importance of regular sex and orgasms for both partners is emphasized: "You'll be joyful and relaxed; your body feels light and you forget all worries." Salma is quiet during all this time; only sometimes does the women's banter make her smile, but mostly she looks scared and embarrassed.

While these collective sessions are usually very humorous, with the women bursting into laughter as they compete to provide the best impressions of sexual acts, the bride often experiences them as awkward. Nevertheless, the *somo's* instructions, especially those given in private, are valued and taken seriously. With virginity being highly valued and marriages often arranged, the bride is expected not to know anything about sex and to be frightened of her wedding night. Many of my informants had never talked to their future husband, and most were terrified of the first night. "I'm scared of my husband," Hafsa, a nineteen-year-old girl, said when we talked about her impending wedding. "I'll be so embarrassed; I've never been naked in front of anybody, and I've never seen a man's penis. Is it really this big? I can't even insert a finger, I'm so tight!" "They say it hurts," eighteen-year-old Aisha exclaimed. "Look at newlywed brides, they can't even sit!" The consummation of the marriage here serves to activate a woman's legitimate sexuality, through a process involving pain and intensive practice. Pain is an integral part of the wedding, as it demonstrates the bride's moral purity, piety, and obedience to the elders: lack of pain during first intercourse is held to suggest prior sexual relations. The consummation of the wedding thus acquires the quality of a moral test, affirming (or denying) the girl's moral character and religious observance. It is therefore regarded as natural and befitting for a bride to display fright during her wedding. Twenty-eight-year-old Zubeida recounted her experiences of her wedding day: "My *somo* said, 'Don't be afraid, I'm just outside the door,' but I was so scared I cried with fear." The older women laugh when they see the bride's fear; though empathetic, they know that "this is a woman's life." One bride evoked suspicion and gossip about her sexual purity by smiling all through her wedding; she was frowned upon by the guests.

During the first night, the women stay at the house, waiting for the stained bed sheet to be displayed. The first intercourse is supposed to "open up" the bride—its purpose is not one of sexual satisfaction. Indeed, the husband is advised not to ejaculate during the intercourse: "Slowly, slowly you penetrate her," explained a *somo*. "When the hymen breaks, pull out! Wipe the blood with a white piece of cloth. You rest, then you do it again, to get used to it—every time you do it she gets wider, until she doesn't hurt again."

After the first night, sexual intercourse is supposed to proceed along a steep learning curve: "You practice it again and again, until you run toward your husband by yourself," an older woman who had been *somo* for several girls described the process. The *somo* stays with the couple for seven days and provides advice, washes the bride, calms her down, and teaches her. Complete openness is encouraged, the partners being allowed to ask anything they want to know. "Tell your partner what you like. You have to study each other's desires, and love will grow over the years, when you get to know each other—don't be lazy and stop trying to please your partner," the same *somo* emphasized.

Sexual initiative in both men and women is desired, and except for anal intercourse virtually all known positions are allowed; the goal is to experience pleasure. Older women in particular emphasize female agency, encouraging the younger women to be their husbands' teachers: to show where and how they enjoy being touched.

In addition to education sessions, bride and groom are also sometimes presented with a booklet on "Muslim marriage" that provides details about the benefits of marital sex, the erogenous zones of the body, different positions and techniques to arouse the partner, and the signs to know when the woman is ready for penetration. The latter is deemed particularly important, since all benefits from sexual intercourse, the book warns, turn into detriments and finally will result in divorce if the husband does not wait until the wife is ready. He is therefore reminded to delay his own orgasm until the woman also reaches her climax. Experimenting and ongoing learning about sex is encouraged and may even include watching porn movies. One woman in her midthirties, for example, had found a couple of porn DVDs in the shop she worked in, asked me to test them on my computer, and took them home in order to watch them with her husband for inspiration and new positions. The underlying motivation is to enjoy the full array of sexual relations at home, so that neither of the partners feels the urge to have extramarital affairs.

The extent to which this idealized image of marital sexuality translates into reality is difficult to establish. The education sessions emphasize that the success of the marriage is largely the wife's responsibility, by ensuring that the husband is satisfied, as Kjersti Larsen also shows in her chapter. This, together with the strong cultural prescription to take pleasure in sex and to initiate sexual intercourse regularly puts a lot of pressure on the woman. While many of my female informants seemed to genuinely enjoy having sex, others described sex as "work," a wife's duty, which they performed but did not enjoy much, emphasizing that the husband would feel betrayed if "he had married you and then you refuse him his rights."

FOOD, BLOOD, AND THE BODY: CONTAINING THE FORCE OF SEXUALITY

While sexual desire is heavily regulated as dangerous and uncontrollable except when channeled through marriage, substances like blood and certain types of aphrodisiac food represent another means to control desire. According to Zanzibari tradition, the amount and quality of blood in a person at a given time plays a vital role in physical and mental well-being and in the regulation of sexuality.

As in other societies across sub-Saharan Africa, heat is associated with sexual desire.[11] Having too much blood—perceived as common in young people—is said to create heat in the body and thus heighten libido and, consequently, make the person rebellious or aggressive. Being "cool" (*baridi*) on the other hand is associated with a desirable calm, controlled disposition (from *kutulia,* to calm down), and contrasts with the "heat" (*joto*) that sexual desire entails. People strive for a healthy balance, mainly achieved through a diet that balances blood-increasing food against blood-reducing conditions and actions. Much of this knowledge about the impact of food on the body is passed on through generations, but it is also heavily intertwined with what is understood as Muslim practice: many religious-advice booklets are dedicated to the art of treating diseases and ensuring well-being through the use of food, emphasizing Muslims' obligation to look after their body and keep it healthy.

Thus, the loss of blood through consuming illnesses, accidents, childbirth, and menstruation is countered through the intake of blood-increasing foods. The amount of blood in the body can also be reduced through physical exercise, sexual intercourse, the renunciation of blood-increasing foods, and masturbation. Views on the permissiveness of masturbation differ; most consider it sinful and classify it as *zinaa*. This might be connected to the fact that during masturbation a substance—semen—is spilled outside its designated place. "Semen should be planted into the woman's womb," a young man explains; "that's its natural place." Masturbation is therefore *haramu,* though usually weighed as a lower-level sin (*dhambi*) than "real" adultery: in line with the principle of *ijtihad* (interpretation), choosing the lesser of two evils,[12] if a man cannot contain himself it is better to masturbate than to seduce a woman, which would give him a much higher level of *dhambi.*

Blood in general is *najisi* (ritually unclean), but not inherently harmful. There are different qualities of human blood, and the blood that circulates in the body is perceived as different from that which leaves the body. Circulating blood appearing, for example, from a cut, is described as bright red and fluid, and contact with it requires only *udhu* (simple ablution). The blood of virginity, too, is not experienced as polluting or dangerous for the man, because it does not originate in the uterus, and its quality is light red and fluid. Blood coming from the uterus, however, is perceived to be polluting and dangerous and to cause *janaba* (major impurity).

While vaginal bleeding transfers the woman into a state of pollution, prohibiting her from sexual intercourse, praying, entering a mosque, fasting, or touching the Qur'an until she performs the ritual ablutions, menstruation and lochia (the first vaginal discharge after childbirth) also offer the opportunity to clean the body of the dirt that accumulates there. Every human body, both men and women argue, contains dirt, and menstruation and postpartum bleeding gives women the unique opportunity to rid their bodies of this dirt regularly—which is widely held to help women survive longer with HIV and AIDS. Directly after the end of menstruation women are said to be in their purest state, and thus most fertile.

The status of menstrual blood itself is ambiguous; it is inherently dirty, but also carries special positive qualities, holding the possibility to generate life. The menstrual cloth is a symbol of women's potential fertility and childbirth, and failure to menstruate means to be ill.[13] The uterus thus constitutes a seat of dirt and danger, radiating pollution and disease, but at the same time represents creation, and women who do not have a functioning uterus are regarded with pity. "If you don't have sex, a child won't develop," Zahra, a thirty-one-year-old woman, recounted, "therefore this special blood [of menstruation] does not stay, it has to leave the woman's body, otherwise it creates an infection." In this moment, devoid of its sacred purpose, menstrual blood turns into dirt. The same argumentation also holds in the case of postpartum blood, semen, and vaginal fluid. I suggest, following Mary Douglas's classification of dirt as "matter out of place,"[14] that these fluids are inextricably linked with the reproduction of life, and only when their goal is fulfilled—or missed—do they become dangerous and polluting: according to God's plan vaginal fluid and male semen should meet inside the woman to form a child, and for this to occur the man has to place his semen in exactly the right place. Whether or not conception takes place, the rest of the sperm is of no use any more and flows out of the body. This fluid must be washed off quickly, because it is perceived as dirty and causing disease. The same is true for vaginal fluid, especially that which is discharged without engaging in sexual activities. This substance is not the fluid that creates a fetus, it is *manii muongo* (fake semen), *uchafu* (dirt), and thus particularly dangerous. It plays the principal role in a female form of witchcraft called *kuramba* (from *kulamba*, to lick), where a jealous or malevolent woman is thought to be able to kill a child by rubbing some of her vaginal fluid into its mouth. The impurity of vaginal fluid is also the reason why women wash their vaginas in order to achieve ritual purity (*udhu*) and some women remove their underwear before performing the daily prayers.

Body fluids are considered especially impure in the case of extramarital affairs: sexually transmitted diseases, for example, are thought to originate in the woman's vagina, by the mixing of different men's semen. Children's disability, prolonged labor, miscarriages, and stillbirths are often attributed to extramarital affairs or to sex during menstruation. Apart from social condemnation, unsanctioned sexuality is thus associated with disease and suffering resulting from a state of ritual and physical impurity, since Muslim virtue is closely bound up with notions of purity in mind and body. David Parkin asserts,

> The underlying idiom for notions of Muslim virtue and holiness among Swahili-speakers is that of the person being cleansed of evil thoughts and emotions, and as bodily and ceremonially cleansed in the presence and site of God, . . . and that this idiom of cleansing underlies not only holiness, but also physical and mental well-being: the semantic pattern being premised on the notion that to cleanse is also to cure.[15]

Muslim norms here combine with pollution beliefs found all over East Africa, even among non-Muslims: the breach of norms leads to ritual pollution, which in turn leads to disease and suffering.[16]

SEX IN THE TIME OF AIDS

HIV infection in Zanzibar is believed to result from immoral behavior, but manifests itself as *damu chafu* (dirty blood), and

HIV-positive people acknowledge the dangers of mixing their blood with that of others through sexual intercourse. The difficulties posed by sex in the time of AIDS are reflected in frequent demands for education on "life skills," including sex education and ways to negotiate sex with partners. In response to the increasing threat of AIDS in local communities, and to large-scale HIV awareness campaigns, people talk increasingly openly about HIV/AIDS (see Pat Caplan's chapter this volume for examples from Mafia Island). I witnessed many such conversations in the context of sessions provided by healthcare professionals to groups of HIV positive people in hospital settings and in the offices of nongovernmental and community-based organizations.

These sessions provide an extraordinary space where local norms of speaking about sex are broken. Attended by married and unmarried adults of all ages, hierarchies of knowledge and authority are overturned when young and old, men and women are instructed together in new ways of negotiating sexual relations and engaging in sexual encounters. Knowledge that is considered dangerous and thus prohibited for unmarried people is discussed openly in the space of the HIV support group. Local norms of secrecy and privacy and the need to avoid explicit talk about sex are suspended: in the name of *elimu* (education) even the detailed discussion of specific sexual practices and individual examples is possible in these sessions. Men and women get up in front of the large crowd, asking how often they could have sex without exhausting their bodies, at which CD4 level sex was inadvisable,[17] how the antiretroviral medications would influence their ability to have sex, whether it was safe to have oral sex without a condom, or if masturbation was allowed. The questions meet widespread approval and are discussed openly in a serious manner. Emphasis is placed on responsible behavior in these sessions, the teacher never getting tired of pointing out that "the brain is the most important organ involved in sex" and drawing on the Qur'anic commandment to protect human life.

Responsible sexual behavior here does not necessarily translate into safe sex in the Western sense (i.e., condom use) but rather implies sex that complies with socially prescribed, Muslim norms. This is enforced within the Zanzibari HIV support group ZAPHA+ (Zanzibar Association for People with HIV/AIDS) through internal control mechanisms and sanctions designed to curb "immoral behavior" among the group members. Two members, for example, were banished from ZAPHA+ for three months after being found cheating on their partners.

The question of sex is often discussed informally among ZAPHA+ members, too. Scientific knowledge about the transmission of HIV and its effects on the human body is combined with local concepts and personal experiences of the way substances work in the body. All my informants agreed that they could feel the virus travel inside the body. Depending on one's current health status, one could feel it rise and sink (*vinapanda na vinashuka*). "If you don't have sex," Fatuma, a long-term female member of ZAPHA+ in her midfifties, explained, "the virus goes to sleep; it calms down [*virusi vinalala, vimetulia*]." Sex, it is understood, makes the blood *nyepesi* (light) and circulate, thus "waking up" the virus and spreading it throughout the body (*virusi vinatembea*—the virus travels), which will lead to an early outbreak of AIDS.

Sex is also believed to increase the viral load and—translating the concept of reinfection into local language—when both partners are HIV positive their viruses are believed to mix and develop into a more aggressive form (*inaongeza ukali wa virusi*, it increases the aggressiveness or strength of the virus), thus accelerating disease progression. One potential solution, therefore, is to live in abstinence for a long period—several years at least—to weaken the virus.

Those who engage in sexual relations despite being HIV positive often try to do so in a responsible manner. When the social risks of disclosing one's health status to the partner are deemed insurmountable, other strategies to minimize the number of sexual encounters or to negotiate condom use may be found: several women told their partners that the doctor had instructed them to use condoms because of some other disease, or tried to put off their partners by claiming they were menstruating, an excuse often used by HIV-negative women too. Others found rather creative solutions: twenty-nine-year-old Mwanakhamis, whose boyfriend is HIV negative, told me, "Before having sex my boyfriend rubs his hands with lemon juice to feel whether he has any small wounds before he touches me. We do the same with our mouths, and if one has any wounds we wait until they heal." They had embraced the biomedical approach to HIV transmission through bodily fluids and bodily orifices and invented a strategy to minimize the viral risks involved in their sexual encounters, in a context where persistent condom use is deemed almost impossible to negotiate.

ISLAMIC ESSENTIALISM AND CHANGING VIEWS ON SEX

This chapter highlights the value of studying locally grounded interpretations of Islam, which dispel simplistic tropes about "Muslim sexuality," revealing extensive variation within Muslim interpretations and practices of sex and gender relations. It demonstrates that although gender relations are not based on equality in Zanzibar, ideals of complementarity and female sexual pleasure coexist with a hierarchical concept of gender relations that places responsibility for the success of a relationship largely on the woman's ability to please her partner. The interplay between these notions opens up spaces for negotiation around sexuality and gender and softens the boundaries between what is permissible and what is not, as Sharifa's case demonstrates: her desire for companionship and for agency in choosing a partner is regarded as threatening the moral order and thus had to be kept secret, but is ultimately accepted when sanctioned by marriage. Moral ideologies can be reconciled with lived realities, and new interpretations and practices can arise, as local coping strategies for the HIV/AIDS crisis (e.g., premarital HIV tests, adjustment of sexual practice by HIV-positive people) reveal. I will end with an observation on current transformations that go beyond merely adjusting sexual practices and may in the long run change deeper values attached to the body and sexual pleasure.

Discourses about AIDS in Zanzibar are predominantly framed in terms of a broader rhetoric of moral decline, in which the sphere of sexual mores takes center stage: scantily clad tourists and mainland migrant workers come with money and far more liberal attitudes to nonmarital sex, sexually provocative music clips are screened on TV, pornographic material is freely available on the Internet, numbers of bars and guesthouses are increasing, and HIV prevention campaigns put the discussion of sexuality in the open, so that even children can "know about sex by themselves now," without having their sexuality activated in the appropriate setting. The fact that girls do not enter the premarital education sessions innocently, already "knowing it all," threatens to break down the distinction between "good" marital sex and bad, "ignorant" sex outside wedlock. All this is believed to make young people drift away from accepted Muslim practice, and the increasing rates of HIV infection and the (perceived or real) rise in premarital affairs are taken as evidence for this trend toward immorality.

This sense of decline in sexual morality has been employed by Muslim essentialists in a political discourse lamenting Muslims' marginalization in contemporary Tanzania and promoting a turn toward a more restrictive Muslim lifestyle as perceived to be laid out by the scriptures.[18] Mostly called the *watu wa bidaa* (innovation people) locally, proponents of various Muslim groups and organizations in Zanzibar demand the renunciation of what they call innovations to religious practice, including ritual performances that involve bodily techniques (such as *maulidi,* the ritual recitation of poems praising the life of the Prophet Muhammad, and *zikiri,* the ritual recitation of the names of God).

While such essentialist discourses are becoming increasingly popular, most Zanzibaris are more realistic in their approach, recognizing the need to adapt to changing life worlds. What I have noticed, however, is a more uncomfortable approach to sexuality and the body among those who are drawn toward the essentialists' views. Stricter prohibitions on bodily practices on the one hand have increased the sense of shame associated with nakedness and bodily processes and, on the other hand, considerably limit traditional practices for sexual education: the essentialists consider everything involving bodily movements, dance, drumming, and music as un-Islamic inventions. This includes the collective initiation rituals (*unyago*) that used to be performed for girls at menarche, which are shunned as "backward" and "un-Islamic," particularly in urban areas.

Reminiscent of the individual and private instructions provided for women of the Arab elite in the nineteenth century,[19] teachings at the onset of menstruation today are largely delivered in private and mainly concern matters of hygiene and the importance of sexual purity and restraint. Only immediately before the wedding is the girl initiated into the knowledge on sexuality and physical male-female relations. These instructions still focus on sexual pleasure, but are increasingly private affairs, held in a back room by only a small circle of women, in contrast to the large, very explicit kitchen parties, and send-offs and bridal showers that take place in coastal Tanzania, where the bride is prepared for married life by a public display of sexual positions and techniques through dance and song. Such large events still happen in Zanzibar but are frowned upon as un-Islamic and excessive by those who subscribe to a more essentialist version of Islam.

As a result, there is a trend toward the privatization and individualization of sexuality, to the extent that some members of the older generations complain that their sons and daughters are ashamed even to talk about sex and do not know how to please their partners anymore: "girls these days don't know [how to have good sex]; they aren't instructed" (*wasichana siku hizi hawajui, hawafundishwi*), both men and women often lament, and many men agree that older women are the better lovers, because they were educated appropriately. While the reformists' demand for more restrictiveness certainly appeals to many mainstream Muslims, who deplore the perceived increase in illicit sexual activities, the more body-phobic approach to sexuality employed by essentialist Muslims in Zanzibar may thus be perceived as counterproductive: in a context where the success of a marriage is strongly associated with a wife's ability to restrain her husband's sexual craving by fulfilling all his desires, playing down the role of pleasure in sex can be seen as causing marital dissatisfaction and thus endanger the marriage.

NOTES

This chapter is a revised version of "Pleasure and Danger: Muslim Views on Sex and Gender in Zanzibar," by Nadine Beckmann,

Culture, Health and Sexuality 12, no. 6 (March 2010): 619–32, reprinted by permission of the publisher (Taylor & Francis Ltd, http://www.tandfonline.com). Many thanks to Erin Stiles and Katrina Daly Thompson for their valuable comments.

1. Tom Boellstorff, *A Coincidence of Desires: Anthropology, Queer Studies, Indonesia* (Durham: Duke University Press, 2007); John Richard Bowen, *Muslims through Discourse: Religion and Ritual in Gayo Society* (Princeton: Princeton University Press, 1993); Magnus Marsden and Konstantinos Retsikas, eds., *Articulating Islam: Anthropological Approaches to Muslim Worlds,* Muslims in Global Societies 6 (Dordrecht: Springer, 2012).

2. Cf. Kjersti Larsen, this volume.

3. Cf. Katrina Daly Thompson, "How to Be a Good Muslim Wife: Women's Performance of Islamic Authority during Swahili Weddings," *Journal of Religion in Africa* 41, no. 4 (2011): 427–48.

4. Abdelwahab Bouhdiba, *Sexuality in Islam* (London: Routledge and Kegan Paul, 1985).

5. Ibid., 8.

6. Hansjörg Dilger, "Sexuality, AIDS, and the Lures of Modernity: Reflexivity and Morality among Young People in Rural Tanzania," *Medical Anthropology* 22, no. 1 (2003): 23–52.

7. Marc J. Swartz, "Shame, Culture, and Status among the Swahili of Mombasa," *Ethos* 16, no. 1 (March 1988): 21–51; Kjersti Larsen, *Where Humans and Spirits Meet: The Politics of Rituals and Identified Spirits in Zanzibar,* Social Identities 5 (New York: Berghahn Books, 2008).

8. M. A. S. Abdel Haleem, trans., *The Qur'an,* reissue edition (Oxford: Oxford University Press, 2008).

9. Jennifer S. Hirsch, Sergio Meneses, Brenda Thompson, Mirka Negroni, Blanca Pelcastre, and Carlos Del Rio, "The Inevitability of Infidelity: Sexual Reputation, Social Geographies, and Marital HIV Risk in Rural Mexico," *American Journal of Public Health* 97, no. 6 (2007).

10. Cf. Nadine Beckmann, "AIDS and the Power of God: Narratives of Decline and Coping Strategies in Zanzibar," in *AIDS and Religious Practice in Africa,* ed. Felicitas Becker and Wenzel Geissler (Leiden : Brill, 2009), 119–54.

11. For examples, see T. O. Beidelman, *Moral Imagination in Kaguru Modes of Thought,* African Systems of Thought (Bloomington: Indiana University Press, 1986); A. I Richards, *Chisungu: A Girls' Initiation Ceremony among the Bemba of Zambia* (London: Tavistock, 1982); Harriet Ngubane, "Some Notions of 'Purity' and 'Impurity' among the Zulu," *Africa* 46, no. 3 (1976): 274–84; Suzette Heald, "The Power of Sex: Some Reflections on the Caldwells' 'African Sexuality' Thesis," *Africa* 65, no. 4 (1995): 489–505.

12. Aisha Omar Maulana, Anja Krumeich, and Bart van den Borne, "Emerging Discourse: Islamic Teaching in HIV Prevention in Kenya," *Culture, Health and Sexuality* 11, no. 5 (2009): 564.

13. Mtoro bin Mwinyi Bakari, *The Customs of the Swahili People: The* Desturi za Waswahili *of Mtoro Bin Mwinyi Bakari and Other Swahili Persons*, ed. and trans. J. W. T. Allen (Berkeley: University of California Press, 1981), 55.

14. Mary Douglas, *Purity and Danger: An Analysis of Concepts of Pollution and Taboo* (London: Routledge and Kegan Paul, 1976), 36.

15. David Parkin, "Wafting on the Wind: Smell and the Cycle of Spirit and Matter," *Journal of the Royal Anthropological Institute* 13, no. 1 (2007): 201.

16. Cf. David J. Parkin, *The Cultural Definition of Political Response: Lineal Destiny among the Luo*, Language, Thought, and Culture (London: Academic Press, 1978); Benedicte Ingstad, "The Cultural Construction of AIDS and Its Consequences for Prevention in Botswana," *Medical Anthropology Quarterly* 4, no. 1 (1990): 28–40; Liv Haram, "Tswana Medicine in Interaction with Biomedicine," *Social Science and Medicine* 33, no. 2 (1991): 167–75; Annerose Hammer, *Aids und Tabu: Zur soziokulturellen Konstruktion von Aids bei den Luo in Westkenia*, Spektrum, vol. 54 (Hamburg: LIT Verlag, 1999); Angelika Wolf, "AIDS, Morality and Indigenous Concepts of Sexually Transmitted Diseases in Southern Africa," *Africa Spectrum* 36, no. 1 (2001): 97–107; Hansjörg Dilger, *Leben mit Aids: Krankheit, Tod und soziale Beziehungen in Afrika: Eine Ethnographie* (Frankfurt: Campus Verlag, 2005).

17. HIV destroys the body's CD4 T-helper cells, which are an essential part of the immune system. The CD4 count thus indicates the progression of the disease in the individual's body: the lower the CD4 count, the more susceptible the patient becomes to infections.

18. Beckmann, "AIDS and the Power of God."

19. Laura Fair, "Identity, Difference, and Dance: Female Initiation in Zanzibar, 1890 to 1930," *Frontiers: A Journal of Women Studies* 17, no. 3 (1996): 153.

FIVE

Sex and School on the Southern Swahili Coast
Adolescent Sexuality in the Context of Expanding Education in Rural Mtwara, Tanzania

MEGHAN HALLEY

FOR MANY, THE NOTION that education for girls is good for the girls, their families, and their communities is an indisputable truth. Indeed, this notion is supported by decades of research in the many developing countries that instituted formal education systems during the second half of the twentieth century. In particular, this research has shown a strong correlation between the education of girls and changes in certain markers of girls' reproductive health. As girls' education level rises, their age of childbearing also rises, as does their use of contraception, and their fertility rates typically fall.[1] Further, in most contexts this correlation follows a linear pattern, with each additional year of education for girls associated with incremental improvements in these markers of reproductive health.[2]

When I arrived in rural Mtwara, an isolated region on the southern coast of Tanzania, in the spring of 2009, I was well aware of this well-established relationship between girls' education and improvements in reproductive health, and it was not a topic I intended to particularly focus on during my eighteen months of field research. However, during the course of my stay, I was repeatedly struck by the multiple ways in which the formal education system in rural Mtwara appeared to increase—not decrease—girls' vulnerability to negative reproductive health outcomes, and particularly to unintended pregnancy, which subsequently led to their expulsion from school.

As I began to dig further into this question of the relationship between girls' education and reproductive health, then, I was not entirely surprised to find that in the poorest countries in the world, and particularly those in sub-Saharan Africa, the relationship between girls' education and reproductive health repeatedly documented elsewhere does not appear to follow the typical linear pattern but instead a curvilinear one, with girls exhibiting improvements in their reproductive health only after many years of schooling. In some contexts, this curve even takes on a U shape, such that girls with a few years of schooling exhibit younger ages of childbearing and lower rates of contraceptive use than those with no education at all.[3] As I dug further into this unexpected question, I also realized that although these macro-level associations between girls' education and reproductive health are well documented, there remains little consensus as to *why* they appear to be so closely linked in most contexts, and even less is understood about those contexts—such as rural Mtwara—that do not show consistent improvements in girls' reproductive health with increased education.[4] In this chapter, I draw on the case of rural Mtwara to explore potential underlying mechanisms linking education, gender, sexuality, and childbearing in a remote community on the Swahili coast that appears to be exhibiting this curvilinear pattern in the relationship between girls' education and reproductive health.

Mtwara Region, located on the southern coast of Tanzania, has experienced a rapid increase in access to formal education since 2003. However, this same period has also been marked by persistently high (and, by some measures, increasing) rates of adolescent pregnancy in the region. Available data suggest that adolescent pregnancy rates in rural Mtwara exceed 30 percent, the highest in Tanzania.[5] These trends make Mtwara a particularly interesting context in which to explore how the impact of expanded education is mediated by cultural norms and expectations of gender, sexuality, and marriage, as well as by specific economic and environmental characteristics of the local context.

The close examination of the cultural environment of coastal Mtwara presented here illustrates the shared cultural and historical roots of the people of the Swahili coast while simultaneously highlighting important points of intracultural variation within this large and diverse cultural group. In addition, the story of rural Mtwara, both past and present, has also been intricately shaped by its location on the coast of the Indian Ocean, which, due to the challenging surrounding terrain and lack of overland transportation options, has served as a primary site of contact between Mtwara and the outside world. While its coastal location served to connect Mtwara to the Swahili coast, its relative isolation also fostered unique cultural practices and identities, which have in turn resulted in the complex interplay between existing cultural norms related to girls' sexuality and the newly introduced structures of formal education in recent years.

Drawing on Anna Tsing's concept of "friction,"[6] in this chapter I explore four pathways through which increased access to formal education for girls in rural Mtwara may act to *increase* female students' vulnerability to pregnancy, including (1) inconsistencies between increased years of schooling for girls and normative developmental and sexual pathways in Mtwara; (2) the intertwining of gender, sexual, and economic roles and the structure of the school system; (3) the link between cultural norms of sexual attractiveness and student lifestyles; and (4) the relationship of educational quality and economic opportunities to subjective motivation for school achievement.

FRICTION: A THEORY OF CULTURAL CHANGE

I employ an anthropological approach to the study of cultural change and globalization. In contrast to theories of globalization that take a macro-level approach (for example, those that focus on economic neoliberalism or international political institutions), the anthropological study of cultural change has focused on the articulation of the global and the local in examining "how globalizing processes exist in the context of, and must come to terms with, the realities of particular societies, with their accumulated—that is to say historical—cultures and ways of life."[7] The anthropology of globalization examines the situated and conjectural nature of cultural change, that is, how the impacts of macrostructural processes occurring on a global scale—such as the global expansion of formal education—are mediated by the persistent diversity of cultural environments worldwide.

From the rapidly growing body of anthropological research on globalization, I draw specifically on Tsing's concepts of global "universals" and "friction" to explore points of intersection between the school system in Mtwara and adolescent pregnancy.[8] In her examination of environmental destruction in the rainforests of Indonesia, Tsing advocates for understanding cultural change through an "ethnography of global connections," examining how certain phenomena circulate around the globe and become instantiated in diverse communities.[9] These "universals" include phenomena that were produced within a specific cultural and environmental context but that, in the era of globalization, have become abstracted from their origins and "flow" into diverse cultural environments.[10] As these universals move, they produce "friction" in their encounters with diverse cultural contexts. According to Tsing, it is through this friction that universals become practically effective in diverse contexts. However, it is also because of friction that these universals essentially lose their universal quality, becoming diversified as they are integrated into unique cultural contexts. Tsing contends that an examination of friction can help illuminate "where the rubber meets the road," that is, where the movement of global universals across diverse cultural environments creates new points of conflict or creativity and, ultimately, new cultural forms.[11] This examination of cultural change through the lens of friction is intended to bridge the often dichotomized processes of localization and globalization to examine both the dynamics and outcomes of these processes together in a single analytic framework.[12]

Drawing on Tsing's theory of cultural change, this chapter explores the encounter between a quintessential "universal"—the Western-style formal education system—and specific characteristics of the cultural environment of rural Mtwara. The data presented here suggest ways in which the expansion of formal education in rural Mtwara is creating points of friction in the cultural domains of gender, sexuality, and marriage. This close examination of these points of friction further suggests specific mechanisms through which the expansion of formal education may initially increase, rather than decrease, adolescent pregnancy among girls in Mtwara.

THE MAKONDE OF RURAL MTWARA: PAST AND PRESENT

Rural Mtwara District is one of six administrative districts that make up Mtwara Region. The district is approximately 550 kilometers south of Dar es Salaam, on the eastern coast of the region, bordered by Mozambique to the south. Mtwara Region has often been described as "isolated."[13] Indeed, when compared to the northern regions of Tanzania, the poor state of the roads both leading to and within this southern region has left rural Mtwara both geographically and economically peripheral.[14] However, the description of Mtwara simply as isolated ignores the region's long history of encounters with powerful outsiders, and in particular with the Arab traders, who first crossed the Indian Ocean to arrive in the coastal Mtwara town of Mikindani in the eighth century.[15]

Indeed, the current cultural and religious makeup of Mtwara is the direct result of its location on the coast of the Indian Ocean. The Makonde ethnic group constitutes the majority of the population in Mtwara Region, and the Makonde are predominantly Muslim as a direct result of the history of Arab rule they share with more northern regions of the Swahili coast.[16] However, even among those who identify as Makonde and Muslim, segments of the Makonde population experienced historically different levels of interaction with the coastal Arabs depending on the timing of their ancestors' migration to Mtwara and their location within the region (coastal or inland). Specifically, the subset of the Makonde population who trace their roots to coastal rural Mtwara District, and who therefore lived for many generations in direct contact (and often intermarried) with the Arab traders who occupied the coast, also simultaneously self-identify as Waswahili and speak a dialect of the Makonde language that is distinct from the Makonde who live in (or trace their ancestral roots to) the more inland areas of the region.[17] The inland Makonde historically experienced less intensive interaction with the Arabs because of the treacherous terrain that separated them from the coast, and though they are Muslim, they generally do not identify as Waswahili—indeed, some of the elders I encountered during my fieldwork did not speak Swahili. In this way, the cultural geography of rural Mtwara—past and present—reflects both the interactions made possible through the region's coastal location as well as the limitations of these cross-ocean influences in the more inland portions of Mtwara.

Though the region's coastal location made certain interactions possible, neither the colonial German or British governments nor the new Tanzanian government truly invested in the development of the region, a trend primarily blamed on the ruggedness of the surrounding terrain, which made overland travel excessively difficult. Health statistics in the region also reflected this lack of investment. In 2002 life expectancy in rural Mtwara was only forty-two years, a full twenty-six years lower than that of Arusha Region, in northern Tanzania.[18] Though economic development in postindependence Tanzania as a whole was by no means successful, economic development in Mtwara has continued to lag behind even the modest growth seen in other regions of the country.

Since 2003, however, Mtwara has been undergoing rapid change. The discovery of natural gas in 2000 and the subsequent discovery of oil just a few years later are likely to have the most significant influence on the region. In this time, the government has also made progress toward completing the tarmac road linking Mtwara to Dar es Salaam. Although sixty kilometers remain incomplete, since 2000 the 560-kilometer overland journey has been reduced from up to six days to less than twelve hours (as of January 2011). In addition, as part of President Benjamin Mkapa's Development Plan for Secondary Education, which mandated the building of at least one secondary school per administrative ward throughout Tanzania, the number of secondary schools in the region has increased from one to twenty-two since 2000.[19] Though both male and female students have flooded these schools, adolescent pregnancy rates in Mtwara have remained high, with many girls dropping out or being expelled from school due to pregnancy.[20] Both the historical and modern-day characteristics of rural Mtwara indicate a particularly interesting context in which to explore the relationship between education and reproductive health on the Swahili coast.

METHODOLOGY

A research team consisting of three Makonde research assistants (two male and one female) and myself collected the data presented here during two periods of field research in rural Mtwara, including three months in 2008 and eighteen months from 2009 to 2010. We used multiple methods, including (1) community ethnography and targeted interviews with thirty-four community leaders; (2) participant-observation in the secondary-school environment; (3) sequential, ethnographic interviews with sixty-nine adolescents paired with a quantitative survey; (4) participant-observation in adolescent initiation rituals practiced in rural Mtwara; and 5) a structured survey of 239 households. Both the research assistants and myself primarily conducted the research in Swahili, though Makonde was also used by the research assistants as needed and subsequently translated into Swahili for my understanding. Elsewhere I have provided a detailed discussion of the methodology used in this research.[21] The description below provides a brief overview of the methods used to collect the data presented here.

The data presented below are drawn primarily from sequential interviews with adolescents and from participant-observation in the initiation rituals. The former involved conducting extended ethnographic interviews at four time points with adolescents between the ages of fourteen and twenty-four living in five different villages in rural Mtwara District: Ufukweni, Mlimani, Barabarani, Mchangani, and Mtoni (all village names are pseudonyms). Of the sixty-nine adolescents interviewed, twenty-five were drawn from a random sample of households in the home field site of Ufukweni. An additional twenty participants were drawn from the other four "satellite" field sites, identified using purposive quota sampling[22] stratified by age and by gender to obtain equal numbers. Finally, due to an underrepresentation of secondary-school students in the original two samples, a school-based sample of twenty-four adolescents was drawn from the enrollment records of Ufukweni Secondary School using a stratified random sample to obtain equal numbers of boys and girls.

Though this sample cannot be considered representative of all adolescents living in rural Mtwara, it was designed to capture the viewpoints of adolescents living throughout the area. I conducted all interviews with female participants and three of the four interviews with male participants. As the fourth interview was focused on sexual norms and individual sexual activity, a male research assistant conducted the final interview with all male participants.

Participant-observation was conducted in the female initiation rituals of *unyago* and in the male ritual of *jando* practiced by members of the Makonde tribe of rural Mtwara, including five female rituals and four male rituals. A female research assistant and I conducted the participant-observation for the female rituals, and the male research assistants did so for the male rituals. Because these month-long rituals are primarily conducted from mid-December to mid-January, the entire research team was simultaneously conducting observations to maximize the number of rituals we could observe during my eighteen months in the field. Pairs from the research team (one male and one female) were stationed in different satellite field sites from December to January to conduct the observations. In addition, in the site where I was stationed, a female family member participating in the rituals I was observing provided assistance with translation from Makonde when necessary.

These observations involved intimate participation in every aspect of these month-long rituals together with the large groups of older relatives of the initiates. The research assistants and myself joined in the cooking, drinking, eating, singing, dancing, and even in removal of our clothing during those parts of the ritual when this was expected. We also documented the events as they took place using handwritten notes, photography, and audio recordings (when permitted by participants). We also conducted informal interviews with the young initiates, their families, and the *walombo* who led the rituals to collect data on the meaning and values associated with the many activities and events that make up these complex rituals. All together, our research team observed a total of ninety initiates (thirty-four female and fifty-six male) in five separate female rituals and four separate male rituals, and we interviewed seven male and nine female walombo.

I personally catalogued all handwritten notes taken by the research assistants and myself using a word-processing program, and the research assistants transcribed all audio recordings in the original Swahili. Analysis was conducted in Swahili to retain the integrity of the language. I conducted the qualitative data analysis in NVivo 8.0 using a grounded-theory approach,[23] with regular input provided by the research assistants, and quantitative data was managed in SPSS 17.0 for PC and analyzed using basic descriptive statistics. I translated those portions of the data presented in publication with guidance from Makonde research assistants.

FRICTION WITH THE SYSTEM: FORMAL EDUCATION AND ADOLESCENT SEXUALITY IN MTWARA

The remainder of this chapter is devoted to a discussion of four points of friction in the domain of adolescent sexuality emerging from the interaction of certain characteristics of the formal education system with aspects of the cultural environment of rural Mtwara. This close examination of these points of friction highlights the inconsistencies between the school system and the cultural environment of rural Mtwara and suggests pathways through which the expansion of formal education in rural Mtwara may result in negative effects on adolescent girls' reproductive health.

Normative Developmental and Sexual Pathways and Increased Years of Schooling for Girls

The first point of friction is rooted in the definition of adolescence and the shifting age of marriage relative to the number of years of available schooling. As described in diverse communities around the world, the expansion of educational opportunities often results in a delay in the age of marriage, particularly for girls.[24] This pattern also holds true for Mtwara. However, this rising age of marriage is inconsistent with normative developmental and sexual pathways in this community.

Girls in Mtwara typically begin to marry at or soon after reaching puberty. Among all thirty-three female adolescent interview participants, eight had already been married, and the average age of first marriage was sixteen years, with the youngest married at fifteen and the oldest at eighteen. Though data from this small subsample cannot be assumed to be representative of all adolescents in rural Mtwara, adolescent participants' discussions regarding normative marriage practices for girls were consistent with the experiences of the subsample of girls who had already been married. Female participants estimated the average age of marriage for girls in rural Mtwara to be sixteen years and the youngest age at which girls begin to marry to be around thirteen years. For example, as "Ana" (age nineteen) described:

> *Wasichana wetu wa huku, tunaolewa mapema. Tukishavunja ungo tu, kwenye umri wa kumi na nne, kumi na sita hivi, tunaolewa.*

> Our girls from here, we are married early. Just after we reach puberty, around age fourteen or sixteen, we are married.

In addition, participants also explicitly linked a girl's age of marriage to her years of schooling. Specifically, they described a process in which girls married soon after either dropping out of or completing primary school *unless* they passed the national exam required to go on to secondary school. As "Salima" (age sixteen) described:

> *Wasichana wengi, wale wasiosoma, wakishavunja ungo, kwenye miaka kumi na sita hivi, wanaolewa. Kama wanasoma shule ya msingi tu basi, wanasubiri matokeo tu. Wakishafeli, wanaolewa tu moja kwa moja.*

Many girls, those who aren't studying, once they have reached puberty, around sixteen years or so, they are married. If they are only in primary school, that's it; they just wait for their [test] results. Once they have failed, they just get married straight away.

Indeed, participants reported that girls who are now attending the recently opened secondary schools are delaying marriage, some until they are twenty-one years old. This is consistent with the ages of the sixteen female interview participants who were themselves secondary-school students, eight of whom were over eighteen years old. Given that students are forced to choose between marriage and schooling by the Tanzanian state, which has passed laws making it illegal for students of any age to be married, this later age of marriage for secondary-school students is essentially inevitable.[25]

However, this delay in marriage has not come with a corresponding delay in the age of sexual debut, in part because, in Mtwara, normative developmental and sexual pathways mark the beginning of sexual activity not by marriage but through ritualized initiation in unyago and jando. The terms *unyago* and *jando* are used in many regions of Tanzania to refer to rituals of initiation that take a variety of forms.[26] However, the practice of unyago, in particular, as an initiation into adolescence has all but disappeared in some of the more northern regions of the Swahili coast, including in Zanzibar (see chapters by Nadine Beckmann and Katrina Daly Thompson in this volume) and on Mafia Island (see Pat Caplan's chapter). Instead, in more northern regions of the Swahili coast, many of the teachings of unyago do not take place until the eve of a girl's marriage,[27] and these events, as described in the chapters by Beckmann and Thompson, are considered conceptually distinct and take a very different form from that of the Makonde unyago.

Among the Makonde, these rituals are conducted as young people are approaching puberty. Though the exact age at which boys and girls are initiated varies, cultural norms dictate that the rituals must be conducted before the first signs of pubertal development. Like adolescents in many rural communities across sub-Saharan Africa, girls in rural Mtwara experience puberty at an age significantly later than that experienced by adolescents in Europe and North America.[28] In rural Mtwara, the mean age of menarche for all female adolescent interview participants was fourteen, with the youngest participant reaching menarche at age twelve and the oldest at age sixteen. The average age of puberty reported by male interview participants was sixteen, with the youngest reporting going through puberty at age thirteen and the oldest at age eighteen (details on the method used for calculation of male age of puberty are described elsewhere).[29] Though these data are based on individual recall, and therefore are subject to error, this estimate is consistent with recent data collected on rural populations in northern Tanzania.[30]

Both boys and girls are typically initiated after they have passed the growth spurt in middle childhood but before exhibiting the first signs of puberty. As the first physical sign of puberty in girls—breast development—typically begins two years before menarche, age twelve is generally the latest a girl in Mtwara would be initiated, with the majority of girls initiated between ages ten and twelve.[31] Though boys' age of initiation varies more than girls for a number of reasons detailed elsewhere,[32] they also must be initiated before their initial growth spurt indicating puberty.[33]

In these rituals, boys and girls receive a range of teachings to prepare them for adult life, including lessons and skills related to negotiating sexual activity. Upon completion of these rituals, boys and girls are seen as having left behind the sexual immaturity of childhood, and it is accepted that both boys and girls will be begin to engage in sexual relationships. As Fatuma (age twenty-three) describes,

> Nilianza mapenzi—sijui—kwenye umri kama—kumi na tatu, eeh, kumi na tatu. Nilipokuwa nimeshaaruka, mwaka huohuo. Baada ya kuaruka tu, mvulana akaanza kunifuata, siyo nilikuwa nimearuka! Akanifuata, akaenda kwa wazazi, kawaambia ananipenda, atanitunza, basi. Tuliishi pamoja, baadaye akanioa. Nilizaa naye mtoto wa kwanza.

I started to have sex—I don't know—around age—thirteen, yes, thirteen. When I had been initiated, that same year. After I was initiated, a boy started to pursue me, you know; I had been initiated! He pursued me, he went to my parents, told them that he liked me, and that he will take care of me, that's it. We "lived together," later he married me. I had my first child with him.

In this quote, the verb *kuaruka* (also sometimes spelled and pronounced *kualuka,* as the Makonde do not distinguish between the letters *r* and *l* in pronunciation) is a term from the Makonde language describing the act of being initiated in unyago or jando. It should also be noted that, in interviews with adolescents, participants often used *kuishi pamoja* (lit., to live together) as a euphemism for being in a sexual relationship, even though they were not actually living in the same household.

In Mtwara, girls and boys are prepared for the beginning of sexual activity in unyago and jando, and it is an expected part of normative developmental pathways in this community that adolescents will begin to engage in sexual relationships upon reaching puberty. These cultural norms are also documented in historical accounts of the Makonde, which describe how Makonde women were also reportedly free to accept or reject marriage proposals and in general enjoyed nearly the same level of sexual freedom as men.[34]

The extent to which premarital sexual activity among postinitiation adolescents—and particularly girls—is viewed as normative in rural Mtwara is distinct from other regions of the Swahili coast. For example, as described in the chapters by Beckmann, Thompson, and Erin Stiles, in Zanzibar sex before marriage is considered shameful and contradictory to the teachings of Islam. In Mtwara, on the other hand, the apparent contradiction between the norms and expectations of unyago and of Islam did not appear to be experienced as contradictory by the Muslim Makonde of Mtwara. Though the reasons for this difference have not been definitively examined, potential contributing factors include the historically matrilineal, matrilocal kinship structure of the Makonde tribe before conversion to Islam, as well as the nature of the conversion process itself.[35] In Mtwara the conversion of the Makonde to Islam was more gradual than in other areas of the Swahili coast, including Zanzibar, and was primarily driven by individuals of mixed Arab-Makonde parentage, who were not perceived as true outsiders, and who tended to take a more accepting approach to existing cultural practices, including the rituals of unyago and jando.[36] Further, though the coastal location allowed for interaction with and exposure to Arab influence, the region's remote location and rugged inland terrain made intensive and regular contact arguably more difficult than in Zanzibar and other more northern regions of the coast.

Finally, though sexual activity during adolescence is considered part of normative developmental and sexual pathways for both boys and girls in Mtwara, these normative pathways also include marriage around the age of puberty, a pathway that is now at odds with extended years of education. As girls increasingly attend school well past the age of puberty, the length of time between initiation and marriage—that is, the adolescent life stage itself—is lengthening. The potential for female students to become pregnant during adolescence has increased because the length of these girls' adolescent life stage has itself extended well past the age of reproductive maturity (puberty), while the age of sexual debut has remained tied to normative developmental pathways (unyago). It remains to be seen whether these changes in the timing of sexual debut vis-à-vis marriage will also change community attitudes toward premarital sex to be more in line with Islamic teachings, or perhaps even change the timing and structure of the rituals themselves to resemble the *singo* described by Thompson in her chapter in this volume. Further, this example from modern-day Mtwara bears some resemblance to the situation described by Corrie Decker (also in this volume) in which school administrators in colonial Zanzibar attempted to use the school system to redefine existing local biocultural definitions of "girls" and "women" (defined in part by unyago) in terms of Western standards of numerical age and schooling. However, the inconsistencies in the definition of developmental stages in and outside of school represent only the first source of friction in the relationship between sexuality and schooling in Mtwara.

Despite the way in which these rituals (unyago in particular) are typically portrayed in the popular media, by nongovernmental organizations, and sometimes even by the Tanzanian government,[37] sexuality is only one of a wide range of topics addressed in these rituals. On the contrary, in these rituals sexuality is woven into teaching about a range of issues, including gender roles, marriage, childbearing, family responsibilities, work ethic, the natural environment, and the history and traditions of the Makonde. Indeed, it is this interweaving of sexuality with other aspects of adult life addressed in these rituals that anchors the sexual aspects within the broader developmental transition from childhood to adulthood.[38]

The Intertwining of Gender, Sexual, and Economic Roles and the Structure of the School System

A second source of friction is found in the interaction between local norms surrounding gender, sexual, and economic roles and the still limited number of secondary schools in Mtwara. Though the number of schools has increased dramatically in the last ten years, each school still draws students from the many surrounding villages, such that the majority of students in secondary school must live away from home in order to attend school. Among the twenty-four adolescent interview participants who were secondary-school students, only three were living at home while attending school. The majority of students were renting rooms, often in groups of three of four students, from families who owned additional homes in the village where the school was located. Students would arrive at school with all their supplies for the semester, including food, clothing, and any pocket money their families could afford to spare, and they would live off these provisions until they returned home during school breaks.

Adolescent interview participants reported that this arrangement was often precarious, particularly for girls. Among twenty-four female students interviewed, twenty stated that if a girl is going to school away from home and she runs out of food, she is more likely to get involved in sexual relationships. "Arafa" (age fifteen) explained:

Kama mimi, kwa mfano. Nipo shuleni, na babangu yupo kijijini hukooo. Sasa, nina shida. Inabidi nimwandikie barua kwa sababu sina simu, na yeye hana simu. Basi, barua natuma. Labda mwanafunzi mwenzangu akaenda mjini, akanichukulia ile barua. Lakini inawezekana barua yenyewe haifiki! Au inachelewa. Kipindi kigumu kile, nakuambia! Unga umeisha, wewe upo shuleni, huna jamaa, huna kitu. Na hata kama una uwezo wa kupiga simu, inabidi kwanza baba kuhangaika kutafuta unga, wakati wewe unalala na njaa. Na sisi wasichana tuilivyo, tukiwa na njaa, tupo tayari kukubali vishawishi vya wavulana.

Like me for example. I am at school, and my father is in a village far, far away. Now, I have a problem. I have to write a letter because I don't have a phone and he doesn't have a phone. So I send the letter. Maybe my fellow student is going to town, and he or she takes it for me. But it is possible that the letter itself never gets there! Or it is delayed. That is a difficult time, I tell you! You have run out of flour, you are at school, you don't have any family, you don't have anything. And even if you can manage to call on the phone, your father still needs to trouble himself to find flour, while you are going to bed hungry. And us girls, the way we are, if we are hungry, we are willing to accept boys' temptations [e.g., offers of gifts or money].

As detailed in Halley, gender, economic and sexual roles in Mtwara are tightly intertwined, as they are in other communities in sub-Saharan Africa.[39] For example, women in Mtwara are referred to using the idiom *watu wa kupewa,* or "those who are given (to)" in reference to their economic dependence on men, and in particular on their sexual partners, both in and outside of marriage. Within this context, it is common practice for boys to offer gifts and money—*vishawishi* (lit., temptations)—to girls they are pursuing as potential sexual partners. This is not considered transactional in the sense of trading sex for money but part of broader cultural norms of gender, sexual, and economic roles. Caplan (this volume) documents a similar cultural pattern on Mafia Island, which one of her participants aptly describes as "love comes from giving." Indeed, this interweaving of gender, sexual, and economic roles has been documented in other regions of the Swahili coast and sub-Saharan Africa.[40] However, in the context of an education system that essentially requires students to live away from their families, girls may be increasingly put in a position of having to rely on their position as *watu wa kupewa* not out of choice but out of necessity.

This is not the case for boys, as it is the cultural expectation that the boys will support the girls in sexual relationships. Though homosexual relationships are not unheard of, this was not recognized by participants in my study as a potential source of economic support for boys or girls. Homosexual relationships are also highly stigmatized, and no participants admitted any involvement in homosexual relationships. Overwhelmingly, participants reported that because male students cannot turn to sexual relationships as a potential source of economic support, they are often forced to seek out short-term manual labor when in need.

The conflict between the demands of the secondary-school system, which require girls to live away from their source of economic support, and these gendered and economic norms underlying sexual relationships represents a second source of friction and a second potential driver of continued high rates of adolescent pregnancy in rural Mtwara, despite increased access to education.

Cultural Norms of Sexual Attractiveness and Student Lifestyles

Not only does secondary-school attendance increase a girl's vulnerability to vishawishi by separating her from her source of social and economic support, it also increases her appeal as a sexual partner. Among all sixty-nine participants, forty-seven (68 percent) felt that female students were more actively pursued as sexual partners than girls who were not in school. This is in spite of a law passed in 2003 stating that any man convicted of marrying or impregnating a student may be sentenced to up to six years in prison.[41] Though participants regularly mentioned this law, and in one field site (Ufukweni), participants were aware of a man currently being tried under this law, it still did not appear to act as a significant deterrent to pursing relationships with female students.

When asked to explain why female students were considered so sexually attractive, thirty-eight adolescent interview participants (61 percent), said that this was because "they are attractive" (*wanapendeza*). The verb *kupendeza* (to be attractive) is used to refer to specific characteristics that are considered desirable in a sexual partner, including lighter skin, a full figure, and younger age. The use of the conjugated verb *wanapendeza* with reference to female students was perhaps best described by "Mudi" (age twenty):

Mudi: *Mvulana anafurahi sana akipata mwanafunzi kutembea naye kwa sababu wanafunzi wanapendeza kishenzi!*

Male Research Assistant: *Wanapendeza namna gani?*

Mudi: *Uh huh. Kwanza, umri alio nao mwanafunzi ni mdogo, inapendeza. Halafu hafanyi kazi ngumu kwa sababu hana muda. Mwanafunzi, akiamka asubuhi, ananawa, amenyoa freshi, anavaa nguo za shule, kupiga sketi, blausi, viatu, kila kitu, anatoka smati kabisa, safari ya shule. Mimi, kila siku naenda tu baharini kuvua samaki, kwa hiyo siwezi kupendeza kama mwanafunzi. Yeye anaenda shule, anakaa tu, kuandika masomo yake, basi. Akirudi nyumbani jioni, anakuta chakula tayari, anakula, basi. Mwanakijiji anaenda shambani kulima, jua kali. Mwanafunzi hawezi kukonda, lazima anenepe tu, halafu usoni mweupeee.*

Mudi: A boy is very happy if he has a girlfriend who is studying because students are crazy attractive.

Male Research Assistant: In what way are students attractive?

Mudi: Uh huh. First, the age of the student is young; it is attractive. Then she doesn't do hard work because she doesn't have time. A student, when she wakes up in the morning, she washes her face, she has shaved [her head] nicely, she puts on her school clothes, her skirt, blouse, shoes, everything. She goes out looking totally smart, on her way to school. Me, every day I go to the ocean to fish, so I can't look as nice as a student. She goes to school, just

> sits, writes her lessons. When she goes home in the evening,
> she finds food waiting for her; she eats, that's it. A villager
> goes to the farm; the sun is hot. A student can't lose
> weight; she must gain weight, and then her face is so light.

As Mudi describes, the student lifestyle contributes to the development of physical characteristics that are considered particularly sexually attractive. Though participants' descriptions of their access to food suggest that it is not quite as easy as Mudi perceived, students do spend the majority of their time inside (as opposed to in the fields) and rarely participate in the manual labor that is otherwise a standard part of daily life in Mtwara. In addition, female students do not wear the traditional *kanga* (colored cloth) of village women or the hijab occasionally worn by women in this region but instead must wear Western-style uniforms required in all public schools in Tanzania. The dress, as well as the lifestyle and resultant physical appearance of female students, make them particularly attractive by cultural standards. Similar cultural standards of female beauty have been documented elsewhere in Tanzania.[42]

Although the requirement to live away from home decreases a girl's ability to resist vishawishi, her student status simultaneously increases her sexual attractiveness and the extent to which men pursue her. This represents a third source of friction produced in the interaction between the structure of secondary education as introduced in rural Mtwara and existing cultural norms and values related to adolescent sexuality present in the surrounding cultural environment. Though secondary-school girls are achieving higher levels of education than their peers, these sources of friction represent potential drivers of the continued high rates of adolescent pregnancy in rural Mtwara.

Educational Quality, Economic Opportunities, and Subjective Motivation

The final source of friction also speaks to patterns of globalization and development in sub-Saharan Africa. In recent years, scholars have proposed concepts such as "development enclaves" and "therapeutic globalization" to describe the defining characteristics of globalization in this region.[43] These concepts all reference the piecemeal way in which globalization and development have progressed in many regions of the continent in the last twenty years, such that the citizens of many countries experience only one point of articulation with the institutions of global modernity while their remaining environment remains untouched.[44] In rural Mtwara, the education system now provides adolescents with one such point of articulation, and schooling is touted as *the* pathway toward both individual and national development.[45]

However, the expansion of this system has not come with a parallel expansion of formal employment to absorb this cohort of newly educated youth, as the region has continued to be relatively economically isolated. In Mtwara girls who do manage to obtain a secondary education do not have expanded access to employment or opportunities for economic independence. Though my research did not involve systematically following girls after completion of their education, continued communication with participants revealed that not one female student was working in a regularly paid job after completing school. Furthermore, in interviews and participant-observation in the schools, I observed that female students would often casually refer to the practice of waiting to receive their final secondary exam results (that is, to see that they had failed) and then immediately marrying. This may be facilitated by the fact that, as of 2010, not a single girl in rural Mtwara had passed the secondary exam at the level required to continue on to advanced secondary school.[46] A secondary-level education appears to do little to improve a girl's economic independence in the current economy of Mtwara, and the quality of the education system itself is too poor to facilitate continuing on to higher levels of schooling.

In addition, a small subset of female students did discuss their intention to use their increased years of education to seek economic advancement not through employment but by leveraging their attractive student status to negotiate marriage to a wealthier man, a practice that has been described in other contexts during periods of rapidly expanding educational opportunities.[47] As "Hamida" (age sixteen) describes:

*Bwanangu ni mtu mkubwa kjijini, na ananipa chochote
ninachokitaka, mara zote navaa staili mpya . . . mpaka
nanenepa wakati nipo shuleni! Ameshaniambia anataka
kunioa, nitakapomaliza shule. Lakini mimi mwenyewe
napendelea mwanaume wa mjini. Nikimaliza shule,
wakati huo, nitakuwa na elimu yangu—sipendi kuolewa
kijijini, kama mamangu. Maisha yake ya umaskini
ilikuwa ngumu tu.*

My man is a big person in the village, and he gives me anything I want; I'm always wearing the newest styles . . . I am
actually gaining weight at school! He has already told
me that he wants to marry me, when I am done with
school, but I myself prefer a man from town. When I fin-
ish school, at that time I will have my education—I don't
want to marry in the village, like my mother. Her life of
poverty was just difficult.

In her recent study of the relationship between education and
adolescent sexual behavior in Belize, Eileen Anderson-Fye identifies subjective motivation related to employment and economic
independence as an important causal factor mediating this relationship.[48] She suggests that in Belize the subjective motivation to
score high marks and complete one's education is driven in part
by the expansion of the tourism industry and availability of jobs
for girls with high school degrees, an incentive that is simply not
available in rural Mtwara. Though girls in rural Mtwara often
spoke emphatically about their desire to complete their education, the lack of economic benefit associated with education, in
addition to the other sources of friction discussed above, may
also play an underlying role in reducing girls' subjective motivation to change their sexual behaviors in order to avoid pregnancy. Though the relationship between economic opportunities
and girls' subjective motivation in education warrants further
investigation, it is consistent with existing survey data that suggests that the curvilinear relationship between girls' schooling
and changes in reproductive health behaviors described at the
opening of this chapter becomes more linear in the few countries in the subcontinent that showed significant improvement

not only in education, but also in economic opportunities during the 1980s.[49]

This final source of friction, fueled by the continued lack of economic opportunities in Mtwara, leaves girls with little economic benefit from their education, beyond potentially using their student status to negotiate for their preferred marriage partner. During eighteen months of participant-observation in Ufukweni Secondary School, I regularly received reports of girls who dropped out of school due to pregnancy, and many others simply disappeared from the classroom for unknown reasons. The multiple sources of friction these girls face as they attempt to negotiate their sexuality and their education suggest potential causal factors underlying the persistently high rate of adolescent pregnancy in Mtwara, despite increased educational opportunities for girls.

I have explored here a number of potential factors underlying the curvilinear relationship between girls' education and changes in reproductive health—and adolescent pregnancy, in particular—seen in many countries in sub-Saharan Africa through a close examination of the case of rural Mtwara. Though the specific sources of "friction" outlined above are specific to the cultural context of Mtwara, certain aspects discussed here are relevant beyond this small corner of the world. For example, the interweaving of gender, economic, and sexual roles described above have been documented elsewhere on the Swahili coast (for a discussion of recent changes in these roles on Mafia Island, see the chapter by Caplan in this volume), in other regions of Tanzania,[50] as well as in South Africa,[51] Botswana,[52] and Uganda,[53] among others.[54] In addition, the Makonde of rural Mtwara share much of the cultural history with the more northern regions of the Swahili coast, and this close analysis provides a window for understanding the relationship between education and sexuality throughout this region. However, this analysis also highlights significant differences in cultural norms and expectations of adolescent sexuality in Mtwara, illustrating the significant intracultural variation within the Swahili coast, and between different Muslim communities and suggesting the need for careful consideration of intracultural variation inherent in the cultural geography of this coast of the Indian Ocean.

NOTES

1. John C. Caldwell, *Theory of Fertility Decline*, Population and Social Structure (London: Academic Press, 1982); John Cleland and Shireen Jejeebhoy, "Maternal Schooling and Fertility: Evidence from Consensus and Surveys," in *Girls' Schooling, Women's Autonomy, and Fertility Change in South Asia,* ed. Roger Jeffrey and Alaka Malwade Basu (New Delhi: Sage, 1996), 72–106; Susan Hill Cochrane, *Fertility and Education: What Do We Really Know?* World Bank Staff Occasional Papers 26 (Baltimore: Johns Hopkins University Press for the World Bank, 1979); United Nations, Department for Economic and Social Information and Policy Analysis, *Women's Education and Fertility Behaviour: Recent Evidence from the Demographic and Health Surveys* (New York: United Nations, 1995).

2. Halvor Gille, "The World Fertility Survey: Policy Implications for Developing Countries," *International Family Planning Perspectives* 11, no. 1 (March 1985): 9–17; World Bank, "World Development Report 1980" (New York: Oxford University Press for the World Bank, 1980); World Bank, "World Development Report 1993: Investing in Health" (New York: Oxford University Press for the World Bank, 1993); United Nations, *Women's Education.*

3. Gille, "World Fertility Survey"; Robert A. LeVine, Sarah E. LeVine, and Beatrice Schnell, "'Improve the Women': Mass Schooling, Female Literacy, and Worldwide Social Change," *Harvard Educational Review* 71, no. 1 (2001): 1–51; United Nations, Department of International Economic and Social Affairs, *Relationships between Fertility and Education: A Comparative Analysis of World Fertility Survey Data for Twenty-Two Developing Countries* (New York: United Nations, 1983).

4. LeVine, LeVine, and Schnell, "'Improve the Women.'"

5. United Republic of Tanzania, Ministry of Education and Vocational Training, "Basic Education Statistics, 2010 Regional" (United Republic of Tanzania: Ministry of Education and Vocational Training, 2010), https://openmicrodata.wordpress.com/2010/09/01/tanzania-administrative-data-on-education-2002-2009/; Mtwara Regional Administrative Officer, "Hali ya elimu mkoani Mtwara (The State of Education in the Mtwara Region)," 2007; Tanzania, National Bureau of Statistics, "Tanzania Demographic and Health Survey 2004" (MEASURE DHS, ICF Macro Calverton, MD, 2004); Tanzania, National Bureau of Statistics, "Tanzania HIV/AIDS and Malaria Indicator Survey 2007–08" (MEASURE DHS, ICF Macro, Calverton, MD, 2008); Tanzania, National Bureau of Statistics, "Tanzania Demographic and Health Survey 2010" (MEASURE DHS, ICF Macro, Calverton, MD, 2010); Tanzania, Regional Committee on School Pregnancy, "Utoro na mimba mkoani Mtwara" (Office of the District Executive Officer, Mtwara, Tanzania, 2007).

6. Anna Lowenhaupt Tsing, *Friction: An Ethnography of Global Connection* (Princeton: Princeton University Press, 2005).

7. Jonathan Inda and Renato Rosaldo, eds., *The Anthropology of Globalization: A Reader,* 2nd ed., Blackwell Readers in Anthropology 1 (Malden, MA: Blackwell, 2008), 4.

8. Tsing, *Friction.*

9. Ibid., xi.

10. Arjun Appadurai, *Modernity at Large: Cultural Dimensions of Globalization,* vol. 1 (Minneapolis: University of Minnesota Press, 1996); Tsing, *Friction.*

11. Tsing, *Friction,* 6.

12. Aihwa Ong and Stephen Collier, eds., *Global Assemblages: Technology, Politics, and Ethics as Anthropological Problems* (Malden, MA: Blackwell, 2005).

13. Pekka Seppälä and Bertha Koda, eds., *The Making of a Periphery: Economic Development and Cultural Encounters in Southern Tanzania* (Uppsala: Nordiska Afrikainstitutet, 1998).

14. Ibid.; United Nations, UNICEF, "Basic Profile: Mtwara Rural District, Mtwara Region" (Dar es Salaam: UNICEF Tanzania, 2008).

15. J. Gus Liebenow, *Colonial Rule and Political Development in Tanzania: The Case of the Makonde* (Chicago: Northwestern University Press, 1971).

16. Ibid.

17. Meghan Halley, "Negotiating Sexuality: Adolescent Initiation Rituals and Cultural Change in Rural Southern Tanzania" (PhD diss., Case Western Reserve University, 2012).

18. National Bureau of Statistics, "Tanzania Population and Housing Census 2002" (MEASURE DHS, ICF Macro, Calverton, MD, 2002).

19. United Republic of Tanzania, Ministry of Education and Vocational Training, "Basic Education Statistics 2010."

20. Ibid.; Mtwara Regional Administrative Officer, "Hali ya elimu mkoani Mtwara"; National Bureau of Statistics, "Tanzania Demographic and Health Survey 2004"; National Bureau of Statistics, "Tanzania HIV/AIDS and Malaria Indicator Survey 2007–8"; National Bureau of Statistics, "Tanzania Demographic and Health Survey 2010"; Regional Committee on School Pregnancy, "Utoro na mimba mkoani Mtwara."

21. Halley, "Negotiating Sexuality."

22. H. Russell Bernard, *Research Methods in Anthropology: Qualitative and Quantitative Approaches,* 4th ed. (Walnut Creek, CA: AltaMira Press, 2005).

23. Anselm L. Strauss, *Basics of Qualitative Research: Grounded Theory Procedures and Techniques* (Newbury Park, CA: Sage, 1990).

24. Jeylan Mortimer and Reed Larson, eds., *The Changing Adolescent Experience: Societal Trends and the Transition to Adulthood* (Cambridge: Cambridge University Press, 2002).

25. Children's Dignity Forum, "Report on the Roundtable Discussion with Law Enforcers on the Application of Laws Preventing Pregnancies and Cases of Marriage of School Girls" (Children's Dignity Forum, 2009), http://cdftz.org/reports.php?c=research%20report&p=.

26. T. O. Beidelman, *The Cool Knife: Imagery of Gender, Sexuality, and Moral Education in Kaguru Initiation Ritual* (Washington, DC: Smithsonian Institution Press, 1997); Pat Caplan, "Boys' Circumcision and Girls' Puberty Rites among the Swahili of Mafia Island, Tanzania," *Africa: Journal of the International African Institute* 46, no. 1 (1976): 21–33; H. Cory, "Jando: Part I: The Constitution and Organization of the Jando," *Journal of the Royal Anthropological Institute of Great Britain and Ireland* 77, no. 2 (1947): 159–68; Cory, "Jando: Part II: The Ceremonies and Teachings of the Jando," *Journal of the Royal Anthropological Institute of Great Britain and Ireland* 78, nos. 1–2 (1948): 81–94; Laura Fair, "Identity, Difference, and Dance: Female Initiation in Zanzibar, 1890 to 1930," *Frontiers: A Journal of Women Studies* 17, no. 3 (January 1996): 146–72; M. Fuglesang, "Lessons for Life—Past and Present Modes of Sexuality Education in Tanzanian Society," *Social Science and Medicine* 44, no. 8 (1997): 1245–54; Lyndon Harries, "The Initiation Rites of the Makonde Tribe," in *Communications of the Rhodes-Livingstone Institute,* vol. 3 (Lusaka: Institute for Social Research, 1940); Liebenow, *Colonial Rule;* Amy Stambach, *Lessons from Mount Kilimanjaro: Schooling, Community, and Gender in East Africa* (New York: Routledge, 2000); Katrina Daly Thompson, "How to Be a Good Muslim Wife: Women's Performance of Islamic Authority during Swahili Weddings," *Journal of Religion in Africa* 41, no. 4 (2011): 427–48.

27. Fair, "Identity, Difference"; John Middleton, *The World of the Swahili: An African Mercantile Civilization* (New Haven: Yale University Press, 1992); Thompson, "Good Muslim Wife."

28. Anne-Simone Parent, Grete Teilmann, Anders Juul, Niels Skakkebaek, Jorma Toppari, and Jean-Pierre Bourguignon, "The Timing of Normal Puberty and the Age Limits of Sexual Precocity: Variations around the World, Secular Trends, and Changes after Migration," *Endocrine Review* 24, no. 5 (October 2003): 668–93.

29. Halley, "Negotiating Sexuality."

30. Ningqi Hou, Dezheng Huo, and Olufunmilayo I. Olopade, "Protective Effect of Longstanding Lactation and Reproductive Factors: A Case-Control Study in North Tanzania," *Breast Cancer Research and Treatment* 134, no. 3 (2012): 1349–51; Ewa Rebacz, "Age at Menarche in Schoolgirls from Tanzania in Light of Socioeconomic and Sociodemographic Conditioning," *Collegium antropologicum* 33, no. 1 (March 2009): 23–29.

31. W. A. Marshall and J. M. Tanner, "Variations in Pattern of Pubertal Changes in Girls," *Archives of Disease in Childhood* 44, no. 235 (June 1969): 291.

32. Halley, "Negotiating Sexuality."

33. W. A. Marshall and J. M. Tanner, "Variations in the Pattern of Pubertal Changes in Boys," *Archives of Disease in Childhood* 45, no. 239 (February 1970): 13–23.

34. Jorge Dias, "The Makonde People: Social Life," in *Portuguese Contribution to Cultural Anthropology* (Johannesburg: Witwatersrand University Press, 1961), 21–61; Harries, "Initiation Rites"; Liebenow, *Colonial Rule;* Karl Weule, *Native Life in East Africa: The Results of an Ethnological Research Expedition,* trans. Alice Werner (London: Sir Isaac Pitman and Sons, 1909).

35. Liebenow, *Colonial Rule.*

36. Cory, "Jando: Part I"; Liebenow, *Colonial Rule;* Otto Raum, "German East Africa: Changes in African Tribal Life under German Administration, 1892–1914," in *History of East Africa,* ed. Vincent Harlow, E. M. Chilver, and Alison Smith, 3 vols. (London: Oxford University Press, 1965), 2:144–208.

37. See, for example, Maggie Bangster, "'Falling through the Cracks': Adolescent Girls in Tanzania: Insights from Mtwara" (USAID Tanzania, 2010); Regional Committee on School Pregnancy, "Utoro na mimba mkoani Mtwara."

38. Halley, "Negotiating Sexuality."

39. Mark Hunter, *Love in the Time of AIDS: Inequality, Gender, and Rights in South Africa* (Bloomington: Indiana University Press, 2010).

40. Jo Helle-Valle, "Sexual Mores, Promiscuity and 'Prostitution' in Botswana," *Ethnos* 64, no. 3 (1999): 372–96; Mark Hunter, "The Materiality of Everyday Sex: Thinking beyond 'Prostitution,'" *African Studies* 61, no. 1 (2002): 99–120; A. M. Moore, A. E. Biddlecom, and E. M. Zulu, "Prevalence and Meanings of Exchange of Money or Gifts for Sex in Unmarried Adolescent Sexual Relationships in Sub-Saharan Africa," *African Journal of Reproductive Health* 11, no. 3 (2007): 44; Barbara Nyanzi, Stella Nyanzi, Brent Wolff, and James Whitworth, "Money, Men and Markets: Economic and Sexual Empowerment of Market Women in Southwestern Uganda," *Culture, Health and Sexuality* 7, no. 1 (January 2005): 13–26; Michelle Poulin, "Sex, Money, and Premarital Partnerships in Southern Malawi," *Social Science and Medicine* 65, no. 11 (2007): 2383–93; Margrethe Silberschmidt and Vibeke Rasch, "Adolescent Girls, Illegal Abortions and 'Sugar-Daddies' in Dar es Salaam: Vulnerable Victims and Active Social Agents," *Social Science and Medicine* 52, no. 12 (June 2001): 1815–26.

41. Children's Dignity Forum, "Law Enforcers."

42. Christina Higgins, *English as a Local Language: Post-colonial Identities and Multilingual Practices* (Bristol: Multilingual Matters, 2009).

43. James Ferguson, *Global Shadows: Africa in the Neoliberal World Order* (Durham: Duke University Press, 2006); Vinh-Kim Nguyen, "Viropolitics: How HIV Produces Therapeutic Globalization," in *HIV/AIDS: Global Frontiers in Prevention/Intervention,* ed. Cynthia Pope, Renée

White, and Robert Malow (New York: Routledge, 2009), 539–50; Noelle Sullivan, "Mediating Abundance and Scarcity: Implementing an HIV/AIDS-Targeted Project Within a Government Hospital in Tanzania," *Medical Anthropology* 30, no. 2 (2011): 202–21.

44. Ferguson, *Global Shadows*.

45. Halley, "Negotiating Sexuality"; Stambach, *Lessons from Mount Kilimanjaro*.

46. Ministry of Education and Vocational Training, "Basic Education Statistics 2010 Regional."

47. Robert A. LeVine, S. LeVine, A. Richman, F. Tapia Uribe, C. Sunderland Correa, and P. Miller, "Women's Schooling and Child Care in the Demographic Transition: A Mexican Case Study," *Population and Development Review* 17, no. 3 (September 1991): 459–96.

48. Eileen Anderson-Fye, "The Role of Subjective Motivation in Girls' Secondary Schooling: The Case of Avoidance of Abuse in Belize," *Harvard Educational Review* 80, no. 2 (2010): 174–203.

49. Gille, "World Fertility Survey"; LeVine, LeVine, and Schnell, "'Improve the Women'"; World Bank, "World Development Report 1980"; United Nations, *Women's Education and Fertility Behaviour*.

50. Liv Haram, "'Prostitutes' or Modern Women? Negotiating Respectability in Northern Tanzania," in *Re-thinking Sexualities in Africa*, ed. Signe Arnfred (Uppsala: Nordiska Afrikainstitutet, 2003), 211; Silberschmidt and Rasch, "Adolescent Girls."

51. Hunter, *Love in the Time of AIDS*.

52. Helle-Valle, "Sexual Mores."

53. Nyanzi et al., "Money, Men."

54. Moore, Biddlecom, and Zulu, "Prevalence and Meanings."

SIX

Learning to Use Swahili Profanity and Sacred Speech

The Embodied Socialization of a Muslim Bride in Zanzibar Town

KATRINA DALY THOMPSON

IN DECEMBER 2009, I arrived at my host family's home in Bububu, a short *daladala* ride from Zanzibar Town, and prepared for my wedding to a local man I had met the previous summer while doing research. Eager to be reunited after months apart, we had asked his family and my host family to hasten the wedding preparations so that we might make the most of the few weeks I would be there before returning to the States. The days before the wedding consisted of getting passport-size photographs of me that would be attached to my certificate of conversion to Islam, driving to a court to have my certificate filled out and signed by a local official, buying wedding rings, and getting my henna done. But one thing seemed missing: I had read that women throughout the Swahili coast often receive sex instruction before they are married, and I wondered whether I would as well. During a meal the night before the wedding, my host mother told me, "Kula vizuri! Utahitaji nguvu kesho!" (Eat well! You will need energy tomorrow!) The way she raised her eyebrows and looked at me knowingly told me she didn't mean energy just for the wedding ceremony itself, and we laughed together because, although we had known each other for ten years, it was the first time she had ever raised a sexual topic in conversation with me, even euphemistically. Now that the topic had been broached, I asked her if I should expect to receive any instruction before the wedding. "But you've been married before! You don't need it," she said. "Not so fast," her friend jumped in. "She may be knowledgeable about sex but not about how we do things here." And with that they got to planning who would come to instruct me in how to please my husband and how to talk (and not talk) about sex in Swahili.

Although I was already in my thirties when I first experienced a Swahili premarital instruction ritual, when I returned a year and a half later to research these rituals I learned that most women in Zanzibar Town get married in their late teens or early twenties, transitioning in a relatively short period of time from *wari* (pubescent girls; sing., *mwari*) to *bibiharusi* (brides) to *wake* (wives; sing., *mke*) and adult women (*wanawake;* sing., *mwanamke*). A ritual called a *singo,* which takes place while married women massage the bride, is an important site for a young woman's rapid transformation and socialization into married life. In order to be successful as a married woman, the bride must learn to speak and act in appropriate ways both with her husband and among other married women. Although married women communicate their expectations about marital behavior to girls through many events of socialization, both explicitly and implicitly, expectations for talk about sexuality are delayed until just a few days before a wedding, lest a young woman be tempted into sexual activity before marriage. In this chapter, I use a language socialization paradigm to analyze the interaction between instructors and a bride during a singo, showing how she is socialized into appropriate modes of communication about sex and her development of the identity of "Muslim wife" and "adult woman."[1]

Contextualizing my analysis with reference to interviews with married and unmarried women, my own experience as a Muslim bride in Zanzibar Town, and other instruction ceremonies that I recorded, I show how married women use the singo ceremony to socialize a bride not only *through* a specific way of talking about sexuality, namely the use of profanity and religious invocation, but also to socialize her *into* this way of talking about sexuality. Moreover, my analysis also shows how experienced singo leaders socialize other married women into their role as marriage instructors.

While married women's use of Islamic terminology and intertextual references to the Qur'an and Sunna establish their authority as Muslims knowledgeable about Islamic marriage, their use of profanity to discuss sexuality marks their authority as adult women knowledgeable about how to please their husbands. Moreover, my focus on embodiment provides support for the view that Islam is an embodied practice that extends beyond the public, male-dominated spaces typically considered as religious. For example, Saba Mahmood has shown that for pious Muslim women in Egypt, "religious virtues [acquire] the status of embodied habits,"[2] and Michael Lambek, writing about the Indian Ocean islands of Mayotte, argues that "knowledge is not as fully objectified and abstract as the textual basis of Islam might lead us to suppose. Rather, Islamic knowledge is embodied in speech, acts, ritual performances . . . and in narrative."[3] My analysis of how bodies are treated during a singo shows that a similar status is actively encouraged among Zanzibari Muslim women as a bride is taught the links between sexuality and Islam.

This chapter builds on ongoing research in two intersecting aspects of women's lives in Zanzibar Town: how women who are first-language (L1) speakers of Swahili learn Swahili norms for marriage and sexuality, including normative speech about these topics, and how they practice and talk about Islam. Because sexuality is central to the self-definition of Zanzibari women as Muslims, the premarital instruction offered to a bride during the wedding preparations that precede an Islamic wedding in Zanzibar Town offers a window into both areas.

Sex instruction and puberty rituals are obvious examples of gender socialization and have been studied as such both along the Swahili coast and elsewhere.[4] Other aspects of Swahili socialization have also been studied. For example, Carol A. Campbell and Carol M. Eastman write about, in passing, the socialization of Swahili children into *ngoma* (dance) performances.[5] Similarly, Eastman writes about the socialization of Swahili children through children's songs into not only song structure and content but also sex role distinctions and the structure of adult relationships.[6] Writing about Kigombe, a "Swahili community on the coast of northeastern Tanzania," but generalizing to "Swahili society," Pamela Landberg makes the obvious claim that the Swahili household is "the central locus for the socialization of children."[7]

However, to my knowledge, there has been no research on *language* socialization among Swahili speakers, with the possible exception of studies of *Utendi wa Mwana Kupona,* a nineteenth-century poem that instructs a bride how to treat and speak to her husband (although these studies remain largely speculative about how the poem may have actually been used by Swahili speakers).[8] My argument is that in addition to serving as sites of gender socialization, the sex instruction rituals that precede Muslim weddings in Zanzibar Town also serve as sites of language socialization. In other words, in addition to socializing the bride into the practices expected of her as a married (and thereby adult) Muslim woman, the ritual also teaches her how to speak Swahili like a married Muslim woman—for example, by using profanity to talk about sexuality and to establish joking relationships with other women (for more on the importance of joking relationships on the Swahili coast, see Susi Krehbiel Keefe's chapter in this volume). Elsewhere I have written about how women construct themselves as Islamic authorities during such rituals,[9] and while I will not review that argument here, I hope it remains clear in the data that women's use of profanity exists alongside religious invocation. For these Swahili speakers there is no conflict between explicit talk about sexuality and talk about God; they see specific sexual acts as an integral part of their religiously obligatory roles as Muslim wives.

My analysis of the singo ceremony presented here draws on my experience as the adopted "daughter" of a Muslim family in Zanzibar Town (they later moved to Bububu) whom I have lived with and visited regularly over the past thirteen years; my experience receiving sex instruction before my own Islamic wedding there, in 2009; and research on weddings I conducted in 2011, during which I both participated in and recorded premarital instruction ceremonies and conducted interviews with married and unmarried women. July 2011 was an optimal time to do research on weddings and premarital instruction ceremonies because it was the month of Sha'aban in the Islamic calendar, the most popular month for weddings in Zanzibar Town (because it precedes Ramadan). People joke that young men marry just before Ramadan "ili wapikiwe" (so that they have someone to cook for them), so they can eat well in the evenings after each day of fasting.

The singo on which I focus in this chapter was that of an eighteen-year-old woman, Asha, the niece of my father-in-law's second wife, Chanda.[10] I was invited by my in-laws and Asha herself to observe, participate in, and record every aspect of Asha's wedding preparations, and I spent a week with her doing this. Asha and her future husband lived in Mwera, a semirural *shehia* (location) outside of Zanzibar Town, but she spent that week living at her maternal aunt's home in town so as to heighten the excitement and surprise of her wedding guests when they would see her wearing henna, makeup, and a beautiful gown for the first time at the wedding itself. Because her aunt and uncle were my in-laws and I lived nearby, Asha and I saw each other every day that week and had many opportunities to discuss her impending wedding. One day we went together to the stylist where she had her hair straightened. Another day we went together, along with my mother-in-law, Chanda, to the singo I discuss below. On a third day we spent eight hours at a henna artist's home, where Asha had henna applied to her arms and legs elaborately for the first time and I, as an adult woman who would attend her wedding, had it applied as well, albeit less elaborately. On a fourth day I took part, along with several other female relatives, in the *kupeleka vyombo* (sending the furniture/tools) ceremony, where we delivered new furniture and kitchen tools to the groom's home and were welcomed by the women among Asha's future in-laws. On the day of the *nikaha* (Islamic wedding ceremony), Asha and I spent the afternoon at a stylist's home, where she was dressed in a rented green gown and gold jewelry and had her makeup and hair done. We then drove back to her aunt Fatima's home for the nikaha itself. After the groom and other men left, Asha and I went to a second stylist's home, where she was made up again, this time in a rented Western-style white wedding dress. Finally, I escorted her to a rented hall, paid for by the groom's parents, where she sat on a decorated stage and had photographs taken with female guests and their children. After that, Asha was picked up by her new husband to begin her life as an adult woman, and I spent the rest of the month conducting research among other women.

After recording interviews with Chanda and Asha, Asha's instruction ceremony, our talk with the henna artist, and the nikaha ceremony, I transcribed the talk using modified discourse transcription conventions.[11] While the trend in talk-in-interaction research is to use video recordings,[12] most of the women I interviewed preferred not to be videotaped, often for religious reasons. All the women I worked with wore some form of hijab (Swahili *hijabu;* <Ar. *hijāb*), when around unrelated men, which at a minimum meant clothing that covered their arms to the wrist and legs to below the ankle, and headscarves that covered their hair, ears, and necks. I dressed similarly in public because the few times I did not, both women and men verbally sanctioned me. A few of the women with whom I conducted research, influenced by trends toward more conservative interpretations of Islam, wore the *nikabu* (<Ar. *niqāb*), a face covering that reveals only the eyes, along with gloves and socks; both Asha and my own "mother" were among these women who adopted these embodied signs of modesty. While those women whom I knew well dressed more casually at home and in my presence, they did not want to risk their videotaped images being seen by unfamiliar men. Moreover, after noticing that even those who agreed to be recorded on video spoke less freely than they usually did, I gave

up using video except while recording mixed-gender wedding events such as nikaha. The singo, in particular, was not an appropriate site for video recording because Asha was naked and her instructors wore only *kanga,* large pieces of bright fabric with Swahili sayings on them, tied around their chests. Because video recording was not possible, I took mental notes on participants' positioning of their bodies, gestures, use of the physical space in which the singo took place, and use of physical objects, and wrote down as much as I could remember as field notes as soon as possible after the event.

LANGUAGE IDEOLOGIES

Research throughout the Swahili coast has shown that women's speech has a low status and is often depicted as inappropriate, with its quintessential genres being "complaints, gossip, and loose speech."[13] Gendered-speech prohibitions that restrict women's discursive agency have been well documented along the Swahili coast in both Tanzania and Kenya.[14] For example, linguistic anthropologist Susan Hirsch writes about beliefs about women's speech she collected in Malindi and Mombasa, Kenya: "The prototype devalued speaker in Swahili culture is a woman, specifically a woman who tells tales. . . . Emphasis on the trivial and potentially fictional quality of women's speech merges with emphasis on its dangerous and disruptive qualities to create the impression that women's speech is suspect, not to be counted on, and to be suppressed."[15] Attempts to reify women's speech are the flip side of the same coin. For example, when Khadija B. Juma, a Zanzibari woman and a keen chronicler of Zanzibari culture, writes about women's linguistic prowess in a chapter on the "traditional Swahili" (*Kiswahili cha asili*) of Zanzibari women, she does so by establishing an ideal to which a "cultured" woman should adhere:

> *Kinamama wa visiwani Zanzibar kwa muktadha wa mada yetu hii, ni wale wenye sifa bainifu zinazowapambanua na kinamama wengine kitabia, kimavazi, kimazungumzo, mwenendo, mapambo, madaha ya kusema na mengi*

mengineyo. Ni wanawake mfano wa silka, mila, dasturi na tamaduni ambazo hazijabetuliwa au kuchafuliwa na tamaduni za kigeni. Mwanamke wa Kiswahili wa visiwani hasa yule aliyezalikwa na kuishi ndani ya mazingira ya Uswahilini, anakuwa na lugha maalumu kutegemea na nani anazungumza naye, nini na pahala gani anapozungumza.[16]

Women of the Zanzibar Islands, for the purposes of our topic here, are those with a clear reputation which differentiates them from other women in terms of behavior, clothing, conversation, movement, decorative styles, graceful speech, and much more. They are women exemplary of disposition, customs, traditions, and cultures that have not been reduced or sullied by foreign cultures. A Swahili woman of the islands, especially one who was born and has lived in the environment of Swahililand, develops a specialized language depending on who she is speaking with, about what, and the place where she is speaking.

Juma's depiction of Zanzibari Swahili women presents them as extremely sophisticated in all respects, but especially in their language use. She implicitly contrasts them not only with mainland African women but also with Zanzibari women who are not raised in a culturally Swahili environment (perhaps, for example, women of Indian heritage). By implication, even a Zanzibari Swahili woman's speech would be devalued if it did not live up to this ideal. Her claims are a good illustration of Hirsch's argument that we know more about the "prescribed ideal" of how Swahili women *should* behave and speak than about how they actually do.[17]

Marc Swartz's work on the relationships between Swahili wives and husbands in Mombasa includes descriptions of women's speech that begin to point to the difference between the ideal and reality:

All men avoid talking about "delicate" issues that might bring shame (*aibu*) to anyone present, and there is a pervasive concern with honor (*fakhri*). Another difference between men's and women's gatherings is that in the latter there is little or no reluctance to discuss particular people and their affairs. Tales of who is doing what, and with or to whom, are as common among the women's groups as they are rare among the men's. Also unlike the men's groups, in the women's groups interaction rather often includes heated statements and arguments, and personal remarks including compliments and insults are sometimes traded. The personal character of the conversation at women's gatherings gives them an emotional and interpersonal tone quite different from the men's and, in fact, women's relations with one another generally are far more intimate, expressive, and warm than are men's. Women share their joys, sorrows, and angers with one another rather freely; men hardly do so at all.[18]

Yet, in the absence of examples of women's interaction, we are left to simply imagine the types of conversations Swartz describes. By analyzing transcribed excerpts of such interaction, this chapter thus fills an important gap in our understanding of Swahili language use by first-language (L1) users.

My concern with the discursive reproduction of Muslim femininity raises questions about what constitutes women's speech, profanity, and (to a lesser extent) religious discourse in contemporary Zanzibar. Before presenting my analysis of the singo I recorded, I reflect theoretically on language socialization in relation to these speech genres.

LANGUAGE SOCIALIZATION

Susan Hirsch writes that "Swahili Muslims, operating from subject positions (e.g., wives and husbands) that entail linguistic expectations, act and speak within and against those subject positions in efforts that remake gender, for themselves as individuals and also for society more broadly."[19] Hirsch's work on men's and women's speech during divorce proceedings offers a fascinating window into how these linguistic expectations play out in institutional interactions, yet we know very little about how

Swahili Muslims acquire or learn to operate from these subject positions. A language socialization paradigm can help us understand this process.

Language socialization research typically takes as its focus a novice, or learner, as an apprentice within a community of practice, examining both "socialization through language and socialization to use language."[20] In some respects, a Zanzibari Muslim bride has been learning about her community's understanding of femininity her entire life. As an apprentice within a community of women, a girl observes the language use of women such as her mother, grandmother, aunts, older sisters, and older cousins among themselves and in the company of female friends, as well as, to a lesser extent, how these women communicate with their husbands. In most contexts, normative femininity can be "inferred from performances of conventional, socially co-ordinated activities, and interpretive practices."[21] The social activity of instructing the bride in her religiously sanctioned marital duties differs from typical forms of socialization in that during this ritual the cultural expectations for how a Muslim woman is expected to act, feel, think, and speak are made *explicit*. In this context, the bride is initiated into a new community of practice that she is not meant to have ever participated in or observed before, that of women talking openly, even profanely, about sex and marriage. Children do overhear some of these interactions before their own weddings, but they are treated as if they don't understand them. For example, when I reviewed the singo recording with Chanda, I asked her if she wanted to wait until her young children were out of the house, but she insisted they were too young to understand the women's use of profanity.

At the same time, during a singo the bride is being taught how to speak to and physically interact with her husband within the small and intimate microcommunity of practice that she and her husband will constitute, in which none of her instructors will easily be able to assess her communicative competence. The instruction ceremony, and talk among women at weddings more generally, thus is an occasion where women can display their competence in communicating with their husbands and in embodying the actions—through reconstructed activity—expected of a good Muslim wife within the Swahili culture of Zanzibar Town. The less experienced women who take part in instructing the bride are also being socialized by their elders, though less explicitly, into how to offer premarital instruction.

In any socialization setting, "veteran and novice participants coordinate modes of communication, actions, bodies, objects, and the built environment to enhance their joint knowledge and skills."[22] Examining premarital instruction from this perspective enables us to examine the socialization of the bride not only through the language use of the women involved but also in relation to the activity of physically preparing the bride's body for her wedding, the physical space(s) in which instruction is offered, the objects used as instructional tools, and the participants' bodies (as well as their reference to the absent body of the bride's future husband)—in other words, to their "situatedness [and] participation in a physical and social world."[23] The linguistic evidence I examine—excerpts from transcriptions of audio recordings—is thus embedded in gestures, instructors' shared focus on particular parts of Asha's body, visible displays of emotion, objects, and architectural spaces that I will also address. Goodwin refers to such contextual data as *contextual configurations,* "a particular, locally relevant array of semiotic fields" to which participants demonstrably orient.[24] My analysis shows how participants interweave and orient to several activities and speech genres: explicit instruction is embedded in massaging the bride, and both profanity and religious invocation are embedded in instruction.

The participation of not only a *kungwi* (a woman known for her expertise in sex instruction),[25] but also older women with long-term experience in Muslim marriages, and younger women with just a few months or years of experience as wives, along with the bride herself, who is expected to have no sexual or relationship experience,[26] suggests that there is not a clear dichotomy between the expert and the novice singo participant, but rather a continuum of expertise across the lifespan. One's level of expertise is based on age, how long one has been married, how many instruction ceremonies one has participated in, and sometimes how involved one is in women's classes on Islamic topics, where the *adabu* (manners; <Ar. *adab*) of marriage are regularly taught

by scholars. Research on girls' initiation ceremonies in Swahili cultures uses the title *kungwi* (sometimes interchangeably with *somo*) to mean the ceremonial leader in girls' initiation rites,[27] or the woman who provides private instruction in hygiene and wifely duties after a girl first begins menstruating.[28] In Asha's singo, both the kungwi and Asha's oldest aunt, the singo host, share "expert" status, and their focus is on sex.

TYPES OF SEX INSTRUCTION

My earlier work on sex instruction during Islamic weddings analyzed a type of contemporary instruction that I now understand to be just one type among at least three different forms that premarital instruction rituals may take: (1) an informal ritual conducted by the female wedding guests while the bride is being dressed and made up for the wedding; (2) a formal ritual, styled as Islamic, in which semiprofessional instructors read from prepared notes about *hadithi* (English, *hadith*, stories about the Prophet Muhammad; <Ar. *hadith*) that illustrate the behaviors of a good Muslim wife; and (3) a singo, a formal ritual in which the bride is massaged and instructed by female relatives. There are no rigid distinctions between these different rituals; a particular instruction ceremony may involve a variety of activities. All of them share the goal of teaching "young women about the social, practical, emotional and sexual aspects of married life, and what it means to be considered an adult woman."[29] A singo is the most similar to unyago (puberty initiation) ceremonies, which may be a fourth ritual;[30] unyago is still referred to by other scholars but all the women who participated in my research claimed that it is no longer practiced in Zanzibar Town, a finding that Nadine Beckmann's research also supports.[31]

Singo literally refers to a massage using ground cloves and sandalwood (as well as to the materials themselves used to scrub someone during a massage), but as one woman told me, "Watu wa zamani waliuita unyago. Sasa hivi, vijana tumeubadilisha, tunaita singo. Yaani, singo ni jinsi ya kumfundisha biharusi." (People in the past called it unyago. Recently, we young people have changed it, we call it singo. In other words a singo is the way to teach a bride.) The main difference between "traditional" unyago and contemporary singo is the number of girls being instructed: several for unyago and only the bride for a singo. Some women I spoke with described a singo as more Islamic than unyago, a position Beckmann identifies as essentialist.[32] Writing about Swahili societies more generally, Kjersti Larsen comments that some women claim they do not want their daughters initiated into unyago because they see it as incompatible with Islam. There are certainly important Islamic elements to the singo ritual and other contemporary forms of sex instruction, which may make them more palatably "Islamic," but these elements may have been present in earlier forms of sex instruction as well.[33] As Larsen makes clear, for those who *do* participate in unyago, there is nothing un-Islamic about it.[34]

As the following excerpt reveals, the relative conformity of singo to locally prevalent ideologies of how Muslim women should behave may be exaggerated by the participants in order to keep the content of singo a secret from the bride (and possibly others). For example, in an interview before her instruction ceremony and about a week before her wedding, Asha criticized traditional puberty rituals, where young women wore little clothing:

> *Kwa sababu vile mwanamke unakuwa unadhihirisha mapambo yako. Na mwanamke haifai kudhihirisha mapambo yako kwenye watu wengine. Waliokuwa yaani maharimu zako, waliokuwa wanafaa ya kukuoa au walikuwa hawafai pia. Unatakiwa mwanamke udhihirishe mapambo yako kwa mumeo tu. Haifai kwa watu wengine.*

> Because in that way as a woman you are revealing your ornaments. And, for a woman, it's not appropriate to show off your ornaments where there are other people. Those who are, in other words your *maharimu,* those who are appropriate to marry you, or those who are not appropriate, too. As a woman you should reveal your ornaments only to your husband. It's not appropriate where there are other people.

In this excerpt, Asha echoes the Swahili translation of the Qur'anic verse, "wasionyeshe mapambo yao" (they shouldn't display their ornaments; translated from the Arabic word *zinah*, embellishment, adornment, ornament, decoration, finery). In doing so, she condemns a traditional practice through reference to a conservative interpretation of Islamic law. Given that her aunts do not share her opinion that women must wear hijab in one another's presence, it is likely that Asha has been taught this conservative interpretation at the Islamic secondary school she attends, which requires its students to wear nikabu. Ironically, her own singo ceremony a few days later bore remarkable similarities to the unyago ceremonies she criticizes, with Asha naked and her instructors dressed only in kanga. Later, Chanda told me that she had deliberately avoided telling Asha that her instruction ceremony would entail nudity because she would have been reluctant to go.

SWAHILI PROFANITY

Asha's depiction of unyago as defying Islamic norms marks nudity as a profane or taboo practice. Yet it was not only nudity, but also profane speech, that would be the hallmark of her own singo a few days later. Swahili speakers refer to profanity as *matusi*, which also means insults or abusive language. For example, in a sex education book aimed at Swahili-speaking teens, Mamuya includes an appendix: "Maneno halisi yaliyo matusi" (Accurate words which are taboo). He writes:

> *Haipendezi kutamkatamka maneno haya. Hayaonyeshi adabu na heshima nzuri. Ikiwa hapana budi kutamka neno mojawapo hadharani, basi yafaa uombe radhi kwanza kabla ya kulitoa mdomoni—pengine kwa kutanguliza neno "ashakum" ambalo maana yake ni sawa na kusema "niwie radhi."*[35]

It's not appropriate to go around saying these words. It doesn't show good manners and proper respect. If there is no choice but to say one of these words in public, then it is appropriate to ask for forgiveness first before letting it out of your mouth—perhaps by beginning with the word *ashakum,* the meaning of which is the same as saying "forgive me."

Mamuya's list includes a number of words used by the women at Asha's singo, including *mavuzi* (pubic hairs), *mboo* (cock), *manii* (semen), *kisimi* (clitoris), *kuma* (cunt), *utoko* (vaginal discharge), and *kutomba* (to fuck). It illustrates that Swahili speakers do not make a distinction between *matusi* and more polite words for talking about sexuality. "Accurate" or explicit terms are profane or taboo. The only way to avoid such profanity while discussing sexuality, as Erin Stiles shows in her chapter in this volume, is through euphemism.

Sharing the same root as *matusi,* the verb *kutukana* likewise means both "to insult each other" and "to use profanity with one another."[36] For Swahili speakers, both words have negative connotations; in most contexts, to use taboo words in someone's presence is to insult him or her. Women in Swahili cultures are expected not to engage in kutukana, although they do find other ways to "sound off" to one another.[37] "Wanawake hupasha na kupashana bila ya kutukana" (Women sound off and exchange "sound-offs" without using profanity), Khadija B. Juma writes.[38] *Kupashana* (to sound off to one another) is contrasted with *kutukana* because the former practice involves messages delivered "off the record" through reference to proverbs or written kanga names that veil the speaker's communicative intent and allow her an out.[39]

Despite the restrictions on women's speech that are upheld by language ideologies, there are spaces in which coastal Muslim women do use matusi—not to insult one another but rather to engage in open discourse about sexuality, through talk, written texts, and song. For example, Carol Campbell, cataloguing different types of music performed by Swahili women in the mid-1970s, includes *nyimbo za kuni* (firewood songs) that women sang while collecting wood. She writes that these songs were extremely ribald, full of "vulgar sexual references, both anatomical and operational," shouted at the top of their lungs. Similar songs are performed today by women in Zanzibar Town while they travel en masse to weddings. The presence of young girls during these performances suggests, again, that their exposure to matusi precedes their own weddings, although they are expected to feign ignorance of their meanings.

While it is not clear whether the songs Campbell discusses were memorized and passed on or improvised on the spot, women did use them to express their frustrations with men: "If a lone man ventures near the women he will often be assaulted with verbal abuse and references to his sexual inadequacies."[40] I observed a similar treatment of the male bus driver hired to drive a group of women to a wedding in the neighborhood of Mombasa, just outside Zanzibar Town. In domains where profanity is allowed or even expected, there is a sense of intimacy. Among close friends of the same gender or between a husband and wife, profanity may be associated with "solidarity, shared values, friendship, love, in short the contacts established through common family and group life."[41] When that intimacy is absent (as in the case of the lone man who walks by a group of women or the lone male driver on a bus full of women), profanity becomes verbal abuse. Importantly, as my analysis of the singo data will illustrate, verbal abuse of men (even when men are not present to hear it) can serve as a means of bonding among women.

Profanity is not limited to verbal references to sex but is also referred to through the body. Campbell describes the dances women perform during Swahili weddings, such as the *chakacha,* a dance for unmarried girls in which "older women sometimes instruct the younger girls in the proper movement by placing their hands on their hips and rotating them," with this "proper movement" designed to simulate a woman seated astride her husband during vaginal intercourse. Another dance, *kishuri* or *kiuno* (waist), done by older women "even more explicitly acts out movements of sexual intercourse and is greeted with much laughter and ululation."[42] While unmarried girls may be taught these dance movements, and may guess at their meanings, they are not explicitly taught the relationship to sex until the singo. These movements form an important part of singo sex instruction, where musical accompaniment is replaced with explicit reference to these movements as techniques for pleasing one's husband sexually.

Although Zanzibari women are expected to restrict their topics of conversation in public, local language ideologies depict them as highly skilled in "sweet-talking" their husbands in order to get their needs met. Consider this example from Khadija B. Juma:

> *Mapenzi na mahaba ni sifa nzito walizonazo wanawake wa Kiswahili hususan wanaoishi Zanzibar. Wana lugha tamu na nzito iliyojaa tabasamu na tashwishi za kila aina za kuweza kumtoa nyoka pangoni. Lugha hii maalumu ya mahaba na mapenzi hujichomeza pale inapohitajika, awepo mpenda na mpendwa; haitolewi popote, ina pahali na wakati wake.*[43]

> Sexual and romantic love are a serious reputation that Swahili women have, especially those who live in Zanzibar. They have a sweet and deep language filled with smiles and ambiguities of every kind, which can *coax the snake out of his cave.* This special language of romantic and sexual love emerges when and where it is needed, when the lover and the beloved are present; it is not given out just anywhere, it has its place and its time.

Juma's reference to "coaxing the snake out of the cave" is an allusion to a Swahili proverb, "Maneno matamu humtoa nyoka pangoni" (Sweet words coax the snake out of his cave), which is used to mean that it's easier to get someone to agree with you by talking nicely, even through false flattery or trickery, than by arguing. But the proverb has a double meaning that is relevant to Juma's emphasis on "sweet talk" here, in that the snake represents a penis coaxed into desire through sexual flattery. Juma's emphasis on knowing the right time and place to talk about sexuality also reinforces the locally salient emphasis on Islamic discretion about marital relations and an overarching Swahili concern with privacy.[44] The use of profanity by a woman with her husband can be a form of "sweet talk."

Premarital instruction is not just a rite that initiates a bride into her new life as an adult, a wife, and a sexually active person, but also one that initiates her into a new speech community, that of women who are allowed use matusi to talk openly about sexuality with their husbands and with one another and women who know how to use verbal and nonverbal communication to get what they want from their husbands. In order to preserve the instruction ceremony as the site where a bride's hearing such matusi will begin, women avoid talking explicitly about the intimate aspects of marriage with a young woman before her instruction ceremony. Women agreed to talk with me about their own premarital instruction, and to let me record instruction ceremonies, because they knew that I was already married. While several women expressed hope that I would return to the United States to offer sex instruction to American Muslim women, they reminded me that I should do so only for women who are about to be married.

A few days before Asha's singo, I recorded a conversation in Chanda's living room with both Asha and Chanda about Swahili weddings and premarital instruction ceremonies. In the following excerpt, Chanda recalls her own wedding. In this excerpt and the others I present in this chapter, punctuation is used to transcribe intonation. A period indicates falling pitch, a question mark rising pitch, and a comma a falling contour, as would be found, for example, after a nonterminal item in a list. A colon indicates lengthening of the current vowel sound. An en dash marks the sudden abortion of a projected word. An em dash marks a truncated intonation unit. My own comments (such as descriptions of relevant nonvocal behavior) are within double parentheses. Brackets connecting talk by different speakers mark the points where overlap begins and ends. The "at" sign (@) indicates a single pulse of laughter. The symbols <VOX> and </VOX> indicate the beginning and end, respectively, of a statement in the voice of another speaker. The number sign (#) indicates unintelligible syllables, or when prefixed to a word, an uncertain transcription. A sharp intake of breath is indicated by the letter H inside parentheses (H). In the English translation, italics indicate words that were not in Swahili in the original (e.g., in Arabic or English).

Excerpt 1

Katrina;	*Siku za harusi: yenyewe zilikuwaje?*	The days of the weddi:ng itself, what were they like?
Chanda;	*@@ Siku za harusi wazee walisheheka:, @@ ngoma zikapigwa, nikaolew– nikachukuliwa @@@.*	@@ On the wedding days, my elders celebrated, @@ then dances were put on, then I was marrie– then I was taken @@@.
Katrina;	*Lakini si kwanza:: ulipelekwa kwa mtu kama ~Asha atapelekwa?*	But isn't it the case that at fi::rst you were taken to someone just like Asha will be taken?
Chanda;	*Eh, nilipelekwa kwenda kufundishwa.*	Yeah, I was taken to be instructed.
Katrina;	*Ulipelekwa wapi?*	Where were you taken?
Chanda;	*Nilipelekwa:— Maanake mimi niliolewa Darislam. Kwa hiyo nilichukuliwa nikapelekwa Temeke kwa jamaa zetu. Tena nikafundishwafundishwa mambo ya harusi,*	I was take:n— Because I was married in Dar es Salaam. So I was picked up and taken to Temeke, to our relatives. And then I was taught all about matters related to the wedding,
Katrina;	*Mhm.*	Mhm.
Chanda;	*<VOX>Itakuwa hivi, itakuwa hivi</VOX> @@.*	<VOX>It will be like this, it will be like this</VOX> @@.
	[[...]]	[[...]]
Katrina;	*Na unakumbuka ulivyofundishwa?*	And do you remember how you were taught?
Chanda;	*@@@@@.*	@@@@@.
Katrina;	*Au huwezi kuambia mbele ya ~Asha @ kabla ya yeye @ kufundishwa?*	Or you can't tell me in front of Asha @ before she @is taught?
Chanda;	*@@@@@. Siwezi kukuambia mbele ya ~Asha kwa sababu yeye @hajafundishwa @@*	@@@@@. I can't tell you in front of Asha because she @hasn't been taught yet @@
Katrina;	*@@@@ Sawa.*	@@@@ Okay.
Chanda;	*Atakuja kuogopa. @[@@]*	She'll get scared. @[@@]
Katrina;	*[Eh.]* *@@[@@]*	[Yeah.] @@[@@]
Chanda;	*[@@@@@]*	[@@@@@]
Katrina;	*Sawa. Kwa hiyo @labda @ baadaye @utaniambia.*	Okay. So @maybe @later @you'll tell me.
Chanda;	*E::h, baadaye nitakueleza. Uzuri. @@@@@.*	Ye::ah, later I'll explain it to you. Good. @@@@@
Katrina;	*Sawa sawa.*	All right.
Chanda;	*@@@.*	@@@.

In this excerpt, Chanda is deliberately vague about what she was taught at the instruction ceremony that preceded her own wedding. While she gives voice to her instructors in line 8, she uses the adverbial demonstrative *hivi* (like this) to avoid telling me what they actually taught her. When, in line 10, I explicitly ask her what she was taught, she responds, in line 11, with nervous laughter that suggests my question is not appropriate at this moment. In line 12, I ask her if the reason for her reticence is Asha's presence, and she agrees, explaining that Asha would be scared if she heard the way instructors talk. Ironically (or perhaps intentionally), her reticence seemed to lead to a greater fear on Asha's part. Note that throughout this excerpt Chanda uses passive verbs to describe all her activities before and during her wedding: "I was married"; "I was taken"; "I was picked up"; "I was taught." In my questions to her, I unwittingly take up this grammar as well, having myself been socialized into Swahili gender norms through years of conversations with Zanzibari Swahili speakers as well as in my own sex instruction ceremony, a year and a half earlier. These passive verb forms are linked to a discourse evident in later excerpts in which women's agency is denied.[45]

Unmarried girls demonstrate their awareness that the singo ceremony, and talk about sexuality more generally, is not considered appropriate for them. For example, during Asha's singo, her cousin, a secondary-school student only a few years younger than she, came home from school and passed through the entry room where we were instructing Asha into her bedroom to change out of her school uniform. When the instructors began singing lurid songs, Asha's cousin started coughing loudly from the bedroom, both to remind us of her presence and to avoid hearing us—an act that generated much laughter from her mother, aunts, and myself. Her actions suggest that unmarried girls know more about singo content than older women acknowledge; both girls and women construct the period leading up to the wedding as the time frame where all sexual knowledge is imparted, because to admit knowing anything about sex before one's wedding would be to tarnish one's reputation.

The preparations for a Swahili wedding in Zanzibar Town, as in other urban areas along the coast, take place in various spaces and are often elaborate, beginning on the day that the groom's family sends a male relative to the bride's family's home to seek the bride's hand, culminating in the signing of the wedding certificate, and continuing afterward with additional celebrations.[46] The week I accompanied Asha, summarized above, is a good example of these time-consuming preparations. While the men's legal ceremony takes place at the mosque, the women's ceremonies (including the legal ceremony) take place at private homes, often at the bride's parents' house. Over a period of several days, as the bride undergoes adornment and instruction and finally signs the wedding contract, most of her activities will take place in bedrooms or other exclusively female spaces. In the case of Asha's wedding preparations, except for the nikaha itself, which the groom, an imam, and a few men from the groom's family attended, all the activities to which I accompanied Asha took place in female spaces, such as a *saluni* (styling salon), private homes, and a rented hall to which only women and children had been invited.

The singo must occur in private because only women are involved, because of the bride's nudity and the instructors' partial nudity, and because of the use of profane speech and bodily movements. Asha's singo took place at her Aunt Zuweina's home, in Fuoni, a periurban location outside Zanzibar Town. Asha, Chanda, and I were the first to arrive, and we gathered in the living room waiting for the kungwi and the other instructors to arrive. Initially two of Zuweina's sons were at home, but she soon hurried them off to some other activity outside the house. While we waited, Asha sat in an armchair and buried her face in her arms, her visible embarrassment serving as an "embodied sign" that fulfilled the older women's expectations of her as a novice.[47] Chanda braided Zuweina's hair while both women teased Asha about her obvious nervousness. As is also true of other Tanzanian initiation rituals for young women, the novice is expected to show her nervousness, because to remain calm would suggest that she is sexually experienced.[48]

As the kungwi and the other instructors (Chanda's sisters, Asha's aunts) arrived, each went into one of the bedrooms to take off her clothes and emerged wearing only a kanga tied around her chest. Only Chanda's sister Fatima and I remained fully clothed, I because I wasn't sure what was expected of me, and Fatima because she wasn't feeling well. Finally, Asha was ordered into the bedroom and told to undress completely, including discarding her bra, leaving only her underwear. She returned to the entry room seeming very embarrassed, covering her breasts with her arms.

Typically, bedrooms in Swahili homes are considered the most private parts of the home, associated with women, whereas the open courtyard, entry room, and living room are considered more public areas in which guests must remain.[49] In this case, as female relatives of the home's owner, the instructors had easy access to the bedrooms to change their clothes, but the bedrooms were not large enough for all of us to gather simultaneously.

The singo therefore took place primarily in the entry room of the house (see fig. 6.1), where Zuweina had laid out straw mats on which Asha was instructed to lie down. The rest of us sat in a circle around Asha, with Zuweina at Asha's head and the kungwi at Asha's feet. After Asha was massaged with ground cloves, all of us went out into the open-air courtyard (walled but without a roof) while the women bathed Asha at a spigot. Then we returned inside to the entry room, where the women gave Asha additional instruction.

FIGURE 6.1 Layout of Zuweina's home

During Asha's singo, the instructors first told the bride to lie down on a mat on the floor. Excerpts 2 and 3 include their instructions to the bride as they get ready to massage her. Zuweina is the eldest aunt; Chanda is the aunt with whom Asha has been staying during the week leading up to her wedding; Dawa is the kungwi.

Excerpt 2

1	Chanda;	*Haya, kaa.*	Okay, sit.
2	Zuweina;	*Kaa hivi. #Mwasho ndo [ya nani?*	Sit like this. [Whose # is this?
3	Dawa;	*[Anakaa kinyume.*	[She's sitting backward.
4	Zuweina;	*Eh?*	Huh?
5	Dawa;	*Anaweza kulala ki–kinyume[nyum– #]*	She can lay down ba– backward [backward]
6	Zuweina;	*[We, ukae] hivi!*	[You, get in] this position!
7	Chanda;	*Akae huku, eh? We, uelekee huku au kaa huku.*	She should sit like this, eh? You, face this way or get in this position.
8	Zuweina;	*### Akabili kibla hivi.*	### She should face qibla.
9	Chanda;	*Aelekee kibla.*	She should face qibla.

In line 8, Zuweina, as the eldest and the longest-married woman among the instructors, wields authority, commanding the bride to lie down and face qibla. Her authority is also respected by the other women, evident in lines 7 and 9, when Chanda aligns herself with Zuweina first by restating and then even echoing Zuweina's words. Chanda's repetition of Zuweina's words suggests that Zuweina is not only socializing the bride into the proper position for massaging one's husband (and for being "fucked," as we will see in the next excerpt) but also socializing the other instructors into preparing a bride for her wedding. Their reference to qibla (the direction of Mecca) in lines 8 and 9 both establishes massaging and instructing the bride as a religious act and draws parallels between the instruction ceremony and other sacred acts, including not only making *udhu* (ritual purity) and prayer itself, but also sexual intercourse, which Muslims in Zanzibar Town believe is also meant to be undertaken while facing qibla. The parallel between the massage and the sex act becomes more explicit in excerpt 3. As they continued to position the bride in a comfortable position, the instructors mixed profanity and religious phrases fluidly:

Excerpt 3

1	Dawa;	*Nani anakutomba, unataka mwenyewe?*	Who fucks you, or do you want it yourself?
2	instructors in unison;	*@ @ He! ((ululating)) [@ @ @ @ @ @ @*	@ @ He! ((ululating)) [@ @ @ @@ @ @ @
3	Dawa;	*[Hataki kuolewa, utakuwa [#*	[She doesn't want to get married, you will be [#
4	Zuweina;	*[Sogea huko, eh. Sogea huko.*	[Scoot that way, eh. Scoot that way.
5	Chanda;	*@@@*	@@@
6	Zuweina;	*Haya, nilalie mie hapa. ((claps hands on thighs)) Uso wako nipe mie. Lala, lala saa hivi.*	Okay, lie on me here. ((claps hands on thighs)) Give me your face. Lay down, lay down right now.
7	Asha;	*((softly)) Huku, au?*	((softly)) Here, or?
8	Zuweina;	*No no no no no! Hichi kichwa chinielekee mie hapa. Haya, sogea huku. M-hm. # Haya. Njoo tena. Nakwambia tena. Lala kama unataka kutombwa. Mtombo wa mwanzo. Mtombo [wa mwanzo ulale ### #]*	*No no no no no!* This head should be facing me here. Okay, scoot this way. M-hm. # Okay. Come again. I'm telling you again. Lie down like you want to be fucked. The first fuck. For the first [fuck you should lie down ### #]
9	Dawa;	*[Anajua anaenda kutombwa huyu?]*	[Does she know she is on her way to get fucked, this one?]
10	Zuweina;	*Namwambia. Mtombo wa [mwanzo unakuja]*	I'm telling her. The first [fuck is coming]
11	Dawa;	*[@Ha @ha @ha:::!]*	[@Ha @ha @ha:::!]
12	Chanda;	*(H) @@@*	(H) @@@
13	Zuweina;	*Uweke hapa kichwa. Bismillah i[rahman irahim.]*	Put your head here. *In the name of God [the merciful, the compassionate.]*
14	instructors in unison;	*[irahman irahim.]*	[*the merciful, the compassionate.*]
15	Zuweina;	*((claps)) Bismillah.*	((claps) *In the name of God.*

In line 1, Asha becomes acquainted with the passive sexual role expected of her, not only through the kungwi's positioning of her as the grammatical object of -tomba (to fuck) and as wanting (-taka) to play this role, but also from the way the other instructors respond to the kungwi's questions. In line 2 the novice instructors align themselves with the experienced instructor through their laughter and ululation, confirming the kungwi's stance. The novice instructors' echoing of Zuweina's invocation in line 14 again shows their alignment with her approach to the singo, their affirmation of her status as an "expert" with more authority than they. They do not yet share her participant role but rather are being socialized into conducting a singo ritual. Zuweina's and Dawa's use of humor, evidenced by the laughter of the other instructors in the turns following theirs, makes their presence more strongly felt,[50] thereby further establishing them as the leaders of the singo.

Like telling the bride to face the qibla, invoking God's name before beginning an activity (lines 13–15) imbues the instructors' speech with Islamic significance, undiminished by their use of the word *fuck* in lines 8–10 and their raucous laughter throughout. When I asked Chanda whether there was any conflict between Islamic instruction and the use of profanity, she responded,

> *Ah! Wanafundisha na matusi, kwa sababu ni lazima ukitaje kile kitu. Huwezi kumfundisha mtu ukamwambia "Kitu fulani, hivi, hivi." Lazima ukitaje. @@@*

> Ah! They teach with profanity, because you must name that thing. You can't teach a person and tell her, "Some thing, like this, like this." You must name it. @@@

Naming sex acts explicitly is a means of establishing verbal authority for themselves, since hegemonic ideologies demand that such profanity not be used by unmarried women. Their status as married women as opposed to girls allows them to use profanity with one another and to socialize the bride into its appropriate use, including instructing her to tell her husband, "Mume wangu, umenitomba vizuri leo!" (My husband, you have fucked me well today!) Through their ventriloquation of her voice they are initiating the bride into a situation when it will be appropriate to use such profanity herself.[51] Zuweina's and the kungwi's use of profanity in the presence of the novice instructors and me marks the group's status as intimates—married women who have been through sex instruction and who know each other well. It also inducts the bride into their group of intimates and into the language of intimacy she is expected to use with her husband.

The use of profanity leads to laughter from the other participants. This is insider humor, doing something funny for an insider audience—here with women who are closely related (sisters, their niece, their in-law, and one close friend). Their recognition of profanity as humor is itself a kind of intimacy, an example of what Gaudio calls "faithful irreverence," sacrilegious speech as a form of Islamic cultural citizenship, or in this case Islamic womanhood.[52]

After positioning the bride, her instructors massaged her with singo, a scrub made from cloves, to remove the dead skin on her body, and simultaneously instructed her how she should regularly massage her husband, an embodied form of socialization:

Excerpt 4

1	Zuweina;	*Unaona hivyo inavyofanywa, shoga? Basi na mume ukamfanya kuliko hivi:.*	Do you see how it is done, my friend? Well then, do it even better than thi:s for your husband.
2	Asha;	((crying))	((crying))
3	Zuweina;	*Kila siku [akisharudi melini,] ananuka kwapa za melini, akishachoka na wanawake wahuni wa kimelini, anakuja huko*	Every day [when he comes home from the boat] with armpits stinking of the boat, tired of promiscuous women on the boat, he comes there
4	Dawa;	[*Fanya, fanya, fanya*]	[Do it, do it, do it]
5	Chanda;	@ @	@ @
6	Zuweina;	*Una #kwapa wa #malonge wa melini, msugue kwanza akutombe.*	You have #armpits # of the boat, massage him first so that he'll fuck you.

In excerpt 4, Zuweina presents Islamically sanctioned gender roles, in which the husband has the responsibility to work outside the home and to provide for his wife, who is expected to stay at home, ready to meet her husband's needs when he arrives. In line 1, she asserts how massage "is done," using both a passive verb and the simple present tense to indicate a norm, and explicitly asking Asha to align herself with this norm ("Do you see?"). Although Asha's crying in line 2 may seem incongruous, in this context it actually indicates her acceptance of this imposed norm. She knows what is expected of her, and she is understandably nervous, or at least performs the nervousness that she knows the other women expect from a virgin bride. In line 4, the kungwi aligns herself with this instruction by encouraging Asha to do what Zuweina tells her ("Do it! Do it! Do it!"), and in line 5 Chanda also offers alignment through laughter. The alignment of these three women indicates that Asha's massaging of her husband is not merely, for example, Zuweina's personal recommendation but rather part of the "culture" of married women in general, and of those who have taken part in singo rituals in particular. The entire excerpt also illustrates how women bond through conversational joking about men, similar to women in conversational data from both North and South America.[53] By making Asha's future husband the butt of their humor, they enact a community of women that positions Asha as an insider and her husband (like their own) as outsiders.

Instructors present "being fucked" as not just a duty but also as something to be desired by a new wife, encouraging her to massage her husband in exchange for sex. In doing so they also socialize the bride into the exchange value of caring for her husband; on a number of occasions I heard women talking about using massage or sex as a means of getting what they desired from their husbands—often permission to attend social events outside the home, necessary because of a conservative belief that a wife's Islamic duty is to not leave the house without her husband's permission. Similarly, after the singo, when the bride is decorated elaborately with henna for the first time, she is taught to avoid domestic chores in order to keep her henna bright "mpaka ilipwe" (until it is paid for)—another reference to the exchange value of beautifying oneself for one's husband. The exchange of corporeal intimacy for money or a husband's permission during the course of a Muslim marriage is an extension of the "orderly exchange between women and men" that begins during the wedding, as Lambek has illustrated elsewhere in the western Indian Ocean, on the island of Mayotte: "sexuality and domesticity in return for material wealth, material wealth in return for sexuality and domesticity. Each sex vaunts the valued resources over which it claims to exercise control."[54]

Excerpt 5 further illustrates the relationship between the activity of massaging the bride, her body as a physical object on which the instructors focus their physical and discursive attention, their use of profanity, their socialization of the bride into a passive role, and their establishment of authority.

Excerpt 5

1	Dawa;	*Anti! Bi harusi! Huwakwi moto mwilini? Huwakwi moto?*	Auntie! Bride! You're not getting hot on your body? You're not getting hot?
2	Asha;	*A-a.*	Uh-uh.
3	Dawa;	*Haya.*	Okay.
4	Another instructor;	*Haiwaki moto hi:i. Maanake nyingine tuli–*	This doesn't get hot. Because the other one we–
5	Zuweina;	((addressing the kungwi)) *Ushamaliza?*	((addressing the kungwi)) Are you finished?
6	Dawa;	((addressing Asha)) *Geuka nyuma.*	((addressing Asha)) Turn over.
7	Zuweina;	((addressing Asha)) *Njoo huku. Usije ukanuka kuku.*	((addressing Asha)) Come here. ⟶Don't let yourself smell like chicken.
8	Dawa;	*Hicho kihafu chenyewe ndo cho chote cha sikukuu, cha rangi halafu ndo anakivaa:*	That half-slip itself is just any one from a holiday, a colorful one, and then she just wears it.
9	Zuweina;	((addressing the kungwi)) *Leo nakuheshimu we.*	((addressing the kungwi)) Today I'm respecting you.
10	Dawa;	*Unamheshimu nani? [Hujaninunulia] lo lote.*	Who are you respecting? [You haven't brought me anything.]
11	Zuweina;	*[Nakuheshimu.] Pata zako.*	[I'm respecting you.] Get what's yours.
12	Dawa;	((addressing Asha)) *Geuka, mtoto.*	((addressing Asha)) Turn over, child.
13	Zuweina;	*# na mahafu.*	# and half-slips.
14	Dawa;	*Ananuka mkojo huyo! Akienda chafya [###]*	She smells like urine, that one! If she sneezes [###]
15	Zuweina;	*[###] shoga #*	[###] friend #
16	Other instructors;	*[@ @ @ ((Ululating laughter.))]*	[@ @ @ ((Ululating laughter.))]
17	Zuweina;	*[Allah! ((addressing Asha)) Lala hapa we.] ((Claps hands on her thighs.)) [# # #]*	[Allah! ((addressing Asha)) Lie down here, you.] ((Claps hands on her thighs.)) [# # #]
18	Dawa;	*[Lala kifudifudi!]*	[Lie face down!]
19	Zuweina;	*# # # Mboo inanuka. [Lala! Kifudifudi.] ((Claps twice))*	# # # The cock stinks. [Lie down! Face down!] ((Claps twice))
20	Chanda;	*[@@@]*	[@@@]

21	Dawa;	*[hii mitako aweke hi:vi]*	[These buttocks she should put like thi:s.]
22	Zuweina;	*[Hebu mie] nanuka kum:a!*	[Listen, my cunt stinks!]
23	Other instructors;	*((ululalating laughter))*	((ululalating laughter))
24	Zuweina;	*He nuka we!*	Hey, stink, you!
25	Another instructor;	@	@
26	Zuweina;	*@ Ala!*	@ My goodness!
27	Chanda;	*@@@ Mtihani, jamani! A-a!*	@@@ It's difficult, my friends! A-a!
28	Other instructors;	*@@*	@@
29	Zuweina;	*[addressing the kungwi]* *Haya mtie mkono wa kundu kwa hiyo tundu ya kundu hapa isugue. Mara inanuka ngano.*	[addressing the kungwi] Okay, put the hand you use to clean your asshole on her; so the asshole here, rub it down. It just might smell like grain.
30	Chanda;	*@@*	@@
31	Asha;	*@@*	@@
32	Zuweina;	*((addressing the other instructors)) Mikono ipeleke. Hamjagusa mkono hata mmoja! Usugueni!*	((addressing the other instructors)) Move your hands. You haven't touched even one hand! Rub it, you all!
33	Chanda;	*@@@*	@@@
34	Dawa;	*((massaging Asha's buttocks.)) Matako anayo Mashallah.*	((massaging Asha's buttocks.)) She has a butt, Mashallah!
35	Zuweina;	*Mashallah!*	Mashallah!
36	Instructors;	*@@ ((ululating))*	@@ ((ululating))
37	Zuweina;	*((in stylized voice)) Eh! Jamani eh! ((singing)):* Hiyo #nambima tombatu!	((in stylized voice)) Eh! My friends, eh! ((singing:)) Hiyo #nambima tombatu!
38	Other instructors;	*((singing the chorus)) Tombatu! Tombatu!*	((singing the chorus)) Tombatu! Tombatu!
39	Zuweina;	*He he:! ((ululating))*	He he:! ((ululating))
39	Chanda;	*Woooo!*	Woooo!
40	Zuweina;	*Mikono isugue, ~Chanda, mpaka kisha # We ~Dawa!*	Rub [her] arms, ~Chanda, until #. You ~Dawa!
41	Kungwi;	*Mhm?*	Mhm?
42	Zuweina;	*((addressing Chanda)) Mwache huyu amsugue yeye ~Dawa. Shoga, sugua mkono. Tena ung'are. Kaja kusuguliwa unamchezea. Unachezea mboo wapi?*	((addressing Chanda)) Leave her, let Dawa rub her. My friend, rub her arm. Moreover, it should shine. She has come to be massaged and you're just playing with her. Where are you playing with a cock?
43	Chanda;	*@@*	@@

Excerpt 5 includes one of the few occasions when the instructors directly address Asha and expect a response: in line 1, checking to make sure the clove mixture that the women are using to massage her is not burning her skin. Because Asha does not immediately respond, the kungwi, Dawa, addresses her twice, first as "Auntie" and then as "Bride," to ask her a question, and then to repeat the question with minimal variation. "Auntie" is used by Swahili speakers to refer to an adult woman whose name one doesn't know or whose name it might be inappropriate to use. (For example, my much younger brothers-in-law referred to me as Auntie.) Here Dawa's use of it marks Asha as an adult woman for perhaps the first time in her life. Asha's delayed (and minimal) response illustrates that she does not expect to be addressed directly or to speak during this ritual.

When one of the other instructors begins to explain that the clove scrub she has brought is high quality (line 4), Zuweina interrupts, reestablishing her authority as the host of this ritual and as the oldest (and therefore most "expert") woman present. She also returns the women's focus to massaging the bride, asking the kungwi, "Are you finished?" meaning finished massaging the front of Asha's body, as she has been lying on her back up to now. In response, the kungwi tells Asha to turn over so they can begin massaging her back. While there are two "experts" here, only Zuweina—as the hostess, the older of the two, and Asha's relative—has the final word.

Throughout the excerpt, Zuweina and the kungwi, the two expert instructors, repeatedly refer to odors. While the goal of the clove massage is to remove unpleasant odors from the bride's body and replace them with the pleasant scent of cloves, the goal of their talk is to socialize the bride into the practice of preparing herself for her husband by ensuring that her body emits only pleasant fragrances. As Rosabelle Boswell argues, fragrance is an important theme in the Qur'an and the hadith, and Zanzibari Muslims have a long history of contact with not only the "the complex olfactory discourses" of the Middle East but also the flowers and spices imported from and exported to the Middle East used by Muslim women to create pleasant fragrances on their bodies, in their clothes, and in their bedrooms.[55] Larsen also explores Zanzibari women's use of fragrance in her chapter in this volume. In addition to the clove scrub used to prepare both men and women for their weddings and by married women to massage their husbands, brides are also taught to use corsages made from jasmine flowers dangling from beads around their waist and covering their mons before sexual intercourse, to decorate their beds with flower petals, and to use incense to fumigate their clothing, mouths, armits, vulvas, clothing, and bedsheets, as well as their husbands' clothing.

In the context of this local interpretation of an Islamic emphasis on cleanliness and pleasant fragrance, Zuweina's repeated references to unpleasant odors serve as a reminder to Asha that it is her Islamic duty as a wife to rid herself of these odors. Zuweina does this through profane humor—in line 7 telling Asha, "Don't let yourself smell like chicken," and in line 29 joking that Asha's anus might smell like grain. Although these statements are ostensibly insulting and use lexical items that Swahili speakers consider taboo, such as *kundu* (big asshole), they are interpreted as humorous by the other women involved, including Asha who laughs in line 30. In turning over on her stomach, Asha was forced to lie down with her face in Zuweina's lap, directly over her crotch, which became another source of humor for the women involved. This is direct socialization into bodily contact that she should not have experienced previously and is therefore expected to embarrass her—and it did. In line 14, the kungwi begins jokingly insulting Zuweina, saying, "She smells like urine, that one!" and suggesting that Zuweina's unpleasant-smelling crotch may make Asha sneeze. In line 19, Zuweina takes on the role of Asha's husband-to-be, speaking as if she is a man, saying, "The cock stinks." Here she teaches Asha that even if her husband's "cock stinks" she should not be hesitant to approach him intimately, despite her nervousness as a virgin; indeed it is her duty.

Although the actual physical activity the women are involved in is massaging the bride, their talk repeatedly draws parallels between how they are treating Asha and how they expect her to treat her husband. While the other women wore bras and panties covered with a kanga tied around their chests, both Zuweina and Dawa wore bras and half-slips. In line 8, Dawa makes reference to the visibly new half-slip that Zuweina is wearing for the occasion. Zuweina responds with flirtatious banter in line 9, telling Dawa, "Today I'm respecting you," meaning she has dressed up for Dawa's sake, positioning the kungwi as her husband in a brief role play. "Who are you respecting? You haven't brought me anything," Dawa retorts. "Get what's yours," Zuweina responds suggestively, inviting Dawa in the role of husband to a sexual encounter and supporting an ideology that a wife's sexuality "belongs to" her husband. Their exchange is performed for Asha's benefit, a means of instructing her to dress nicely for her husband, to bring him things, and to initiate sex with him. Later, in line 42, Zuweina positions Dawa in the role of wife, drawing a parallel between how she massages Asha's arms and how she would "play with" her husband's penis.

Zuweina's and Dawa's use of matusi and their ritualized insulting of one another have three functions. First, they contribute to the construction of camaradarie among the women, who laugh and ululate throughout the ritual, especially in the turns immediately after such insults. They display mutual knowledge of sexuality and probe their fellow participants' "willingness to laugh about the subject matter in question." The other women show their appreciation of the humorous matusi through laughter, sharing in "the payoff of amusement and increased rapport."[56]

Second, they initiate Asha into the speech community of married women in which she will now be allowed to use such matusi to strengthen close relationships with other women who are her *watani* (joking partners).[57] Although the humorous insults they make toward one another as well as both toward and about her have the potential of "biting," in fact they establish her as a co-participant, emphasizing her (soon to be acquired) equality of status with them as a married woman.[58]

Third, they offer oblique commentary on the role Asha must take on as a wife: when Dawa and Zuweina joke about the smell of Zuweina's kuma (cunt), they inform Asha that she must take care to clean and make herself fragrant. When Zuweina criticizes Dawa's massage technique, she informs Asha that one must use rigor in massaging, rubbing differently than she would play with her husband's mboo (cock). Mock abuse of the novice and others who perform the role of the bride is found in wedding rituals of other Tanzanian ethnic groups as well, used to teach her that if she does not keep herself clean and please her husband, she will be subject to further ridicule and shame.[59]

ALTHOUGH RESEARCHERS recognize that language socialization is a lifespan phenomenon, there has been relatively little research on how such socialization occurs outside childhood and on how people are socialized into gendered communication, let alone marital communication. This chapter, like Ayala Fader's work on Hasidic brides who are socialized into talk about sexuality and romance before their weddings,[60] focuses on the language socialization of a young woman during the liminal period between childhood and adulthood, virginity and marriage. My work shares with Fader's a recognition that language socialization among "nonliberal religious women" is an embodied practice that involves teaching a novice not only how to talk but also how to use her body in religiously sanctioned ways. Whereas the focus among Hasidic women is on modesty even within marriage, for the Zanzibari Muslim women with whom I worked, the focus of premarital instruction is on teaching the bride to transgress norms of embodied modesty, including appropriate speech, both in the presence of close female friends and relatives and with her husband. My analysis has shown that language socialization is an important component of the transition to adulthood in a community where female adulthood is defined though marriage and the onset of sexual activity. We might look for analogous moments in other cultural contexts, such as Mayan *pixab'*, ritual advice given to brides and grooms before their weddings in Guatemala,[61] bridal showers in the United States, or "kitchen parties" in mainland Tanzania.[62]

Language socialization studies define success "as the ability to communicate in the language of a particular community and to act according to its norms."[63] How do women assess whether the bride has actually acquired the linguistic, behavioral, and physical skills they are teaching her? Because the bride is relatively silent during her instruction, because her later communication with her husband about sexuality will take place in private, and in the absence of a longitudinal study that would track her language use from her wedding throughout her marital life, it is not possible to show how the bride herself enacts the "social relationships and other sociocultural phenomena" that will make her into an expert member of her speech community, an "expert" Muslim wife. Anecdotal evidence from northern Unguja and Mombasa suggests that some women show a marked difference in language use within days of getting married, perhaps eager to assert their new status in relation to unmarried women and girls.[64] More research is needed on these rapid linguistic changes. Yet the instructors' display of expert knowledge that they themselves were taught during a similar instruction ceremony months or years before offers a proxy through which successful language socialization becomes apparent; we see "sedimented traces" of their own experiences being instructed.[65] This chapter thus approached socialization by illustrating how marriage instructors imagine and address the competent Muslim wife inside the inexperienced bride, focusing on "the horizon of her potential abilities"[66] and showing that taking on this identity has a significant linguistic component.

We know, following Margaret Mead, Elinor Ochs, and other socialization researchers, that the bride must be an active agent in her socialization, not automatically internalizing what she is taught.[67] Yet it remains an open question the extent to which women can or do "select images and perspectives" from among those presented to them during premarital instruction ceremonies.[68] Indeed, many of the women I interviewed did seem to have internalized what they were taught, presenting a bride's mastery of sex instruction as utterly axiomatic and completely linked to the identity of "Muslim wife." A different research method, which would study intertextual links between speech events over time,[69] might reveal the extent to which women in Zanzibar Town contest or negotiate the prescribed ways of talking about sexuality and being sexual that are presented during singo ceremonies.

One of the limitations of existing research on women's speech in Swahili cultures is that in public, formal, or mixed-gender settings, women are likely to remain silent, use respectful forms of speech, or speak in ways that reproduce their society's (positive and negative) linguistic expectations of them. For example, in her study of men and women's speech during divorce proceedings in an Islamic court in Mombasa, Hirsch shows that women in unhappy marriages are expected to persevere silently, without complaint, and they show their recognition of this expectation in their testimony: "Women who narrate domestic conflict routinely depict themselves in their stories as persevering silently."[70] One means used to silence women is a language ideology that depicts their speech as dangerous; storytelling is associated with women's inappropriate speech. When women do speak out in court, then, narrating the conflicts that have led them to seek divorce, Hirsch shows that they contradict societal expectations by refusing to silently persevere, and they reproduce the language ideology that depicts women as producing dangerous speech, telling inappropriate narratives, and sharing information that should be kept private. Stiles's work on Islamic courts, in this volume and elsewhere,[71] shows that even when telling these narratives as a last resort to escape an unhappy marriage, women use highly circumscribed speech marked by innuendo in order to maintain their *heshima* (respect). In my own analysis of interviews with Zanzibari women about sex with spirits, I showed that their talk about sex is full of euphemisms and that personal disclosures of sexual practices and desires are fleeting.[72]

In contrast to courtroom discourse, which is constrained by the presence of the judge and other men, and to my own interview data, which was constrained by the presence of a foreign interviewer the participants did not know well, the conversational data I present here is unique in presenting the actual texts of women talking about sexuality and marriage among themselves. While my presence may have had some impact on their talk, my status as a married Muslim woman, the wife of a local man, and a member of the family (by marriage), meant that the conversation was one among intimates. Indeed, this is the goal of ethnographic research even when the ethnographer does not share identity labels or familial relationships with her participants. Certainly, as the data shows, the women with whom I conducted research did not avoid profanity or attempt to uphold local ideologies of appropriate women's speech. At the same time, their speech did not reproduce local negative stereotypes of women's speech as dangerous; rather they made frequent use of Islamic terminology and phrases that marked their speech as sacred.

During the course of this research I was both an insider and an outsider. This distinction is particularly relevant to my focus on socialization, because during my interactions with other Muslim women it was clear to me that I was being socialized, often explicitly, into local interpretations of Islamic gender norms. An outsider to Zanzibar, I was nevertheless an insider at the first instruction ceremony I attended, because I was the bride. No doubt the context in which I have lived and was educated, and my identity as a Muslim feminist, mean that my interpretations of this data are different from the other participants. Yet in some ways I was in a similar position to most brides in Zanzibar Town, only vaguely familiar with the sexual culture of Muslim wives into which I was inducted. At the ceremony I discuss in detail here, I was more an observer than a participant, but my status as in-law to the other women meant that I was treated as an insider, albeit a novice, still learning how to participate in the instruction of a bride. Many of the women I spoke to expressed hope that by sharing information about marriage instruction with me, I would go on to share it with other Muslim women so that they could also begin to practice the good adabu of a Muslim wife. While I do not share that goal or their essentialist interpretations of what it means to be a "good Muslim" generally, let alone a "good Muslim wife," this chapter is nevertheless my good-faith effort to share what I have learned about the marriage instruction offered to Muslim women in contemporary Zanzibar Town. Echoing Zuweina, I ask you, reader: *Do you see how it is done, my friend?*

NOTES

1. Cf. Stanton E. F. Wortham, "Socialization beyond the Speech Event," *Journal of Linguistic Anthropology* 15, no. 1 (2005): 95–112.

2. Saba Mahmood, "Feminist Theory, Embodiment, and the Docile Agent: Some Reflections on the Egyptian Islamic Revival," *Cultural Anthropology* 16, no. 2 (2001): 212.

3. Michael Lambek, "The Practice of Islamic Experts in a Village on Mayotte," *Journal of Religion in Africa* 20, no. 1 (1990): 31.

4. Kjersti Larsen, "Gender Socialization: Sub-Saharan Africa: Swahili Societies," *Encyclopedia of Women and Islamic Cultures: Family, Law, and Politics*, ed. Suad Joseph (Leiden: Brill, 2003).

5. Carol A. Campbell and Carol M. Eastman, "Ngoma: Swahili Adult Song Performance in Context," *Ethnomusicology* 28, no. 3 (1984): 489.

6. Carol M. Eastman, "Nyimbo za watoto: The Swahili Child's World View," *Ethos* 14, no. 2 (July 1986): 144–73.

7. Pamela Landberg, "Widows and Divorced Women in Swahili Society," in *Widows in African Societies: Choices and Constraints,* ed. Betty Potash (Stanford: Stanford University Press, 1986), 124.

8. Carol M. Eastman, "Women, Slaves, and Foreigners: African Cultural Influences and Group Processes in the Formation of Northern Swahili Coastal Society," *International Journal of African Historical Studies* 21, no. 1 (1988): 1–20; Ann Biersteker, "Language, Poetry, and Power: A Reconsideration of 'Utendi wa Mwana Kupona,'" in *Faces of Islam in African Literature,* ed. Kenneth Harrow (Portsmouth, NH: Heinemann, 1991), 59–77.

9. Katrina Daly Thompson, "How to Be a Good Muslim Wife: Women's Performance of Islamic Authority during Swahili Weddings," *Journal of Religion in Africa* 41, no. 4 (2011): 427–48.

10. All names of participants have been changed.

11. John W. DuBois, Stephan Schuetze-Coburn, Susanna Cumming, and Danae Paolino, "Outline of Discourse Transcription," in *Talking Data: Transcription and Coding in Discourse Research,* ed. Jane Edwards and Martin D. Lampert (Hillsdale NJ: Lawrence Erlbaum Associates, 1993), 45–89; DuBois, "Transcription Convention Updates," appendix, July 28, 2006, http://www.linguistics.ucsb.edu/projects/transcription/A05updates.pdf.

12. Charles Goodwin, "Recording Human Interaction in Natural Settings," *Pragmatics* 3, no. 2 (1993): 181–209; Goodwin, "Practices of Seeing, Visual Analysis: An Ethnomethodological Approach," in *Handbook of Visual Analysis,* ed. Carey Jewitt and Theo Van Leeuwen (London: Sage, 2000), 157–82; Sigrid Norris, "The Implication of Visual Research for Discourse Analysis: Transcription beyond Language," *Visual Communication* 1, no. 1 (2002): 97–121.

13. Susan F. Hirsch, *Pronouncing and Persevering: Gender and the Discourses of Disputing in an African Islamic Court,* Language and Legal Discourse (Chicago: University of Chicago Press, 1998), 33.

14. See, for example, Saida Yahya-Othman, "If the Cap Fits: Kanga Names and Women's Voice in Swahili Society," *Swahili Forum* 4 (1997): 135–49; S. Hirsch, *Pronouncing and Persevering;* Rose Marie Beck, "Texts on Textiles: Proverbiality as Characteristic of Equivocal Communication at the East African Coast (Swahili)," *Journal of African Cultural Studies* 17, no. 2 (December 2005): 131–60; R. Beck, "Gender, Innovation and Ambiguity: Speech Prohibitions as a Resource for 'Space to Move,'" *Discourse and Society* 20, no. 5 (September 2009): 531–53.

15. S. Hirsch, *Pronouncing and Persevering,* 67.

16. Khadija B. Juma, "Kiswahili cha asili cha kina mama wa visiwani Zanzibar," in *Utamaduni wa Mzanzibari,* ed. Juma (Zanzibar: Baraza la Kiswahili la Zanzibar, 2008), 28.

17. S. Hirsch, *Pronouncing and Persevering,* 38.

18. Marc J. Swartz, "The Isolation of Men and the Happiness of Women: Sources and Use of Power in Swahili Marital Relationships," *Journal of Anthropological Research* 38, no. 1 (1982): 31–2.

19. S. Hirsch, *Pronouncing and Persevering,* 18.

20. Elinor Ochs, introduction to *Language Socialization across Cultures,* ed. Bambi B. Schieffelin and Ochs (Cambridge University Press, 1986), 2.

21. Elinor Ochs, "Becoming a Speaker of Culture," in *Language Acquisition and Language Socialization: Ecological Perspectives,* ed. Claire J. Kramsch, Advances in Applied Linguistics (London: Continuum, 2002), 103.

22. Claire Kramsch, "Introduction: 'How Can We Tell the Dancer from the Dance?,'" in Kramsch, *Language Acquisition,* 18.

23. Ibid., 11.

24. Charles Goodwin, "Action and Embodiment within Situated Human Interaction," *Journal of Pragmatics* 32, no. 10 (2000): 1490.

25. Mtoro bin Mwinyi Bakari, *The Customs of the Swahili People: The* Desturi za Waswahili *of Mtoro bin Mwinyi Bakari and Other Swahili Persons,* ed. and trans. J. W. T. Allen (Berkeley: University of California Press, 1981); Farouk M. Topan, "Vugo: A Virginity Celebration Ceremony among the Swahili of Mombasa," *African Languages and Cultures* 8, no. 1 (1995): 87–107; Margaret Strobel, *Muslim Women in Mombasa, Kenya, 1890–1975* (New York & London: Yale University Press, 1979); Sarah Mirza and Margaret Strobel, eds., *Three Swahili Women: Life Histories from Mombasa, Kenya,* trans. Mirza and Strobel (Bloomington: Indiana University Press, 1989); Laura Fair, "Identity, Difference, and Dance: Female Initiation in Zanzibar, 1890 to 1930," *Frontiers: A Journal of Women Studies* 17, no. 3 (1996): 146–72; Corrie Decker, "From Hygiene to Biology: Talking around Sex in Zanzibar's Colonial Girls' Schools" (presented at the African Studies Association, San Francisco, November 19, 2010).

26. Topan, "Vugo."

27. Mary Ntukula, "The Initiation Rite," in *Chelewa, Chelewa: The Dilemma of Teenage Girls,* ed. Zubeida Tumbo-Masabo and Rita Liljeström (Uppsala: Nordiska Afrikainstitutet, 1994), 96–119; Fair, "Identity, Difference."

28. Mtoro bin Mwinyi Bakari, *Desturi wa Wasuaheli na khabari za desturi za sheri'a za Wasuaheli,* ed. C. Velten (Göttingen: Vandenhoeck & Ruprecht, 1903); Decker, "Hygiene to Biology"; Topan, "Vugo."

29. Kjersti Larsen, *Where Humans and Spirits Meet: The Politics of Rituals and Identified Spirits in Zanzibar,* Social Identities 5 (New York: Berghahn Books, 2008), 7.

30. On historical forms of unyago and in other parts of the Swahili coast, see Bakari, *Desturi za Wasuaheli;* A. H. J. Prins, *The Swahili-Speaking Peoples of Zanzibar and the East African Coast (Arabs, Shirazi and Swahili)* (London: International African Institute, 1967); Pat Caplan, *Choice and Constraint in a Swahili Community: Property, Hierarchy, and Cognatic Descent on the East African Coast* (London: Oxford University Press, 1975); Caplan, "Boys' Circumcision and Girls' Puberty Rites among the Swahili of Mafia Island, Tanzania," *Africa: Journal of the International African Institute* 46, no. 1 (1976): 21–33; Caplan, "Perceptions of Gender Stratification," *Africa: Journal of the International African Institute* 59, no. 2 (1989): 196–208; Strobel, *Muslim Women;* Decker, "Hygiene to Biology"; Minou Fuglesang, "Lessons for Life—Past and Present Modes of Sexuality Education in Tanzanian Society," *Social Science and Medicine* 44, no. 8 (1997): 1245–54; Patricia Romero, "Does Being 'Sexy' Keep a Marriage Going in Lamu?" (paper presented at the African Studies Association annual meeting, 1992).

31. Larsen, "Gender Socialization"; Larsen, *Where Humans and Spirits Meet;* Nadine Beckmann, "Pleasure and Danger: Muslim Views on Sex and Gender in Zanzibar," *Culture, Health and Sexuality* 12, no. 6 (August 2010): 619–32.

32. Beckmann, "Pleasure and Danger."

33. Thompson, "Good Muslim Wife."

34. Larsen, "Gender Socialization."

35. S. J. Mamuya, *Jando na unyago* (Nairobi: East African Publishing House, 1972), 239.

36. R. E. Moreau, "Joking Relationships in Tanganyika," *Africa: Journal of the International African Institute* 14, no. 7 (July 1944): 391; Jonathon Glassman, "Sorting Out the Tribes: The Creation of Racial Identities in Colonial Zanzibar's Newspaper Wars," *Journal of African History* 41, no. 3 (2000): 415.

37. Yahya-Othman, "If the Cap Fits."

38. Juma, "Kiswahili cha asili," 35.

39. Penelope Brown and Stephen C. Levinson, "Universals in Language Usage: Politeness Phenomena," in *Questions and Politeness,* ed. Esther N. Goody (Cambridge: Cambridge University Press, 1980), 256–89.

40. Carol A. Campbell, "An Introduction to the Music of Swahili Women," Seminar Paper no. 68, Institute of African Studies, University of Nairobi, 1976, 3.

41. Einar Haugen, *The Ecology of Language,* ed. Anwar S. Dil, Language Science and National Development (Stanford: Stanford University Press, 1972), 329.

42. C. Campbell, "Music of Swahili Women," 14.

43. Juma, "Kiswahili cha asili," emphasis in original.

44. Katrina Daly Thompson, "Zanzibari Women's Discursive and Sexual Agency: Violating Gendered Speech Prohibitions through Talk about

Supernatural Sex," *Discourse and Society* 22, no. 1 (January 2011): 3–20; S. Hirsch, *Pronouncing and Persevering.*

45. Cf. Thompson, "Zanzibari Women's Agency"; Thompson, "Good Muslim Wife."

46. See, for example, Gearhart, this volume.

47. Ayala Fader, *Mitzvah Girls: Bringing Up the Next Generation of Hasidic Jews in Brooklyn* (Princeton: Princeton University Press, 2009), 19.

48. Ntukula, "Initiation Rite."

49. For example, on Lamu homes, see Patricia Romero, *Lamu: History, Society, and Family in an East African Port City* (Princeton: Markus Wiener, 1997), 39.

50. Neal R. Norrick, "Issues in Conversational Joking," *Journal of Pragmatics* 35, no. 9 (2003): 1333–59; Deborah Tannen, *Conversational Style: Analyzing Talk among Friends* (New York: Oxford University Press, USA, 1984).

51. Ochs, "Speaker of Culture," 103.

52. Rudolf Gaudio, *Allah Made Us: Sexual Outlaws in an Islamic African City* (Chichester, UK: Wiley-Blackwell, 2009), 124.

53. Diana Boxer and Florencia Cortés-Conde, "From Bonding to Biting: Conversational Joking and Identity Display," *Journal of Pragmatics* 27, no. 3 (1997): 275–94.

54. Michael Lambek, "Virgin Marriage and the Autonomy of Women in Mayotte," *Signs* 9, no. 2 (1983): 280.

55. Rosabelle Boswell, "Scents of Identity: Fragrance as Heritage in Zanzibar," *Journal of Contemporary African Studies* 26, no. 3 (2008): 295.

56. Norrick, "Issues in Conversational Joking," 1342; Cf. Norrick, *Conversational Joking: Humor in Everyday Talk* (Bloomington: Indiana University Press, 1993).

57. Moreau, "Joking Relationships"; A. R. Radcliffe-Brown, "On Joking Relationships," *Africa: Journal of the International African Institute* 13, no. 3 (1940): 195–210.

58. Boxer and Cortés-Conde, "Bonding to Biting"; Norrick, "Issues in Conversational Joking."

59. Penina O. Mlama, "Digubi: A Tanzanian Indigenous Theatre Form," *Drama Review* 25, no. 4 (1981): 3–12.

60. Fader, *Mitzvah Girls.*

61. Robin Shoaps, "Morality in Grammar and Discourse: Stance-Taking and the Negotiation of Moral Personhood in Sakapultek (Mayan) Wedding Counsels" (PhD diss., University of California, Santa Barbara, 2004); Shoaps, "'Moral Irony': Modal Particles, Moral Persons and Indirect Stance-Taking in Sakapultek Discourse," *Pragmatics* 17, no. 2 (2007); Shoaps, "Ritual and (Im)moral Voices: Locating the Testament of Judas in Sakapultek Communicative Ecology," *American Ethnologist* 36, no. 3 (2009): 459–77.

62. Sheryl McCurdy, "Fashioning Sexuality: Desire, Manyema Ethnicity, and the Creation of the 'Kanga,' ca. 1880–1900," *International Journal of African Historical Studies* 39, no. 3 (2006): 461n61.

63. Kramsch, "'How Can We Tell the Dancer?,'" 24.

64. Erin E. Stiles, pers. comm., June 28, 2012; Stiles, "Unsuitable Husbands," chap. 8, this volume; Susan F. Hirsch, pers. comm., August 31, 2012.

65. Kramsch, "'How Can We Tell the Dancer?,'" 23.

66. Ibid., 20.

67. Margaret Mead, *Coming of Age in Samoa: A Psychological Study of Primitive Youth for Western Civilization* (New York: Morrow, 1961).

68. Ochs, introduction to *Language Socialization*, 1.

69. Wortham, "Socialization beyond the Speech Event."

70. S. Hirsch, *Pronouncing and Persevering*, 31.

71. Erin E. Stiles, "When Is a Divorce a Divorce? Determining Intention in Zanzibar's Islamic Courts," *Ethnology* 42, no. 4 (October 2003): 273–88; Stiles, "'There Is No Stranger to Marriage Here!': Muslim Women and Divorce in Rural Zanzibar," *Africa: Journal of the International African Institute* 75, no. 4 (2005): 582–98.

72. Thompson, "Zanzibari Women's Agency."

SEVEN

Pleasure and Prohibitions

Reflections on Gender, Knowledge,
and Sexuality in Zanzibar Town

KJERSTI LARSEN

ADDRESSING THE QUESTION ASKED by the editors of this
book—that is, how ideologies of normative Swahili sexuality
and gender are discursively constructed, performed, negotiated, or
rejected within and outside marriage—I shall explore notions of
prohibitions and pleasures. My argument is that these notions are
not necessarily everywhere morally organized in the same way that
we may expect from a so-called Western convention. Seen from a
Zanzibari perspective, prohibitions and pleasures are accommodated differently according to contexts and social relationships.
That would imply that notions of gender and sexuality encompass values, attitudes, and practices that may, from the outside,
appear contradictory, even transgressive. Through ethnographic
material, my aim is to convey that what could otherwise be understood in terms of inherent moral contradictions, or even ritual subversions concerning notions of gender and sexuality, may
rather relate to a problem of context and logic of translation.

I have conducted ethnographic fieldwork in Zanzibar Town, including both Stone Town, or Old Town (Mji Mkongwe), and its suburbs (Ng'ambo) since 1984. The people I have worked with belong to different communities and economic categories. They are all Sunni Muslims, and thus Islam and Islamic teachings are thoroughly incorporated into their everyday and ritual lives. With the aspiration of being good Muslims, most would understand and negotiate their lifestyle and activities with reference to the Qur'an and the hadith as well as to translations provided by local religious scholars (walimu and mashehe). In general, people with whom I am acquainted would participate in a wide spectrum of activities that they do not necessarily consider to be commendable according to Islam (dini), such as spirit possession (ngoma ya sheitani), local healing practices (uganga), divination (ramli), and ritualized sex instruction (unyago). While they continuously discuss whether their lifestyle is or is not in accordance with Islam and in which situations they actually may sin (fanya dhambi),[1] they do not consider participation in such activities to be contrary to Islam and to being good Muslims.[2] Likewise, in the various neighborhoods and milieus where I have worked, preparation for marriage (ndoa) remains a crucial part of socialization. The significance of this religious and social institution, and the aspiration to become a good Muslim wife or husband, cannot be underestimated. A wedding is, however, not just an event for transferring norms of gender and sexuality but also for negotiating them.

In my discussions of socialization of girls with women of different age groups, they all contend that themes related to sexuality—including the onset of menstruation—should never be explicitly dealt with between mothers and daughters. For example, among women of Muslim Indian origin, mothers would ask either a married sister or a sister-in-law to teach the daughters about physical puberty and how to behave during menstruation; most mothers from other milieus would appoint a somo (instructor) for their daughters. In fact, in preparing their daughters for puberty and married life, both the appointment of a somo and, later, the arrangement of the ritual called unyago are considered important. Both somo and unyago are educational institutions by and for women. Before a girl reaches the age of physical puberty the mother will chose a somo for her daughter.³ The one who becomes a somo must be (or must have been) married and is usually a close friend or relative of the mother. The responsibility of a somo is first to teach the girl, that is, *mwari* (here, this means virgin; in general, it is a term referring to the period from the onset of menstruation until first marriage), how to behave during menstruation, and later how to approach matters relating to sexuality.

The relationship is formalized and it is the somo—not the mother—who brings the girl to unyago. Again, Muslim women of Indian origin would not be initiated nor participate in any form of unyago. Rather, a married aunt would stay with the bride in her bedroom while she is being adorned and prepared for the marriage ceremony (*nikaha*). During this period she will teach the bride about sex and how to "live with a husband" (*kukaa na mume*). Such an arrangement could also be preferred by other women. Women who practice unyago likewise say that the purpose of unyago is to teach a young woman how to live with a husband.

Unyago was probably introduced to Swahili societies by women brought as slaves. After the abolition of slavery, the ritual groups were joined by women who were previously freeborn and who in their turn brought their daughters for initiation.⁴ Over the years the ritual has continued to undergo modifications according to social and religious practices and ideals prevalent in the Swahili region.⁵ Although unyago was never universally performed, its existence plays an important role in the formation of female gender identity.⁶ Generally, I would say that those who do not participate, or who do not want their daughters to be initiated, claim that it is against Islam, saying that what women learn and do during the rituals is incompatible with being a good Muslim. Others argue that the rituals are old-fashioned (*ya zamani*), that girls today can learn all they need to know from school and from television, videos, magazines, and the Internet.⁷

In anthropological terms, unyago could best be described as an initiation ritual where girls or young women learn about sexuality before entering their first marriage. When I initially conducted research on unyago, in 1985–86, it was called *unyago wa siri* (secret unyago). Currently there exist in Zanzibar Town various forms of unyago: the one I first encountered, which is now referred to as *unyago wa kutapisha* or *unyago wa mwari,* a more recent version called *unyago wa kusinga* or *unyago wa harusi* and *unyago wa ngoma.* In unyago wa kutapisha, the verb *tapisha* (from *tapika,* vomit) refers to a crucial section within the ritual where the mwari must drink and then vomit a special emetic soup. *Unyago wa harusi* literally translates into "wedding unyago." *Singo,* or *unyago wa kusinga,* can be translated as "unyago to massage the bride." *Singo* (from the verb *singa*) refers to the process of rubbing and smearing the bride's body with a scrub made from cloves and different oils and perfumes before the wedding (for a detailed analysis of a singo ritual, see Katrina Thompson's chapter in this volume). *Unyago wa ngoma* are events where certain unyago dances, or *msondo,* are enacted as "cultural shows."[8] Although Thompson reports from fieldwork in Zanzibar Town that the women she worked with differentiated between unyago and singo, contending that only singo, or what I refer to here as unyago wa kusinga, is currently performed,[9] I found that Zanzibari women I have known from the mid-1980s and who are themselves initiated in unyago wa kutapisha seem eager to ensure the continuation of this ritual practice, despite its declining popularity.

The underlying idea behind these various forms of unyago is that sexuality and gender are embedded in particular modes of knowing and must be learned in order to manage the passage from youth to adulthood: from being unmarried to entering a first marriage. Also notable is the precept that significant knowledge about womanhood and sexuality should not be an issue between mother and daughter but rather between a somo and her mwari and within the unyago group, especially in the context of unyago wa kutapisha. At the unyago wa kusinga that I attended only the *nyakanga* (ritual expert) and the somo represented what could be referred to as the unyago group, or group of instructors, and only these women were together with the mwari inside her room while the other women invited to participate in the occasion remained outside. During initiation the mwari is told not to reveal any of the teachings she received to uninitiated women or to men. It is said that those who have previously revealed unyago secrets to outsiders have become mad—a curse that builds on the idea that access to knowledge implies a moral responsibility regarding the sharing and application of acquired knowledge. This, precisely, suggests the importance attached to knowledge and knowledge transmission in matters of gender and sexuality—in particular, knowledge in the form of secrecy.

Questioning the manner in which gender and sexuality are articulated, rejected, and constructed, I shall elaborate from the meaning of songs performed during unyago wa mwari or unyago wa kutapisha and during weddings (arusi), two separate yet interlinked occasions. Having presented and discussed certain songs, I shall briefly examine in what manner the songs' representations of gender and sexuality correspond to normative ideology and the experiences and practical engagements of women and men in daily life. Although the messages conveyed during the two different contexts may appear contradictory, they also supplement one another.

These songs are composed and regularly revised by women in order to convey relevant learning about married life and sexuality. The messages are formulated in accordance with the way these different contexts are organized: one public and one private. When referring to the public-private distinction, I wish to emphasize that in this sex-segregated society many arenas where only women are present should equally be considered public. Activities in which only women participate—such as home visits in the afternoon and early evening, social gatherings within neighborhoods, as well as several sequences of wedding celebrations—constitute public space.[10]

The songs referred to here were collected during fieldwork in the mid- and late 1980s, when initiation rituals were the main focus of my research. Since then I have, however, continued following the evolution of unyago and of weddings. The songs are about both prohibitions and pleasures. The term *pleasure* refers to expressions of sexual needs and satisfaction. *Prohibitions* as I see them are not pure abstractions but acts of restrictions and avoidance involving social relations. This means that practice is taken to be equally significant as the norm in the constitution of society and for its moral order. It also means that prohibitions are not seen to be exclusively restrictive but something that may also grant value to the person who maintains them. People achieve their social identity and value not only because of what they do but equally from what they refrain from doing. Notions of what you and others do and do not do are all involved in differentiations between self and other and thus engender and mark identity. It also means, following Michael Lambek and in line with Michel Foucault's approach to power, that prohibitions are understood to incorporate creativity and carry positive moral implications in the sense that they grant value to the person who maintains them.[11] Such an understanding implies, however, that there is a recognized relationship between knowing and doing. In this sense, morality is one aspect of what constitutes a social person.

To seek knowledge—whether religious or mundane—is perceived to be important and exigent among women and men in Zanzibar Town, and the use of knowledge—especially esoteric knowledge—is a moral issue. Knowledge is recognized as a source of potency and acquisition depends not only on access and capacity but also on curiosity. For instance, in contexts of locally constituted healing practices, an apprentice will gain access to what is considered a hidden meaning only if she or he is able to show interest by asking relevant questions.[12] The same pedagogical principle is, to my knowledge, followed by a somo and in the context of unyago. Words and actions seem to have, at least, two levels of meaning: one open and straightforward and one hidden and to be disclosed or detected. This approach to learning and communication should be seen in the light of a private-public distinction that extends beyond the organization of social space. It also means that learning understood in terms of potency and potential social disruption involves a link to social responsibility.

KNOWLEDGE, MORALITY, AND SEXUALITY

Besides being linked to social responsibility and thus morality, learning also implies authority. A private-public dimension is significant not only in an exploration of sexuality, gender, and marriage in this society, but also in relation to knowledge and what is perceived as its hidden or "inner" meaning (*maana ya ndani*). The distinction shapes understandings concerning the kind of experiences and learning to be disclosed and concealed in different arenas. Moreover, it has consequences for the organization of space and conduct in this society and is explicitly expressed in sex segregation. In daily life, distinctions between what may be said and done in public (*hadharani*) and what may only be known and acted in private (*ndani*) are major concerns. Daily communication and interaction are unavoidably connected with the problem of concealment and disclosure. These concerns take various forms. Women and men alike do their best to protect their secrets while, simultaneously, trying to detect those of others. Furthermore, irony (*maneno ya kinyume*) forms part of daily communication. When meeting, women as well as men will usually comment on each other's appearance and conduct and on that of their relatives or friends in seemingly flattering ways. Yet, by applying irony they may concomitantly use the opportunity to criticize each other or their respective relatives' behavior, dress, and relationships. For example, one evening I attended a party together with women I have known for many years; one among them suddenly turned toward a woman named Zuwena to praise her dress and how well it suited her. She said, "Your dress is really nice. Whenever I see you in this dress, you look beautiful" (*Kanzu yako nzuri sana. Kila ukivaa nguo hii inakupendeza*). However, by saying this, the woman was, in fact, offending Zuwena in front of the other guests. According to Zuwena, what the woman actually did was to announce that Zuwena had been wearing the same dress at several occasions. To be seen in the same dress at different occasions is taken as an indication of insufficient maintenance and thus, by extension, that the woman's husband or boyfriend has lost interest. This attitude is, I hold, prevalent in some milieus where people strive to keep up with an image of affluence such as living in comfort. The episode is meant to illustrate that through irony people can point to an alternative reading of a situation while avoiding the challenge of direct dissent.[13] In a Zanzibari context, this approach to communication is linked to the idea of the hidden meaning of knowledge and also to "backward" (*kinyume*) words and acts.[14] The names of the special kind of women's cloth called *kanga* represent another way of speaking one's heart while at the same time remaining silent. Wearing kanga cloths may also allow women to communicate about sex in an appropriate and discreet way.[15] The kanga bear messages in Swahili and the messages are said to be the "name" (*jina*) of the kanga, like: "A loving heart has no patience" (*Moyo wa kupenda hakuna subra*) or "Stop with your hatred; I will not eat at your place" (*Komeni na chuki zenu mimi sili kwenu*). Kanga are worn by women in their immediate neighborhoods within Stone Town as well as in Ng'ambo. Kanga names are considered when offered as gifts and, moreover, referred to in situations where someone wishes to communicate a particular message. On most occasions women seriously consider which saying to "wear" in relation to whom they expect to meet, where they are going, and whom they want to confront. Others will notice and read the name of the kanga worn as well as who are present and the way they relate to each other and make their own deductions concerning the messages conveyed. The names of some kanga are formulated in response to the names of other kanga. Still, because messages are not explicitly uttered but only worn, nobody is openly challenged and no relationships are publicly exposed. It is again the one who reads and, potentially, reacts who in the end "suffers the meaning" of the message, especially if its reading leads to an action or reaction. Before entering a discussion of the songs, I shall present some points referring to the interpretations of text and performance.

TEXTS, ENACTMENTS, AND MEANING

Ritual, enactments, puns, irony, and songs are significant means of communication, production, and transfer of knowledge as well as of negotiation and contestation of social life in Swahili society. This has been shown by several scholars of Swahili society[16] as well as in other African societies.[17] Examining these forms of communication with the aim to explore aspects of society means that performance and text are not only seen to represent an already constituted ideological viewpoint. Rather, performance and textual meanings are creative and as such form part of what produces society while at the same time being produced by society. Exploring such contexts may enhance an understanding of how people view and represent society to themselves, how they perceive and debate norms and practices, while also taking into account the social context within which such forms are created and deployed. Speech act theory reminds us about the need to question what a speaker is doing in uttering certain words because what the performer is doing is indeed part of the social realm. This implies that performative acts and their context should be approached as social arenas where knowledge of society is both created and communicated between people.[18]

The messages of the texts sung at two different but related ritual events—the initiation ritual unyago wa kutapisha and the wedding—are, I argue, formulated more in accordance with the way in which the different contexts are perceived—one private arena and one public—than with experiences of gender, marriage, and sexuality more generally. The songs are neither found in the form of written texts nor composed in a fixed form. They are produced, memorized, and reproduced in more or less revised versions. During one of my early stays in the field, I was initiated in unyago wa kutapisha and later I had the opportunity to participate briefly in unyago wa kusinga and unyago wa ngoma. Over the years I have participated in numerous weddings in different communities. Within the ritual settings, I have never found myself in a situation where I could write down songs or any other information nor have I insisted on the use of a tape recorder. However, outside the ritual context, women would sing and recite songs for me, which I would then write down. In these particular settings, there would usually be three or four women present who would comment on the songs, often reminding and correcting each other. They were discussed in Swahili while I took notes. Many of the words used were unfamiliar to me, especially words used in the unyago repertoire. Whenever I looked puzzled and asked them about the meaning of certain words or phrases, women would carefully explain to me in Swahili the meaning of those words or phrases. Afterward, I translated them into English. In certain cases, I would confirm my English translations with women whom I knew had a good command of both Swahili and English. Inspired by Karin Barber, I have chosen to explore the songs as a form of text that may disclose notions and practices not otherwise made explicit.[19] The meanings of songs, texts, and performances are not self-evident. To grasp the meaning of songs or texts involves, "not merely a problem of information, but a problem of comprehension."[20] Songs, in line with other types of performance, require interpretations that can be conducted only with reference to a broader understanding of people and relationships and how these are constituted and experienced in other social arenas, events, and relationships. As I will show, performance may present differing messages at different phases of one single performance or also during performances that refer to one another.[21]

UNYAGO WA KUTAPISHA AND ITS SONGS

Being an initiation ritual, unyago wa kutapisha is understood to mark social puberty and to produce social, not physical, maturation.[22] These are private or exclusive occasions, only accessible for already initiated women in addition to the one to be initiated, the mwari. Whether it is unyago wa kutapisha or the more recent version of it called unyago wa kusinga or unyago wa harusi, the ritual takes place before the young woman's first marriage. But while unyago wa kutapisha should be performed outside in a deserted place over several days, the recent version is performed during a single evening inside a house and focuses only on sexual intercourse and on what are and are not acceptable sexual practices. The bride may, for instance, receive instructions by a somo and nyakanga in her bedroom while being adorned and prepared for the marriage ceremony (nikaha).[23]

There is a hierarchy of knowledge and thus ritual authority among initiated women where the ritual leader called nyakanga ranks first before the ritual expert, called the *kungwi*. During unyago the already initiated women dance while singing the particular songs known only to them. The mwari should, at this point, make an effort to memorize the songs by heart. While dancing, the mwari is requested to move in certain prescribed ways by the ritual leader (nyakanga), the ritual expert (kungwi), and other initiated women (warombo) present. They sanction her when she fails by tapping her with thin sticks (*fimbo*) on her legs while singing:

Fimbo ya kwanza, hewallah Bwana Juma	The first beat, by God, Bwana Juma,
Fimbo ya pili, hewallah Bwana Juma	The second beat, by God, Bwana Juma,
Fimbo ya tatu, hewallah Bwana Juma	The third beat, by God, Bwana Juma,
Bwana ananiumiza mtwana	Bwana is hurting me, the rascal.

The interpretation of this song provided by the women I worked with is that although sex is pleasurable for women, there are limits to what a woman could accept from her husband. She should, they say, not accept sex to the extent of feeling pain; intercourse must not harm her physically. In local parlance, the expression *hewallah* (from Arabic *wallah* and Swahili *wallahi*) is often pronounced either in connection with a positive surprise or in order to underscore one's modesty even when confronted with something unpleasant. By including the term *hewallah* (by God), the song confirms not only the significance of sexual pleasure within Islamic marriage (Erin Stiles, this volume), but also the importance of respect and modesty. In terms of prohibitions and pleasures, the mwari is instructed not to turn her husband away but rather to respond to his approaches.[24] Yet she is also told that a good man should not exaggerate his sexual advances to the point where penetration hurts. The stick (fimbo) can thus be interpreted as a metaphor for the man's penis.

During her initiation, the mwari has to pass through a series of trials, all supposed to enhance her understanding concerning matters of sexuality, fertility, and reproduction. Even so, she will understand, women explain, only if she is already motivated or able to ask questions about the meaning of the various trials or teachings she is being exposed to, which are here referred to as *mizungu*. Through dance movements called *kukata kiuno* women express sensuality and pleasure and, at times, imitate sexual intercourse. Additionally, the mwari is supposed to learn about fertility and reproduction through various ordeals, exposure to certain paraphernalia, and their secret names. Women hold that a mwari would never be able to realize the full meaning of the songs and teachings during the initiation itself. After her initiation a mwari has access to knowledge about adult life and thus about sexual relations. Still nothing regarding the teaching received will be explained to her by the ritual leader, the expert, her somo, and the other initiated women if she does not ask relevant questions. The idea is that later, after having participated in the unyago of other young women and having gained in experience and practical engagements with other women and men, she will eventually grasp the genuine meaning of the unyago teachings. What is learned then will mature and can only make sense to her in all its wealth through repetition and with the outcome of lived experience.

Having been initiated, a woman becomes a member of the unyago group. From then on she can participate in unyago and may potentially become a ritual expert. A ritual leader told me, "Life will teach her and make her understand, while the initiation can only expose her to that which lies ahead of her." Below, I present two songs expressing the problem of gender, sexuality, and adult life more generally.

Kuota mvi si utu uzima	To grow gray hair is not old age,
Kungoka meno si utu uzima	To lose teeth is not old age,
Huyu mashine iwe nzima	[As long as] this one [your] machine is working.

According to the women I have worked with, this song celebrates women's sexuality and conveys that old age is not a question of physical maturity but of whether you remain sexually active or not. It emphasizes the importance of acknowledging one's sexual desires. I was told that the message of the song is that being sexually active and celebrating your sexuality is what makes you alive. In terms of prohibition, the song implicitly tells women never to ignore the pleasure of sexual desires. Subsequently, I shall discuss how the meaning conveyed through this song relates to a wedding song saying that a problem of women is that they avoid too much intimacy with their husbands. Yet another wedding song also conveys that avoiding sexual intimacy would be wrong, for the sake of the husband's desires. Even so, the unyago song below describes a woman wanting her pleasure, scolding a man for not making love with her.

Mavuzi yangu nimeyanyoa	I have removed all hairs,
Na kuma yangu nikaisuguwa	I have cleaned my cunt,
Kumbe ni hanisi sikumtambuwa	Gosh, I didn't realize that he's a homosexual.
Wacha kukoroma babu,	Stop snoring, old man,
Wacha kukoroma babu,	Stop snoring, old man,
utombe kuma,	Fuck the cunt.
Kila nikimwita	Every time I call him,
Ananyamaza kimya	He remains silent.
Chukua mapumbu kayaweke nyuma	Pick up your balls and place them behind.
Wacha kukoroma babu	Stop snoring come, old man,
ulitombe kuma	Have intercourse
Kichinichini nake, kichinichini nake	This small thing, this small thing,
Nilidhani mboo,	I thought you had a penis.
Kumbe mswaki	Lo and behold, it is a toothbrush.

In this song, addressed to a man or to his penis, a woman complains because the man or his penis sleeps while she wants to make love. Thus the song presents the woman as sexually active while the man is the one who is trying to escape the woman's approaches or is without desire. Realizing that the man is not interested or able, the woman criticizes the man. She ridicules him for being indolent and for the size of his penis, and therefore his inability to please her. The song presents an image of a sexually active and desiring woman in contrast to a sexually uninterested man—an image that again, as will be discussed below, opposes the one presented in the wedding where the man is considered the sexually active one. The unyago song illustrates a man not able or willing to satisfy a woman.

Songs performed during unyago could be said to represent women's point of view or one among several approaches to sexuality held by women. During unyago the teachings focus on women being sexually active and embodying sexual pleasures. The teachings also encompass representations of pleasure in sexual relations. Women are portrayed as active and demanding, different from their depiction in the songs performed in the weddings I have attended. In one of the wedding songs, as I will later illustrate, it is said that one of women's defects is that they will try to avoid sexual intimacy with their husbands. Still, in the unyago song cited above it is rather men's sexuality and their ability to provide pleasure that is questioned. The song thus indicates that women may actually experience a husband's inability to satisfy them. Again, it is the pleasure of sexuality and the problem of sexual passivity that are emphasized. The song cited above does not explicitly focus on prohibition, but it does talk about sexual desire and the problem of not being sexually satisfied.

While exploring the differing content of women's songs during unyago and wedding celebrations, I emphasize that unyago constitutes learning for and by initiated women, without implying that it concerns all women or that even all women involved in unyago actually live and act according to these teachings. Thus, what is conveyed during unyago should be seen to represent one among various understandings about gender and sexuality. Let me now turn to wedding songs and see the way they illustrate and represent gender and sexuality in this more public, social arena.

WEDDING SONGS AND NOTIONS OF MARRIAGE

For women and men in Zanzibar Town, a first marriage is a public marking of change in status and social positioning, for the individuals in society and in social relationships at large. It is what enables them to enter into adulthood. Likewise, to marry and to have children is the aim of both women and men and the main concern of their families and relatives. The celebration of a first marriage—although relative to the involved families' economic standing—is a significant and elaborate event. At this point the bride is not expected to have experienced any intimate relationship with a man. Even if initiated in unyago she would still, ideally, have received only teachings. The expectation is that, still lacking in experience, she would not yet have understood the full meaning of the received teachings. The bride's somo would, nevertheless, have provided her with more specific information about the forthcoming intercourse and the importance of virginity. In the wedding as in unyago it is women who teach women about morality, respectability, sexuality, and reproduction and thus women, not men, who through their teachings are responsible for the conduct of women.[25] In this sense women are in this society both controlling and controlled—a dimension that is silenced in dominant gender norms where only men's authority is emphasized. This latter view on the position ascribed to women and men is, for instance, reflected linguistically in how the act of marrying and divorcing is grammatically to be formulated either in the active or passive form according to the gender of the subject. While a man marries (*anaoa*), a woman is married (*anaolewa*); while a man divorces (*anaacha*), a woman is divorced (*anaachwa*).

The various songs performed for the bride by women during weddings I have attended emphasize a wife's expected admiration for and generosity toward her husband. Moreover, the songs often portray a husband's strong sexual desires. Representations of women's sexual desire and activity seem absent in these songs. This is in contrast to the unyago songs presented above, where women's sexual desire and activity is in focus. Let me now provide examples of three songs I have heard performed for the bride in several weddings.

Mwari usiwache ufunguo	Mwari, do not lose the key,
Ukiacha ufunguo	If you do lose the key,
watachukua wenzio	The other women will steal it.
Mume ndugu ya muengeenge	A husband is similar to broken glass
kama kioo	like a mirror.
Amanallahu, amanah rasuli	*Amanallahu, amanah rasuli*[26]
Bismillahi ndiyo	"In the name of God" is indeed
ya kwanza ya kuondokea	the first [words] to be pronounced.

The song says that a woman should do her best in order to please her husband and make him feel comfortable. If not she may lose him to another woman—because, according to the song, men are fragile and easily seduced. The bride is reminded about the prohibition of resisting the husband because then he would be seeking sex outside marriage. Her pleasure, it is sung, can only be achieved if she makes him feel good. Furthermore, the bride is reminded about the importance of requesting God's protection. When having intercourse she should request God to protect the husband from committing adultery and, by implication, protect her own well-being.[27] The text of the song captures the way a relationship between wife and husband is commonly represented and reasoned with reference to East African Islam.[28] The instructions provided by this song could, however, also be understood in the context of the frequency of divorce in Zanzibar and, more generally, in Swahili societies. Given that divorce is relatively common, there is, in principle, no shame associated with being divorced either for women or men.[29] Yet it could be embarrassing for a wife if it becomes known that her husband is to divorce her for another woman. This would lead to gossip about the other woman being more attractive and that the wife is not able to satisfy her husband. Such rumors would make a wife feel ashamed. Thus, the song also emphasizes the importance of treating the husband with respect, flattering him, and, I was told, not openly opposing him. This message is linked to the idea that a man will be content and happy only if the woman manages to make him feel attractive and desirable. In the wedding song cited below the focus is precisely men's sexuality and the importance of satisfying a husband's sexual needs.

Kuna ila, ila ya mume,	One defect, the defect of a husband,
kila mara nipe nayo ila.	All the time, "Give me that [vagina or sex]," but . . .
Nyama yote ukanipa	All your "flesh" [slang for vagina] you give
kidogo kuonja	[only] a little to taste
Ila moja ya mwanamke,	One defect of a woman,
leo nimechoka ila,	"Today I am tired, but. . . . ,"
Ila moja ila ya mwanamke	One defect, the defect of a woman,
ila leo nimeumwa	"But today I am sick."

In this song the bride is told about men's strong sexual desires and their need for intimacy with their wives. Moreover the bride is informed that it is a mistake of women to make excuses in order to escape having sex with their husbands. Both constant sexual approaches from the husband and excuses made by women are said to be defects. My interpretation of this song addressed to the bride is, however, that the bride is told that her husband would constantly be in need of her. The bride is advised against what is here said to be the shortcoming of women, namely to use excuses in order to avoid sexual intimacy with the husband. This message could be interpreted as a prohibition in the sense that a wife should never refuse her husband's sexual advances. Besides the emphasis on pleasures and prohibition, the advice provided in this song is interesting in another way. The song expresses the idea that although men possess strong sexual desires, women do not. Still, it might be that the song is not questioning women's sexual pleasures but rather advising a bride to respond attentively to a husband's sexual approaches even in situations where she does not desire him or is not in the mood for intimacy; Stiles (this volume) also discusses how sexual satisfaction is perceived as an essential aspect of marriage. It is commonly understood that if a husband remains satisfied he will be kind to and provide well for his wife. By connecting the advice provided in this latter song to the previous one, it seems that brides, at least in weddings I have attended, receive the instruction that if they wish to keep their husbands they have to respond actively to their advances whatever the women may feel or wish. This is not necessarily advice about subordination, but about how to ensure that a husband will remain kind and generous.

The interpretations above are based on successive exchanges I have had over many years. In discussions about marriage, both married and divorced women and men often mention the importance of making men feel content and cared for. This requires, according to most women, that they make an effort to acquire special skills and competence. If, on the contrary, women wish to obtain a divorce it is said that they should start by ignoring the husband's needs. The idea is that in such cases men would soon look for another wife. One song sung to the bride during wedding preparations goes as follows:

Kidomo katiti kama kasiba	Small mouth, like a little round tube,
Mke siti mume haiba	The wife is a lady, the husband likable,
Atoaji watu muhadharani	[He is] the one who provides [her] permission to be in public.

Again, the song repeats the prohibition of contesting or quarrelling (being big mouthed) with the husband. Rather, the wife should keep a small, round mouth, uttering only sweet words. The women I worked with explain that if a wife has manners and behaves as a respectable and loving Muslim wife, she will ideally receive support and generosity from her husband. Only then will she be able to leave the house and be in public and thus participate in society.

It is difficult to say to what extent the teaching received during the wedding and unyago actually influence women's daily life practices and their relationships with their husbands and with other men. Nevertheless, my focus on the interconnection between pleasures and prohibitions and their positive moral implications reveals how the same moral ideals may be assigned different meanings in different relations and in various social arenas. If not opposed to each other, the messages of the songs presented above are, at least, divergent. While the songs I cited from unyago emphasize women's sexuality and pleasures, the wedding songs I presented focus on men's sexuality and needs and what women should refrain from doing in order to keep their husbands and protect a good marriage. The fact that the songs carry divergent meanings does not, however, imply that they contradict each other or that one is a subversion of the other. It might be that the messages are addressing different dimensions of the very same ideals and experiences, rather than being an expression of what may appear to be contradictions internal to society. There are, I insist, different versions of gender and sexuality.

While relatively dramatic political, economic, and social changes have taken place in Zanzibar during the last few decades, it seems that basic values related to gender and sexuality have proved rather resistant to change, a reflection also brought up by Pat Caplan in this volume. Notions about what it means to be a woman and a man and what is emphasized during the socialization of girls and boys have, in my experience, not changed much during the last thirty years, except, perhaps, by a recent importance ascribed to girls' formal education. Several virtues such as assiduity in religious devotion, formal and religious education, generosity to the poor, and hospitality are endorsed and said to be essential ideals for both genders. Simultaneously, from an early age, girls and boys are assigned different activities and positions. Much more than boys, girls are expected to be involved in domestic tasks and to care for younger children. Boys have more time than girls to spend outside playing with their age-mates. Important in this context is that in contrast to boys, girls in Zanzibar Town are continuously reminded about the significance of respectability and modesty and, as an extension, virginity and chastity.[30] This form of socialization into a gendered morality seems to be found in most Swahili societies. Similar observations are made throughout the Swahili coast by, for instance, Stiles in rural northern Unguja, Caplan on Mafia Island, and Farouk Topan with regard to Swahili societies more generally.[31]

Islam and the Qur'an are constitutive moral reference points for both women and men and thus in the socialization of children.[32] Besides the importance of attending Qur'anic school (*chuo,* or *madarasa*) and reading the Qur'an, rules, regulations and responsibilities, prohibitions, and pleasures are most of the time explained by referring to particular verses in the Qur'an, with reference to various passages in the hadith or simply by stating what is and is not considered acceptable behavior for a good Muslim. Regarding girls and young women's conduct, moral concerns are, as mentioned above, often expressed in relation to whether they act according to norms of shyness and shame (*haya*) and behave respectably (*kwa heshima*).[33] Men are equally exposed to moral evaluations, but not as systematically. Criticism concerning a lack of shyness, modesty, and respectability has an unquestionable negative effect on a woman's reputation, but not necessarily on that of a man. Approaching puberty, girls are constantly reminded about these ideals. Contrary to the current importance ascribed to girls' education, I observed and heard complaints regarding a number of them leaving school. This practice tends to be explained with reference to the idea of sex segregation and a protection against what, in this period in life, is seen as potential threats in arenas where genders are mixed. Although just as many boys drop out of school, the observance of sex segregation is mainly perceived to be girls' and women's responsibility, and from early puberty girls are repeatedly commented upon if they are seen in the company of boys. Gradually it seems that gestures and movements marking distance from, or avoidance of, any explicit contact with boys or men become more or less internalized.

Sex segregation is a distinctive value shared by women and men in Zanzibar Town, although no emphasis is placed on purdah in the sense of concealing women from men and vice versa. Sex segregation is mainly managed through an organization of social space, of the material environment, division of labor, and through gestures, manners of avoidance, and clothing.[34] Regarding clothing, the headscarf (*mtandio*) or the hijab are important and for adult women the garment called *buibui* plays a significant role in protecting their respectability, making them sexually inaccessible while moving outside "in front of people" (*mbele ya watu*). Women would often say that without their buibui they feel as if they are naked (*kama uchi*) when in public. Nakedness can have different connotations. The sense of being naked can mean that a person feels that the body or intimate aspects of their personhood are exposed. It may also mean that women, as in this case, perceive that without their buibui not only their body but also their clothes and carried goods would be exposed. In the urban area women often put on a buibui on top of, for instance, their kanga, when moving beyond their immediate neighborhoods. Sometimes they would also wear kanga so as to cover their head and shoulders—that is, as a shawl. Women's modesty seems to be a constant matter of concern for both women and men. By implication this means that their sexuality in its apparent yet silent, or "veiled," form remains a constant point of concern with regard to both the meaning and formation of social relations—between women and men, among women themselves, and in particular among women belonging to different age groups (*rika*). Women's sexual attractiveness and pleasure should never be a focus of public attention and therefore should not be exposed in public. Yet in urban areas attention is indeed paid by both women and men to women's elegance, sensuality, and beauty through bodily movements, fragrances, clothing, and decoration. In addition to forming part of feminine aesthetics, refinement in conduct and appearance also conveys something about the relationship between women and men: the aesthetics, in its turn, signal whether a woman is well provided for and thus appreciated by her husband. Aesthetics is here involved in the enactment, contestation, and negotiation of gender and sexuality.

Ideally speaking, men are represented by both women and men in terms of being providers and heads of households, including holding authority in relation to wives and children and for their unmarried sisters. In one of the wedding songs cited above, the bride is told to be attentive in order not to lose her husband to other women. In my understanding, the importance of not losing the husband is partly linked to his role as a provider and head of the household. "A husband is medicine (*Mume ni dawa*), Amina, a divorced woman in her late forties, told me. She continued by explaining that while being divorced is not in itself a problem for a woman, it may easily lead to problems both economically and socially. "Living alone you would still be considered respectable," Amina explained, "but it becomes difficult because you are without the respect and (moral) authority (*heshima na uwezo*) of a husband as well as even the minimal economic support." More generally, women and men argue that men ought to hold authority in the household and family and that women should respect the authority of men. They add, however, that this is only possible if the husband is ensuring the well-being of his wife and children. Still, most women, whether divorced, widowed, or still married usually run small enterprises (*biashara ya pesa ndogo*) in order to earn their living, including the preparation and selling of food from the house or to restaurants, tailoring, and flower decorations. According to both Islamic teachings and more general understandings along the Swahili coast, women's property includes their jewelry, household goods received when married (*vyombo*), everything acquired through their own work, or property inherited, like coconut palms, fruit trees, and land.[35] Moreover, in terms of daily experience it is clear that women who have been divorced or widowed often become heads of households and form new relationships without formally seeking the consent of a father, uncle, or brother. Thus women's social, political, and economic activities are recognized. This recognition, together with the fact that many adult women are breadwinners, means that the normative gender representations are constantly being challenged by experience. Still, the ideals are certainly perpetuated.

From time to time, women would emphasize in conversation that a marriage followed by a divorce is what eventually provides some escape from social scrutiny, an escape that, as Elisabeth McMahon shows in her chapter in this volume, has historical roots. Women often say that when divorced they can move about and interact with other women and men without being morally questioned in the way young, unmarried, or even still married women are. I am time and again told sentiments similar to this one: "Before being married you have no freedom (*uhuru*), after having been married it becomes better, if you are divorced you have your freedom" (*Kabla ya kuolewa huna uhuru kabisa, baada ya kuolewa hujambo, na ukiachwa unapata uhuru wako*). *Freedom* is, however, a problematic term. Unmarried women are under the authority of elder women (sisters, mother, aunts, and grandmothers) as well as male relatives. What they refer to in this case is that after having been married a woman escapes some of the authority of her own natal family. Talking about how in the wake of marriage and divorce they gain "freedom," women acknowledge that with age they will be assigned responsibilities and are expected to make decisions about how to organize their life and relationships. To most women, nevertheless, it seems that remarrying and thus living again with a husband is socially and emotionally perceived to be the most favorable situation. Most women perceive that sexual activity should form part of women's and men's life—and this, preferably, within the context of marriage, although the presence of lovers is far from unknown.[36] Still, unmarried, divorced, or widowed women would not easily expose their intimate relationships publicly, because that would easily provoke "talk" (*maneno*) about them behaving like prostitutes (*malaya*) or, at least being morally loose (*wahuni*). In this sense they face a number of restrictions in their daily lives. It seems rather difficult to maneuver within the field of adult courtship and chastity. Women convey different ways and strategies of avoiding compromising situations. In their fear of being gossiped about they usually make a point of not being seen with any man. Yet avoiding male friends and cultivating only women friends would not necessarily be seen as a sign of their chastity. A few years back I was discussing what is perceived as the problem of "talk" (maneno; lit., words) or gossip with a woman I have known since I first started my fieldwork in Zanzibar Town. She said, "If you are divorced, like me, you are still seen as a respectable woman, but life is not easy. People easily talk. If you visit women friends or go out only with other women, they say that you are a lesbian. If you are with men, they claim that you are a prostitute [*malaya*]." Following from this exchange, I have paid some attention to this issue and on several occasions heard that adult women spending time with women are referred to as lesbians (*wasagaji*) by women and men alike.

This brief presentation of gender norms and practices suggest that the way relationships between women and men are portrayed in the context of unyago does not necessarily correspond to women's experiences in daily life, nor does the image presented in the context of weddings. This indicates how the very same prohibitions and pleasures may be comprehended and enacted differently in differing situations and relationships. They are open to interpretation and have to be accommodated according to the persons and values involved. Proclamations referring to moral ideals and abstractions do not necessarily mean that these are the main references for people's daily actions, relations, and concerns. Different kinds of restrictions are more or less open to adaptation according to a given context and to the persons and relations involved.

In the beginning of this chapter, I argued that in Zanzibar Town there is an appreciation of the ability to differentiate between private and public space. It includes awareness of what kind of practices, experiences, and knowledge are allowed to be openly stated and what should only be hinted at or even silenced in public. This delineation between private and public arenas supports the contention that there is no contradiction between what women express through the songs performed during weddings and unyago. One fact that may explain the difference in the messages would be that the bride's mother is present during the wedding and thus, in this context, there is less explicit emphasis on the bride's sexual pleasure. Nevertheless, both messages are equally significant and sincere. The above-mentioned divide could, however, be interpreted as a moral contradiction: one emphasizing women's sexuality and pleasures, the other focusing on women's responsibility of satisfying and comforting the husband. From such a reading the unyago teachings would be seen as subversions of the representations conveyed in wedding songs. Furthermore, because the content of the wedding songs are more in line with what women and men in Zanzibar Town usually present as the dominant Muslim, Swahili gender ideology, unyago teachings could easily be interpreted in terms of "ritual of rebellion," "tension release," or "protest."[37] However, when apprehended within a wider social and cultural context, the divergent messages expressed in the different social arenas should rather be seen to illustrate the range of knowledge and experience inherent in this society and, moreover, the level of sophistication characterizing moral discourses more generally. This understanding would be in line with Richard Rorty's argument that knowledge cannot be brought under a set of rules constituting a single system.[38] What may appear to be contradictions are not necessarily problems to be eliminated through rationalization. They rather constitute different messages or practices that actually make sense in relation to distinct social and performative contexts.[39] What women reveal in the context of unyago corresponds as much to their experience as does the content of the marriage songs. Interesting in this regard is Ivan Karp's study of women's marriage rituals among the Iteso in Kenya as performative action. Karp argues that the use of humor and irony allows the participants to assert different and contradictory messages about marriage.[40] Therefore the various contradictory voices should not, according to him, be understood in terms of subversion, but rather as different readings—an insight already conveyed by Victor Turner.[41] "If experience can be full of contradictions," Karp writes, "so can the comments made upon it in performance."[42] During unyago, riddles should be learned by heart as well as names of objects and actions associated with women's daily life tasks and activities. These objects include the mortar and pestle (*kinu na mchi*) and dishes (*vyombo vya nyumbani*), beads worn around the waist (*shanga*), and the white cotton cloth (*sodo*) that women used to wear during menstruation and to clean the husband's penis after intercourse. These objects are, however, in different ways associated with sexual intimacy and likewise the names or terms memorized mainly concern sexuality, reproduction, and fertility—encapsulating knowledge a woman could unfold only after having been exposed to married life. In contrast to a mwari, already initiated women are said to comprehend the complexity of sexual prohibitions having been exposed to married life.

Zanzibari women speak with many voices, being at once both controllers and controlled, performers and audience. Moreover, in many situations they may convey contradictory messages. This is a characteristic of ritual communication in a variety of societies.[43] In most cases these voices, contradictions, and paradoxes are equally incorporated in people's daily life experiences. As such, knowledge gained through unyago does not allow women to ignore the norms of public life represented in wedding songs. Yet according to contexts and to different forms and levels of knowledge, prohibitions may also be mitigated or reinterpreted. Knowledge perceived as a form of secrecy is potentially powerful precisely because it sustains possibilities and potentialities of transformation through reinterpretation of established orders. Knowledge transferred through hints, riddles, songs, and signs must be decoded; the messages deduced through a combination of curiosity, experience, contextualization, and interpretation. As already discussed, in Zanzibar there seems to be a more or less shared conception that things are never only what they appear or, what they are said to be. This involves a subtle dialectic between transmitted and acquired knowledge. Such an approach to learning encompasses a belief in the dynamics of disclosure and secrecy, revelation and concealment. It also opens up implicit contradictions and multiple moral messages, each seen as meaningful when explained in relation to a specific problem.

Teachings about sexuality and in this case womanhood are transferred in the distinctive relations of somo and mwari and mwari and the unyago group. The somo relation is an important one because it is the somo, not the mother, who takes the girl to her unyago and who, eventually, is responsible for the sexual well-being and performance of the bride after the wedding. The teachings and instructions received through these relationships— somo and unyago—are normative in the sense that certain skills and forms of conduct are, at this point in life, expected to be known by the young woman. This is expected by other women, her husband, and her husband's family. Women's knowledge about sexuality, sexual intimacy, and married life is evaluated on the basis of their conduct and their husbands' satisfaction. Of interest for the discussion here is that this kind of knowledge is transferred in settings and relationships characterized by trust and through oral discourse, song texts, riddles, and bodily imitation and practice. In this sense, the contexts of unyago and weddings do not entail fixed bodies of unambiguous instructions but rather teachings relating to specific relationships and experiences that, again, induce spaces for critical reflection and revision. Hence, what should be highlighted regarding unyago and wedding songs is not whether there is an authoritative and exclusive interpretation of them, but rather how the contexts and social relations involved are associated with a plurality of configurations and meanings in the public as well as in the private domain. Questioning which version of gender and sexuality captures the "women's version" could easily lead to another problem of ideological positioning. It seems clear that the instructions and teachings presented above complement and comment on the more normative ideology of gender and sexuality, but so do the experiences of daily life, for instance, when contrary to the idea that men are providers, women have to secure the household's income or when women, despite their efforts, are confronted with their husband's lack of interest and support. Thus in order to comprehend the complexity of gender and sexuality in this society, the various contexts and relations involved should be analyzed and combined.

PROHIBITIONS, PLEASURES, AND WAYS OF KNOWING

Ritual language is limited in comparison with ordinary spoken language and thus the dynamic interaction between text and context is crucial when it comes to meaning. Participants enter into ritual events with prior ideas, expectations, and experiences. The layers of meaning displayed in performance refer back to the context of everyday life in an inescapable and constitutive way.[44] In the same way, ritual knowledge enters into daily-life situations. Let me conclude with a brief illustration.

One afternoon, having gathered jasmine flowers, I wanted to give them to my friend Dada to take to her room. At the time of this particular incident she lived with her aunt, whom I have known for several years. Jasmine flowers are picked just before dusk, when the fragrance is at its strongest. This flower is used to fragrance women's clothes as well as beds and to clean and fragrance their skin. The smell of jasmine flowers is said to enhance sensuality and to attract the husband's attention. Scent is intimately intertwined with desire and allure, as Thompson and Rebecca Gearhart show in this volume. At that time Dada was only fifteen years old and still a mwari. Her aunt immediately told me, "You want to expose her to jasmine flowers? She does not understand their meaning; she is only a mwari." Dada's aunt criticized me for exposing Dada to the effect of jasmine when she had not yet been taught the meaning and use of the flowers and their fragrance. At this point in a girl's life, exposure to what concerns sexuality and sexual intimacy is, according to normative views, considered harmful. It is prohibited. In such situations shame (aibu) is ascribed to those who are responsible for a girl's upbringing and education—her somo and the immediate circle of adult women. However, in this case, where I impulsively wanted to introduce Dada to the jasmine flower, the aunt prevented the potential damage. Still, she scolded me for my thoughtlessness.

This incident underlines how perceptions of sexuality and gender, along with references to the significance of learning transferred in ritual contexts, are brought into and activated in daily life. Both weddings and unyago place women equally as "knowers" and controllers of behavior regarding pleasures and prohibitions. In fact, women are the main producers of these social arenas and their meanings. What is communicated in both wedding and unyago songs no doubt refers to moral ideals and prohibitions. Still, the songs are performed in different social arenas and therefore the messages are formulated in accordance with these different contexts: one focuses on sexuality in terms of prohibitions while the other emphasizes its pleasures. Perceptions of a private-public dimension are significant in the organization of space and conduct and thus of morality in this society. It also means that the very same prohibitions are differently perceived according to contexts and other relationships.

Exploring prohibitions in the light of knowledge shows how the character of the acts and the relations they imply can change as a person moves through life, gains access to learning and experience, and thus obtains different social and moral positions. Particular forms of learning seem to allow for alternative interpretations of certain kinds of pleasures and prohibitions and, moreover, appear to accommodate different readings of, for instance, the meaning of gender and sexuality. Following this, the presence of prohibitions are understood to protect those who lack knowledge or are not yet seen to have reached an adequate understanding or maturity to receive learning about how life and relationship are meant to be lived—and by implication, not yet appropriate to ensure reproduction of a particular moral order. Situations and practices entail implicit claims about what to know and when to know it. Knowledge here is meaningfully potent as well as a potential source of disruption. Having access to both wedding and unyago teachings, and the personal relationships involved, women comprehend and control the multifaceted meaning of the existing prohibitions concerning sexuality, including their inherent pleasures. In such a venture, social life is at the same time a complex set of contradictions, of pleasures and prohibitions best understood as relative to contexts and existing relationships.

Recently, women of my acquaintance have begun to worry because many of the most prominent unyago experts are aging. Responding to this situation, they have currently started to bring girls to unyago wa kutapisha or unyago wa mwari at the age of only eight or nine years. The young girls are able to learn, they say, because they are not yet shy like those who are between fifteen and seventeen years old. Once when attending a small wedding celebration in a private home, lasting only one afternoon and evening, some young girls between six and eight, suddenly danced in ways particular to unyago wa kutapisha. Zakia, a woman in her early fifties, looked surprised and asked their aunt whether the girls were actually already initiated. This was confirmed and a discussion started among several women who had gathered in the kitchen. The mother of two of the girls said, "They will learn and they will get accustomed to it" (*watajua na watazoea*). Others agreed with her view. Khatija explained that it was crucial to transfer "the authentic unyago knowledge" (*unyago hasa*) to the very young girls because soon the old women would be gone and there would be nobody left to teach them. She said, "When the old people have left this world, nobody will be able to teach and to have the initiation done. The knowledge will be lost" (*Watu wazima watakapoondoka duniani, hakuna atakayeweza kufundisha au kuchezewa. Maarifa itakuwa hayapo*). There seems, however, to be an ongoing discussion concerning whether it is appropriate to initiate girls into unyago wa kutapisha at this young age. Nevertheless, most women tend to agree that girls are able to use what they learn from the dance movements, riddles, and songs and from the particular etiquette and hierarchy through which initiated women relate to each other. Furthermore, young girls are openly praised for their ability to keep secret what they learn during the ritual. However, it is still unclear to me whether the meaning of unyago is maintained or transformed through teaching young girls.

Through what is still considered to be the proper unyago version, sexual prohibitions are taught and pleasures are celebrated. It is, however, time and again emphasized that these teachings should not be exposed in front of other people—because then the moral order of society could be threatened. On another level, such exposure could also put at stake the honor of those involved and the value of their relationships. Prohibitions are complex phenomena precisely because they are situated in specific social and ideological contexts.[45] Those explored in this chapter refer to acts of restrictions and avoidance and concern sexuality and the formation of gender within a particular moral system. My aim here has, however, been to illustrate how prohibitions as well as pleasures carry positive moral implications by granting value to the person in terms of what she or he does and refrains from doing. It is therefore crucial to address the practical interpretations and implications of prohibitions and their inherent pleasure within the context of a particular social and cultural universe. Only then may we understand the way in which prohibitions are practiced in order to reverberate positively back on persons and relationships.

NOTES

1. Kjersti Larsen, "Fastens materialitet: Ramadan som bemerkelsesverdig begivenhet på Zanzibar," *Norsk antropologisk tidsskrift* 3–4 (2011): 208–23.

2. Kjersti Larsen, *Unyago: Fra jente til kvinne,* Oslo Occasional Papers in Social Anthropology 22, 1990; Larsen, "Morality and the Rejection of Spirits: A Zanzibari Case," *Social Anthropology* 6, no. 1 (1998): 61–75; Larsen, "Knowledge, Astrology and the Power of Healing in Zanzibar," *Journal des africanistes* 72, no. 2 (2002): 175–86; Larsen, *Where Humans and Spirits Meet: The Politics of Rituals and Identified Spirits in Zanzibar,* Social Identities 5 (New York: Berghahn Books, 2008).

3. Larsen, *Unyago.*

4. Margaret Strobel, *Muslim Women in Mombasa, Kenya, 1890–1975* (New Haven: Yale University Press, 1979).

5. Pat Caplan, "Boys' Circumcision and Girls' Puberty Rites among the Swahili of Mafia Island, Tanzania," *Africa: Journal of the International African Institute* 46, no. 1 (1976): 21–33; Lena Eile, *Jando: The Rite of Circumcision and Initiation in East African Islam* (Lund: Plus Ultra,

1990); Larsen, *Unyago;* John Middleton, *The World of the Swahili: An African Mercantile Civilization* (New Haven: Yale University Press, 1992).

6. Caplan, "Boys' Circumcision"; Larsen, *Unyago;* Eile, *Jando.*

7. Larsen, *Unyago;* Kjersti Larsen, "The Other Side of Nature: Expanding Tourism, Changing Landscapes and Problems of Privacy in Urban Zanzibar," in *Producing Nature and Poverty in Africa,* ed. Vigdis Broch-Due and Richard A. Schroeder (Uppsala: Nordiska Afrikainstitutet, 2000).

8. Larsen, "Other Side of Nature."

9. Katrina Daly Thompson, "How to Be a Good Muslim Wife: Women's Performance of Islamic Authority during Swahili Weddings," *Journal of Religion in Africa* 41, no. 4 (2011): 427–48; Thompson, "Learning to Use Swahili Profanity," chap. 6, this volume.

10. Larsen, *Unyago;* Kjersti Larsen, "Kunnskap, kjønnsidentitet og sosial endring: Ulike former for kunnskap i Zanzibar Town," *Norsk antropologisk tidsskrift,* 1993; Larsen, "Other Side of Nature."

11. Michael Lambek, "Taboo as Cultural Practice among Malagasy Speakers," *Man* 27, no. 2 (1992): 245–66; Michel Foucault, *The History of Sexuality* (New York: Vintage Books, 1990).

12. Kjersti Larsen, "Dialogues between Humans and Spirits: Ways of Negotiating Relationships and Moral Order in Zanzibar Town, Zanzibar," in *The Power of Discourse in Ritual Performance: Rhetoric, Poetics, Transformations,* ed. Ulrich Demmer and Martin Gaenszle, Performances 10 (Berlin: LIT Verlag, 2007).

13. James W. Fernandez and Mary Taylor Huber, eds., *Irony in Action: Anthropology, Practice, and the Moral Imagination* (Chicago: University of Chicago Press, 2001).

14. Katrina Daly Thompson, "Zanzibari Women's Discursive and Sexual Agency: Violating Gendered Speech Prohibitions through Talk about Supernatural Sex," *Discourse and Society* 22, no. 1 (January 2011): 3–20.

15. Thompson, "Good Muslim Wife."

16. T. O. Ranger, *Dance and Society in Eastern Africa, 1890–1970: The Beni Ngoma* (London: Heinemann Educational, 1975); Strobel, *Muslim Women in Mombasa;* Susan Geiger, "Women in Nationalist Struggle: TANU Activists in Dar es Salaam," *International Journal of African Historical Studies* 20, no. 1 (1987): 1–26; Larsen, *Unyago;* Larsen, "Morality and Rejection"; Larsen, *Where Humans and Spirits Meet;* Laura Fair, *Pastimes and Politics: Culture, Community, and Identity in Post-abolition Urban Zanzibar, 1890–1945* (Athens: Ohio University Press, 2002); Pat Caplan, "'Law' and 'Custom': Marital Disputes on Northern Mafia Island, Tanzania," *Understanding Disputes: The Politics of Argument,* ed. Caplan (Oxford: Berg, 1995), 203–22; Kelly M. Askew, *Performing the Nation: Swahili Music and Cultural Politics in Tanzania* (Chicago: University of Chicago Press, 2002); Askew, "As Plato Duly Warned: Music, Politics, and

Social Change in Coastal East Africa," *Anthropological Quarterly* 76, no. 4 (2003): 609–37.

17. Karin Barber, *I Could Speak until Tomorrow: Oriki, Women and the Past in a Yoruba Town,* International African Library 7 (Edinburgh: Edinburgh University Press for the International African Institute, 1991).

18. Johannes Fabian, *Power and Performance: Ethnographic Explorations through Proverbial Wisdom and Theater in Shaba, Zaire* (Madison: University of Wisconsin Press, 1990); Erin E. Stiles, "When Is a Divorce a Divorce? Determining Intention in Zanzibar's Islamic Courts," *Ethnology* 42, no. 4 (October 2003): 273–88.

19. Barber, *I Could Speak.*

20. Ibid., 21.

21. Ivan Karp, "Laughter at Marriage: Subversion in Performance," in *Transformations of African Marriage,* ed. David J. Parkin and David Nyamwaya, International African Seminars 3 (Manchester: Manchester University Press for the International African Institute, 1987); Larsen, *Unyago;* Larsen, *Where Humans and Spirits Meet.*

22. Larsen, *Unyago.*

23. Thompson, "Good Muslim Wife."

24. See also ibid.

25. Larsen, *Unyago;* Larsen, "Kunnskap, kjønnsidentitet."

26. This line is in Arabic. The literal meaning is "Trust is with God, trust is with the Prophet." Its figurative meaning is "From now on, what happens is between you and God, together with the Prophet."

27. See also Thompson, "Good Muslim Wife."

28. Pat Caplan, "Perceptions of Gender Stratification," *Africa: Journal of the International African Institute* 59, no. 2 (1989): 196–208; Erin E. Stiles, *An Islamic Court in Context: An Ethnographic Study of Judicial Reasoning* (New York: Palgrave Macmillan, 2009); Thompson, "Good Muslim Wife."

29. Larsen, *Unyago;* Larsen, *Where Humans and Spirits Meet;* Stiles, *Islamic Court.*

30. Larsen, *Unyago.*

31. Stiles, *Islamic Court;* Caplan, "Boys' Circumcision"; Farouk Topan, "From Mwana Kupona to Mwavita: Representations of Female Status in Swahili Literature," in *Swahili Modernities: Culture, Politics, and Identity on the East Coast of Africa,* ed. Patricia Caplan and Topan (Trenton: Africa World Press, 2004).

32. Larsen, "Fastens materialitet."

33. Larsen, "Dialogues."

34. Larsen, *Unyago.*

35. Pat Caplan, "Women's Property, Islamic Law and Cognatic Descent," in *Women and Property, Women as Property,* ed. Renée Hirschon (London: Croom Helm, 1983), 23–43; Stiles, *Islamic Court.*

36. Larsen, *Unyago.*

37. Max Gluckman, "Les rites de passage," in *Essays on the Ritual of Social Relations,* ed. Gluckman (Manchester: Manchester University Press, 1963); Gluckman, "Rituals of Rebellion in South-East Africa," in *Order and Rebellion in Tribal Africa,* ed. Max Gluckman (New York: Free Press of Glencoe, 1963); Ioan M. Lewis, *Religion in Context: Cults and Charisma* (Cambridge: Cambridge University Press, 1986).

38. Richard Rorty, *Philosophy and the Mirror of Nature* (Princeton: Princeton University Press, 1979).

39. Michel Leiris, *La langue secrète des Dogons de Sanga (Soudan français),* Travaux et Mémoires de l'Institut d'Ethnologie 50 (Paris: Institut d'Ethnologie, 1948).

40. Karp, "Laughter at Marriage."

41. Victor W. Turner, *The Forest of Symbols: Aspects of Ndembu Ritual* (Ithaca: Cornell University Press, 1967).

42. Karp, "Laughter at Marriage," 143.

43. Turner, *Forest of Symbols;* Bruce Kapferer, *A Celebration of Demons: Exorcism and the Aesthetics of Healing in Sri Lanka* (Bloomington: Indiana University Press, 1983); Karp, "Laughter at Marriage."

44. Barber, *I Could Speak.*

45. Jean Comaroff, *Body of Power, Spirit of Resistance: The Culture and History of a South African People* (Chicago: University of Chicago Press, 1985).

PART THREE

Defining Masculinity in Ritual and Marriage

EIGHT

Unsuitable Husbands

Allegations of Impotence in Zanzibari Divorce Suits

ERIN E. STILES

IN MY CONSIDERATION OF how marital dispute cases involving impotence claims are handled in an Islamic court in rural Zanzibar, I explore the way in which people in rural northern Unguja understand the legal ramifications of sexuality and the physical dimensions of marriage. In the court in which I conducted research, a wife's lack of sexual fulfillment, most commonly attributed to a claim of her husband's impotence, is generally regarded by the judge as grounds for divorce. Both lay people and legal professionals draw on their understandings that a satisfying sexual relationship is a necessary element of a marriage in determining when a woman can sue for divorce in court. However, as we shall see with the court cases I consider herein, taking a husband to court often results not in the judge's decision to dissolve the marriage but a husband's decision to divorce his wife unilaterally through repudiation. Therefore, a woman may decide to pursue an impotence claim in court not simply because she expects a favorable ruling but in order to encourage her husband to divorce her through repudiation. Throughout this chapter I draw contrasts and parallels to the workings of Islamic family courts elsewhere in the Indian Ocean region. In her chapter for this volume, Elisabeth McMahon similarly examines how women slaves and ex-slaves on colonial Pemba Island strategized about marriage and divorce.

In Zanzibar, Islamic courts have been an official part of the state legal system since 1985. The legal system of mainland Tanzania differs from Zanzibar in a few ways; on the mainland, there are no Islamic courts. The Islamic courts have jurisdiction over family law matters for all Muslim residents of Zanzibar; Muslims must take family law disputes to the Islamic courts, while non-Muslim Zanzibaris handle family law matters in civil courts. The primary Islamic courts hear cases concerning marriage, divorce, inheritance, and some child custody matters. Unlike many other states today that incorporate Islamic law into the legal system, Islamic law in Zanzibar is not codified. Therefore, procedural law in the Islamic courts, which concerns court proceedings, is regulated by the Zanzibari state, while substantive family law, which deals with rights and duties, is in the hands of the *kadhi*s. Kadhis (<Ar. *qadi*) are Islamic judges and base their decisions primarily on the Qur'an, the Sunna (the way of life of the Prophet Muhammad, which Muslims strive to emulate), and Shafi'i legal sources. The Zanzibari kadhis working today are Sunni and have generally been trained in the Shafi'i tradition, although some have told me they would reference another *madhhab* (Ar., school of legal thought) if necessary.

THE LAWS OF MARRIAGE

In rural Unguja, both lay people and legal professionals talk about a satisfying sexual relationship as an essential aspect of marriage. If a woman has a complaint about the sexual dimension of her relationship with her husband, she may phrase this euphemistically in a number of ways. For example, she might say that her husband *hana uwezo,* which can be translated as "he doesn't have the ability" or "he doesn't have the power." She might also say about him, *hafai* (he is not suitable; useless). Alternatively, she might simply refer to him as *mgonjwa* (a sick person). In courtroom discourse, lay people and legal professionals also often frame sexuality as a legal requirement of marriage and use legal euphemisms for sex. A woman with an impotence claim may describe this unfortunate situation using words indicating her legal right to a sexual relationship by telling the court, *sipati sheria zangu*. This phrase can be translated into English as "I'm not getting my rights" or "I'm not getting my legal due." The Swahili term *sheria* is derived the Arabic word *sharī'a*. In Swahili, however, the term *sheria* is used to refer to law of all types, religiously derived or otherwise. Thus, *sheria za dini* refers to religious law, and *sheria za kanuni* refers to state law. The term *sheria* is also used colloquially to refer to legally granted rights and duties, as in the rights and duties of a marital relationship. In Zanzibar, husbands are expected to provide many things to their wives, including a home, food, clothing, and money for incidentals. When they fail to provide, women may come to court to sue for adequate maintenance or claim lack of maintenance as grounds for divorce. In court, and in everyday discourse about marriage, women typically describe such claims as "I don't have a house to live in"; "My husband does not provide food"; or "I don't receive adequate clothing." However, in the courtroom, if a woman says simply *sipati sheria* (I don't get sheria), she is usually referring to lack of sexual activity within the marriage. A woman might also use more specific language by stating that she does not get *sheria za mke na mume* (the rights of a wife and husband) or *sheria za ndoa* (the rights or law of marriage).

In isolation, we cannot always assume that euphemisms such as *sheria* and *uwezo* reference sexuality, but in the context of the courtroom, it was clear to me and the court staff that a woman was discussing her sexual life. A woman would explain that she had been married for years but still had no children, for example, or would discuss how her husband had received treatment for an illness. Furthermore, the kadhi and clerks would follow up with questions about the marriage, the health of the husband, or whether there were children. Also, as will be evident in the following case studies, women were not making any formal claims against their husbands other than impotence. When women brought other claims against husbands, they were typically phrased in other ways. For example, although the phrase *hana uwezo* may be understood to refer to a lack of financial ability, women with financial claims against husbands did not use this term but rather detailed where a husband was falling short by specifying that she did not have a house to live in, that the house was unsound, or that she was not provided with adequate food or clothing.

In court, the kadhi and the clerks often used similar legalistic terminology. I will call the kadhi with whom I worked most Sheikh Hamid; I also use pseudonyms for the other individuals named in this chapter. Although only a handful of Sheikh Hamid's cases involved claims of impotence or lack of sexual fulfillment, he often made it clear to litigants and those coming in to seek informal advice that this was a necessary part of an Islamic marriage. To one husband, for example, Sheikh Hamid instructed, "You are required to follow sheria za ndoa—the law of marriage. Do you understand? This means that you have to satisfy your wife." Similarly, in his frequent written rulings that required a disputing husband and wife to attempt reconciliation, he might order a husband to "sleep at home with your wife in order to fulfill the sheria of marriage." As we shall see, he reasoned that lack of sexual fulfillment would be grounds for divorce. However, although Sheikh Hamid considered impotence or lack of sexual fulfillment (or both) grounds for divorce, he rarely had to rule on this matter.

Other Islamic courts and Islamic scholars in East Africa, as well as in other times and places, have similarly understood impotence as grounds for divorce.[1] Writing about divorce in Zanzibar in the early twentieth century, Harold Ingrams notes that impotence was considered a valid reason for divorce among Sunni Muslims, but it is not clear if he saw it used as grounds for divorce in Zanzibari practice.[2] Jurists from all Sunni madhhabs have contended that impotence or lack of consummation of marriage is grounds for divorce. Significantly, this has most often been because of the absence of sexual fulfillment, an essential dimension of marriage, and not the impossibility of procreation.

In her work on eighteenth-century Hanafi Ottoman courts, for example, the historian Judith Tucker finds that impotence was indeed considered grounds for the annulment, although a woman had to testify that she was still a virgin after a full year of marriage. She observes that "all discussion of sex in these cases by judges referenced sexual desire, not procreation."[3] A more contemporary example that illustrates similar reasoning about the purpose of marriage is explained by Vardit Rispler-Chaim, in her examination of a 1990s fatwa from Kuwait.[4] A woman asked the mufti (an expert in Islamic law) if she could divorce because of her husband's sterility. In the fatwa (<Ar.; legal opinion), the mufti reasoned that sterility was not grounds for divorce on its own—particularly if the husband could still perform sexually. Again, marriage was not solely about procreation but also sexual fulfillment. However, the mufti in this case also reasoned that if the woman grew to despise her husband because of his sterility, then she could divorce by compensating him financially; this is in reference to the type of Islamic divorce known as *khul'* (Ar.).

RESEARCH LOCATION AND METHODOLOGY

This chapter is based on data I collected during approximately twenty months of ethnographic research in Zanzibar in four research trips between 1999 and 2008. Research was conducted in a rural Islamic court on the island of Unguja and in the surrounding community. The court in which I worked most is in the village of Mkokotoni, about one hour's drive north of Zanzibar Town on the western side of the island, well known for a thriving fish market. The Mkokotoni court has jurisdiction over a region of over one hundred thousand people, most of whom subsist by farming, fishing, and engaging in small business or the informal economy, although some work in tourism or in professional capacities as teachers and government workers. Although parts of northern Unguja are densely populated, most people live in villages clustered together in the lush farming areas in the west or along the eastern coastal strip; there are no large towns. Many people in the region describe themselves as Watumbatu, referring to what is locally understood to be one of the original ethnic groups of

Unguja. Sheikh Hamid was from the island called Tumbatu, which is just north of Mkokotoni and is reachable only by boat.

When I conduct research in the area, I live in a village I call Kinanasi, which is about three kilometers from Mkokotoni by road. Villages in this region may consist of a few houses or several hundred, and because the area is so densely populated, it is perhaps easier to think of villages as neighborhoods within the larger political unit known as a *shehia,* which normally consists of between three and six thousand people in northern Unguja. Some of the villages, like Kinanasi, line the main road north. Others are situated far off the main roads and are reachable only by foot or bicycle.

Most people in this part of Unguja live in modest houses of coral brick, concrete, or wattle and daub; roofing is typically of tin or thatch. Most people are of very modest means; few houses have electricity, and I knew no one who owned a car and only one or two men who owned a Vespa. However, many men owned Chinese-made bicycles; when women rode bicycles, it was nearly always as the passenger of a man. Litigants would come to court by bicycle, on foot, or by the *gari ya abiria* (passenger vehicles) that sped along the roads during daylight hours.

In court, my research methods consisted of observation and occasional participant-observation; semistructured, unstructured, and informal interviews; and the analysis of court-produced documents, such as plaintiffs' claims, defendants' counterclaims, and judicial rulings. Out of court, my research methods included a household census, participant-observation in all manner of daily activities and special events; and unstructured and informal interviews. All research was conducted in Swahili; all court proceedings were in Swahili and all court documents were written in Swahili, save occasional citations of Arabic sources (such as the Qur'an, hadith reports of what the Prophet Muhammad said and did, and legal literature) in Arabic. I was not permitted to tape-record court sessions and so took careful notes on a laptop; as a result, I do not have full transcriptions of court proceedings. However, I was fortunate to work with a generous judge and court staff, who often stopped court proceedings to explain points to me and to make sure I was following along. I was permitted to copy court documents, and they are included in this chapter in both the original Swahili and my English translations.

SEXUALITY, MARRIAGE, AND DIVORCE IN NORTHERN UNGUJA

In rural Unguja the importance of the sexual dimension of marriage is stressed not only in court but also in everyday discourse. Many chapters in this book, as well as the research of other scholars, have addressed the nature of the sexually relevant instruction a young woman receives before her first marriage, which has been and remains quite widespread in various forms along the Swahili coast, including northern Unguja.[5] During my fieldwork, as a woman (and at that time unmarried), I was not privy to the conversations of men about such topics, but I was generally able to participate in married-women's activities, and I found that married-women's songs, banter, talk, and performance are clear indicators of the cultural importance of a robust sexuality in marriage.

Ideally, a Zanzibari woman will be a virgin at her first marriage, and the cultural definition of bride as virgin shapes women's wedding activities. Of course, not all brides are virgins, and some women become pregnant before marriage. Although this is regarded as regrettable in rural Unguja, it was not generally considered a disaster but simply viewed as something that is bound to happen when young women and men mature. This is a contrast to what Nadine Beckmann reports from her research in Zanzibar Town, where she observed that extramarital sexuality is sharply condemned.[6]

As a virgin, a bride needs instruction in the sexual dimensions of marriage. At puberty, a girl becomes known as a *mwari*. Here, the term is used to refer to a girl who is physically mature and is theoretically considered to be marriageable; however, most young women do not marry until many years later, when they have finished their schooling. The term *mwari* may be used differently elsewhere on the Swahili coast; John Middleton, for example, writes that *mwari* refers to a young woman who is betrothed and thus has begun a process of initiation.[7] In northern Unguja, a mwari should not wear makeup, use henna, or attend weddings. Ideally, she should be neat, quiet, and modest. Of course, many girls do not meet this ideal, and I have seen girls teased or lightly scolded for being untidy or boisterous. Once she becomes a mwari, girls are assigned a somo. This is an older female relative or a friend of her mother, who is responsible for teaching her about the physical changes of puberty and how to care for herself.[8] Eventually, this instruction will include her sexual education, which begins in earnest before her first marriage and may extend to the wedding night itself, since a somo may supervise the first few days of marital intercourse.[9]

Also, because of the provocative nature of married women's dances, songs, and playfulness at weddings, young unmarried women are discouraged from attending weddings. They have not "tasted the stew," as one woman phrased it, and thus should not be exposed to the antics of sexually active married women; elsewhere in this volume, Beckmann also notes that food metaphors are a common way to describe sex. However, the situation changes as soon as a young woman is married. Once she has joined the coterie of sexually active women by marrying, she can—without judgment—wear makeup, use henna, and participate in joyful banter, play, and teasing about sexual matters. I have observed marked contrasts in the public demeanor of newly married women, even after only a day or two of being married. I recall one young woman, perhaps twenty-one years old, flirting and joking with a man old enough to be her grandfather days after marriage; before that, her interactions with the older man had been much more reserved.

As the chapters in this volume by Kjersti Larsen and Katrina Thompson show, much sexual instruction for a young woman focuses on how she can please her husband. However, as we shall see in the cases discussed below, litigants and the court staff also view a fulfilling sexuality as important for women: it is a legal requirement of marriage, and lack of a marital sex life is grounds for divorce. In her chapter, Pat Caplan describes the importance of women's sexual enjoyment as a "right" in marriage on Mafia Island in the 1960s through the 1980s. This also resonates with the emphasis on female pleasure in sexuality that is emphasized in the unyago songs analyzed by Larsen in her chapter in this volume.

Divorce is very common in Zanzibar, as it is elsewhere on the Swahili coast.[10] Men in Zanzibar maintain the right to unilateral divorce through repudiation, and most divorces take place outside court in this manner. Classical Islamic law permits a type of divorce known in Arabic as *talaq* and in Swahili as *talaka*, in which a man may simply divorce his wife through "repudiating" her by stating that he divorces her. Although in many Muslim-majority countries the ability of men to divorce their wives unilaterally through repudiation has been circumscribed by state law,[11] in Zanzibar, this type of divorce is legal.

Zanzibari women may file for divorce in court and may receive a divorce on a variety of grounds. It is not uncommon for men and women to divorce and remarry several times throughout their lives, and in rural Unguja, I have found little stigma associated with divorce. Because most divorces take place out of court through repudiation, men are more likely to be viewed negatively after divorce: a man who divorces wives frequently through repudiation may acquire a bad reputation, for example. The majority of cases opened in the kadhi courts are brought by women, and nearly all of them concern marital disputes. Among such cases, claims for maintenance are most common, followed by suits for divorce.[12]

IMPOTENCE CLAIMS IN COURT

Sheikh Hamid presided over the Mkokotoni court from 1995 through 2005, when he died suddenly at about age seventy. Before being selected to be a kadhi,[13] he was a teacher of religion in a government school for many years. Sheikh Hamid came to court every Monday through Thursday. In the Islamic tradition, Fridays are reserved for communal prayer, and although government offices in Zanzibar—including the Islamic courts—are open on Fridays, Sheikh Hamid and most other kadhis did not work on Fridays. On the kadhi's days in court, he talked with visitors to the court, heard litigants, and worked on open cases from about eight in the morning until noon or one o'clock. During the time I conducted research at the court, the court staff was composed of several clerks and a typist. Bwana Fumu was the head clerk, and he assisted Sheikh Hamid with nearly every aspect of the cases opened in the court. He also frequently helped visitors and potential litigants with legal issues.

On average, about forty total cases are opened per year in the court. Women open about 80 percent of the cases in the Mkokotoni court, and this majority is not unusual for Islamic family courts in Zanzibar and elsewhere in the Indian Ocean region: Anna Wurth has noted similar patterns of court usage in Yemen, as has Ziba Mir-Hosseini for petitioners in both Iran and Morocco, Susan Hirsch for Kenya, and Michael Peletz for Malaysia.[14] In Mkokotoni nearly all cases opened by women involve marital disputes, but claims focusing specifically on a husband's impotence or a lack of sexual fulfillment are few. When a case does feature such a claim, it is typically the primary or sole argument supporting a woman's request for a divorce. During Sheikh Hamid's ten years at the court, only nine or ten cases were brought forward with a sexual problem as the primary claim for a divorce. Although the number of cases involving impotence is very small, an analysis of the cases is fruitful for several reasons. For one, the cases show the breadth of reasons women give the court for requesting a divorce—in addition to impotence, women claim divorce for lack of maintenance, a husband's absence, and incompatibility. Furthermore, cases involving impotence illustrate the importance of sexuality in understandings of marriage in Zanzibar. The claims also show not only that the court handled them in similar ways but that husbands responded to their wives' claims in very similar ways, as we shall see in the analysis below.

During my research in the court in 1999 and 2000, I observed three cases involving impotence claims and was thus able to collect ethnographic data on them; in subsequent field trips, which were much shorter, I did not witness any cases involving impotence, although I collected data on many other impotence cases from the court records. Nearly all the cases Sheikh Hamid heard that involved claims of impotence resulted in divorce. Most often, the husband voluntarily divorced his wife after she brought her claim to court. In one case, court records show that the kadhi ordered the husband to divorce his wife, and in only one case does it appear the wife was ordered to return to her husband. This chapter will discuss in detail only the three cases for which I have ethnographic data.

Raya's Case

One case involving an impotence claim was brought to the court by a young woman called Raya in May 2000. On her first day in court, she was accompanied by an aunt a few years older than she was. At this point, I had been working in the court for several months, and although I did not know these women personally, it was likely that they had heard about the foreign researcher in Mkokotoni; most people who came to court were not surprised to see me there, but were rather friendly and curious. As the two women approached the kadhi's desk, the aunt turned to me and whispered loudly, "Mgonjwa!" with a knowing expression on her face. As noted previously, *mgonjwa* can be translated as "sick person" and in the context of marital disputes, it may be used to indicate a husband's lack of sexual ability. The fact that Raya's aunt whispered the problem to me—the only other woman in the room—indicated to me that the illness was likely of a sexual nature. The two women sat in front of the kadhi's desk, and Sheikh Hamid asked Raya what the problem was; he had likely noticed the stage whisper of Raya's aunt. She said, simply, "Mgonjwa!" The kadhi then asked, *Hawezi?* (He can't?) and paused. Raya answered yes. Sheikh Hamid asked if they lived together and if her husband had received any *matibabu,* or treatment, for the problem. Raya said that they did indeed live together and that he had sought and received a great deal of treatment, but to no effect. She noted that he did not want to divorce her, indicating that this was why she was in court. The kadhi announced that she undoubtedly had a serious problem and that she should open a case.

After the kadhi had finished with his initial questions, he sent the women to talk to me. On my days in court, I sat in a chair near the kadhi's desk. I listened to the proceedings, took notes on my laptop, and talked with the kadhi, clerks, and litigants like Raya. If the litigants did not already know who I was, the kadhi would explain that I had come from America to study sheria za dini (religious law) and that I would ask just a few questions about the case. Raya had a quiet and gentle manner. She was eighteen years old; she explained that she had been married for about eight months and that this was the first marriage for both herself and her husband, a man called Juma. When I asked if she had children, Raya's aunt laughed and told me that Raya's husband had no *kazi* (work—here, another euphemism for sex), so how could she possibly have children? Raya added that her husband had been "sick" since the day they married. I asked if her husband was elderly. The aunt answered that he was young but that he was still unable to perform. Together, the women explained that Raya had asked Juma for a divorce but that he had refused. He had been several times to an *mganga,* a healer with expertise in local medicine (often known as Swahili medicine), but to no avail. When I asked her if she would like to remain married if he was successfully treated and the illness resolved, she laughed quietly and said, "Basi, tena!" (No, I've had enough!).

Raya then went to talk to the head clerk about opening her case. Bwana Fumu asked what her primary claim was, and Raya again said her husband was mgonjwa. The clerk then asked what *homa* (fever, illness) he had, but he and Raya's aunt laughed knowingly together at the question, and it was clear that Bwana Fumu knew the nature of his illness—he had been in the room for their discussions with the kadhi. Bwana Fumu asked Raya several more questions, including whether her husband had been sick since the beginning of their marriage. Raya said that he had. Bwana Fumu then prepared the claim document, called the *madai.* In the claim, Juma's impotence was stated as preventing Raya from receiving the sheria of husband and wife. Note that the document, as prepared by the clerk, includes the word *uyume,* a nonstandard spelling of the Swahili word *uume* (penis). This term is more explicit than the euphemisms used by women like Raya, and although I did not discuss the use of the term with the clerk, there was no hesitation or awkwardness in preparing the document, and it appeared that the term was considered fine for use in the formal context of the court. Note also that line 5 includes reference to "those rights of wife and husband"; the demonstrative *hizo* (those) indicates the euphemism discussed earlier.[15] Court documents are written in very formulaic language; for example, the final two points of each claim document are written according to a formula, usually with similar wording. Before the numbered points of the madai that I begin with below, the names of plaintiff and defendant are recorded. Also, within documents, spelling of certain words can vary, and I have retained these spellings. Place-names are identified only by the first letter to maintain privacy.

Madai	*Plaintiff's Claim*
Mdai amefika mbele ya mahakamni na kueleza kama haya yafuatayo hapo chini	The plaintiff has come before the court to explain the following:
1. Kwamba mdai ni mwanamke, 18, Mwafrika wa C——.	The plaintiff is a woman, aged 18, African, from C——.[16]
2. Kwamba mdaiwa ni mwanaume, 23, Mwafrika wa K——.	The defendant is a man, 23, African, from K——.
3. Kwamba mdai na mdaiwa ni mke na mume na wameoana kiasi miezi 8 na hawana watoto.	The plaintiff and defendant are wife and husband and have been married for eight months. They have no children.
4. Kwamba mdai anadai talaka kwa kudai mumewe ni mgonjwa wa uyume hafai kwa kipindi chote cha 8 miezi.	The plaintiff requests a divorce because her husband has an illness affecting the penis, he is not suitable; the problem has continued [since they were married] eight months ago.
5. Kwamba chanzo cha madai haya ni ugonjwa wa uyume wa mdaiwa na mdai anadai hapati sheria hizo za mke na mume na kustahamili hawezi tena.	The source of this claim is the illness of the husband, the defendant, and the plaintiff claims that she does not get those rights of husband and wife and she can no longer persevere.

6. *Kwamba madai haya yametokezea C——.*	This plaint took place in C——.
7. *Mdai anaomba mahakama yako tukufu ya Kadhi kutoa hukumu kwa mdaiwa kama ifuatavyo hapo chini:*	The plaintiff asks your esteemed court of the kadhi to pass judgment on the defendant as follows:
a. *Mdaiwa atiwe talaka ya mdai kwa vile ni mgonjwa uyme wake hafai.*	a. To order the defendant to divorce his wife because his illness makes him unsuitable.
b. *Gharama za mahakama zilipwe na mdaiwa.*	b. To order the defendant to pay all court fees.[17]
c. *Amri nyengine yeyote ili itakayotolewa na mahakama iwe na muafaka na mdai.*	c. [To fulfill] any other orders that are issued by the court in an agreement for the plaintiff.

Juma was then summoned to court, and he appeared a few days later. The clerks read Raya's claim document to him. Juma prepared a counterclaim, called the *majibu ya madai* (response to the claim), with Bwana Fumu. The document stated that he was not able to divorce his wife as she requested because he had no desire to do so. He also claimed that he was indeed fulfilling the "sheria of marriage." The document made no mention of an illness, and simply asked the court to dismiss the plaintiff's claims. In Juma's hearing with the kadhi, however, he said that although had been well when they married, he became sick somewhat later. He explained that he had received treatment and had recovered, but his wife no longer wanted him. At this, Sheikh Hamid ordered Juma to visit a doctor in a nearby hospital to determine if he was indeed sick, and if that was causing impotence. Juma agreed to do so. However, two days later, Raya was back in court. Juma had divorced her through repudiation, and she was there to obtain a certificate of divorce.

Patima's Case

In Sheikh Hamid's court, similar cases had similar outcomes. In one case opened in 1999, a thirty-year-old woman called Patima requested a divorce on the grounds that her elderly husband was mgonjwa and that she was not getting her sheria. The claim document, again prepared with the help of Bwana Fumu, stated that every time she "wanted her sheria" from her husband, he told her go find someone who could fulfill her needs.

Madai	*Plaintiff's Claim*
Mdai amefika mbele ya mahakamni na kueleza kama haya yafuatayo hapo chini	The plaintiff has come before the court and explained the following:
1. Kwamba mdai ni mwanmke, 30, Mtumbatu wa K——.	The plaintiff is a woman, aged 30, Mtumbatu, from K——.
2. Kwamba mdaiwa ni mwanamume, 80, Mtumbatu wa C——.	The defendant is a man, aged 80, Mtumbatu, from C——.
3. Kwamba mdai na mdaiwa ni mke na mume wameoana kiasi miaka 2 iliopita hawana watoto.	The plaintiff and defendant are wife and husband; they have been married for the past two years and have no children.
4. Kwamba mdai anadai talaka yake kwa kudai mume wake ni mgonjwa hapati sheria za mke na mume kwa muda wa 2 miaka sasa tokea alipoolewa.	The plaintiff claims a divorce; she claims her husband is mgonjwa and has not been able to fulfill the sheria of wife and husband for two years now, since they were first married.
5. Kwamba mdai anadai kuwa wakati anapotaka sheria zake kwa mdaiwa humwambia mdai aende nje akatafute watu ili apate haja yake.	The plaintiff claims that when she requests her sheria from her husband, she is told to go elsewhere, outside, to find people who can fulfill her needs.
6. Kwamba mdai anadai amekaa kwa muda mrefu sana kustahamili ili mume wake ikitibu lakini bado hajapoa nakustahamili hawezi tena.	The plaintiff claims that she has persevered for a very long time in order for her husband to find treatment, but he has not yet recovered and she can no longer persevere.

7. *Kwamba mdai anaiomba mahakama kusikiliza shauri hili kwa vile tokeo hili limetokezea hapo C——.*	The plaintiff asks the court to hear this plaint, which happened in C——.
8. *Mdai anaomba mahakama yako tukufu ya Kadhi kutoa hukumu kwa mdaiwa kama ifuatavyo hapo chini:*	The plaintiff asks your esteemed court of the kadhi to pass judgment on the defendant as follows:
a. *Mdaiwa atowe talaka mara moja kwani yeye ndie asiyeweza kukamilisha sheria za mke na mume.*	a. To order the defendant to divorce [his wife] at once because he is unable to fulfill the sheria of wife and husband.
b. *Gharama za mahakama zilipwe na mdaiwa.*	b. To order the defendant to pay all court fees.
c. *Amri nyengine yeyote ili itakayotolewa na mahakama iwe na muafaka na mdai.*	c. Any other orders that the court issues in a ruling for the plaintiff.

Patima's husband was summoned, but instead of appearing in court, he sent a letter indicating to the court that he had divorced her.

Mwajuma's Case

In another case from 1999, a young woman called Mwajuma claimed that her husband, Machano, had been impotent the entire four years of their marriage. She had asked him to divorce her, and he agreed, providing that she compensate him by returning some of her marriage gift, *mahari* (<Ar. *mahr*). His request for money was in reference to a type of Islamic divorce known as *khuluu* (<Ar. *khul'*). Generally, in khuluu, a woman compensates her husband for a divorce she desires; in Zanzibar, this is known colloquially as *kununua talaka* (buying a divorce).[18] Mwajuma claimed that she had given the requested sum of money—25,000 Tanzanian shillings—to her husband, but he had not divorced her.

Before Mwajuma opened her case with Bwana Fumu, she and I talked. She told me that she was in court to ask for a divorce because her husband *hana nguvu za kiume* (does not have masculine strength). Like Raya and Patima, Mwajuma explained that she had persevered throughout their marriage, but that she had finally had enough and so decided that it would be better if she was divorced. Her claim document, again prepared by Bwana Fumu, emphasized both the impotence claim and the payment she had made to her husband for the requested divorce.

Mdai	*Plaintiff's Claim*
Mdai amefika mbele ya mahakamni na kueleza kama haya yafuatayo hapo chini:	The plaintiff has come before the court and explained the following:
1. Mdai ni mwanamke, 28, wa K——.	The plaintiff is woman, aged 28, from K——.
2. Mdaiwa ni mwanaume, 38, wa C——.	The defendant is a man, aged 38, from C——.
3. Kwamba mdai na mdaiwa ni mke na mume wameoana kiasi miaka 4½ iliopita hawana watoto.	The plaintiff and defendant are wife and husband and have been married for the past four and a half years; they have no children.
4. Kwamba mdai anadai mume wake ni mgonjwa hafai (mume wake) kwa kipindi chote hicho cha minne na nusu sasa.	The plaintiff claims that her husband is sick and has been unsuitable for four and a half years.
5. Kwamba mdai anadai mnomo mwenzi wa mfungo tatu katika mwaka wa 2000 mdai alidai mdaiwa amuache kwa hali yake hiyo ya ugonjwa.	The plaintiff claims that in the third month of the year 2000 she asked the defendant to divorce her because of his illness.
6. Kwamba mdai anadai alipe mdai mdaiwa auache ndipoka mdai alipwe nusu ya mahari aliyemualeya na zilikuwa 25,000/-.	The plaintiff claims that the defendant wanted her to pay him half of her marriage gift to divorce her, and indeed she paid him TSh 25,000.

7. *Kwamba mdai anadai akabidhiwe fedha hizo 25,000/- na kaka wa mdai ujudi J—— hapo C——, mbele ya mjomba wakeili mdaiwa mwinyi S—— na mama wa mdaiwa C—— ili mdaiwa atowe talaka ya mdai.*

The plaintiff claims that she entrusted this money, in the amount of TSh 25,000, to her elder brother J——, here in C——, in front of her maternal uncle and a representative of the defendant, B——, and the defendant's mother, M——, in order for the defendant to issue the divorce.

8. *Kwamba mdai ana mdaiwa ameshalipa 25,000/- alivyotaka alipwe lakini hadi hii leo bado mdaiwa hajatoa talaka ya mdai.*

The plaintiff claims she already paid the defendant the TSh 25,000, that he wanted to be paid but that until today the defendant has not divorced the plaintiff.

9. *Kwamba mdai anadai apewe talaka yake na mdaiwa kwani hawana sababu tena ya mdaiwa kuzuia talaka ya mdai.*

The plaintiff demands that the defendant divorce her because he has no further reason to refuse the divorce.

10. *Kwamba chazo cha mdaiwa haya ni mdaiwa kupokea fedha alizotaka apewe ili atowe talaka na baadae asitowe talaka ya kupokea fedha hizo.*

The source of this plaint is that the defendant received money that he requested in order to divorce his wife, and he has not divorced her after receiving this money.

11. *Kwamba mdai haya yametokea hapo C——.*

This plaint took place in C——.

12. *Mdai anaomba mahakama yako tukufu ya Kadhi kutoa hukumu kwa mdaiwa kama ifuatavyo hapo chini:*

The plaintiff asks your esteemed court of the kadhi to pass judgment on the defendant as follows:

a. *Mahakama imemuamuru mdaiwa atoe talaka ya mdai mara moja.*

a. The court orders the defendant to divorce the plaintiff immediately.

b. *Gharama za mahakama zilipwe na mdaiwa.*

b. The court fees must be paid by the defendant.

c. *Amri nyengine yeyote ili itakayotolewa na mahakama iwe na muafaka na mdai.*

c. Any other orders that the court issues in a ruling for the plaintiff.

When Mwajuma and Machano eventually came to court to- gether, Machano immediately agreed with all her claims about the problems of the marriage and confirmed that Mwajuma had given him the sum that he had requested to divorce her. He then divorced her right there in the court, and the case was closed— again without a judicial ruling.

ALL THREE cases described in this chapter involve a woman re- questing divorce on grounds of her husband's impotence. Each of the three women claimed that illness was causing impotence and preventing her husband from fulfilling his marital duties. As we have seen, this claim is commonly framed in discourse as his failure to fulfill a woman's right to a sexual relationship, phrased as *sheria za mke na mume,* or *sheria za ndoa.* All three women noted that they had persevered for some time but that now the time had come to ask for divorce. All three husbands agreed to a divorce after their wives opened cases in court, and all three divorced their wives unilaterally: Raya and Mwajuma's husbands both came to court before enacting the divorce, and Patima's husband divorced her after receiving the summons and did not appear in court. Therefore, none of the cases resulted in a judicial decision. As noted earlier, court records indicate that this was also a typical outcome for other cases involving impotence.

Nevertheless, I have a fair idea how Sheikh Hamid would have reasoned under the circumstances. As noted previously, the kadhi occasionally explained to litigants that a sexual relationship and fulfillment was a legal requirement of marriage. And he viewed lack of such a relationship as potential grounds for divorce. On slow days in court, Sheikh Hamid often took it upon himself to give me somewhat formal lessons in Islamic law, which in- cluded more explicit theoretical instruction than what I learned in my observation of the daily proceedings of the court. On one occasion, he described the various grounds on which a woman could get a divorce. First, he told me that beating was justifica- tion for divorce. Then, he explained that if a woman simply did not want her husband, she could "buy" a divorce from him by returning some of her mahari (<Ar. mahr); here, he was using the colloquial phrase to describe the type of Islamic divorce known

as khuluu. I asked the kadhi if a woman could get a "free" divorce without her husband agreeing to it; in Zanzibar, the term *free divorce* can refer to a judicial *fasikhi* (<Ar. *faskh*) divorce, akin to an annulment. Sheikh Hamid replied that this was sometimes possible—for example, if the man was ill. He elaborated by noting that a husband's contraction of a contagious disease like leprosy was grounds for divorce, as would be a medical condition that prevented him from working to support her. Finally, he explained a woman could get a *talaka bure* (free divorce) if she married a man who was impotent or one who preferred the company of other men.

Sheikh Hamid's contention that impotence is grounds for divorce is certainly not unusual: judges and legal scholars in other times and places have similarly argued for dissolution of marriage on such grounds. Most often, this has been because of the lack of sexual enjoyment as an essential dimension of marriage and not the impossibility of having children. As we have seen, a discussion of procreation was not central in any of the three cases from Sheikh Hamid's court. Although all three claim documents noted that the plaintiff and defendant did not have children, this information was sought and included in any type of marital dispute case and thus was not specific to the nature of the claim.

Comparing Sheikh Hamid's rulings to similar cases elsewhere in what Gwyn Campbell describes as Indian Ocean Africa sheds light on the importance of understanding variation of Islamic practice and interpretation even with the general region.[19] Carolyn Fluehr-Lobban's research on Islamic law and courts in Sudan presents both parallels and contrasts to the Zanzibari cases. In Sudanese courts, Fluehr-Lobban finds that impotence is indeed grounds for divorce but that the burden of proof is on the wife.[20] The cases that Fluehr-Lobban researched primarily involved a woman's claim that her husband had been impotent since the beginning of the marriage and that she thus remained a virgin. In such cases, Fluehr-Lobban observes that a woman would likely be sent to a hospital to ensure that she was still a virgin; furthermore, in Sudanese law, a claim of impotence would be met in court with a requirement that the couple cohabit for a year in order for them to consummate the marriage. Procedure in Egypt appears to be similar, and Essam Fawzy notes that such requirements may prevent many women from bringing impotence claims to court.[21] This is a notable contrast to Sheikh Hamid's court. As we have seen, although he did not need to rule on any cases involving impotence in my tenure with him, the burden of proof was clearly upon the accused husband. As we saw in Raya's case, her husband was asked to submit to a medical examination. Vardit Rispler-Chaim and Judith Tucker both note that some jurists argue that divorce is possible on grounds of impotence only if a husband was not able to perform from the time of the marriage and if the wife thus remained a virgin.[22] Although all three women in the cases examined here claimed that their husbands had been impotent from the time of marriage, none was asked to submit to a medical examination to certify their virginity. The women were asked, however, how long their husbands had been unable to perform.

Both lay people and legal professionals in Zanzibar consider sexual fulfillment a legally essential part of marriage. A young woman's first marriage is a time for sexual instruction, which often emphasizes the pleasure of marital sexual relations. As other chapters in this volume show (e.g., Thompson and Larsen), the instruction focuses primarily on the way in which a wife can increase the enjoyment of the husband. However, the court cases presented here also show that a wife's sexual fulfillment is important and is even viewed as a legal requirement of marriage. As we have seen, lack of sexual gratification due to a husband's impotence is used as grounds for divorce. In Zanzibar, because men maintain the right to unilateral divorce, most divorces take place out of court. Unsatisfied women may ask husbands to divorce them or may file for divorce in court on grounds of impotence. The kadhi agrees that this is grounds for divorce and will order medical testing for proof of the husband's impotence.

However, in the three cases presented in this chapter, the husbands in question divorced their wives upon being summoned to court, or after appearing in court and then being ordered to the hospital for an examination. In other types of divorce suits, this rapid recourse to divorce was unusual. Normally, a case would proceed through weeks or months of court dates, after which

Sheikh Hamid would issue an attempt at reconciliation; such cases typically only resulted in divorce after the reconciliation fell though. And, in such cases, a woman might end up with a court-ordered khuluu divorce, in which she compensates her husband financially for the divorce. In a divorce by a husband's repudiation, a woman does not bear any financial responsibility for the divorce, since it is by her husband's initiative. Although a divorce through repudiation does not lawfully require a woman to transfer any money or property to her husband, some women in this part of Unguja are divorced through a means that is locally termed *kuandikia pesa* (writing for money). In such a divorce, a man asks his wife for money to divorce her through repudiation, which is considered unlawful by scholars and legal professionals.[23]

Earlier in this volume, Elisabeth McMahon shows in her chapter on women in colonial Pemba that careful strategizing about marriage and divorce is nothing new on the Swahili coast. Thus, although the number of cases involving claims of impotence for divorce in this Zanzibari court is small, the sample suggests that opening a court case featuring a claim of impotence can be an effective means of persuading a husband to enact an immediate divorce. Women may use a claim of impotence strategically to encourage husbands to divorce them.

NOTES

A shorter version of this chapter first appeared in *Dossier: Journal of Women Living under Muslim Law* 32–33 (2014). Here, the discussion has been extended. Thanks to WLUML for permitting the use of this material.

1. Carolyn Fluehr-Lobban, *Islamic Law and Society in the Sudan* (London: Routledge, 1987); Sarah Mirza and Margaret Strobel, eds., *Three Swahili Women: Life Histories from Mombasa, Kenya*, trans. Mirza and Strobel (Bloomington: Indiana University Press, 1989); Valerie J. Hoffman, "Islamic Perceptions on the Human Body: Legal, Spiritual and Social Considerations," in *Embodiment, Morality, and Medicine*, ed. Lisa Sowle Cahill and Margaret A. Farley, Theology and Medicine 6 (London: Kluwer Academic Publishers, 1995); Vardit Rispler-Chaim, *Disability in Islamic Law*, International Library of Ethics, Law, and the New Medicine 32 (Dordrecht: Springer, 2006); Judith E. Tucker, "Muftīs and Matrimony: Islamic Law

and Gender in Ottoman Syria and Palestine," *Islamic Law and Society* 1, no. 3 (1994): 265–300; Tucker, *Women, Family, and Gender in Islamic Law*, Themes in Islamic Law 3 (Cambridge: Cambridge University Press, 2008).

2. William Harold Ingrams, *Zanzibar: Its History and Its People* (London: H. F. and G. Witherby, 1931), 238.

3. Tucker, "Muftīs and Matrimony," 272; see also Tucker, *Women, Family*.

4. Vardit Rispler-Chaim, "Hasan Murad Manna, 'Childbearing and the Rights of a Wife,'" *Islamic Law and Society* 2, no. 1 (1995): 92–99.

5. Pat Caplan, "Boys' Circumcision and Girls' Puberty Rites among the Swahili of Mafia Island, Tanzania," *Africa: Journal of the International African Institute* 46, no. 1 (1976): 21–33; Mirza and Strobel, *Three Swahili Women*; John Middleton, *The World of the Swahili: An African Mercantile Civilization* (New Haven: Yale University Press, 1992); Laura Fair, "Identity, Difference, and Dance: Female Initiation in Zanzibar, 1890 to 1930," *Frontiers: A Journal of Women Studies* 17, no. 3 (1996): 146–72; Nadine Beckmann, "Pleasure and Danger: Muslim Views on Sex and Gender in Zanzibar," *Culture, Health and Sexuality* 12, no. 6 (August 2010): 619–32, and chap. 4, this volume; Katrina Daly Thompson, "How to Be a Good Muslim Wife: Women's Performance of Islamic Authority during Swahili Weddings," *Journal of Religion in Africa* 41, no. 4 (2011): 427–48, Thompson, "Learning to Use Swahili Profanity," chap. 6, this volume; Larsen, "Pleasure and Prohibitions," chap. 7, this volume.

6. Beckmann, "Pleasure and Danger."

7. Middleton, *World of the Swahili*, 143.

8. For a discussion of somo and more elaborate public dances involved in instructing young women in Zanzibar in the first part of the twentieth century, see Fair, "Identity, Difference." Fair describes different approaches to training in different ethnic and socioeconomic communities and traces changes in the instruction process over time.

9. For examples, see Beckmann, "Pleasure and Danger"; Thompson, "Good Muslim Wife."

10. J. N. Anderson, "Islamic Law in Africa," *Journal of African Law* 21, no. 2 (1977): 137–38; Margaret Strobel, *Muslim Women in Mombasa, Kenya, 1890–1975* (New Haven: Yale University Press, 1979); Marc J. Swartz, *The Way the World Is: Cultural Processes and Social Relations among the Mombasa Swahili* (Berkeley: University of California Press, 1991); Middleton, *World of the Swahili*; Susan F. Hirsch, *Pronouncing and Persevering: Gender and the Discourses of Disputing in an African Islamic Court*, Language and Legal Discourse (Chicago: University of Chicago Press, 1998); Pat Caplan, "Monogamy, Polygyny or the Single State? Changes in Marriage Patterns in a Tanzanian Coastal Village, 1965–94," in *Gender, Family and Household in Tanzania*, ed. Colin Creighton and Cuthbert K. Omari (Aldershot, UK: Avebury, 1995); Erin E. Stiles, *An*

Islamic Court in Context: An Ethnographic Study of Judicial Reasoning (New York: Palgrave Macmillan, 2009).

11. Ann Elizabeth Mayer, *Islam and Human Rights: Tradition and Politics,* 4th ed. (Boulder: Westview, 2007); John L. Esposito, *Women in Muslim Family Law,* with Natana J. DeLong-Bas, 2nd ed., Contemporary Issues in the Middle East (Syracuse: Syracuse University Press, 2001).

12. Stiles, *Islamic Court;* Anna Würth, "A Sana'a Court: The Family and the Ability to Negotiate," *Islamic Law and Society* 2, no. 3 (1995): 320–40; Ziba Mir-Hosseini, *Marriage on Trial: A Study of Islamic Family Law: Iran and Morocco Compared,* Society and Culture in the Modern Middle East (London: I. B. Tauris, 1993); S. Hirsch, *Pronouncing and Persevering;* Michael G. Peletz, *Islamic Modern: Religious Courts and Cultural Politics in Malaysia,* Princeton Studies in Muslim Politics (Princeton: Princeton University Press, 2002).

13. Kadhis are nominally appointed to their posts by the president of Zanzibar. Most are nominated by the chief kadhi.

14. Stiles, *Islamic Court.*

15. Thanks to Katrina Daly Thompson for pointing this out.

16. Litigants opening cases are asked to state their ethnicity (*kabila*) for the clerk. Most in this area identify as Watumbatu, though some occasionally say they are "African," "Swahili," or "Arab."

17. This is a typical part of a plaintiff's claim. Normally, the plaintiff will pay a fee to open a case; during the time these cases were opened, the fee was TSh 1,250, which was about $2. Although this statement appears in most plaintiffs' claims, I did not regularly see a losing defendant reimburse the plaintiff for this fee, nor was it mandated in written rulings.

18. For an extended discussion of khuluu in Zanzibar, see Stiles, *Islamic Court.*

19. Gwyn Campbell, "Islam in Indian Ocean Africa," in *Struggling with History: Islam and Cosmopolitanism in the Western Indian Ocean,* ed. Edward Simpson and Kai Kresse (New York: Columbia University Press, 2008).

20. Fluehr-Lobban, *Islamic Law,* 165.

21. Essam Fawzy, "Muslim Personal Status Law in Egypt: The Current Situation and Possibilities of Reform through Internal Initiatives," in *Women's Rights and Islamic Family Law: Perspectives on Reform,* ed. Lynn Welchman (London: Zed Books, 2004), 14–91.

22. Rispler-Chaim, *Disability in Islamic Law;* Tucker, *Women, Family.*

23. For an extended discussion, see Stiles, *Islamic Court.*

NINE

Forming and Performing Swahili Manhood
Wedding Rituals of a Groom in Lamu Town

REBECCA GEARHART

BEFORE HE REACHES THE door of his dressing room, the groom (*bwanaharusi*) can smell the burning incense (*udi*) coming from within. Now cleanly shaven after the barber ceremony, he enters the room looking more dapper than ever. Inside, two of his uncles, his older brother, a cousin, and a family-appointed groomsman[1] chatter excitedly as they lay out the groom's Omani-style ceremonial attire:[2] a new white robe (*kanzu*), a hand-embroidered cap (*kofia*), a gold-trimmed black robe (*joho*), and colorfully striped pieces of fabric that will serve as a turban and a waist sash. Each of these articles, having carefully been cleaned, ironed, and permeated with incense, is now ready for the bwanaharusi to don.

The groomsman begins by wrapping one end of the sash around the bwanaharusi's waist; he tucks in the brass dagger (*jambia*) before the last go-round. Then he ties the other end of the sash so that it neatly hangs down the front of the groom's kanzu. Several men are involved in the fitting of the turban, as it needs to be positioned just so as it is wound around the kofia in order for one end to hang down to the bwanaharusi's left shoulder. After an hour of wrapping and tucking and positioning, the bwanaharusi's uncles hold up the joho for him to wear. As the entourage jokingly gives the bwanaharusi a few last words of advice and he is dabbed with a last round of perfume, a surge of anxiety overcomes him. Beads of sweat trickle down the sides of his face as the heaviness of the robe takes effect. The bwanaharusi's brother hands him a ceremonial sword, he takes a deep breath, the door opens, and the bwanaharusi begins his march toward manhood.

Though Swahili brides get more attention than do grooms in the literature,[3] weddings also serve as a critical rite of passage for Swahili men. Drawing on my experience as a guest and as a photographer-videographer at dozens of Swahili weddings in Lamu Town, on Lamu Island, Kenya, over the past twenty-five years, the insider's perspective I gained during my own Swahili wedding, in Lamu Town in 2005, and interviews I conducted with Swahili men in Lamu Town in 2011, this chapter focuses on the wedding rituals that define Swahili masculinity and prepare men to meet the social and religious obligations that are required of them as adult Muslim males in Lamu Town society.

PREMARRIAGE ARRANGEMENTS

Teenage boys (*barobaro*) in Lamu Town typically enjoy a high degree of mobility and spend the majority of their time outdoors and in the company of other males. Swahili boys are couriers; they walk, ride donkeys, and sail in boats to carry food and messages between houses, and pick up and deliver goods to and from the farms, the market, and local shops. They juggle schoolwork and religious studies with income-generating activities that often make them pivotal contributors to their families' economic stability.[4] As unemployment waxes and the benefits of a high school education wane, older barobaro in Lamu Town increasingly leave school to concentrate on learning a trade that will provide them with some financial stability into adulthood.

The pressure to meet family expectations as a wage earner becomes greater as barobaro move into their late teens, when talk of marriage begins. Obtaining the money or goods (or both) required of a groom at marriage can be a substantial obstacle depending on the family into which a young man wishes to marry. Generally, the transfer of wedding gifts (mahari) a groom or his family makes to the bride or her family fluctuates with the times; as flashier and more expensive weddings have come into and gone out of fashion, so too has the asking price of the mahari ebbed and flowed.[5] If the bride's family expects a large, expensive wedding, the mahari might be quite modest and vice versa. Margaret Strobel suggests that at the turn of the twentieth century, weddings among the Mombasa elite lasted four or five months, "giving them time to accumulate necessary funds between feasts and dances."[6] Today, big weddings last but four days, though now as in past decades, young men in Lamu Town find marriage to be a financially daunting proposition.[7]

The great sums amassed for large weddings hosted by the elite is separate from the mahari, which is a legal transfer made according to Islamic law. The money collected to pay for the wedding is a second type of transfer from the Swahili groom's family to the bride's family that is customary, not required by Islam.[8] A third kind of payment the groom makes comes in the form of clothing, jewelry, and cash that the bwanaharusi gifts the bride (bibiharusi) and her female relatives throughout the wedding celebration.[9] That many Lamu Town families retain the cohesiveness and desire to pool their resources to finance weddings that launch young people into society in an impressive manner is quite astonishing in today's economic climate. While Jane Bristol-Rhys's research in the United Arab Emirates found that extended Emirati families continue to work cooperatively to assemble the money necessary for putting on their four-day weddings,[10] Adeline Masquelier's research in Niger suggests that young Nigerien men can no longer rely on the strong family networks that used to ensure the mobilization of resources (land, labor, capital) necessary for putting on a wedding and demonstrating the groom's ability to support the bride and their future children.[11] One Swahili man with whom I spoke recalled his 2003 wedding; a four-day celebration that was very respectable but not lavish by Lamu Town standards. To pull it off, he borrowed KSh 600,000 ($8,500) from relatives and spent the first years of his marriage working to pay off his debts.

Accessing that kind of money depends on how well connected the groom is to relatives who have resources to give or to loan. Once the young man's family has made its selection of a bride and carefully discussed the kind of wedding they can afford, the young man's closest male elders personally deliver the marriage offer (*maneno* or *posa*) to the young woman's father. Since news of the impending proposal has cautiously passed back and forth between close relatives of the prospective groom and bride, this occasion makes the proposal official and is necessary before any wedding arrangements can be made. The significance of the maneno cannot be overstated; the manner in which the proposal is made by the groom's male relatives and received by the father of the bride (or his proxy) signifies the respect (*heshima*) each family has for the other, and it must be handled delicately and in the proper way. The prospective groom's entourage (made up of his grandfather, father, elder brothers, and uncles) dress formally, in kanzus and kofias, and are greeted warmly by the father of the prospective bride and his male relatives in their home. Though the mahari can be paid in cash, material goods, or both and is the bibiharusi's to keep, it is negotiated between the prospective groom's father (or his proxy) and his future father-in-law (or his proxy). Since mahari in the form of cash is less likely to find its way to the bride herself (as it is commonly used by her parents to cover wedding expenses), many women in Lamu Town prefer locally handcrafted, wooden bedroom furniture, which is a popular form of both mahari and dowry. The groom and bride's passivity in this exchange, marked by their absence from the negotiation itself, is countered by the active involvement of the groom's male representatives and the involvement of the bride's female relatives, who ratify the proposal with a specially prepared meal that seals the deal.

In Lamu Town, it is still considered uncouth for a couple to meet without a chaperone before they are married. The relaying of love poetry between the female relatives of the bride and groom used to be the only socially sanctioned mode of communication between the betrothed. Today, cell phones and computers have made private communication between unmarried youth much more feasible than it was, and text messaging has become the preferred medium with which lovers transmit romantic messages.

PREWEDDING FESTIVITIES

If the period between the marriage proposal and the wedding includes the month of Ramadan, the bibiharusi's family prepares an elaborate meal made up of a variety of different dishes known as *bembe* and delivers it to the family of the bwanaharusi to eat after the fast is broken in the evening. This is typically the first time a Swahili man is feasted in such a way, and he often invites male relatives and friends to share the dinner. It is customary for the groom's guests to help compensate the bibiharusi's family for the cost of the meal, and young men often joke about this tradition by teasing, "Usile bembe kama huwezi kulipa" (Don't eat the bembe if you can't afford it). The bembe offers the groom a first taste of the quality of the cooking he can expect from his new wife and allows him to imagine himself a married man. The reference to eating also serves as a sexual metaphor, not unlike those discussed in Katrina Thompson's and Erin Stiles's chapters in this volume.

The presentation of the trousseau is the groom's first demonstration of his ability to support his future wife in the manner she is accustomed to or in the manner she aspires to live.[12] This event is called the "sending of the bag" (*kupeleka begi*), at which the groom's female relatives ceremoniously deliver a large suitcase of fine dresses, matching shoes and adornments, and expensive perfume for the bride to wear after the wedding, when the bride and groom visit and receive relatives and friends as a new couple. That the contents of the bag have been carefully selected for the bride by the groom's female relatives explains why the items are typically passed around for all the women present to scrutinize. This event features the singing of love poetry composed for the groom and the bride by their close female relatives, in particular those who are known for their poetic talents. One such exchange that was shared with me by a Lamu groom named Majid and his betrothed, Thuweba, provides an example.

Majid's Message to Thuweba:

Kwanda mutie fatiha, wahishimiwa wazee	We begin with prayer, respected elders.
Kwa mola wetu ilaha, dua muziombolee	To our perfect God, say a prayer.
Kwa hini yetu furaha, Rwabi atutimizie	For our happiness, may God bless us with it.
Nimekuja Bi Thuweba, kwako wewe maridhiya	I have come to you, Ms. Thuweba, modest one.
Wala sio matilaba, yangu nilokusudiya	It is not my plan or intention (to be here; it is fate).
Tunu yangu hini haba, nyonda wangu nipokeya	This gift for you, my love, please accept it.
Mpenzi nilitamani, zaidi kukuleteya	My love, I wish I could have given you more.
Vizuri va duniani, nisibakishe kimoya	All the best things in the world, bar none.
Kwa nia zetu mwendani, mola tatubarikiya	With our good intentions, go; God will bless us.
Kikupa wangu ukweli, huba zanipa udhiya	To tell you the truth, my love for you is torturing me.
Hata usiku silali, huwaza tuko pamoya	I cannot even sleep at night, I think only of us together.
December huona mbali, ni basi tavumiliya.	December seems so far away, but anyway, I will wait.

Thuweba's reply to Majid:

Mazuri twatumaini, kwa dua zenu wazazi.	We hope good things come from your prayers, our parents.
Furaha iko moyoni, kuja kwetu mpumbazi.	My heart is filled with happiness; you are coming to our home to be my consoler.

Sijui namna gani, nikopokee mpenzi.	I don't know how I can welcome you enough, my love.
Majidi nimeinyosha, mwili	Majid, my body is outstretched to receive you.
Kwa furaha na bashasha, na Mungu kikuombeya.	With happiness and exhilaration, and to God I pray for you.
Tunu ya kufurahisha, shukurani kikwambiya.	Your gifts made me happy, and to you I say thank you.
Nyonda usiwe na dhiki, nakweleza uwelewe.	My love, don't be distressed; I'm telling you so that you understand.
Nisemayo ni ya haki, vitu uloleta wewe.	What I'm saying is the truth about the things that you've sent.
Hakuna kilichobaki, ila ni wewe mwenyewe.	There is nothing left for me to receive now except you.
Sichoke kuvumiliya, kwake Mola tulingane.	Do not be tired of waiting until God pairs us together.
Nami pia naumiya, mawazo sina mengine.	I'm also in pain and all my thoughts are about you.
Miezi ilobakiya, epite tudirikane.	May the remaining months pass so we can be united.

WEDDING EVENTS

Perhaps the most highly celebrated of male wedding events in Lamu Town is the stick dance, known locally as both *ngoma ya simbo*[13] and *kirumbizi*. This much-anticipated, all-male affair, performed for grooms whose personal preference warrants the ceremony, takes place in an outdoor public space in which men from the whole town are invited to participate. Musical accompaniment for the stick fighters is provided by an ensemble led by a double-reed woodwind instrument called *zumari ya mtapa,* locally made double- and single-headed drums, and a brass plate struck with raffia braids that adds an electrifying sound that encourages the players to increase the speed and energy of their maneuvers.

About half an hour of musically accompanied sparring occurs before the groom is escorted onto a stage that has been erected at the edge of the arena. Flanked by an entourage of bachelors made up of younger brothers, cousins, and friends, the groom is invited to sit upon a handcrafted wooden "king's chair" (*kiti cha enzi*), which is ornately carved and inlaid, to oversee the spectacle. In contrast to the competitive drama unfolding in the stick dance circle is the genteel treatment that the bwanaharusi receives on stage by preadolescent female relatives of the bibi-harusi. As the stick dancers entertain the bwanaharusi from the sparring ground, the girls festoon him with a lei made of fresh jasmine and roses (or a red-and-white paper version), serve him rose-flavored milk with nutmeg (considered an aphrodisiac), and dab him with perfumed oils[14]—all to prepare him for the impending union with his new bride, later in the evening.

There is quite a bit of mystical symbolism related to the stick dance, which is associated with protecting the groom from evil spirits, as his social status betwixt and between bachelorhood and adulthood makes him particularly vulnerable to attack. The lei the groom wears and the food he consumes permeate him with the protective properties of the colors red and white, discussed in more detail below. Though rarely sung anymore, kirumbizi lyrics welcome evil spirits to the stick dance so that the dancers and musicians can confuse and divert them from attacking the groom. Reference to these spirits also signifies any ill will harbored by disapproving relatives, who are not supportive of the marriage. Anyone with a grievance is encouraged to get it out of his system at the stick dance. Anyone with an enemy is invited to challenge his foe to a duel that allows for the public expression of the conflict and its resolution.

After the bwanaharusi has had a chance to spar with his friends and relatives, the musicians signal the grand finale. Each draped with a twin half of a new piece of cloth (*leso*) across his shoulder, the groom and the father of the bride face off against each other. Though the script of this final scene is well known in Lamu Town, several of the men with whom I spoke said they found dueling with their fathers-in-law to be more stressful than anticipated. Hitting the stick hard enough to maintain dignity among one's peers while simultaneously exhibiting a certain degree of deference to one's elder turns out to be more precarious than it looks. Inevitably, each bwanaharusi overcomes this challenge by publicly appeasing his male elder by graciously accepting defeat. And with that symbolic gesture, the stick dance ceremony is deemed a success and officially comes to close.

If the wedding includes a stick dance, it immediately precedes the marriage ceremony (*nikaha*) itself. A Swahili nikaha, like all Islamic marriage rituals, requires the verbal consent of the bride before the ceremony can proceed. Though the wedding official often obtains the bride's consent prior to the nikaha, the scholar who officiated my marriage came by the house in which I was being beautified to ask my consent on his way to the ceremony. In the company of my fiancé's close male relatives, I was instructed to sit next to my husband-to-be and confirm that he was the man I wished to marry. Only after receiving my affirmation did the gentlemen continue on their way to the nikaha. According to Islamic tradition, Swahili weddings consist of the exchange of vows between the groom (or his male proxy) and the father of the bride (or his male proxy). The nikaha can be as public or private, and as big or small, as the groom and his family desires. It can be held inside or outside, in the morning, daytime, or evening, before or after a meal, and is deemed legal as long as an Islamic judge (*kadhi*) or Islamic scholar (*mwalimu*) officiates.

In Lamu Town, a bwanaharusi's preparation for the nikaha begins a month before the event, when he stops shaving or cutting his hair to honor a tradition known as *kufuga ukuti* (growing the raffia).[15] The day before the nikaha, the bride's female relatives "send the toothbrush" (*kupeleka mswaki*) to the groom, a ceremony that includes delivering a collection of toiletries that the groom will use for his shave. With these items, the bwanaharusi's female relatives pamper the groom, giving him a facial treatment and washing his feet as they sing wedding songs and playfully tease him about how his new wife will indulge him. Soon thereafter, a barber comes to the house to give the groom a much-needed haircut and shave.

Some families make quite a spectacle out of the barber's visit, and the event is accompanied with drumming and singing. At such celebrations, locks of the groom's shorn hair are displayed on a woven tray used for cleaning rice and on which male relatives toss shilling notes in the groom's honor, traditions similar to practices in other areas of the Muslim world such as Morocco and Yemen.[16] Since a Swahili groom is expected to let himself become quite scruffy in the weeks leading up to the wedding, these treatments are meant to alter his appearance significantly; his physical transformation reflects the psychological and social transformation he is making as he passes out of boyhood and into manhood, from a relatively unconstrained, carefree, outdoor existence, to a more controlled and refined state of comfort inside the home.

In the days leading up to the wedding, the bwanaharusi is informally taken aside by male elders, who offer advice on how to foster his wife's religious development, and by recently married male peers, who explain how to treat her during various phases of her menstrual cycle. Since young Swahili men are not privy to such information before this time, being let in on family secrets and the private lives of women can be quite overwhelming. Several men explained that while the advice they were given was helpful in many respects, some of it was shocking and took time to process. Perhaps most helpful are the tips young men receive from their female elders. As one groom recalls his grandmother's advice:

> In a lifetime, things will happen between you and your wife that you never expected to happen. If you hear your wife has done something bad, don't believe it and don't listen to what people say. Unless you see it with your own eyes or find a way to discover if it's true or not, do not believe it. Don't let anyone come between you and your wife.

When the day of the nikaha finally rolls around, the bwanaharusi has had every opportunity to seek counsel from his married relatives and friends and usually feels fairly well prepared for the big day. The tying of the kilemba, the placement of the jambia, and the final fitting of the joho, connects the groom to all his male relatives, who have donned the same accoutrements on their wedding day. As one bwanaharusi described,

I didn't realize that I would look so good in the wedding outfit. When I was getting dressed, I said to myself, "Wow, this is a very special day for me!" They put so much perfume in the clothing and on me that when I walked outside, everyone could smell that a groom was passing. I was very proud!

After being pampered and dressed up by his relatives, the bwanaharusi is led to the mosque or a family home for the nikaha in an all-male musical procession that includes the reciting of Qur'anic verses to the beat of tambourines (*matwari*). The nikaha is a covenant made between the groom and the bride's family, represented by the bibiharusi's father or another close male elder. The ceremonial handshake between the bwanaharusi and the father of the bibiharusi symbolizes the vow and signals the conclusion of the nikaha. In Lamu Town, the recitation of maulidi verses that honor the birth (<Ar. *maulid*) and life of the Prophet Muhammad often immediately follows the nikaha. At the conclusion of the ceremony, the groom circulates among the elders, thanking them for attending and receiving their blessings for a prosperous marriage. And as with all significant Swahili occasions, the successful completion of the marriage ceremony is celebrated with food, sometimes simply with *halwa,* or *halua* (locally made sweetmeat), and *kahawa* (strong Arabic coffee) among immediate family members, and sometimes with a feast shared by guests numbering in the hundreds, depending on the groom's financial situation.

If the groom is wealthy, his male relatives serve bottles of soda and huge platters of freshly cooked flavorful beef or goat meat and potatoes cooked in coconut milk-flavored rice (*pilau*), raw-vegetable salad (*kachumbari*), and a variety of spicy sauces and chutneys to rows of men seated on woven floor mats. The labor that this meal entails includes the groom's female relatives, friends, and neighbors who clean, cut, and season the food by hand, hired hands and family clients who cook the food in enormous cast-iron kettles over wood fires, and servants who help prepare as well as carry the food from one place to another as needed. When the groom sneaks a glance at how well everything is being carried off and overhears a compliment about how efficiently the food was served, his heart fills with pride, though he cannot allow himself to express it. Humility and grace at such moments demonstrate the groom's personal integrity as well as his family's honor. Moreover, the groom is not in a position to boast, as several major challenges still await him.

KUTIA NDANI

The next obstacle to confront the groom occurs when he proceeds to the home of the bride to consummate the marriage. The name of this ceremony, *kutia ndani* (to put inside) is a double entendre, referring to the bwanaharusi's attempt to get into the area of the house where the bibiharusi is waiting for him and to his deflowering of the bride soon thereafter. Unmarried male relatives of the bride blockade the entryway of the house, and the groom and his male escorts help push against these adversaries, who jokingly jostle the groom and thwart his advances. The intensity of the theatrics involved in this tradition varies depending on how committed the bride's male relatives are to making the groom work for his betrothed.

After making their way into the house, the bwanaharusi and his party are invited to a special meal for the groom and his close male relatives and friends known as *kombe*. If the nikaha ceremony occurred at lunchtime and pilau was served, the kombe is typically quite modest, consisting of sweetmeat and coffee. If the nikaha occurred in the evening, the kombe includes pilau and is as elaborate as the bride's family can afford. While this meal is a customary sign of affection toward the groom by his new in-laws, it is also meant to strengthen the groom for his first sexual encounter with their virgin daughter (*mwanamwali*). As the groom and his close relatives and friends enjoy the last of the kombe, the groom's thoughts turn to the imminent meeting with his bride.

Behind the door of the room in which the bibiharusi awaits, her female relatives (married aunts and elder sisters) instruct the bwanaharusi to pay an entrance fee and open only when satisfied with the number of shilling notes that have been slid under the door or pushed through ventilation ducts above it. After appeasing his female in-laws, the bwanaharusi makes his way through the crowd to approach his new wife. It is customary for the bwanaharusi to place his right hand on the bibiharusi's head and recite the *ayat al-kursi* (Throne Verse), a Qur'anic verse believed to ward off evil spirits (*jini*), practices found in Morocco as well.[17] It is also customary for the groom to adorn the bride with a gold necklace or bracelet,[18] symbolic compensation for the bride's soon-to-be confirmed virginity. After the bwana- and bibiharusi are seated next to each other, the couple is served a glass of rose-flavored milk that they ceremoniously share, each holding the glass while the other takes a sip.[19] Over the past fifteen years, these traditions have increasingly become photo opportunities for relatives eager to pose with the new couple. Depending on the size of the gathering, visual documentation of this event can go on for over an hour, especially if a professional photographer has been hired. The nervous tension in the air as the newlyweds make small talk and try not to fidget is palpable. Just one thing is on their minds—the only deed that remains undone.

Finally, after photographs have been taken and pleasantries shared between members of the newly joined families, the couple moves to a bedroom to consummate the marriage. The anxiety that this phase of the wedding causes Swahili men is generally overshadowed by the focus on the virginity of the bibiharusi.[20] Although the bwanaharusi receives advice on various deflowering strategies from married relatives and friends, he is often personally inexperienced in sexual matters, if not a virgin himself. Calming the nerves of his new wife is the first challenge, especially if the two have spent very little time becoming acquainted in person, which is often the case, even today. Knowing how to perform the sex act quickly and without too much unpleasantness for the bibiharusi is the second step. The third is reporting the bibiharusi's virginity to female relatives waiting outside. Before the 1980s it was customary for Swahili women in Lamu Town to parade the bride's blood-stained bedsheet around the immediate neighborhood to publicly share the news of the bride's virginity and receive coins that were tossed into the sheet in celebration. Today, less emphasis is placed on the physical evidence of a bride's virginity and the sheet no longer leaves the marriage bed. Evolving notions of social etiquette more in line with less conservative coastal communities allow the contemporary Lamu Town groom the freedom to share the virgin status of his new wife with a female relative awaiting the news. Boisterous ululation immediately ensues among the women who have congregated in the home, where dancing and singing among the new couple's female relatives continues into the late hours of the night.

If such news does not come in a timely fashion and the delay is caused by the groom's impotence, he faces humiliation equal to that of a bride whose virginity is questioned. In this case, the bwanaharusi is given a short grace period for further coaching and to overcome his anxiety. People say that if he is unable to perform the sex act due to impotence, it is very likely that the marriage will be called off and he will be forced to live with the shame. However, if he and his new wife consummate the marriage within the week, the marriage is deemed a success and the groom escapes the ordeal relatively unscathed, except for his notoriety as the victim of performance anxiety in the stories that will be told to future grooms.

POSTMARRIAGE CUSTOMS

Lamu Town families point to Sunna (the body of custom and practice based on the life of the Prophet Muhammad) when explaining the wedding feast (known as *lima ya harusi* in Swahili) hosted by the groom after the consummation of the marriage. The feast is considered a religious obligation rather than a local or family custom, a difference that warrants future research in coastal Kenya, as it demonstrates variation in Swahili Islamic practice, even in a relatively small region.[21] In Lamu Town, this meal is a private affair to which the close family members of the bibi- and bwana-harusi are invited. Until about a decade ago, this feast was a Lamu groom's final wedding obligation. The bride's coming-out party, known as *kutoleza nje* (to put outside), which always occurs the day after the marriage is consummated, was strictly a female affair at which the bibiharusi was welcomed into the company of her new peer group. Due to the popularity of making this occasion an opportunity to take photos and video of the new couple, the bwa-naharusi and his male escorts make an appearance toward the very end of the ceremony, disrupting the otherwise sexually stratified nature of Swahili weddings and marking quite a dramatic deviation from the "traditional" wedding script.

When the bwanaharusi arrives, typically dressed in a Western suit and tie to match his new wife's white bridal gown, he mimics the bibiharusi's entrance by slowly proceeding his way past the all-female guests to the stage on which the bride is seated. The glamorous stage is typically draped in silk fabric, decorated with hanging party lights, and adorned with flower girls and boy attendants dressed like miniature grooms and brides. For the rest of the evening and as the majority of the guests take their leave, female relatives wait their turn to pose with the new couple on stage, thus becoming part of the family's wedding album. These days, photographs are instantly added to Facebook pages, and videotapes are copied and distributed for private viewing by relatives and friends near and far. The showing of the bride marks the official end of the wedding. Yet though the event is the bibi-harusi's entrée into adult society, the groom's official entrance comes after the wedding, when he and his wife are welcomed as special guests into the homes of relatives and friends in which he was rarely if ever invited as a bachelor.

The honeymoon period for Lamu newlyweds lasts about three months, and during that period the new couple is invited for lunches and dinners and generally treated as celebrities wherever they go. As one newly married bwanaharusi explained,

> Whenever I go to someone's house, they are so respect-ful. I've never been treated like that before. All my uncles who I am visiting and who are inviting my wife and me to eat with them are so welcoming. I can tell that they really want her to be part of our family. They are treating her like a queen—not like she is from another family, but like she is already part of our family. And her family is treating me the same way. It feels very nice to be married!

Though honeymoons in Lamu Town last longer than they do in many societies, they do not last forever, and soon the couple is pressured to move into the next phase of life: parenthood. When reminiscing about the advice he received on his wedding day, one Swahili man remembered, "My uncle told me that there are three groups in the male Swahili hierarchy: (A) bachelors, (B) married men, and (C) fathers. He said, 'Welcome to group B and enjoy it while you can. Only when you get to group C will you become a full member of our society. Each group has its challenges and its benefits.'"

IT IS not a subtle irony that although grooms are largely responsible for footing the bill, Swahili weddings in Lamu Town are arranged by female elders; most men have a limited role in the selection of their wives, aside from the power to veto a particularly bad choice. Young men choose a bride from among a handful of young women deemed eligible by their aunts and grandmothers, who spend a considerable amount of time scrutinizing the marriage pool. Young ladies from families not recently married into are top priority for the women, as sustaining linkages to the most prestigious Lamu Town families is strategic in terms of maintaining or enhancing social rank. Such calculation is particularly important to the Lamu elite, who see marriage as one way to control their social status, be it based on religious piety or wealth, or both.

Marriage between first cousins is still quite common in Lamu Town, particularly among the elite. John Middleton has proposed the following marriage statistics among Swahili "patricians": 65 percent of firstborn daughters married paternal parallel cousins (children of paternal uncles or maternal aunts), 25 percent of those were marriages between first or second cousins.[22] The rationale behind this system is that it allows members of the upper class to retain purity of lineage, wealth, and property within the family rather than diluting it. In practical terms, when a couple's parents (usually their fathers) are siblings, they constitute a united front when marital problems arise and do not hesitate to step in to prevent the conflict from breaking up the family. As one Lamu woman, who married her father's brother's son, explained, "If I do something wrong to my husband, he calls my father (his uncle) to talk with me, and if my husband does something wrong to me, I call his father (my uncle) to talk with him. The elders demand that we apologize, change our behavior, and move on from there." Elders often claim that arranged marriages and marriages between close relatives mitigate against divorce, although unfortunately this does not bear out in reality.

Though the Swahili recognize that polygyny is sanctioned by Islam (marriage to four wives simultaneously is allowed under certain conditions), fewer men in Lamu District in 2005–6 indicated having more than one wife (8.1 percent) compared to other districts, such as Kilifi (15.4 percent) and Malindi (26 percent), and Coast Province generally (12.8 percent).[23] The infrequency of polygyny is especially true among Lamu families of higher status that support a woman's prerogative to divorce her husband if he takes a second wife.[24] This family support for elite women who wish to divorce polygynous husbands may be the cause of the high divorce rate among people in Lamu District (10.8 percent) compared to other districts in Kenya. This supports Susi Krehbiel Keefe's argument in this volume that polygyny is rare among the Swahili due in part to the effectiveness of women's strategies to thwart the practice. A combination of challenges— including financial insecurity, high unemployment, jealousy, and ill will (hasida) among family members—puts a strain on couples in Lamu.[25]

The issue of hasida is particularly relevant when it comes to Swahili marriage. Like other rites of passage, the Swahili consider marriage to be a transition that makes the bride and groom susceptible to harm instigated by the ill will and jealousy of others, usually directed in the form of a curse (fitna) or "the evil eye." "Since the Swahili believe that those in a pure spiritual state are able to deflect malice more effectively than those in a state of impurity," would-be targets of such assault need extra spiritual protection.[26] In the case of the groom, one way this protection is offered comes in the form of food.

The practice of combining foods that are red, black, and white on ritually significant occasions is still common in Lamu Town. Abdul Hamid el-Zein's Lamu informants explained this combination as one that symbolizes the impurity of humans, who emerged from red and black dust, and the purity of celestial beings such as angels, prophets, and saints, represented by white.[27] Pilau, including red meat and black peppercorns; and halwa, a reddish-tinted sweetmeat prepared with slivered almonds and served with black Arabic coffee, are wedding foods especially prepared for the groom that by combining the powerful color triad provide a ward against evil. As in Pakistani weddings, the presence of red and white in the flowers and the milkshake offered to the groom at the kirumbizi ceremony provides other examples of how the colors are employed to deter spiritual assault against the groom.[28]

In addition to battling unseen nemeses, a Swahili groom must also face human adversaries, sometimes in the form of his own relatives. As the Swahili men and women with whom I have spoken explain, the patriarchs of the family are ultimately responsible for ameliorating family discord, a duty first recognized by the groom at his wedding. The physical strength the groom and his male relatives demonstrate at the kirumbizi and during the kutia ndani ceremony, as well as the military attire and weaponry the bwanaharusi dons to ward off supernatural and human obstacles, are outward expressions of the inner fortitude men must draw on when dealing with family conflict. As weddings bring relatives from near and far together for days at a time, family strife is inevitable and must be handled appropriately. Until their own weddings, young men are largely incognizant of family disputes and are not party to conflicts or how they are resolved. Upon reflection, one newlywed shared what he had learned about dealing with family squabbles at his recent wedding:

> Not everyone is happy that my wife and I are together; there are people we should be wary of. Not everyone invited to our wedding was happy for us; some don't want the marriage to last. As a man, I need to face all these situations eloquently—not rudely. A man needs to be able to handle any situation smoothly; that is the man's responsibility. For example, at my wedding, I knew that some of the guests were not happy for us, but I did not show them that I was aware of that. I showed them that I was happy that they were able to attend.

In considering what masculinity means among the Swahili of Lamu Town and how weddings serve to articulate that meaning, it is helpful to consider wedding traditions that involve the groom as a set of introductory lessons that teach him what it means to be an adult Swahili man. Though some ceremonies are held according to family or personal preference (e.g., the shaving ceremony and the kirumbizi), and the lavishness of a wedding depends on the family's wealth, these customs and others (e.g., bembe, kutia ndani, lima ya harusi) have been preserved by Lamu families over time and are imbued with illustrations of how adult men in Lamu society should behave. The tact with which a young man collects wedding funds from his male elders, the dignity he demonstrates when interacting with his male relatives as they decide upon the proposal, and the kindness he showers on his female relatives to ensure that the food and gifts they prepare for the bride are of the highest quality indicate whether or not the groom is ready to accept his role as head of his household and perform the duties prescribed for his new status.

Though scholars have described a masculinity crisis among African men whose wives have assumed the traditionally male role as breadwinner,[29] economic downturn in Lamu Town has not significantly impacted gender roles, leaving intact the rights and responsibilities husbands and wives have maintained for centuries. Men and women's spheres of influence remain separate; women enjoy freedom and control of the domestic sphere and men enjoy freedom and control of public space. These spheres are maintained and indeed celebrated in the majority of the wedding ceremonies described in this chapter. Transgression of men and women's space during the wedding is marked linguistically to de-emphasize the volition of the actor and emphasize the strength of the custom: the groom is "put into" the house during the kutia ndani ceremony; the bride is "put out" of the house during the kutoleza nje ceremony.

During the first months of marriage, Swahili men are introduced to a host of new responsibilities that they are asked to take on by their natal family and their new in-laws. Being welcomed into the circle of adult males means being consulted about business ventures, performing annual rituals, and contributing financially to cover school fees, medical expenses, and the cost of weddings and funerals of extended family members. As one Swahili proverb explains, *Mwenye kuowa haowi mke tu. Huowa na jamaa zake* (One doesn't marry a wife alone. One marries her whole family).

Though the groom is well aware of the competitive nature of Lamu weddings, especially among the Lamu elite,[30] his own wedding is his first direct exposure to how family politics, wealth, and social status intersect. A bwanaharusi soon learns that the combination of willpower and finesse that he mustered to negotiate the first night with his new wife is a recipe for how he will become a well-respected man in Lamu Town. As one newly married man explained, the wedding itself—all the pressures and family tensions—is like a test for the rest of your adult life!

NOTES

My thanks to Zainab Ahmed and her entire family in Lamu Town for their support of my research, and to each of the men whose thoughts and experiences are conveyed in this chapter. Even with the assistance I have received, especially from my husband, Munib Said A. Mafazy, it is inevitable that I have failed to get everything right. Any errors or confusions in this narrative are entirely my own.

1. For analysis of the social compact between descendants of former slaves and masters in Lamu Town, see Mbarak Ali Hinawy, "Notes on Customs in Mombasa," *Swahili* 34, no. 1 (1964): 17–35; John Middleton, *The World of the Swahili: An African Mercantile Civilization* (New Haven: Yale University Press, 1992).

2. For more on how the Swahili incorporated this ensemble as a marker of status, see Laura Fair, *Pastimes and Politics: Culture, Community, and Identity in Post-abolition Urban Zanzibar, 1890–1945* (Athens: Ohio University Press, 2002).

3. See Françoise Le Guennec-Coppens, *Wedding Customs in Lamu* (Lamu Society, 1980); Patricia Romero Curtin, "Weddings in Lamu, Kenya: An Example of Social and Economic Change (Mariages à Lamu [Kenya]: Un cas de changement économique et social)," *Cahiers d'études africaines* 24, no. 94 (1984): 131–55; Minou Fuglesang, *Veils and Videos: Female Youth Culture on the Kenyan Coast* (Stockholm: Almqvist and Wiksell International, 1994); Patricia W. Romero, *Lamu: History, Society, and Family in an East African Port City* (Princeton: Markus Wiener, 1997); Katrina Daly Thompson, "How to Be a Good Muslim Wife: Women's

Performance of Islamic Authority during Swahili Weddings," *Journal of Religion in Africa* 41, no. 4 (2011): 427–48; Larsen, "Pleasure and Prohibitions," chap. 7, this volume; Thompson, "Learning to use Swahili Profanity," chap. 6, this volume.

4. Rebecca Gearhart, "Seeing Life through the Eyes of Swahili Children of Lamu, Kenya: A Visual Anthropology Approach," *AnthropoChildren* 3, no. 3 (2013), http://popups.ulg.ac.be/2034-8517/

5. Curtin, "Weddings in Lamu," 140–41.

6. Margaret Ann Strobel, "Muslim Women in Mombasa, Kenya. 1890–1973" (PhD diss., UCLA, 1975), 37.

7. Curtin, "Weddings in Lamu," 135.

8. Middleton, *World of the Swahili*, 128.

9. Ibid., 129.

10. Jane Bristol-Rhys, "Weddings, Marriage and Money in the United Arab Emirates," *Anthropology of the Middle East* 2, no.1 (2007): 20–36.

11. Adeline Masquelier, "The Scorpion's Sting: Youth, Marriage and the Struggle for Social Maturity in Niger," *Journal of the Royal Anthropological Institute* 11 (2005): 59–83.

12. For discussion on how Swahili women in Mombasa manipulate their husbands by equating how much their husbands love them with how loose they are with their wallets, see Marc J. Swartz, "The Isolation of Men and the Happiness of Women: Sources and Use of Power in Swahili Marital Relationships," *Journal of Anthropological Research* 38, no. 1 (1982): 26–44.

13. *Simbo* (Amu dialect) is also referred to as *fimbo* in other parts of the coast. See Richard Skene, "Arab and Swahili Dances and Ceremonies," *Journal of the Anthropological Institute of Great Britain and Ireland* 47, no. 2 (1917): 413–34.

14. See the comments on scent, and related cited literature, in chapters by Thompson and Larsen this volume.

15. Cf. Middleton, *World of the Swahili*, 151.

16. Edward Westermarck, "Marriage Ceremonies in Morocco," *Sociological Review* 5, no. 3 (July 1912): 192; Robert B. Serjeant, "Recent Marriage Legislation from al-Mukallā with Notes on Marriage Customs," *Bulletin of the School of Oriental and African Studies* 25, no. 3 (1962): 489.

17. Westermarck, "Marriage Ceremonies," 198.

18. In reference to Swahili weddings in Lamu, Le Guennec-Coppens refers to this gift as *hidaya* [<Ar. *hadiya*] and suggests it is generally presented after the wedding night. *Wedding Customs in Lamu*, 14.

19. Cf. Thompson, "Good Muslim Wife," 440.

20. Curtin also makes this observation in "Weddings in Lamu," 144.

21. Ed van Hoven's study of *zakat* (almsgiving, one of the five pillars of Islam) practices at Soninke Manding marriage ceremonies in eastern Senegal offers a good model for comparing notions of religious obligation and

social or family custom. "Local Tradition or Islamic Precept? The Notion of Zakāt in Wuli (Eastern Senegal)," *Cahiers d'études africaines* 36, no. 144 (1996): 703–22.

22. Middleton, *World of the Swahili*, 123.

23. Kenya National Bureau of Statistics, *Kenya Integrated Household Budget Survey, 2005/06* (Nairobi: Kenya National Bureau of Statistics, 2006).

24. Curtin, "Weddings in Lamu," 137–38; Middleton, *World of the Swahili*, 123.

25. Middleton, *World of the Swahili*.

26. Rebecca Gearhart and Munib Abdulrehman, "Purity, Balance and Wellness among the Swahili of Lamu, Kenya," *Journal of Global Health* 2, no. 1 (2012): 43.

27. Abdul Hamid M. el-Zein, *The Sacred Meadows: A Structural Analysis of Religious Symbolism in an East African Town* (Evanston: Northwestern University Press, 1974), 184.

28. Pnina Werbner, "The Virgin and the Clown: Ritual Elaboration in Pakistani Migrants' Weddings," *Man* 21, no. 2 (1986): 227–50.

29. Margrethe Silberschmidt, "Disempowerment of Men in Rural and Urban East Africa: Implications for Male Identity and Sexual Behavior," *World Development* 29, no. 4 (2001): 657–71; Donna L. Perry, "Wolof Women, Economic Liberalization, and the Crisis of Masculinity in Rural Senegal," *Ethnology* 44, no. 3 (2005): 207–26.

30. Curtin, "Weddings in Lamu"; Middleton, *World of the Swahili;* Romero, *Lamu*.

TEN

Spirit Possession and Masculinity in Swahili Society

LINDA L. GILES

THE RELATIONSHIP BETWEEN GENDER, ritual, and the body is central to many studies of spirit possession. Spirit possession is inherently connected to the body, which provides the vehicle for possession. Many studies have also suggested that spirit possession is often connected with gender. They point out that in many societies women make up the majority and sometimes the totality of those possessed. Most studies point out that this is an unintentional result of women's sociocultural position,[1] but others have pointed out that societal views often assign women possessive roles.[2] In both cases, one of the major factors in female affinity toward possession is engendered notions of the body and its associated character traits, which Janice Boddy explored in-depth in her influential case study of *zar* possession in Sudan.[3]

I conducted fieldwork on spirit possession guilds (*vyama* or *vilinge*) in the Swahili coastal society of East Africa from 1982 through 1984, supplemented by short visits in 1992, 2001, 2006, 2007, and 2011. Beliefs in spirits and spirit possession are widespread among the Swahili. While oral traditions within the spirit guilds and written accounts from the late nineteenth and early twentieth centuries suggest that spirit guild activity was more common in the past,[4] today only a minority are actively involved with spirit guilds. I found that the majority of possession cases, guild members, and clients of guild leaders are indeed female but that a significant number of men also participate. (The exceptions are two atypical spirit guild types found in Zanzibar Town, the *Habeshia* and the *Kibuki,* which both have origins in non-Swahili areas and have very low involvement from men.) Within the spirit guilds themselves, men play a specialized role as musicians and are well represented as leaders and upper-level officials. They can also be found among the regular initiated members in most guilds. Even more significantly, men in all these spirit guild positions undergo varying amounts of possession. In addition, contrary to the situation reported in many other possession studies,[5] male guild members and participants cannot be typified either as low-status individuals or as homosexuals. While Kjersti Larsen and Mohamed Saleh both note that effeminate and homosexual men participate in kibuki ceremonies in Zanzibar Town but heterosexual men do not,[6] I found no evidence at all of any relationship with homosexuality in the spirit guilds I studied.

This is not to say, however, that gender has no effect on the majority of possession cases or possession guilds in Swahili contexts. This chapter explores how the act of spirit possession is conceptualized in relation to the body and self and relates this to societal views about gender characteristics and behavioral ideals as well as possible sexual implications. I explore how these factors affect male attitudes toward possession, expressions of possessive relationships, and the development of case histories and possessive careers. I then focus on two particularly interesting cases of male possession and initiation that I encountered in the Tanga area of northern Tanzania in 1983–84 and make some comparisons to the female cases more commonly encountered throughout my field area. I explore how both men came to accept spirit possession under personal duress, how they were especially resistant to being initiated into spirit guilds for non-Islamic spirits, and how they used their Islamic possessive spirits to pursue a masculine career as Islamic ritual specialists and distanced themselves from further associations with the spirit guilds.

I conducted research in a number of urban and rural field sites, primarily in the city of Mombasa and the small towns of Vanga and Wasini in southern Kenya; the Tanga and Pangani areas in northern Tanzania; Zanzibar Town; and the Wete and Chake Chake areas of Pemba. Field data was collected through participant-observation and by formal and informal interviews with ritual specialists who treat spirit possession, members and other participants in spirit possession guilds, and members of the general public. I conducted interviews in the Swahili language, sometimes with the assistance of local field assistants. Most interviews were taped and later transcribed. I also attended and documented a number of spirit guild ceremonies and gathered life histories of various types of people who were treated for or experienced spirit possession.

SWAHILI SPIRIT POSSESSION AND POSSESSION GUILDS

Spirit possession has a long history on the Swahili coast, and like many other aspects of Swahili culture, it represents a synthesis of indigenous African and Middle Eastern (predominantly Arab) beliefs and practices. Possessive spirits are commonly called *pepo* (also the Swahili word for wind), or, according to Arabic terminology, *sheitani* (pl., *masheitani*), or *jini* (pl., *majini*). Although spirits resemble humans in many ways, they are a separate form of creation. They interact with people because of an inherited relationship, personal attraction, anger, or ritual manipulation by knowledgeable humans. Spirits may possess people so that the human body becomes a vehicle for the spirit, but usually spirits first manifest themselves through illness, bad luck, barrenness, and other misfortunes. Diagnosis and treatment requires the services of a ritual specialist known as *mganga* (pl., *waganga*) or *fundi* (a general term for someone who possesses any type of expertise), who practices the arts of *uganga* (divination, curing, and magic). Waganga who deal with spirits are generally differentiated into two basic types. Those using traditional Middle Eastern Islamic methods are often known as *waganga wa kitabu* (waganga of the book—that is, the Qur'an and other written Arabic texts) and frequently given the title Mwalimu, Mwalim, or Maalim (all meaning teacher or scholar); I refer to these as Qu'ranic waganga in my subsequent discussion. The second type are waganga who use possessive spirits and ceremonies involving music (generally focusing on drumming) and dance (*ngoma*). This latter type of waganga are known by various terms, including *waganga wa pepo/sheitani* (waganga of the spirits), *waganga wa kichwa* (waganga of the head, since spirits are believed to settle in and take over a person's head), or *waganga wa ngoma* (waganga of the drum/dance/ceremony); I will refer to these as "spirit waganga" throughout this chapter and examine career choices between the two types of uganga in the case studies that follow.

Whereas I did not hear of or encounter any female Qu'ranic waganga at any of my field sites,[7] I readily found both men and women as spirit guild waganga. Although most Muslim scholars claim that spirits should be exorcized using Qur'anic methods, many types of spirits are appeased with the assistance of spirit waganga (waganga wa pepo), especially if they can enter into useful relationships with humans. Such spirits are often possessive, in which case they usually ask that the patient be initiated into an appropriate spirit guild group that engages in rituals (including ngoma) for spirits of its type. Spirits may further request that the initiate advance to higher ranks within the guild. The highest rank is that of the mganga or fundi, who has acquired a full range of spiritual skills and may head his or her own spirit guild.

Spirit beliefs and rituals vary according to societal position, spiritual knowledge, and locality. They also vary between the two types of waganga, individual waganga, and the different types of possession guilds. Nonetheless, there are some general patterns that can be discerned from my field research in conjunction with other literature on the topic. Swahili spirit practitioners divide spirits along two key dimensions, contrasting Muslim (*Kiislamu*) spirits with pagan (*kafiri* or *shenzi*) spirits, and coastal (*pwani*) spirits with those from the African interior (*bara*). Within these broad divisions, they break spirits into more specific categories that are the foci of particular spirit guilds. Many of these categories are identified with certain human ethnic groups who have impinged on Swahili experience throughout their history, either as outside groups or as groups that have become integrated into Swahili communities. The Swahili prefix *ki-*, which designates manner, is often used to refer to such spirit types, thus Arab spirits are known as *pepo wa Kiarabu,* Maasai spirits as *pepo wa Kimasai,* and so on. The category of "Arab" spirits is often extended to other types of spirits from the Middle East or northeastern Africa, especially those that show a highly Islamic character, such as *pepo wa Kisomali* (Somali spirits). Only one spirit type is identified as Kiswahili in nature. These are the *pepo wa Kipemba,* who originally came from the island of Pemba but now reside throughout the Swahili region. Most contemporary cases of possession involve Arab and Pemban spirits, but other types assume secondary importance in certain areas, including Maasai spirits in Tanga; Ethiopian and Malagasy spirits in Zanzibar Town; and Nyamwezi and Shambaa (Tanzanian ethnic groups) spirits in Pemba. Various categories of spirits, especially the more common ones like Arab and Pemban spirits, are further subdivided into more specific types based on the songs and rhythms they require, other ritual requirements, and perceived character. Names for types of spirits may vary somewhat according to locality; thus in Mombasa Pemban spirits are called pepo wa Kipemba or simply Wapemba (Pembans), in the Tanga area and Zanzibar Town they are often called *bwengo,* and in Pemba itself they are often simply called *wenyeji* (native residents or owners of the land) in addition to Wapemba, or referred to only by their subtypes.[8]

Possession, Gender, and the Body

In spirit possession, an exterior nonhuman entity intrudes into the human realm and interferes with human affairs. It results in a loss of human control, including control of the individual self. During full possession, one's body is not only troubled by but also actually taken over by the spirit. Thus the human body becomes the spirit's body, through which the spirit acts and communicates within the human world. According to the Swahili, the spirit takes control of the mind or will by physically coming into one's head. In Swahili this is expressed by saying that the spirit *anapanda kichwani,* which literally means that it climbs onto or into, or rides on, the head—a conception that is common in many spirit possession traditions. Once the spirit is fully settled in the head, it is possible to communicate with it through the agency of the one possessed. This condition, however, can be difficult to achieve. The spirit must be convinced to make itself available in this form, and the possessed human must also learn how to accommodate the spirit. Full contact is established only when the spirit speaks verbally through its human medium and enters into a two-way conversation.

In spirit possession, an outside being not only interferes in one's affairs but also ultimately takes over one's body, mind, and behavior. This loss of control is more problematic for men than women, as self-control and restraint are highly valued male attributes in Swahili societies, especially among the upper classes. Rebecca Gearhart's chapter in this volume exemplifies these issues in Lamu Town. Similarly, Marc Swartz identities formality, honor, and restraint as male behavioral ideals among Mombasa Swahili. Women, he reports, are viewed by men and also many women as less logical and possessing less emotional control.[9] Larsen finds similar views in Zanzibar Town, where she notes that women and men are defined as psychological opposites. Men are viewed as having "more strength, rationality, and reason than women" and thus "to have more self-control and to behave in morally and socially acceptable ways. . . . Lack of self-control is more tolerated in women."[10] Elsewhere she describes a case of an educated and religious Zanzibari man who refused to accede to the demands of spirits troubling him in order to preserve his image of being "knowledgeable, respectable, and possessing the ability to exercise self-control."[11]

Michael Lambek writes that spirit possession is also detrimental to male self-image among Malagasy-speaking Muslims in Mayotte in the Comoro Islands, because the spirits themselves, and thus the spirits' possessed human mounts, behave in ways that clash with male behavioral roles. The Comoros are closely linked to mainland Swahili societies: there has been much interaction and migration between them and there are many cultural, religious, and linguistic similarities. Spirits in Mayotte are often undignified, selfish, irresponsible, intemperate, sensual, and demand gifts and favors, characteristics that are seen as more typical of women and viewed as antithetical to adult male ideals.[12] These same problematic behaviors are also typical of most spirits in Swahili society.

Perceived masculine gender characteristics and behavioral ideals are also related to men's greater association with what is considered orthodox Islam in terms of public performance, leadership roles, and societal expectations, which adds to the difficulty of spirit possession, since submitting to spirits' demands is often condemned by religious authorities as compromising Islam's monotheistic requirement. Lambek also points to this distinction in his 1981 study of Mayotte, noting that "access . . . [to possession] for men is restricted to the degree that their status is dependant upon participation in Islam."[13] He later refines this statement, writing that "Islam is embodied and reproduced largely and most saliently by men, possession by women" but astutely adding that this division should be viewed more as a "division of labor in historical production than . . . an ideological division."[14]

John Middleton sums up these gendered impediments in Swahili society by noting that even as spirit guild leaders, males "risk being classified with transvestite musicians and other anomalous yet powerful figures outside the formal mosque-centered male networks of scholarship, dignity, and honor."[15] Spirit guild waganga often noted it was more difficult for men to accept possessive relationships and go through initiation because they feel more shame (*aibu*) about it than women do. For example, when I asked a female spirit mganga if her father had the same powerful spirit (a male *ruhani*, see below) that she did, she replied: "anaye lakini hamukubali yeye. Wajua wanaume si sana wakubali haya mambo. Sharti augue sana hata akubali." (He has him but he [her father] did not agree to him. You know men do not often agree to these things. It is necessary that he suffer a lot before he agrees.) Similarly, the granddaughter of the female mganga who took me to a spirit initiation for Shale (one of the two male case studies explored below) reported that her grandmother's brother also had spirits but had not been initiated. When I asked if it was true that men often did not want an initiation ceremony, she agreed and explained, "waona aibu" (they feel shame).

Parallels with Human Sexual Actions and Their Implications

Possession as a temporary physical entry of one entity into another also has many parallels with human sexual intimacy. The spirit assumes the active role of entering, generally associated with the male in human heterosexual relations, and moreover "climbs on top of" the human recipient. Spirits are also the ones who initiate the relationship and often they do so because of physical attraction. These sexual implications probably add to the society's uneasiness about possession and also help explain why women are considered more vulnerable. In the case of a male, the usual heterosexual gender roles are reversed, which may add to the perception that it is more problematic for males to undergo possession.

Several scholars, however, note that homosexuality, especially among males, is not unusual and not necessarily disapproved of in Swahili society. Larsen paints a complex picture of male homosexuality in Zanzibar Town in her 2008 book. She believes all men who have sexual relations with other males are labeled as male homosexuals (*hanithi*) and observes that the term can also be used as a general insult to suggest lack of manliness. Larsen observes that homosexuals of both sexes are criticized for "lacking modesty or shame" but points out that they are tacitly accepted as long as they do not call public attention to their homosexuality. In contrast, male homosexuals who fail to perform expected masculine gender roles or who mix gender markers in public are not respected, although the latter are often accepted in female company. "The masculine gender image," she adds, "has no room for what is seen as feminine behavior."[16]

In Gill Shepherd's 1987 study of homosexuality in Mombasa, she suggests that only the male partner who is paid for the act with another male is considered a homosexual (*shoga*) and that, although "the paid partner usually takes the passive role during intercourse . . . his inferiority derives from the fact that he is paid to provide what is asked for, rather than the role he adopts." Shepherd adds that "homosexual relations in Mombasa are almost without exception between a younger, poorer partner and an older, richer one" and that "financial considerations are always involved."[17] The paid partner thus is put in a position of dependence, and males gain status by having dependents that they support and control, as Susi Krehbiel Keefe, in this volume, also shows in relation to men's desire for polygamous marriages.

Shepherd's interpretation of homosexuality in Mombasa has since been contested by later ethnographers, who point out that her research was conducted among Comorian immigrants and not the larger Swahili community. Mary Porter, who also conducted fieldwork in Mombasa, found that the Mombasa Swahili view homosexuality as "highly problematical." She posits a cultural hierarchy of sexual behavior, with "normal" heterosexual sex most valued, followed by the "'active'" homosexual male (the *basha*), then the female homosexual, and at the very bottom, the "passive" male homosexual (*shoga*), who is sodomized. She notes that basha are much less publicly noticeable than other homosexuals, since they are often powerful married men who fulfill most gender expectations, including the "sexually 'active'" role in homosexual encounters. The shoga's low status derives from the fact that he transgresses gender roles the most visibly by attending women's events, sometimes taking women's roles, behaviors, and dress, and taking the passive (sodomized) role in sexual activity, activities that compromise honor (*heshima*).[18]

Contrary to Shepherd and Porter, Deborah Amory conducted fieldwork among "homosexuals" themselves in an undisclosed East African coastal city. She agrees with Porter that the shoga (or khanithi/hanisi) is much more stigmatized than the basha, and adds that "the definitions of the *shoga* and *basha* identity rely on the 'active' versus 'passive' roles in sex, that are specifically gendered in coastal society and that correlate with other gendered behaviors."[19] Both Porter and Amory note that the experience of passive anal sex is said to "ruin" a Swahili male, in the same terminology applied to a Swahili female who has sex before marriage.

These latter studies suggest that, in spite of Shepherd's finding to the contrary, the passive role in male homosexual relations (including being mounted and penetrated), which is similar to that adopted in spirit possession, does indeed appear to be highly problematic for masculine identity and status among the Swahili. Moreover, as Larsen points out, the amount of stigma attached to this role as well as others that transgress gender norms is greatly augmented in public contexts; thus, the more public spirit possession becomes, the more it can be expected to threaten masculinity.

Shepherd's alternative analysis of stigma in male homosexual relations as resulting from accepting payment would not seem to apply to Swahili (or most other) patterns of spirit possession in that gifts are usually given *to* the spirit by its human partner and his or her family to placate it, although it is also important to remember that during possession the person acts as the spirit and thus takes on the role of accepting and soliciting gifts. The issue of human dependence that Shepherd highlights also arises in many other ways in human-spirit relationships, since the spirit is usually the one who initiates the relationship and the one who is at least initially in control. The spirit makes demands that it tries to force the possessed person to accept. Moreover, the welfare of the person possessed depends on the spirit and its goodwill and thus puts the person in a position of dependence and submission.

Spirit Guild Initiations: The Pungwa

The possessive relationship usually remains tenuous, incipient, and troublesome until an initiation ceremony into a spirit guild is held. This ceremony, known as the *pungwa,* transforms the initiate into a suitable mount or "chair" (*kiti*) for the spirit. It is chiefly concerned with drawing the spirit to take full possession of the initiate and developing a cooperative relationship between them. In addition to the usual rebirth-redevelopment metaphor found in most rites of passage, the pungwa also uses the metaphor of the wedding. Accordingly, female initiates are often referred to as the bride (*bi arusi,* a variant of *bibiharusi*) of the spirit.[20] In the only pungwa ceremony for a male initiate that I attended (discussed in the case studies), the central participants stated that the same wedding metaphor was applicable, comparing the male initiate to the groom, or *bwana arusi.*

There are many parallels between Swahili weddings and spirit initiations. The relationship between the spirit and its chair is similar to those established in marriage. Both set up and legitimize physical intimacy on a regular basis between two individuals from different family groups within a long-term, institutionalized, and formally consecrated interpersonal relationship. This relationship, moreover, binds together the respective families of the individuals as well as the individuals themselves, as Lambek and Lesley Sharp also point out for spirit possession in Mayotte and northwestern Madagascar, respectively.[21]

In Swahili weddings, however, the role of the groom is perceived as different from that of the bride; the former is seen as more active, the latter more passive. As Larsen and Katrina Thompson both discuss in this volume, this difference is explicitly encoded in the Swahili language: whereas a groom marries (*anaoa*), a bride can only be married (*anaolewa*). In the spirit guild, the human role thus seems more equivalent to that of the bride. Moreover, just as the male (or, more often, his family or others representing him) proposes to the female in a human marriage, the spirit is the one who asks for the *initiation* ceremony. The role of the possessed human is merely that of accepting or refusing. Refusal, however, causes considerable difficulty, thus giving the spirit quite an advantage. Most people show considerable resistance to undergoing a spirit initiation ceremony, since it is the critical step that institutionalizes the spirit-human relationship. Although many people eventually submit, it is particularly difficult for men to do so.

The initiation process itself also has many parallels to the marriage ceremony. Like many Swahili weddings, spirit initiation ceremonies are major community celebrations involving dancing, feasting, and requiring a considerable outlay of funds. In addition, the preparation of the spirit guild initiate is very similar to the preparation of the bride and groom for their first wedding. They become the center of attention and are washed, scented, decorated, and dressed in finery, as both Gearhart and Thompson show in this volume. Once again, however, the process has more parallels with the preparation of the bride than the groom, due to its intensity, the emphasis on making the initiate physically attractive and receptive to the spirit, the need for careful instruction, the passive role of the initiate, and her behavioral and social restriction, including almost complete seclusion. Moreover, in the past, weddings often took place after the conclusion of a more encompassing rite of passage, the female puberty ceremonies (*unyago*) discussed by Larsen, Pat Caplan, and Thompson in this volume. The use of the wedding metaphor therefore draws symbolically from both the female initiation rites held at puberty and the wedding ceremony itself. Thus the spirit guild initiate is often referred to as the *mwari*, the same term used for the initiate in the puberty ceremonies. This association also helps explain the otherwise puzzling inclusion of the unyago rhythm played during the female puberty rites (and also incorporated into women's wedding celebrations)[22] during the ceremonies for Kipemba spirits. I found a similar association with the traditional male puberty rites (which included circumcision), called *jando* on the island of Pemba, where Kipemba ceremonies sometimes included the jando rhythm locally called *unjuguu*, in reference to the circumciser. Jando rites were once widespread in the Swahili area[23] but have now largely disappeared, as we see in Caplan's chapter in this volume. In many cases boys undergoing jando would not be ready to marry until later, but the rite was considered a prerequisite to sexual maturity, marriage, and life as an adult male.

Gender and Islam among the Spirits

The possession experience is also affected by the gender of the spirit involved. Most possessive spirits seem to be conceptualized as male. Lambek and Sharp note that this is also true of the *trumba* spirits found in the Comoro Islands and Madagascar and relate this to their association with women—Sharp pointing out that male spirits are naturally attracted to women and that the relationship of mediumship is viewed as marriage,[24] and Lambek observing that transgender possession highlights the separation of spirit and host and "heightens reflection" about the spirit world and its relation to human society.[25] Nonetheless, some spirits are viewed as female, in both the Swahili and the trumba contexts. Moreover, I found that among the Swahili there are cases where gender of the spirit is not seen as very important and that sometimes guild members are not even sure whether their spirits are male or female.

There are some types of spirits, however, that typically form cross-gender relationships with their human partners. Many spirits typified as jini behave in this fashion. Jini include a number of generalized and often rather minor spirits who rarely form regular possession relationships and are not one of the spirit types associated with spirit guilds. They also usually include, however, one of the most powerful and important types of spirits in spirit guilds as well as in other religious and cultural contexts—Middle Eastern ruhani. Ruhani have the most Muslim character of all spirit types. They require both spiritual and physical cleanliness and hence dislike their human associates to be involved with babies or physical sexual relations, and some ruhani object to their human associate's getting married to another human or cause them to be uninterested in humans of the opposite sex. Such objections are not only because of uncleanliness but also often attributed to jealousy. Ruhani tend to interfere with the person's sexual and reproductive activities. They often cause infertility, miscarriage, menstrual problems, and impotence, but they can also cause other types of serious physical and mental problems.[26] After the initial problem has been addressed through the appropriate ritual, the ruhani often requires its human partner to set aside one or more nights per week exclusively for him or her. At this time, one must bathe and wear clean, religiously appropriate (usually white) clothes, isolate oneself in a clean room, and conduct appropriate prayers or other devotional activities before sleeping. Although human sexual and child-rearing activities are prohibited at such times, ruhani will often allow their chairs to engage in them at other times. Important spirit practitioners of both sexes, including Qur'anic waganga as well as those associated with possession guilds, often have powerful ruhani as primary spirits. It should be noted though, that not all such relationships are thought to be cross-sexual, especially by those with the most Islamic training.[27]

TWO CASE STUDIES

I now turn to two particularly interesting case studies of male spirit possession. These cases involved two men whom I was able to interview and observe during research in the Tanga area of northern Tanzania in 1983–84. Both Rajabu and Shale (pseudonyms) seemed unlikely candidates to be possessed by spirits or, even more so, initiated into spirit guilds. Rajabu was a relatively young man who lived in Tanga but had previously traveled in the Middle East and studied in Europe. After returning from Europe, he became possessed and totally reversed his lifestyle to become a Qur'anic mganga. Later, but before our acquaintance, he was initiated into several different spirit possession guilds. Rajabu was an especially valuable informant because his international experience and Western education made him more aware of the kinds of information I would find relevant. The second man, Shale, was younger than Rajabu but had less Western-style education. He had strong reasons to resist initiation into a spirit guild because as a teacher in a Qur'anic school (*madarasa*), he considered it highly inappropriate on religious grounds. Yet he, too, eventually found it necessary to be initiated. I was able to attend Shale's second initiation ceremony, which was held for three different kinds of spirits. This was quite significant for my research, because, although I attended many spirit guild initiation ceremonies, almost all of them were for female initiates. Shale's initiation was the only one for a male initiate that I was able to study closely.

Rajabu

Rajabu's ancestors came to the Swahili coast from Oman. An elderly informant in Wasini identified them as members of the el-Mandhry clan, which had a reputation for their proficiency in Islamic learning. Many of Rajabu's direct ancestors had been Qur'anic waganga, including his father and grandfather. Rajabu noted that both his father and grandfather had great magical powers and that his grandfather was also a spirit mganga as well as a witch (*mwanga*). Although Rajabu studied the Qur'an, he chose "the sporting life" as a young man. He was both an athlete and a musician, and he drank alcohol and smoked *bangi* (marijuana) with his companions. He soon left for the Middle East and then went on to Europe to study electrical engineering. When his father died, he returned to Tanzania and soon became ill with stomach problems. He lost weight for two years, until he was taken to a Swahili mganga, who found that he had inherited a female Arab ruhani spirit from his grandfather. This spirit, which like most ruhani was very religious, was offended by his non-Islamic lifestyle. The ruhani asked Rajabu to give it a ring, prayer beads, a white plate and ink bottle to prepare *kombe* (an Islamic medicine made from washing off the ink of selected Qur'anic texts), and a white goat. Most spirits want specific types of animals as sacrificial offerings; they do not usually eat the meat but drink the blood, a practice considered offensive to Islam. However, some very religious Islamic spirits, like Rajabu's ruhani, do not drink the blood but request that the animals be kept alive. In accordance with the spirit's wishes, Rajabu also gave up his sporting life and began to practice as a Qur'anic mganga under the tutelage of his ruhani. At first he "hid" his practice of uganga by pursuing it only at night, but later he gave up his work as an electrician and became a full-time mganga.

Other spirits, which he describes as the servants of the ruhani, possessed him later, making him ill until he gave them what they wanted. The first of these was a *rubamba,* a type of Pemban spirit that is not only pagan but also extremely unsavory in character, specializing in witchcraft. This spirit had been his mother's but she had never given it an initiation ceremony, as she had promised. Thus it had come to Rajabu and afflicted him with impotence. Rajabu gave it the ceremony it desired and it now provides him information about those practicing witchcraft. Later he was afflicted by two other spirits that were extremely aggressive and offensive to Islamic behavioral norms, this time Maasai. Maasai spirits are portrayed throughout the Swahili area as aggressive warriors with immodest and dirty personal habits. Those possessed by them do not wash themselves during spirit ceremonies and are sometimes said to smear themselves with ghee, foul-smelling plants, and animal urine. They are also often reported to drink the blood of the sacrificial animals themselves, either alone or mixed with honey. Rajabu described one of his Maasai spirits as especially fierce (*jehuri sana*), who carries a bow and arrow, boasts about killing people, and brings him frightening dreams. Rajabu agreed to provide an initiation ceremony for both Maasai spirits but had not yet done so. He was also possessed by two other types of Islamic spirits that he rarely mentioned because they played a minor role in his practice of uganga—a *subiani* (part ruhani) and a female sea jini (*jini bahari*), a "love" spirit. Rajabu had given both these spirits rings and given the sea jini an initiation ceremony in the form of a *zikiri,* a type of ceremony associated with Sufi *tariqa* (religious orders) that involves rhythmic chanting.

Although it is not unusual for a Qur'anic mganga to have a strong relationship with a ruhani spirit, it is unusual for this type of mganga to be initiated into a spirit guild. It is even more unusual for a Qur'anic mganga to be initiated into spirit guilds for pagan spirits, especially those that are so non-Islamic in behavior and character as Maasai and rubamba spirits. Given these circumstances, one would expect Rajabu to practice as a spirit guild mganga as well as a Qur'anic mganga, but he did not. Moreover, he did not attend spirit guild ceremonies, although he may refer patients to them. He himself used only "Qur'anic" methods in the Middle Eastern tradition, practicing divination (*ramli*), astrology, and preparing medicines from incense, herbs, and pieces of paper on which he wrote Arabic ritual phrases and formulas. He did this by consulting his Arabic instruction books and through the help of his ruhani and its servants. He continued to be attentive to the ruhani and devoted two nights a week to its ritual requirements, dressing in white, burning incense, and sitting alone on his prayer mat reciting the Qur'an until dawn.

Rajabu seemed to have come to terms with his spirits and adjusted to his life as an *mganga.* He was sought out by both male and female clients and employed several male assistants. He appeared to make a relatively modest but decent living from his practice and had a successful marriage with several young children.

Shale

Shale appeared to be quite young and was married to the granddaughter of a female spirit guild leader in Tanga who brought me to his spirit initiation ceremony. The couple had two young children. Shale was from a small coastal village of farmers and fishermen. In contrast to Rajabu, he was dark skinned and did not mention any Arab ancestry. People at the spirit initiation said that the villagers were of mixed Digo and Swahili origin but considered themselves to be Swahili and spoke the local Swahili dialect instead of Digo.[28] Shale moved to the city of Tanga to teach at a Qur'anic school.

Shale's family had a history of spirit possession, especially on his paternal grandmother's side. This grandmother's father, sister, and brother Kombo were reported to have been spirit waganga. These individuals were all deceased except for Shale's grandmother's sister, who acted as the head mganga at Shale's initiation. Shale's grandmother had a Maasai spirit and had been initiated into the spirit guild but she was not an mganga. His father was possessed by two Islamic jini, one of which possessed him when his boat overturned at sea. He had refused to give them their initiation ceremony and thus they still troubled him greatly. A number of other relatives, including many young men, also had possessive spirits although most had not yet been initiated. One of these was the grandson of Kombo, who had inherited his grandfather's spirits. Shale's mother, on the other hand, did not have any possessive spirits.

Shale's first spirit, Jini Longi, began to trouble him when he had not yet married. Shale and the waganga at the ceremony identified this spirit as a Muslim Somali spirit that is categorized as a ruhani but is said to be of mixed descent. Spirit names, which give a line of descent and place of origin, are hard to ascertain, especially as the initiate is usually not aware of the name he or she says during the name giving, but it seems from its non-Swahili name, Longi (and its father's name, which sounded like Longiyo), that it is mixed with up-country (bara) spirits and probably more specifically Maasai. This spirit made Shale very ill both physically and mentally. He reported that he acted as if he were mad and repeatedly poured rosewater, the favorite item desired by Muslim spirits, over his head. Some informants said that he inherited this spirit from his great-grandfather but others, including Shale himself, said that it had not appeared in his family before. The spirit was called and asked for a *zikiri*, a white cloth to cover its head, and white animals. Shale reports that it also wore a costume that consisted of a white *kanzu* (a gown often worn by coastal Muslim men) with red stripes, trousers, and a red-and-white turban. The colors are significant, since the color white is typical of Muslim spirits and the addition of the color red generally signals a more complex identity. After the spirit was given its requirements, Shale recovered and practiced as a Qur'anic mganga with the spirit's aid.

After one year Shale became ill again and was tiring extremely easily. Jini Longi was called and reported that several of its companions were causing the illness. These were identified as another Muslim jini/ruhani and two pagan spirits—a bwengo (the local term used for most Pemban spirits) and a Maasai. All three of these new spirits were said to be of mixed descent and thought to be from the same family lineage as Shale's first spirit. Whereas some of these spirits have an up-country (bara) character, others have coastal Islamic traits. The second jini/ruhani lives in the sea but is closely associated with non-Muslim Pemban spirits, which tempers its Islamic character. All three of the new spirits were called by an mganga to possess Shale and said that they wanted an initiation in the form of a regular spirit ceremony (ngoma) with drums and dancing. Shale did not want to have this kind of non-Islamic ceremony because of his religious profession, but after he saw that he was not getting well, he finally agreed. He began making preparations and about two years later gave all three spirits their initiations during a week-long ceremony held in his home village, most of which I was able to attend and observe.

Many people attended the initiation ceremony at various times, both as participants and onlookers. The head mganga supervising the ceremony was Shale's paternal great-aunt, and a number of other waganga, both male and female, participated. Most of the dancers were women, but male musicians, family members (including Shale's father), and waganga often joined them and became possessed. Shale's father and a number of young men, including Kombo's grandson, often went into rather violent and hysterical possessions because their spirits were upset that they had not had an initiation ceremony.

Shale himself was treated in the same way as the female initiates I had seen at other initiation ceremonies. He was secluded between the public parts of the ritual and kept in a passive state except when fully possessed. When he was not dancing, he sat or lay down quietly, not talking and often with a cloth over his head that covered much of his body. Whenever he needed to get up and go anywhere, he was led by a companion. Various guild members, most of whom were female, attended to him during and between ceremonies. In addition, one woman who had recently undergone initiation herself was assigned as his special guide and attendant during the initiation for each spirit type. Shale was dressed in elaborate costumes and smeared with protective medicines, and a stick was put in his mouth, which prevented him from speaking. At the start of each ceremony an appropriately colored cloth was put over his head and he was fumigated with incense and steam from pots of medicine to draw and settle the spirit on his head. During certain points in the ritual, he was even held on the laps of senior guild members and sometimes carried over their backs as a sign of his position as a young child learning how to function as a spirit chair and guild member. This was done even though it resulted in extremely close contact with a number of female guild members. When he was fully possessed, he often joined the ranks of the dancing female guild members. Sometimes other men joined the group of female dancers, but at other times Shale was the only one dancing among them.

The first part of spirit initiation was devoted to the Maasai spirit, Longi wa Malongi (the child of Malongi; compare to the name of the ruhani Jini Longi). It was given an ngoma with drums, rattles, and gongs and song texts focusing on Maasai symbolic themes emphasizing the up-country landscape, pastoralism, and the warrior age grade. Two colors out of the three primary ritual colors were used—black, which is symbolically associated with pagan spirits, and red, a color preference associated with the Maasai ethnic group. Shale's basic costume was black with red highlights, but at times he added several coastal spirit characteristics—a braid turban (usually associated with pagan coastal spirits) and a tan gown (kanzu). He sometimes held a knobbed club (*rungu*), a characteristic of Maasai and some other up-country spirits. He behaved in a bold manner that was occasionally aggressive, at times shouting at the other dancers, jumping up and down, stalking about with his club, and occasionally pairing off with another dancer to stalk each other and thrust their clubs at each other. The spirit was given a red goat and cock as sacrificial animals. At the end of the ceremony Shale and the other guild members went off to a spirit shrine (*mzimu*) where I was told they would kill the goat and drink its blood mixed with honey.

The Pemban bwengo spirit displayed a typical non-Islamic coastal character but with some up-country and Maasai-like traits. Its ceremony used a regular ngoma style with non-Islamic songs and instrumentation. Its costume used the typical red, white, and black color scheme of Pemban spirits, in this case a black costume trimmed in red and white and a tricolor-braid turban. At other times, Shale also donned the same tan gown as the previous spirit and replaced the braid turban with a free-flowing Arab-style head cloth. The bwengo was given black sacrificial animals, including a male goat. The spirit, acting through Shale, engaged in rather obscene actions with the goat (grabbing its testicles and acting as if drinking the urine) that would be considered ritually polluting from an Islamic standpoint, actions that were said to derive from the Maasai aspect of its ancestry.

The last spirit called was Shale's second jini/ruhani, whose name, Sufian wa Longota, signals its hybrid character. Sufian is a name frequently given Middle Eastern spirits, whereas the name of the spirit's father, Longota, is again suggestive of a non-Swahili up-country name and resembles the name of the Shale's Maasai spirit. This spirit is Islamic but shows a more syncretic nature than Shale's first jini/ruhani, Jini Longi. Instead of the more standard Islamic zikiri ceremony, it required a regular spirit ngoma, employing drums and gongs, but adding a tambourine (*tari*, an instrument permitted in some Islamic religious ceremonies) and using song texts with Islamic and Middle Eastern themes. Although it showed the usual Islamic preference for white sacrificial animals, its costume showed a more complicated color scheme—a white costume trimmed in red and black and a white Arab-style head cloth with a red-and-white band. It held a sword, a weapon associated with Arab spirits.

At the conclusion of the ceremony for the jini/ruhani, everyone rushed to the shore with a model boat containing offerings and the sacrificial goats to be given to the spirits. A number of men and women who were possessed by their spirits threw themselves wildly into the water and had to be dragged back to shore. When the throat of the goat for the Pemban bwengo spirit was cut, Shale became very excited at the sight of the blood and also jumped into the sea.

The following day, each spirit was called to possess Shale and be introduced to his children and wife so that it would not harm them but look after their welfare. The next day Shale returned to Tanga with the instructions that he was to rest for seven days since his spirits were still very close to him and would still have an unsettling effect on his mind. The following week he resumed teaching at the Qur'anic school but devoted Thursday and Friday to his practice as a Qur'anic mganga. His possessive spirits helped him with this by explaining things to him about each client's case. The information would suddenly come into his mind as soon as the client appeared.

DISCUSSION

Most people on the Swahili coast do not develop possessive relationships with spirits voluntarily. Case histories generally follow a common pattern of long-term afflictions that do not respond to other treatments and are eventually diagnosed as spirit induced, initial reluctance to develop a long-term spirit relationship and be initiated into a spirit guild, and eventual agreement after the patient comes to view this course of action as the only way to find relief. Although this type of case history is typical of both sexes, it tends to be more extreme in male cases—their initial opposition to spirit activities is more pronounced; their afflictions, though often similar to those of female initiates, are among the more severe and persistent; their resistance to entering into spirit relationships, and especially initiation, stronger; and their eventual change of attitude and behavior greater.

The cases of Rajabu and Shale are complicated not only by their gender but also by their personal positions and lifestyles, which also relate to their generational status. Neither showed any interest whatsoever in spirit activities before their affliction and diagnosis. In addition, both seemed to consider spirit possession objectionable. Whereas Shale considered it inappropriate on religious grounds, Rajabu's objections were probably primarily intellectual—he questioned its very existence. Nonetheless, both had to reevaluate their beliefs when their afflictions did not respond to nonspirit remedies. They not only came to accept the possibility that their problems were spirit induced but also agreed to seek treatment from spirit guild waganga rather than Qur'anic waganga and to accede to the spirit's demands even though it meant entering into a permanent relationship with the spirit.

Note that in spite of their initial rejection of spirit interactions, there was a powerful predisposing factor present in both cases—a family history not only of spirit possession but also of uganga. Even more significant, many of the family members involved had been males, including a number of waganga in previous generations. Rajabu's family, with their Arab ancestry and training in the Islamic textual tradition, had emphasized Qur'anic uganga in the male line, whereas Shale's family had been more involved with spirit uganga affecting both males and females. However, in Swahili coastal society these two traditions of uganga tend to overlap, in spite of the assertions of Islamic scholars and many Qur'anic waganga to the contrary. Qur'anic waganga like Rajabu's ancestors often have special relationships with ruhani and other types of Middle Eastern jini, which may take the form of possession, and spirit waganga together with their guild members and clients are often possessed by these same types of spirits. Moreover, both types of waganga frequently employ many of the same methods of dealing with spirits of various kinds. Although it is much rarer in recent times, I often heard of male waganga in previous generations who practiced both traditions of uganga, as Rajabu's grandfather seems to have done. It is not clear if Rajabu's grandfather had personal relationships with non-Islamic as well as Islamic types of spirits. Nor is it clear if his relationship with his ruhani took the form of actual possession or if he also gave this spirit an initiation ceremony according to possession guild ritual. Nonetheless, we do know that it was this very same spirit that later possessed Rajabu (precisely because it wanted him to be a Qur'anic mganga) and that, in this case, it did require an initiation ceremony.

Many members in Shale's descent line, including a number of waganga, had been possessed by various types of Islamic and non-Islamic spirits, usually ruhani, other types of coastal jini (including many "Islamic" spirits that use "Swahili-style" ngoma), Pemban bwengo, and Maasai spirits (*jini bara Kimasai*). All these spirit types possessed both men and women, but males had more interaction with Islamic types of spirits, especially ruhani, than did females. This included a number of Shale's young male relatives in addition to several generations of male ancestors. All possessed male relatives had at least one Islamic spirit, although often in combination with other types. Moreover, whereas none were identified as Qur'anic waganga, male waganga stressed their relationships with ruhani. The ruhani of Shale's male ancestors, however, were inherited by other relatives, including at least one female. Shale's first spirit, the powerful ruhani Jini Longi, like his subsequent spirits, appears to be making its first appearance in his family.

There is little doubt that Rajabu and Shale found it easier to accept their initial possessive relationships because of the nature of the spirits involved. As ruhani, they are the most prestigious type of spirit in terms of power as well as Middle Eastern and, especially, Islamic associations. Moreover, they not only made it possible to define the possessive relationship itself as Islamic but also allowed both men to redefine themselves as Qur'anic waganga. Rajabu and Shale could thus become skilled high-ranking spirit practitioners who pursued uganga as their vocation rather than merely spirit guild initiates; however, they did so not as spirit waganga but as less objectionable Qur'anic waganga. Ironically, they can claim their skills in this "Islamic" profession precisely because of their spirit possession. Their possession validates their position as Qur'anic waganga and at the same time makes it a "choice" that is, in fact, required. Since Rajabu's relationship is further identified as inherited from his grandfather, he can claim even less personal responsibility for his decision: it is part of his patrimony. For Shale, on the other hand, his new ruhani allows him to strike out in a new direction.

During the initiation ceremony into the spirit guild for ruhani, both men had to accept the passive role by accepting the spirit's demand for establishing an intimate relationship and allowing the spirit to enter them bodily. After initiation, however, neither seemed to regularly undergo this type of physical possession. Rajabu devoted his cross-sexual ruhani its weekly night and later acquired the female sea love spirit, but their interactions did not seem to take the form of bodily possession. The ruhani of both men aided them in their practice of uganga, through dreams and telepathy, but neither did so through possession.

Moreover, although both Rajabu and Shale could claim themselves to be simultaneously Qur'anic waganga and spirit waganga, they explicitly rejected the latter association. Although the extent of Shale's future participation in spirit ngoma was not yet evident, Rajabu made it clear that he did not even attend such events. Nonetheless, he did leave open a possibility that he might redefine his position in the future, since he explained his avoidance not in terms of religious or status impropriety but in terms of safety; other spirit practitioners present could try and use their spirit powers negatively against him in order to advance their own position and that might result in harm to his family members, especially his children, who were very vulnerable because of their young age.

Another important attribute of the initial possessive spirits of both men was their individual personalities. Whereas ruhani are typified as pious Muslims, individual ruhani can vary considerably in their moral and religious character and sometimes behave like other types of spirits. Deviations or mixed behavior patterns are especially likely if the spirit itself is not a *ruhani safi* (a pure or true ruhani) as a result of mixed descent or influence from other spirit types. Thus it is significant that Rajabu's and Shale's initial ruhani both exhibited the pious attitudes and behavior of ruhani safi, even though Shale's spirit was of mixed ancestry. Hence both spirits insisted that the initiation ceremony take the Islamic ritual form of the zikiri rather than the non-Islamic ngoma. Moreover, they extended their demands outside the ritual context and demanded that their human associates lead an exemplary Muslim lifestyle. Thus, paradoxically, although spirit possession is often seen as non-Islamic, possession by this type of ruhani often results in their chair's exhibiting more rather than less Islamic religious behavior. In the case of Rajabu, possession by his grandfather's ruhani caused a complete turnaround in his life, causing him to reclaim an ancestral heritage of Islamic learning and Qur'anic uganga that he had previously rejected for a modern secular life. For Shale, on the other hand, possession by his first ruhani probably helped him follow a more Islamic life-style, claim more access to the Islamic scholarly tradition, and claim higher status in Swahili society than other members of his family had previously.

The spirit histories of both men do not end at this stage, however. Both were subsequently forced to enter into relationships with other types of spirits—one by one in the case of Rajabu and as a collective group in the case of Shale—through the same process of forced recruitment through persistent illness. Except for the two additional Islamic spirit types that eventually appeared in Rajabu's spirit retinue (six in all), these other spirits differ significantly from the first ruhani spirits. They require non-Islamic ngoma ceremonial form and most are extremely non-Islamic in character in terms of their symbolism as well as their actions, diet, and hygienic practices, which are viewed as highly immoral or polluting: not only non-Muslim coastal Pemban spirits (which often appear in possession cases throughout the coastal area) but also Maasai spirits from the African interior. Rajabu's Pemban spirit (the second of his six spirits to appear) is the most non-Islamic type of Pemban spirit possible, a rubamba spirit specializing in witchcraft, inherited from his mother instead of his father's family. Whereas she had never dealt with this rubamba effectively, Rajabu was forced to do so, thus recognizing the non-Arab aspects of his coastal heritage through his mother's side.

Neither man wanted to extend his spirit relationships into the area of non-Muslim spirits but both again submitted under physical duress. Rajabu pointed out he had been initiated for his first pagan spirit in order to cure his problem of impotence, which was itself a threat to his masculinity, and he still owed the next two their initiation. Shale, who was currently undergoing initiation for his non-Muslim spirits during my research, stressed that he had been even more opposed to it than he had initially been to his first initiation but had eventually relented, as previously, when his illness continued unabated.

Although both men have had to come to terms with non-Islamic spirits, they nonetheless continued to define themselves as Qur'anic waganga, whose primary spirits are extremely Islamic in character. The non-Islamic spirits are clearly secondary—they possessed them after the Islamic ruhani and are defined as the ruhani's servants or companions. Once they have been acknowledged, such spirits can be settled into the spirit arsenal under the dominion of the ruhani, and both men can still define themselves in spirit terms as Islamic practitioners.

Both Rajabu's and Shale's array of spirit thus express Arab, Swahili coastal, and African up-country, as well as Islamic and non-Islamic, aspects of their cultural and ancestral environment, yet allow them to claim primary importance and personal identification with the Islamic, and to a somewhat lesser degree, Arab, aspects of their Swahili heritage. Rajabu's spirits are diverse but each is an unmixed type—Islamic or pagan; coastal (pwani) or up-country (bara); Arab, Pemban (Swahili), or Maasai. In contrast, all Shale's spirits are from a single lineage of mixed coastal/up-country, Islamic/pagan, Arab/Maasai descent, thus resembling Shale's own family ancestry to a large extent. (Whereas Shale did not mention any specific Maasai ancestry, his spirits' Maasai attributes could serve as an especially potent symbol of the African aspects of his ancestry and cultural heritage.) This distinctive hybrid identity also probably related to all these spirits being claimed as uniquely his own rather than inherited from any individual ancestor. The character of each spirit thus depended on its own preferences so that it could favor any side of its heritage yet still display hints of its hybrid nature.

The cases of Rajabu and Shale are good illustrations of the unique difficulties that spirit possession presents for males, the conditions that lead to their acceptance of this relationship, and the type of spirit careers that some men subsequently pursue. Both cases highlight the important role that family history can play in possession and the practice of uganga in spite of extensive personal resistance. Their initial possession by ruhani was consistent with male spirit relationships in both families, and their later possessions by other types of spirits reflected other aspects of their family and cultural heritage, including those that were not often stressed or overtly acknowledged. Moreover, although these spirit relations were largely involuntary at the outset, they could be consciously restructured in certain ways in order to be more compatible with the individual's preferences and assigned gender role. Both Rajabu and Shale turned the possessive relationship into a source of prestige and power by stressing their Islamic spirits and becoming Qur'anic waganga, which is not only a suitable male profession but also avoids the more problematic gender implications of the experience of possession.

NOTES

This chapter has developed from "Body and Spirit: Gender Relationships and Swahili Spirit Possession," a paper I presented at the African Studies Association meeting in Orlando, Florida, on November 4, 1995.

1. For example, John G. Kennedy, "Nubian Zar Ceremonies as Psychotherapy," *Human Organization* 26, no. 4 (1967): 185–94; Michael Onwuejeogwu, "The Cult of the Bori Spirits among the Hausa," in *Man in Africa,* ed. Mary Douglas and Phyllis Kaberry (London: Tavistock, 1969), 279–305; Roger Gomm, "Bargaining from Weakness: Spirit Possession on the South Kenya Coast," *Man,* n.s., 10, no. 4 (December 1975): 530–43; Clive S. Kessler, "Conflict and Sovereignty in Kelantanese Malay Spirit Seances," in *Case Studies in Spirit Possession,* ed. Vincent Crapanzano and Vivian Garrison (New York: Wiley, 1977), 295–331; and esp. Ioan M. Lewis, "Spirit Possession and Deprivation Cults," *Man* 1, no. 3 (1966): 307–29; Lewis, *Ecstatic Religion: A Study of Shamanism and Spirit Possession* (London: Routledge, 1971); Lewis, *Religion in Context: Cults and Charisma* (Cambridge: Cambridge University Press, 1986).

2. For example, Jacqueline Monfouga-Nicolas, *Ambivalence et culte de possession: Contribution à l'étude du Bori Hausa* (Paris: Éditions anthropos, 1972); Michael Lambek, *Human Spirits: A Cultural Account of Trance in Mayotte* (Cambridge: CUP Archive, 1981); Bruce Kapferer, *A Celebration of Demons: Exorcism and the Aesthetics of Healing in Sri Lanka* (Bloomington: Indiana University Press, 1983); Janice Boddy, *Wombs and Alien Spirits: Women, Men, and the Zar Cult in Northern Sudan* (Madison: University of Wisconsin Press, 1989); Lesley Alexandra Sharp, *The Possessed and the Dispossessed: Spirits, Identity, and Power in a Madagascar Migrant Town,* Comparative Studies of Health Systems and Medical Care 37 (Berkeley: University of California Press, 1993).

3. Boddy, *Wombs and Alien Spirits.*

4. For example, Emily Ruete, *Memoirs of an Arabian Princess from Zanzibar,* ed. Pat Romero (New York: Marcus Wiener, 1989); Mtoro bin Mwinyi Bakari, *The Customs of the Swahili People: The Desturi za Waswahili of Mtoro bin Mwinyi Bakari and Other Swahili Persons,* ed. and trans. J. W. T. Allen (Berkeley: University of California Press, 1981); Richard Skene, "Arab and Swahili Dances and Ceremonies," *Journal of the Anthropological Institute of Great Britain and Ireland* 47, no. 2 (1917):

413–34; William Harold Ingrams, *Zanzibar: Its History and Its People* (London: H. F. and G. Witherby, 1931); Hans Koritschoner, "Ngoma ya Shetani," *Journal of the Royal Anthropological Institute* 66, no. 1 (1936): 209–19. For discussion of both the decline and persistence of Swahili spirit possession guilds and the societal factors involved, see Linda L. Giles, "Sociocultural Change and Spirit Possession on the Swahili Coast of East Africa," *Anthropological Quarterly* 68, no. 2 (April 1995): 89–106; Giles, "Societal Change and Swahili Spirit Possession," in *Knowledge, Renewal and Religion: Repositioning and Changing Ideological and Material Circumstances among the Swahili on the East African Coast,* ed. Kjersti Larsen (Uppsala: Nordiska Afrikainstitutet, 2009), 85–106.

5. For example, Lewis, *Ecstatic Religion;* Pat Caplan, *Choice and Constraint in a Swahili Community: Property, Hierarchy, and Cognatic Descent on the East African Coast* (London: Oxford University Press, 1975); Pamela Constantinides, "Ill at Ease and Sick at Heart: Symbolic Behaviour in a Sudanese Healing Cult," in *Symbols and Sentiments: Cross-Cultural Studies in Symbolism,* ed. Ioan M. Lewis (London: Academic Press, 1977), 61–84; Peter Fry, "Male Homosexuality and Spirit Possession in Brazil," *Journal of Homosexuality* 11, nos. 3–4 (1986): 137–53; James Lorand Matory, *Sex and the Empire That Is No More: Gender and the Politics of Metaphor in Oyo Yoruba Religion* (New York: Berghahn Books, 2005).

6. Kjersti Larsen, *Where Humans and Spirits Meet: The Politics of Rituals and Identified Spirits in Zanzibar,* Social Identities 5 (New York: Berghahn Books, 2008); Mohamed Saleh, "Les Comoriens de Zanzibar et le culte des esprits kibuki malgaches," in *Madagascar et l'Afrique—Des liens et des appartenances historiques,* ed. Didier Nativel and Faranirina V. Rajaonah (Paris: Karthala, 2007), 425–37.

7. Michael Lambek reports that on the Comorian island of Mayotte, Islamic cosmology and associated magic and medicines (*ilim dunia,* which I would equate with Qur'anic *uganga*) is much more associated with men, though women are not officially precluded. Lambek, *Knowledge and Practice in Mayotte: Local Discourses of Islam, Sorcery and Spirit Possession* (Toronto: University of Toronto Press, 1993), 200n14.

8. For discussion of various spirit types and their symbolic connection to Swahili society, see Linda L. Giles, "Spirit Possession on the Swahili Coast: Peripheral Cults or Primary Texts?" (PhD diss., University of Texas, Austin, 1989); Giles, "Sociocultural Change," and Giles, "Spirit Possession and the Symbolic Construction of Swahili Society," in *Spirit Possession, Modernity and Power in Africa,* ed. Heike Behrend and Ute Luig (Madison: University of Wisconsin Press, 1999), 142–64. See also Kjersti Larsen, "Spirit Possession as Historical Narrative: The Production of Identity and Locality in Zanzibar Town," in *Locality and Belonging,* ed. Nadia Lovell (London: Routledge, 1998), 125–46.

9. Marc J. Swartz, "The Isolation of Men and the Happiness of Women: Sources and Use of Power in Swahili Marital Relationships," *Journal of Anthropological Research* 38, no. 1 (1982): 26–44.

10. Larsen, *Where Humans and Spirits Meet*, 35.

11. Kjersti Larsen, "Morality and the Rejection of Spirits: A Zanzibari Case," *Social Anthropology* 6, no. 1 (1998): 68.

12. Lambek, *Human Spirits*, 61, 121.

13. Ibid., 63.

14. Lambek, *Knowledge and Practice*, 62–63.

15. John Middleton, *The World of the Swahili: An African Mercantile Civilization* (New Haven: Yale University Press, 1992), 178.

16. Larsen, *Where Humans and Spirits Meet*, 116–18; 121.

17. Gill Shepherd, "Rank, Gender, and Homosexuality: Mombasa as a Key to Understanding Sexual Options," in *The Cultural Construction of Sexuality*, ed. Pat Caplan (London: Routledge, 1987), 250.

18. Mary A. Porter, "Talking at the Margins: Kenyan Discourses on Homosexuality," in *Beyond the Lavender Lexicon: Authenticity, Imagination, and Appropriation in Lesbian and Gay Languages*, ed. William Leap (New York: Gordon and Breach, 1995), 134, 145.

19. Deborah P. Amory, "Mashoga, Mabasha, and Magai: 'Homosexuality' on the East African Coast," in *Boy-Wives and Female Husbands: Studies of African Homosexualities*, ed. Stephen O. Murray and Will Roscoe (New York: St. Martin's, 1998), 78.

20. Cf. Sharp's description of *trumba* spirit possession in northwestern Madagascar (Sharp, *Possessed and Dispossessed*) and various descriptions of the zar spirit complex in northeastern Africa—for example, Kennedy, "Nubian Zar Ceremonies"; Constantinides, "Ill at Ease"; Lucie Wood Saunders, "Variants in Zar Experience in an Egyptian Village," in *Case Studies in Spirit Possession*, ed. Vincent Crapanzano and Vivian Garrison (New York: Wiley, 1977), 177–91.

21. Lambek, *Human Spirits;* Sharp, *Possessed and Dispossessed.*

22. For a study of the history of unyago and weddings in Mombasa, see Margaret Strobel, *Muslim Women in Mombasa, Kenya, 1890–1975* (New Haven: Yale University Press, 1979).

23. For descriptions, see Bakari, *Customs of the Swahili People;* Mbarak Ali Hinawy, "Notes on Customs in Mombasa," *Swahili* 34, no. 1 (1964): 17–35; Peter Lienhardt, introduction to *The Medicine Man: Swifa ya Nguvumali* (London: Oxford University Press, 1968), 1–80; Pat Caplan, "Boys' Circumcision and Girls' Puberty Rites among the Swahili of Mafia Island, Tanzania," *Africa: Journal of the International African Institute* 46, no. 1 (1976): 21–33. See also Hans Cory's detailed description in "Jando: Part I: The Constitution and Organization of the Jando," *Journal of the Anthropological Institute of Great Britain and Ireland* 77, no. 2 (1947): 159–68; Cory, "Jando: Part II: The Ceremonies and Teachings of the

Jando," *Journal of the Anthropological Institute of Great Britain and Ireland* 78, nos. 1–2 (1948): 81–94. Though mostly pertaining to non-Swahili groups, the terminology and ritual structure is very similar to that found on the Swahili coast.

24. Sharp, *Possessed and Dispossessed.*

25. Lambek, *Human Spirits,* 61; cf. Larsen, *Where Humans and Spirits Meet.*

26. For an example of a woman's traumatic experience of ruhani, see Katrina Daly Thompson, "Zanzibari Women's Discursive and Sexual Agency: Violating Gendered Speech Prohibitions through Talk about Supernatural Sex," *Discourse and Society* 22, no. 1 (January 2011): 3–20.

27. For a detailed discussion of jini and ruhani and various case studies of people possessed by them, see Giles, "Spirit Possession on the Swahili Coast."

28. For a discussion of the problem of identifying ethnicity in Shale's (and the villagers') case and throughout the East African coastal area, see Linda Giles, "Complexities of Identity in the East African Coastal Area," in *Contesting Identities: The Mijikenda and Their Neighbors in Kenyan Coastal Society,* ed. Rebecca Gearhart and Linda Giles (Trenton: Africa World Press, 2014).

ELEVEN

Being a Good Muslim Man

Modern Aspirations and Polygynous Intentions in a Swahili Muslim Village

SUSI KREHBIEL KEEFE

MEN IN PEPONI DESIRE polygyny, the practice of having more than one wife at a time, while women despise it. Peponi is a pseudonym for a Swahili Muslim fishing village south of Tanga Town on the coast of Tanzania where I spent all of 2004. Although most husbands never have more than one wife at a time in this village, men tirelessly boast, brag, and plot toward this end. They invoke Islamic doctrines when discussing their desires and justification for multiple wives. Some Islamic scholars argue that polygyny is not a rule or right but an exception and maintain that the notion that it is compulsory or preferred for a Muslim man to have more than one wife is a misconception.[1] While popular conceptions of polygyny treat the reasons behind polygyny as having to do with satiating men's sexual appetites, in actuality many scholars argue that the Qur'an permitted polygyny as a solution to the pressing social-welfare problems during the time of revelation, roughly fourteen hundred years ago.

In Peponi men argue the practice is part of their rights and privileges as Muslims. In contrast to scholarship on Islam and Africa that presents polygyny as a tradition declining in the face of modernization, this chapter demonstrates that male desire for polygyny is still strong, and it argues that men's desire reveals local perceptions of both the dynamic and enduring values of Islam as well as quintessential signs of masculinity, success, and modernity in this Swahili Muslim community. As structural-adjustment policies and other neoliberal reforms leave ordinary Tanzanians vulnerable to economic and social insecurity, polygyny serves as a conspicuous symbol of prosperity and virtue. However, while kinship and community ties have become increasingly critical to people's survival strategies as state protections have declined, these same political-economic forces have undermined men in their efforts to carry out their marital plans because they do not have the means to support multiple wives. Moreover, men's largely unfulfilled hopes for multiple wives exacerbate gender-based power inequities by precipitating divorce, abandonment, and the neglect of their current wives.

In the village of Peponi, Islam forms an essential axis on which everyday activities, communications, and transactions turn. Decisions about whom and when to marry, whether to stay married, divorce, or remarry, as well as what behaviors constitute wifely or husbandly behavior, are informed by people's relationship to Islam. It is long established that Muslim identity is central to the ways that Swahili people constitute themselves as persons and in shaping their relationships over the course of their lives.[2] As scholars such as Katrina Daly Thompson, citing Joan Russell, assert, Islam in East Africa is "not just an intellectual exercise, but a way of life."[3] In Peponi, Swahili men and women have culturally specific, personalized strategies through which they navigate their relationships throughout the life course. As Adeline Masquelier does in Niger, I focus "on actors rather than institutions and tracing the meanings Islam has for people instead of assuming that Islam always determines their choices and constraints."[4] This chapter, following Masquelier, aims to elucidate how Swahili men in Peponi "relate to doctrine in practical ways and how they selectively use Islam"[5] with a particular focus on their understanding of Islam as it relates to their marital choices. First, I engage with previous studies of polygyny and Islam in Africa to establish how to include men in studies of polygyny and Islam. Second, in an effort to explore polygyny more fully, I provide a background to marriage practices, expectations, and values among Swahili Muslims of Peponi, Tanzania. Third, I examine how the polygynous aspirations of men contribute to gender inequality in marriage and divorce practices and experiences among Peponi residents. Fourth, I consider how men's aspirations for polygyny are inextricably linked to discourses of Islam, kinship, modernity, and success. Finally, I demonstrate these links by providing three extended ethnographic portraits of men in Peponi.

WHERE ARE THE MEN IN STUDIES OF POLYGYNY? GENDER AND METHODS

In Tanzania, the largest percentage of polygynous unions is among Muslims. The Tanzania Marriage Act of 1971 prohibits polygyny for Christian marriages but still permits it for civil, Islamic, and traditional unions. Higher polygyny rates among men and women are associated with rural residence and low educational attainment,[6] and according to the 2005 Tanzania Demographic and Health Survey, about 25 percent of currently married women and 10 percent of men are in polygynous unions.[7] However, these rates vary significantly by region. In Tanga Region, where Peponi is located, 23 percent of women are said to be in a polygynous union with 20.9 percent with one cowife and 2.1 percent with two or more cowives.[8] In the Tanga Region 19.7 percent of men have two or more wives. These are among the highest rates of polygyny for men in Tanzania, rivaled only by Zanzibar and Mbeya Region.

Until recently, most large-scale demographic surveys in Africa focused exclusively on women of reproductive age, with limited information on men.[9] Practical political interests and ultimately the financial impact of high fertility rates in poor countries often drive academic and popular interest in reproduction and fertility. Changes in marriage and sexual relationships influence the demographic trajectories of reproduction and fertility;

demographic studies of marriage have consequently resurged in recent years, with a focus on high fertility.[10] In this research, polygyny is constructed as a valuable research topic, not because of an interest in nuptiality but due to a concern with fertility and population levels. This results in an emphasis on women, and an exclusion of men, indicating that women are considered the only significant variable impacting population. These studies are limited and lead to an incomplete picture. Where are the men? And why are men's expectations, desires, and realities ignored when they clearly have a considerable impact on not only demographic outcomes but also the experience and process? In response, anthropologists note the importance of considering marriage and relationships in a more fluid and gendered manner and not just within the context of narrow policy-oriented questions.[11] I argue that men are essential to understanding population processes.

Despite many academic studies on polygyny, there is a noticeable lack of research regarding peoples' attitudes toward polygyny.[12] Remarkably, the academic literature reveals little about how polygyny affects people's lives and, particularly, ignores men's lives.[13] The experiences of women in polygynous unions, especially as they negatively impact women's sexual and reproductive health, continue to dominate the research on polygyny.[14] Furthermore, the little information available about men was gathered through consultations with women.[15] Understanding why women choose or end up in polygynous unions, or why men find the practice appealing (with some spending nearly a lifetime chasing polygynous status) is rarely addressed. In this chapter, I depart from women-centered approaches to polygyny by drawing out men's perspectives. I also consider motivations for, attitudes toward, and experiences of polygyny.

WHEN I first arrived in Peponi, I introduced myself and my research to people vis-à-vis my connections to Pamela and Leif Landberg, a husband-and-wife team of anthropologists who conducted their dissertation research in Peponi in the 1960s. Recollections of the Landbergs helped me tremendously; their work had made many people in Peponi, particularly the older generation, familiar with what anthropologists do. Like Pamela

Landberg, I presented myself as interested in *kina mama* (lit., women), which people interpreted as "things that interest women." This made sense to men and women in my community. From the first day I arrived in the village, I was bombarded with questions about divorce proceedings in America, presented with scenarios of bad husbands in Peponi, asked for help tracking down an errant husband. (Women routinely asked to use my cell phone to "beep" their husbands, which entailed calling and hanging up before the call was answered. This is understood to be a request to call back. There are elaborate systems of beeping to communicate different messages. Women expect that if they beep their husbands, the husbands will call back, and thus the cost of the call will be the responsibility of the husband, as most cell phones in Tanzania are on a prepaid system). Women often talked to me about marriage and divorce without even knowing my specific research interests, as these are topics that women discuss frequently and openly.

During my fieldwork in Peponi, I used a mixed-methods approach, combining quantitative surveys and a census with a range of qualitative techniques. My central focus was to assess social changes occurring in Peponi over the past forty years. This also informed my design of a household survey of 350 ever-married men and women, community census and map, interviews with twenty-three female entrepreneurs (small restaurant owners in particular), and life history narratives with twenty couples/unions who were married or formerly married. The latter resulted in interviews with twenty-three women and twenty men for a total of forty-three interviews; when I interviewed the parties to three polygynous unions, I interviewed both wives. I worked with a team of research assistants at various stages of research, primarily in collecting quantitative data. I conducted all in-depth interviews with women by myself; the in-depth interviews with men were conducted using a combination of techniques. Anthropologists have long noted the ease of conducting same-sex interviews and the difficulties associated with conducting interviews with members of the opposite sex. When I had a strong rapport with a male interviewee, I conducted the entire interview by myself. Other interviews, in particular initial ones, were conducted by a research assistant (a twenty-five-year-old Swahili Muslim man from the community), who also assisted me in determining research and interview questions, phrasing, and translation. Based on his interviews, I conducted follow-up interviews by myself or with him. Collecting both quantitative and qualitative data enabled me to collect more representative, complete, and meaningful data on marriage, divorce, and polygyny than one method alone would have allowed and uniquely enabled me to attend to men's perspectives in a way that is missing from previous scholarship.

Through its location on the Tanga-Pangani road, Peponi residents have ready access to urban markets and to the amenities provided by a large urban center. Given the size and location of the community, it is neither peripheral nor flourishing. In many ways life remains quite similar to what the Landbergs described in the 1960s.[16] The community is rural and life is, for the most part, relaxed in a way Tanzanians often associate with the Swahili coast. Fishing, trade with Zanzibar, and farming continue to be the most common means of livelihood. Since the 1960s, with the near tripling of the population of the village, many more houses, roads, small stores, small restaurants, small businesses, and mosques make up the community. In the late 1960s, Peponi had a primary school and one madrasa (Islamic school for children), a small health clinic, a few small stores, one restaurant, and one operating mosque. The newest sections of Peponi are those above the beach. The newer section is bisected by the Tanga-Pangani road, which runs from north to south following the coastline. Leif and Pamela Landberg both noted the importance of building up from the beach (and nearer to the road) during their fieldwork in the late 1960s.[17] They cite construction near the road as indicative of its economic, political, and social importance to the village. Almost forty years later, I can affirm this is still true. While the waterfront of the village is important to the fishermen, the center of activity of the village is that area which runs parallel to the road. Of the thirty-one small stores in the village, all but three are located on or near the main road. Also, of the twenty-six restaurants and six tea and coffee shops in the village, all but seven are located on or near the main road.

The focus of the road reflects the orientation of the villagers to that which lies beyond the village. The school, government court building, government offices, hospital, produce market, soccer field, and main Friday mosque are all located on the main road. All main village-level activities (political rallies as well as religious and cultural celebrations such as Maulidi) are held near to the main road (in front of the mosque, political-party buildings, school, hospital, or on the soccer field).

In February 2004, early on in my fieldwork, a cell phone tower was installed in the village and many more people began to purchase cell phones. There are numerous signs such as these indicating engagement with the "signs and styles of a global order."[18] Young men and women, particularly those who have completed secondary school and advanced technical-training programs, lament the lack of jobs and opportunities promised them if they completed their education. They desire opportunity, success, and engagement with the wider world; they articulate feeling left without purpose, unsure of how to apply their education and skills to a simple life in Peponi. One young woman named Asha (all names in this chapter are pseudonyms) is a twenty-three-year-old secondary-school graduate who also completed an expensive secretary course. Neither her secondary-school degree nor her secretary certificate yielded a job opportunity. She complained, "I worked so hard, and yet here I am back in the village. I am a not a farmer or a wife. My family spent so much money on my education. We all expected that I would be earning a salary as a secretary in Tanga by now. Instead, I am here with nothing to do, and I'm not prepared to live a village life. I don't want that." Juma, a twenty-four-year-old secondary-school graduate with strong English-language skills, was delighted to be hired by expatriates who built a small backpackers' beach resort near Peponi. After working at the beach resort for four years, Juma became restless, despite acknowledging he was one of only a few people from the village with steady employment and a salary. He earned $50 a month, a substantial income for a young single man living in a village, and he outwardly displayed signs of his relative wealth, such as a cell phone, new Western-style clothing, and a newly constructed home of his own (most men his age live with extended family or rent a small room in someone's house). Juma regularly discussed quitting his job so that he could move to Arusha, where he might have more opportunities. When I asked him what he would look for there, he replied, "I want to find a more fulfilling job, not just pour another rum and coke, not have the same conversation over and over again with another traveling *mzungu* [Westerner]. Also, I want to meet a wife, a partner, someone to love. I cannot find that person here. This is just a village." I inquired about his girlfriend, Mwantuum, a twenty-three-year-old tailor who sews clothing from her home. I was aware of their relationship and knew she had high hopes for marriage. "Oh, she is a nice girlfriend, but I have goals; she knows that I do not want to marry her." Over the course of my year in Peponi, Juma articulated, numerous times, the desire for a relationship that was a partnership and for an occupation that was fulfilling. His education prepared him for a different life, and he felt cheated that opportunities he expected were not available.

Discussions of weddings, and their importance, are common among Peponi residents, and ideals of premarital relationships, marital payments, and weddings are widely understood to be grounded in principles of Islamic law. However, while weddings and marriage continue to have an important role in Swahili society, research on these topics reveal tensions between the ideals and realities of premarital courtship, weddings, and marriage itself. Peponi residents regard weddings as a tremendous rite of passage for young people. However, the reality of premarital pregnancies, the postponement of marriage, and young unmarried mothers with no intentions of marrying the father challenge local ideals of the first marriage as the key rite of passage resulting in adulthood. Although local notions of proper Muslim behavior are understood as prohibiting premarital relationships, people in Peponi do not harshly condemn such relationships, courtship, dating, and even sexual relations. They do prefer to avoid conception and pregnancy outside marriage, but even this consequence is not unusual and is accepted by most as a feature of modern life since age at first marriage is delayed by increased schooling, particularly for girls.[19] Despite these changes, marriage remains a respected and desired goal of all young people.

My research in Peponi directly contradicts the official demographic portrait of Tanga Region (presented above). Although most men support polygyny, few are able to attain this dream. My research indicates the average number of wives for the 597 men captured in the village census is 1.09. In all of Peponi, there were only thirty-one men with two wives (5.1 percent), one man with three wives (0.02 percent), and no men with four or more wives. Furthermore, twenty-four of the thirty-one men with two wives (77 percent) were over the age of fifty—demonstrating that polygyny is something a man may realize with age and with the assistance of his grown sons, as I will discuss later in this chapter. A 1960 census of Peponi also indicated a low prevalence of polygyny, with only 6.5 percent of men with two wives.[20] This reveals polygyny, though desirable among men, has consistently been difficult to attain over the past fifty years.

THE IMPORTANCE OF BEING MARRIED, THE IMPORTANCE OF BEING MUSLIM

The most frequent question people asked me, especially in the beginning of my field research, was: Are you married? I quickly assessed this was a twofold question: first, knowing my status as a married adult helped people determine how to treat me. Second, it helped men know how to approach me in their frequent marriage proposals. People in Peponi assumed I was Christian and, for the most part, were uninterested in my religious beliefs. Neither my religion nor my marital status was an impediment to my marrying a Swahili Muslim man. "Divorce that husband of yours and marry me! You can become Muslim and *tuna umuhimu pamoja*—we could be useful together." This was a frequent refrain from men and the phrase "useful together" in this context was a thinly veiled sexual reference.

Everyone in Peponi desires marriage, although not always for the same reason. Asani explained to me about his father, whom the community widely acknowledged as homosexual. "He married my mother when he was young and they have six children together. They are still married. My father has relationships with men in the village, sometimes with married men, sometimes with younger unmarried men. He does not prefer women, but this is not a reason to not get married and have children. This is not a reason to not have a wife." Regardless of reason, and in Asani's father's case sexual orientation, everyone marries at least once. Marriage is a valued institution, yet the importance of marriage among Swahili Muslims might misleadingly suggest that partnerships are static and stable over time. In fact they are highly fluid for both men and women, as much research on the Swahili coast has shown.[21]

MEN'S POLYGYNOUS ASPIRATIONS AND THE REVITALIZATION OF ISLAM

When asked, most young men state that they do not expect their first marriage to endure and that they do not imagine being married to just one woman for their entire lives. Furthermore, 18 of 20 unmarried men stated they want to be in a polygynous union at some point. In fact, they look forward to exercising certain rights that they describe as not only part of their Muslim identity but endorsed and even encouraged by Islam. These rights include both polygynous unions and the right to divorce by repudiation. Specifically, men described with pride how they are allowed four wives at any given time, as long as they can equally maintain each wife. Men in Peponi see polygyny both as part of being a devout Muslim and as a status symbol. Men describe the ideal and respected Muslim man as one who can afford to maintain multiple wives. Affluence, rather than any other factor, usually determines whether a man has the ability to fulfill his desire for a polygynous marriage. As a man becomes more prosperous, he is better able to afford multiple wives. Some men even see polygyny as a religious obligation for those who can afford it.

Men's expectations of polygynous marriage reflect a revitalization of Islam in the community since the late 1960s, when Pamela Landberg conducted her research. When I showed the Landbergs my photos of contemporary school children in Peponi, they commented that the community appears "more Islamic than before." Today, for example, most schoolgirls wear a head covering as part of their primary school uniform; they did not in the 1960s. While this is not necessarily a reflection of an increase in commitment to Islam on the part of each young girl, it is certainly an outward expression of a cultural and religious influence of Islam that did not exist previously. The Landbergs pointed to other signs, such as a dramatic increase in the number of mosques and madrasas.

Stories from my own experience also indicate this change. During my time in Peponi I was, not surprisingly, compared to Pamela Landberg quite often, usually as a commentary on my behavior, dress, or approach to research. People would ask me what I ate for lunch or dinner and I quickly learned they wanted me to be eating local foods. If I said I ate coconut rice or cassava they were delighted. If I reported eating something ambiguous in origin, like eggs or noodles, they said: "Oh Pam, she ate and learned to prepare all our foods!" One day I joined some older men for a cup of coffee by the main road. In the village, I usually wore skirts or dresses and a *kanga* (printed cotton cloth) around my waist and shoulders, and sometimes over my head. However, on this day I wore a pair of long, dark, loose pants because I was on my way to the city to run errands. The men chastised me. They said: "You know, Pam never wore pants. She always wore long skirts and dressed only in the local style, like a good Muslim woman." When I returned to the United States and actually met Pam, she showed me photographs from her own time in Peponi. I was quite surprised to see her wearing knee-length skirts and tank tops, revealing a lot of skin! While I was willing to stretch the "rules" a bit and wear pants, I would never wear clothing that revealed my legs and arms (even though Peponi women, while working, routinely reveal skin on their legs and arms). I wore conservative clothing out of respect for local customs but also because of the unwanted attention I was certain to receive if I were to wear such revealing clothing. People remembered Pam as a behaving like a good Swahili Muslim woman, although she is a Christian American. People in Peponi knew Pam and I were not Muslim, but they found our investment in abiding by their customs, respecting their values, and learning their way of life important and a sign of respect. Members of the community seemed to transpose contemporary ideas of Islam and dress onto the past, and onto Pam. And while the goal of polygyny has not changed since the Landbergs' research, it is now more concretely connected to discourses of Islam.

GENDER INEQUALITY AND POLYGYNY

In previous work, I demonstrate that men and women in Peponi are likely to engage in serial monogamy and have multiple spouses over the course of their lives, but not often simultaneously, as polygyny permits.[22] This is the case both because women find the practice undesirable and because men cannot afford it. Instead, because wives prefer it, men are formally married to one woman and have informal relationships with other women. Men and women have divergent feelings about polygyny and this is related mostly to their differing expectations of marriage. Women's opposition to polygyny is not strong enough to prevent men's active pursuit of other women, such as secret wives, girlfriends, lovers, or "outside wives" (women who live in another area, usually rural or poorer, than a man's primary residence in an unofficial relationship that nevertheless resembles a marriage).[23] However, women have devised their own coping strategies. First, most women make their preference for a monogamous marriage known to their husbands, their families, and other women. Second, they make every effort to block a polygynous union.[24] And, failing the first two options, they will seek a divorce through any means possible to get out of a polygynous marriage. Many if not all women who faced polygyny in their previous marriage(s) do not wish to remarry if widowed or divorced. For most women, this is achievable because of the possibility of entrepreneurial work or living with other women (or both), mainly relatives, to share costs. Women are resigned to, but frustrated by, the practice of polygyny and skeptical that a change will ever occur. Men in Tanzania, however, have political, cultural, and religious support for polygyny.

In my work, I have found that local interpretations of Islam and, in particular, older men's expectations that their sons will help them afford polygynous marriages late in life directly fuel younger men's expectations about the practice itself. These conflicts highlight the context of dramatic gender inequality within

Peponi. Gender inequality derives not only from cultural and Islamic interpretations of gender roles but also from political and economic structures that privilege men with regard to marriage, divorce, and polygyny. Associated with the unrealized dreams of polygyny is the fact that men frequently exercise what they perceive to be their rights to divorce and serial monogamy. Men view themselves to be entitled by Islam to the unilateral right to divorce a wife for any reason at any time. This is done through a process of repudiation called *talaka* (<Ar. *talaq*). Husbands can either pronounce a talaka or write a talaka. Even in this small community there are various understandings of how repudiation should work. Some cases involved a man taking a second wife, then giving his first wife a talaka when she persuaded him to do so; often the husband divorced the second wife and returned to the first wife. We'll see an ethnographic example of this type of case in the next section.

POLYGYNOUS INTENTIONS: ISLAM, KINSHIP, AND SUCCESS

Portraits of three men illuminate the experiences and thoughts of men in Peponi. These men reference both Islamic discourses and modern notions of success, development, and wealth as they discuss their life goals, experiences with marriage, and expectations for their future.

Modern Marriage and Multiple Wives

During my fieldwork, I developed a friendship with a newly married young woman, Saba, who was the sister of the wife of the family I lived with during my first three months in Peponi. Saba's marriage took place on my first day in Peponi. Because of my relationship with her family, I was invited to participate in the wedding and had access to Saba during her weeks of confinement following the wedding. As a result, we developed a close relationship and I was particularly interested in her experience as a new bride. I wanted to know about her courtship and expectations of marriage as well as the realities of her married life. During Saba's confinement, a period of approximately two weeks after a wedding when a bride must remain at home but can receive visitors, her husband, Asani, stopped by to see his new brother-in-law, Jumbe, quite frequently. I lived in Jumbe's household at the time and was able to witness and participate in the interactions that took place with the new husband. The first time he came there was much to-do and enthusiasm; everyone cheered for him and also teased him about leaving his bride alone so soon, implying that she could not be trusted to be faithful while he was away. His demeanor was confident and nonchalant. Jumbe made a big production of sending one of the older girls to fetch sodas; "An Arab soda for me!" Asani shouted after the girl—referring to a soda produced in Tanzania rather than imported from the United States. Looking directly at me, he said, "I don't like American cola. I am an Arab Muslim man," thumping his chest.

People in Peponi routinely make connections to what they view as a pure Swahili identity; those who can connect their family history to Zanzibar and Oman see themselves in a superior position because they perceive themselves to be Arab, or more Arab, than those who are not. This practice of directly claiming an Arab identity or lineage is about connecting to Islam and making powerful claims to purity and authenticity. By saying he is an "Arab man," Asani attempts to demonstrate what he thinks of as his family connections to Zanzibar and his allegiance with the Muslim world beyond Peponi. He forges his claims to an "authentic" Islam, and participates in a global discourse about modern Muslim lifestyles and their superiority to American, or even African, ways of living.[25]

The next time Asani stopped by to visit it was late afternoon. Jumbe was not present since he was at the mosque for the *alasiri* (late afternoon) prayer. Asani, however, the "Arab Muslim man," was out visiting instead of attending afternoon prayers. I was sitting in the living room writing field notes when Asani entered, and I saw a different side of him that day. Instead of Swahili, he spoke in stilted English and said things that, at first, sounded a bit like gibberish. After listening closely I realized he was impersonating and performing what he thought a "cool American guy" would sound like. He ignored proper Swahili greetings and did not show me any of the usual signs of respect, which others (including Asani) afforded me on a regular basis.

By Swahili standards he was quite rude. I asked him why he was neglecting the typical greetings and interacting with me in an inappropriate way. He gave me a big smile and explained: "I'm like Arnold; don't you like it?" It took me a second to sort out his reference; then it dawned on me: he meant Arnold Schwarzenegger. I told him that, no, in fact, I did not enjoy the way he was acting and pointedly asked him why he was not at afternoon prayer. His response: "Oh, I don't always have time to go."

Asani and I eventually developed a rapport and settled into *utani,* a "joking relationship."[26] The joking relationship is common among many Swahili communities and exists in relationships considered ambiguous, allowing for a type of institutionalized familiarity meant to mitigate the ambiguity.[27] For example, John Middleton notes that joking relationships are particularly present between cognatic and fictive kin, as well with people from different ethnic groups. Pamela Landberg explains further: "*watani* [those in a joking relationship] can behave in ways which are otherwise not appropriate to the proper social and moral order. Nonetheless, it is precisely the ambiguities inherent in transitional states and symbolized in these social categories which provide the basis for *utani* ritual action."[28] For the duration of my year in Peponi, Asani frequently ignored culturally appropriate greetings and means of interactions and choose to interact with me in a way he learned and adopted from the action movies he had seen, such as *Terminator* and *Rambo.* This also involved bossing me around, something no other man or woman in Peponi ever truly attempted. Usually, people in Peponi spoke to me with respect and even deference. He described this way of acting and talking as cool and modern, the manner of a man who knows things and is successful in development. Development, in this context, is similar to what Christine Walley describes: "Many coastal residents felt they lacked sufficient opportunity to benefits from tourism and sought a range of formal and informal means to convert the presence of rich foreigners in their midst into personal *maendeleo* or development for themselves and their families."[29] In addition, many Tanzanians, such as those discussed in Brad Weiss's ethnography of hip hop culture in Arusha, feel left behind by development, particularly with respect to tourism and industry.[30] When residents of Peponi discuss maendeleo they mean the chances to improve themselves and their lot in life. It was clear from the start that my role in my relationship with Asani was to reprimand him and attempt to teach him some manners; he expected and wanted this. I found our interactions somewhat bizarre, but he stuck to this pattern of behavior and to performing his paradoxical Arab Arnold. His wife, Saba, on the other hand, was always courteous and polite. In keeping with the joking relationship, I would thank her, deliberately in front of Asani, for her respect. During these interactions she would talk back to Asani, tongue in cheek: "See, I'm polite, and she likes it!" Asani would always treat Saba heavy-handedly in front of me—performing his "cool/American" and "Arab/Muslim" hybrid masculinity for me.

Once, Asani barged into my house, after dark, with Saba and said, "*Lete kamera!*"—ordering me to bring my camera. When I asked him why, he said, "I want pictures of my wife and me!" Despite being slightly annoyed that he would "order" me about, I retrieved my camera and agreed to take photos. When I returned to the living room, Asani was instructing Saba to put on her *buibui* (a black, formal robe and headdress or veil usually reserved for the most pious and wealthy members of the village and for formal events or travel to the city). I asked why she was putting on the buibui, and Asani replied, "My wife is a good Muslim woman. Let your pictures show this." I took pictures and what transpired was unusual. Asani adopted poses and mannerisms atypical of a Swahili husband. Swahili married couples in Peponi generally do not spend time together in public spaces, they do not go visiting together, and they certainly do not exhibit public displays of affection. Even their presence together at my house, this time and many others, was unusual behavior for a Swahili couple. On this occasion Asani wrapped his arms around Saba, held her hand, held her hand up so it was visible in front of their faces, and performed his version of an American/Western/ modern romantic husband. These poses were reminiscent of a Swahili wedding photo shoot, a time when the usual male and female behavior in public is suspended and romantic poses are adopted. The paradox between his heavy-handedness, his "good Muslim wife," and the romantic poses for the photographs was spectacular. Asani and his desire for an Arab soda, expectations of his wife, commitment to speaking to me in an Arnold-esque manner, and the poses he adopted for our impromptu photo shoot all indicate a mixing of global discourses. Asani openly discusses his interest and commitment to a globally relevant Islam, desire for "development," and admiration for hypermasculine American men such as those portrayed by Arnold Schwarzenegger. Men reference and look to each of these discourses for direction about their values, preferences, and ideals. What it means to be a contemporary Swahili Muslim man is influenced not by just one global discourse but by many.

Asani is a self-described businessman engaged in illegally importing sugar from Zanzibar. There is a profitable smuggling business between Zanzibar and the community. Men deliver goods, food, produce, grains, livestock, and people intending to visit Zanzibar in their dhows (sailboats, some with motors, most without) and return with items (such as sugar, refrigerators, freezers, televisions, DVD players) that are taxed heavily on the mainland but have a much reduced tax, or no tax, in Zanzibar. When I asked him why he chose this as an occupation, he said, "I saw that people who did this business were able to develop, they have money and nice things, so I chose to do it too." There is some risk involved because smuggling items from Zanzibar is illegal, and mainland Tanzanian authorities occasionally conduct raids, mainly for sugar. During my time in Tanzania there were five separate sugar raids on the village by mainland authorities. Asani, and others, describe the profession as exciting and profitable. It allowed men with some education and no hope for a reliable job of another type a chance to attain some of their goals, goals that are informed by neoliberal ideologies that motivate these kinds of aspirations.[31] Asani is an example of a young man at the start of his adult life in Peponi: his risky and profitable business is part of his efforts to attain the local ideal of contemporary Swahili manhood.

Nine months after his wedding, and my arrival in Peponi, I conducted an in-depth interview with Asani, who explained:

> I chose Saba [as my wife] because she has nice behavior. I liked her because she is not concerned with having many

things. I love my wife a lot. I like the life of a married person; I was not that useful [*umuhimu*] before marriage. Together we are useful. After deciding to get married to this wife, I waited a long time to marry. I was unable to marry directly because my ability to raise the mahari was small, and so I had to save. But my wife was my lover before marriage. The mahari I paid was TSh 50,000, ($50), along with furniture for our room. I paid all that they asked for; I did not hold anything back, not one single thing. Before my marriage I had several lovers, but now I have one wife.

Asani takes pride in his ability to pay the full amount requested for the mahari. He does his best to fulfill the expectations of conspicuous consumption that evidence his identity as a good modern Muslim husband, by paying all the mahari and "not holding one thing back." "Not holding one thing back" (*sikubakisha hata kimoja*) is commonly articulated among men and women as a positive attribute of men who meet the agreed-upon mahari payments. These men are "good Muslims," are considered successful, have support from their kin, and take their obligations seriously. Men who do not pay the entire mahari are viewed as stingy; it is a sign of a poor man who cannot keep his commitments. In a previous study in Mombasa, Marc Swartz argues that men acquiesce to women's needs and desires for material goods because "only in marriage can men find the emotional relationship at least some of them want and their reluctance to use their ability to control their wives is due to their unwillingness to endanger the unique emotional rewards they get from them."[32] Asani discusses why he likes the life of a married man, emphasizing that he felt adrift, not useful, before marriage. As a married person he describes himself as "useful," which is how I translate the word *umuhimu* here, both as an individual, and as a couple. Asani describes the contributions of married people as useful to their families and their community.

Asani acknowledges that he chose his wife because she is not the type of woman to demand many things from him in terms of conspicuous material consumption. Men repeatedly point to frugality as a desirable quality in a wife, citing it as a Muslim virtue.

But if a husband is not required to continually spend lavishly on his wife or wives, he may have money to spend elsewhere, including on girlfriends, lovers, outside wives, or additional wives. I asked Asani if being married was important, and he said, "As a good Muslim man, I must say yes." He continued, describing the importance of being married to attain adulthood and to fully realize his Muslim male identity. "As a Muslim man, I must marry; it is my duty, and I would not want it any other way." And yet, another young man, Juma, laughed when I asked about men's marital goals, and summed up men's approaches quite nicely: "You know us, we are a bit crazy; we are permitted four wives, and unlimited girlfriends, and we take full advantage." Juma's assessment of Swahili men has little to do with their interpretations of Islam and more to do with men's use (and abuse) of patriarchy. When I asked Asani directly about fidelity and polygyny, he replied, "Yes, I have a lover outside my marriage. She lives in Zanzibar; you know, I am there every week for sugar. Before my marriage I had several lovers, but now I have one wife, and one lover. My lover in Zanzibar is just a lover. I will not consider her for a wife. I am not ready for another wife, not yet." I asked him if he expects to take a second wife in the future: "In my life I think I will marry three times: as a youth, as an adult, and as an old man. It is necessary to be with various wives. It would be nice to never divorce, and if I have good luck, I will stay married to each wife." Asani acknowledges the need for luck in achieving polygyny, referencing, indirectly, the fact that women do not like the practice. Although Asani does not explicitly divulge these goals to his new wife, he is open with me about his infidelity and his desire for additional wives once he attains more financial stability. The fact that he has a girlfriend, but cannot afford another wife, raises the question: What is the difference between a girlfriend and a wife? It is important to note that sex is not condoned outside marriage for Muslims, but like premarital sex and relationships, extramarital affairs are common among residents of Peponi. Girlfriends and lovers require gifts and financial support, but these expenditures are much smaller than those required by a wife, making extramarital affairs a less-expensive simulation of polygyny. The extramarital affairs of young men unable to afford and attain polygyny, their expressed goal, can be seen as approximating polygyny, allowing men to feel they are achieving parts of the ultimate goal as a modern Muslim man. Girlfriends and lovers are valued by men for the short-term feelings of love that they may not be getting from their wives. For example, Dotto justified his infidelity: "Yes, I had *hawara* [lovers]. When things at home are bad a man must look elsewhere for love." Lovers earn them respect from other men for having multiple women depend on them; they confer the status of a man who cares for, and is cared for by, more than one woman; they even allow a man to imagine a life in the future as modern, virtuous, and successful. Asani, then, bides his time, saves his money, builds his business, and invests in his kin networks in ways that will help him in the future and potentially secure a second wife. His case illustrates, however, that despite his relative economic success, polygyny is not an easy accomplishment.

Achieving Polygyny Late in Life

Mzee Issa, in his early seventies, completed secondary school in an era when few men or women received formal education. At the time, stable well-paying jobs were available for these educated men in the lucrative sisal industry, with sisal grown in an estate at the southern edge of the village. Mzee Issa was hired as an accountant and maintained this position for the next thirty years while the sisal industry thrived. Mzee Issa's position afforded him a type of wealth and power that was largely inaccessible to most men who engaged in subsistence activities such as fishing and farming. As a young, affluent man, Mzee Issa married Fatuma, a beautiful woman from a respected family in Tanga. He rescued her from an abusive marriage, paid for her divorce, and gave her a large lavish wedding in Peponi. Mzee Issa is passionate about local and national politics, and during that time he sought and held local political positions in the village, such as village secretary and treasurer. He continues to participate actively in local politics. As a result of his salary, he was able to build a large concrete, aluminum-roofed house with electricity (one of the few in the village) and his seven children received a secondary education—both highly visible signs of his success.

Mzee Issa's success as a young man permitted the possibility of polygyny at a young age, which is unusual for men in this village. Indeed, he sought to marry a second wife several times in youth and middle age. The two times he carried out his plans and married a new bride, Fatuma insisted Mzee Issa give her a talaka, effectively ending their marriage. She could not tolerate sharing her husband with another woman and had no intention of splitting the resources he directed her way with another wife. Both times, Mzee Issa eventually divorced the second wife and came back to Fatuma. He says, "As much as I wanted a second wife, it was not worth the fighting and losing Fatuma." I asked him why he wanted a second wife in his younger days: "I am a good Muslim man. I had the capital to provide nicely for my wife and children, help my relatives, and also take a second wife." Mzee Issa explains that his priorities, and obligations, are to take care of his wife, children, extended family members, and then pursue a second wife. This forty-year marriage of Mzee Issa and Fatuma illustrates the role of polygyny in the fluidity of marriage and divorce among couples in Peponi, and women's roles in limiting polygyny.

In the 1980s nationalization, mismanagement, and the rise of synthetics brought about widespread declines in sisal production. Consequently, Mzee Issa lost his job. When discussing this period he expressed bitter disappointment and how difficult it was on him as a husband, man, and community leader to lose his income, purpose, and what he perceived as his power. In what appeared to be an effort to salvage his masculinity and hide the depletion of his savings, Mzee Issa sought, once again, to remarry. Unlike his previous attempts at polygyny, Fatuma did not insist on a divorce. He remains married to both Fatuma and his second wife, Hidaya, today. Both Mzee Issa and Fatuma explained to me that their current relationship is a marriage in name only. Mzee Issa describes his first wife as an old lady. At sixty-five, she is younger than he is, but is overweight and has difficulty with her hips and knees and finds it challenging to move about. Mzee Issa, in turn, reports that she is unable to perform the "duties" of a wife because of her health and age; specifically, she is no longer able to have sex with him. I replied, "But you are also an *mzee* [old man]." His reply: "Yes, but she is a woman, and I AM A MAN!" He clarified that he believes old men continue to have sexual desires and needs, while old women do not.

Mzee Issa speaks with authority about Islam and the Qur'an and what is permitted with regard to marriage. He enjoys discussing how a man is required to behave toward his wives. While he professes to treat both his wives equally, his wives challenge this point. For example, while Fatuma continues to live in the large, modern home, Hidaya lives in a mud-and-thatch two-room house. She routinely apologized for being unable to offer me a more comfortable room to sit in when visiting her. Second, Mzee Issa is quick to point out that he treats his wives equally when it comes to daily expenditures. Fatuma, however, angrily complains Mzee Issa contributes almost nothing to her household needs. She insists the only reason she is able to survive is because her children and grandchildren take care of her. As an older man with no job, Mzee Issa has no regular income. He has already passed on his assets—land and property—to his children so they might attain their own goals. His sons helped him afford his marriage to Hidaya (by providing mahari payments and materials for building a second home), and they do provide him with a modest amount of cash for daily living. Mzee Issa spends the bulk of his limited resources on Hidaya's household expenses. I asked Mzee Issa about the obvious difference in what he provides his wives, and he explained: "I do not find it necessary to give Fatuma money; it is our children's responsibility to provide for her. I provided them with an excellent education and they live with her in the house I built rent-free." In other words, because he supported his children in their early life, he now views their contributions to Fatuma's maintenance as his own. Although he continues to frustrate her, Fatuma ultimately resigned herself to this unequal treatment and stated that she did not have the energy or need to fight his second wife. She acknowledges that if she is going to be in a polygynous union, she is pleased that she is the first wife, not the second wife, because it gives her a higher status in the village.

Finally, Mzee Issa understands that, according to the Qur'an, he should treat his wives equally in all ways, including sexual relations. He acknowledges the need to spend equal time with each wife; he suggests a man should alternate which house he sleeps and eats in as a means of achieving emotional equality. He claims to pass by the house of the wife he is not staying with each morning to ask if there are any problems or needs, suggesting that he alternates between households. In fact, he sleeps and eats exclusively with Hidaya, the second wife, and both wives indicated that they prefer this arrangement. As Fatuma explains, "I cannot deny him access to his house, but I do not want him sleeping or eating here. He should just stay with her." Fatuma will not even say Hidaya's name, or reference her as a cowife or second wife. She repeatedly calls Hidaya "her" or "that woman." Mzee Issa is upfront that he no longer has a sexual relationship with Fatuma. However, it is not because of her age, health, or sexual drive, Fatuma argues. She declares that she refuses to have sex with him: "[These days] I am not interested in getting any of the diseases we now know about." She is certain her husband already has or will one day contract HIV or another sexually transmitted infection.

By successfully marrying multiple wives and claiming to treat his wives as specified by the Qur'an, Mzee Issa presents himself as a "good Muslim man." He no longer has a sizeable income, nor is he actually able to support his wives equally, but his polygamous relationship provides other villagers a symbolic reminder of the status he once possessed. He continues to be a respected elder in the community, heavily involved in local government, and "a good Muslim man." His pride in achieving this social position is not lessened by the contradictions his wives point out. Indeed, as we have seen, he creatively interprets Islamic requirements to justify his practices. Polygyny, as practiced in Peponi, however, rarely resembles the visions that men craft.

Choosing Islam: Kinship, Piety and Polygyny

Jumbe is an economically successful, twenty-eight-year-old Peponi man. He buys seafood from local fishermen and sells it to a European export business operating out of Tanga. Jumbe describes how he began his business as a middleman:

> I was lucky to meet a European man from Italy when I was in secondary school. Knowing a little English from

school helped me with this man, who wanted to bring our fish to Europe. I convinced him I could organize the fishermen in Peponi and provide him with the fish. I tell the fishermen what type of seafood we need, weigh the fish and seafood, pay the fishermen each day, and keep the fish on ice. It is a big job to keep track of all of this. I make a good profit selling the fish, as the Italian is not stingy. You see that I have built a new house with all the modern conveniences, I have a cell phone, and now I have a motorcycle. I am twenty-eight and not the firstborn son. I have the respect of a firstborn son, because of my success and my seriousness. I am the head of my father's family now. My father was a successful man, but now I take care of him.

As a prosperous businessman, Jumbe is in a position of both power and obligation to his kin and the poorer villagers of Peponi. Jumbe notes that his success and seriousness afford him a greater level of respect, akin to that of a firstborn son. His "seriousness" references his piousness and devotion to Islam. On Friday afternoons, the Muslim day of communal prayers, there is a steady stream of people coming to his house requesting food, money, and assistance. As a man who considers himself a good Muslim, Jumbe considers it his duty to help others. In the quotation above, he said *seriousness* in English to reference his piousness and devotion to Islam. He provides small sums to most of the people who humble themselves by coming to his home. He also feels obliged to assist his extended family members. For example, Jumbe routinely provides work opportunities for his paternal cousin Waziri, a thirty-two-year-old twice-divorced woman with a three-year-old son in her care. Jumbe is the closest relative of means and she frequently asks him for financial help. He knows that she is unlikely to receive help from others. He assigns Waziri odd jobs helping his wife, Saumu, with household duties such as laundry. Jumbe, however, is conflicted over this practice of supporting his kin. He wants to help but also cannot afford to give money to everyone. He prefers to think of ways they can help him and his family. Another paternal cousin, Mohammedi, benefits from Jumbe's generosity. Two years ago Jumbe offered to finance his university education. He pays for all of Mohammedi's educational and living expenses, but fully expects Mohammedi to repay the money when he graduates. Jumbe is pleased that he can help his cousin; it is an additional opportunity to help his kin, invest in his future, and demonstrate his success to the community. All these actions demonstrate to the entire community his status as a good Muslim, a good relative, and a good man.

Jumbe also considers his obligations to his father, Mzee Rama, as part of his duty as a good Muslim son. When Jumbe married, his father sold him his house. Although he offered him the house at a reduced rate as a gift and early inheritance, Jumbe's father also had an ulterior motive: Mzee Rama sought to secure enough capital to acquire a second wife and provide her with a separate, smaller house. This trade benefited both men, and they received public acknowledgment for doing the right thing: Mzee Rama for providing his son and daughter-in-law with a nice home, and Jumbe for helping his father attain his goal of a second wife. However, this move by Mzee Rama and Jumbe effectively displaced Binundu, Jumbe's mother, from the home she lived in at the time. And as Mzee Rama was an old man with no job, it was highly unlikely that he would be able to provide for two wives. Like Mzee Issa, Mzee Rama expects that his children, particularly Jumbe, will provide for their mother. Initially, Binundu continued to live in the house, but soon after Jumbe married his wife Saumu, it was clear it was not a good arrangement. Binundu moved out to live with other children. However, she continued to spend most of her time each day at Jumbe and Saumu's house, as did Mzee Rama, despite having a separate household and a new wife. He stated that he was there to spend time with his namesake grandchild, Rama, and, like his wife, he also frequently ate meals prepared by Saumu and paid for by Jumbe.

Saumu and Jumbe were married three years before I arrived in Peponi. Their relationship was not an easy one. While Saumu describes their early relationship in romantic terms, she got pregnant before marriage and her mother threatened to place a curse on Jumbe if he did not marry her. Jumbe does not consider the marriage a love match. Although he married her, his treatment of her did not reflect the caring, monogamous, romantic relationship she desired. Jumbe describes Saumu as demanding and frivolous. He explains that he was extremely generous with the mahari he provided her and her family. He argues that providing items such as furniture and household goods provided at their marriage, and paying for electricity and daily food costs, adequately fulfill his obligation as a husband. He finds her ongoing requests for a new dress for each wedding she attends extravagant. "Why can't she wear one of the many dresses she already has? Why must it always be a new dress?" For weddings, female guests often buy the same fabric and have matching dresses made by a local tailor. This is an important element of the wedding celebration for women that communicates their importance in the community, their solidarity with other women in their family, and their ability to secure resources for luxury items like a new dress.[33] Jumbe declares that he has countless responsibilities and that many people make demands on his income; "buying my wife a new dress is not a priority." The wife he envisions does as she is told, takes care of the home and children without questioning him, and is a pious Muslim who is uninvolved in what he describes as *mambo ya mila* (traditional practices and customs). Jumbe regards some mila practices like dancing and drumming as rooted in African cultures, not Islam; the chapters in this volume by Pat Caplan, Kjersti Larsen, and Katrina Thompson also address debates over mila and Islam.

Saumu describes Jumbe as ungenerous and goes further to say he should take better care of her and their two-year-old son because he has the means to do so. She says he has threatened to divorce her if she does not obey him in all things. In particular, he insists that she not leave their house and courtyard, not even to do errands or visit family. He routinely denies her requests to visit relatives and friends and to participate in community events, celebrations, and activities. She must rely on other people to do errands and visiting for her. On one occasion, she thrust her dressed-up and powdered son at me and insisted I carry him to an eid celebration. Even her informal entrepreneurial efforts making and selling juice require she hire a young girl to actually sell the juice. But this allows her to purchase luxury items, such as baby powder, a lacy bra from a traveling salesman and, most important, the fabric to have a new matching dress made for each family wedding. Unlike the situation Swartz describes in Mombasa thirty years ago, Swahili wives in Peponi are no longer exclusively dependent on the goodwill of their husbands to purchase items that aid them in "gaining and maintaining prestige."[34] Women's informal entrepreneurial activities, particularly in food preparation, have had a significant effect on women's options within and outside marriage.[35]

Although it irritates her to do so, Saumu reluctantly defers to her husband in both small and large matters. Despite her anger, she does not want Jumbe to divorce her, nor to remarry. She explains:

> I do not want to be divorced and on my own. But I also do not want to be treated with disrespect and I do not want a second wife in this family. I will leave my husband before that happens. I know he will take another wife someday and then I will take our son and go to my parents' house. They will have me. I will make juice and sell it at my sister-in-law's small restaurant and that will be all that we need. I will be able to take care of myself. I'd rather be on my own than have a husband with a second wife. I have respect for myself.

Jumbe is aware of his wife's feelings and says that he would feel disappointed if his marriage to Saumu ended because he remarries. He admires the fact that his own parents have stayed married for forty-five years. However, he also approves of his father's second wife; "As long as I can maintain them independently, why wouldn't I have four wives? I am a good Muslim man and Islam permits up to four wives." As a "good Muslim man," he believes he has to wait until the time is right, and he does not intend to take a second wife until he can afford it: "It's not even that I want the hassle or demands of a second wife. And you know things here [with Saumu] will get more difficult. But, as an important successful businessman and as a good Muslim man, having a second wife is important. People [men] expect me to show my success in this way; they would be suspicious if I did not try for a second wife." Jumbe is aware of the discord in his father's relationship with his mother. He knows his mother feels betrayed and disrespected, yet it does not dissuade him from considering a second wife. His desire to maintain his reputation in the community as a successful, virtuous Muslim supersedes these ambivalent feelings.

The relationship between Jumbe's parents was obviously strained. The only time Mzee Rama indicated, in my presence, that Binundu was his wife was on the day that my own husband, Dan, arrived in Peponi. Upon his arrival, in my ninth month of fieldwork, I took him to Jumbe's house for an introduction and both of Jumbe's parents were present. Mzee Rama jumped up and heartily shook Dan's hand. Although I had never heard him mention having two wives before, on this day he introduced himself, saying: "Yes, I am Mzee Rama. I have two wives; this woman is my first wife, the mother of my children [while saying this he pointed to Binundu, and then beckoned to her to join him]. I also have a second wife, who is not here." The enthusiasm and delight with which Mzee Rama delivered this brief speech stunned me. He had not made this speech to me upon my arrival, nor did he introduce Binundu as his wife when he met other visitors I brought to meet his family. Interestingly, and perhaps not surprisingly, polygyny was a topic that villagers were eager to discuss with Dan. Men and women alike enjoyed teasing us about his prospects for a second wife in the village. They knew full well that he was not a Muslim, but like they did with me, they saw no obstacle to his converting to Islam.

This multigenerational view of polygyny in Peponi highlights the complexity of these relationships. Young men help their fathers attain polygyny by providing them the capital to do so, and by taking care of their mother's needs. This, in turn, frees their fathers of the responsibility to care for their first wives financially. Fathers help their sons by providing them with a house or gifting them other assets of value. Jumbe is a man with a successful business, he takes his rights and responsibilities as a Muslim man seriously, and he dismisses what he describes as his wife's extravagant and unnecessary demands for his resources. He believes he is a good Muslim man because he fulfills his duty to his family and because he plans to take a second wife. He values his wife but privileges his responsibilities to his father and extended family, as well as his reputation in the community. All this is framed by his interpretations of Islam and his desire to construct himself as virtuous. He is careful and deliberate about considering when it is the right time to take second wife. For him, being a "good Muslim" is looking cautiously toward his economic position in the future and not rushing into polygyny before he can afford it.

Polygyny is difficult for men to achieve: systemic poverty and a lack of industry and jobs make accumulating the necessary resources for mahari payments, weddings, and maintaining two separate households extremely difficult. Second, a myriad of kin obligations further divide men's meager resources. And finally, when men do find the resources available to marry a second wife, their current wives often thwart their polygynous plans. Despite the obstacles, most men continue to articulate a desire for multiple wives. Men's ambition for multiple wives is a frequent topic of discussion and a defining characteristic of their identity as modern Muslim men. This research highlights the gendered expectations of marriage, in particular men's desire for polygyny and women's aversion to the practice. Men and women readily discuss their relationship plans and preferences. Women are known to initiate a divorce if they suspect their husband is making moves to acquire a second wife. The actual number of men with multiple wives is quite low, and despite the various obstacles men encounter to achieve polygyny, women's role is undoubtedly a large factor. It can be argued that polygyny, the reality of men's desire for it, and the fear it incites in women have real consequences as it is among the most frequent reasons given for the cause of divorce in Peponi.[36]

Asani, Mzee Issa, and Jumbe all define their desire for polygyny through their understanding of Islam. They desire to become modern, successful, and virtuous Muslims; polygyny is the most conspicuous means of doing so. Men clearly state the attributes of a "good Muslim man." They describe their obligations to kin and community and their rights to polygyny as an essential component of this identity. Men who attain financial success are expected to pursue polygyny, or to help others, such as their fathers, achieve it. Polygyny, then, is both a symbol of success and an Islamic virtue. A man is prosperous and a "good Muslim" if he successfully attains multiple wives and treats them as the Qur'an stipulates. For men in Peponi, a man's priorities, and obligations, are to take care of his wife, children, and extended family members and then pursue a second wife. Each of these actions is construed as part and parcel of his rights and responsibilities as a Muslim man.

NOTES

1. Amira Mashhour, "Islamic Law and Gender Equality: Could There Be a Common Ground? A Study of Divorce and Polygamy in Sharia Law and Contemporary Legislation in Tunisia and Egypt," *Human Rights Quarterly* 27, no. 2 (2005): 562–96.

2. John Middleton, *The World of the Swahili: An African Mercantile Civilization* (New Haven: Yale University Press, 1992).

3. Joan Russell, *Communicative Competence in a Minority Group: A Sociolinguistic Study of the Swahili-Speaking Community in the Old Town, Mombasa* (Leiden: Brill, 1981), 25, quoted in Katrina Daly Thompson, "How to Be a Good Muslim Wife: Women's Performance of Islamic Authority during Swahili Weddings," *Journal of Religion in Africa* 41, no. 4 (2011): 428.

4. Adeline Masquelier, *Women and Islamic Revival in a West African Town* (Bloomington: Indiana University Press, 2009), 25.

5. Ibid., 24.

6. Riley Bove and Claudia Valeggia, "Polygyny and Women's Health in Sub-Saharan Africa," *Social Science and Medicine* 68, no. 1 (2009): 21–29.

7. National Bureau of Statistics and ORC Macro, *Tanzania Demographic and Health Survey 2004–5* (Dar es Salaam: National Bureau of Statistics, 2005).

8. Ibid.

9. Ann K. Blanc and Anastasia J. Gage, "Men, Polygyny, and Fertility over the Life-Course in Sub-Saharan Africa.," in *Fertility and the Male Life-Cycle in the Era of Fertility Decline,* ed. Caroline H. Bledsoe, Jane I. Guyer, and Susana Lerner (Oxford: Oxford University Press, 2000), 163.

10. Ibid.; Stephen Obeng Gyimah, "Polygynous Marital Structure and Child Survivorship in Sub-Saharan Africa: Some Empirical Evidence from Ghana," *Social Science and Medicine* 68, no. 2 (2009): 334–42; Milly Marston et al., "Trends in Marriage and Time Spent Single in Sub-Saharan Africa: A Comparative Analysis of Six Population-Based Cohort Studies

and Nine Demographic and Health Surveys," *Sexually Transmitted Infections* 85, supplement 1 (2009): 164–171; Bernard Njau, Sabina Mtweve, Rachel Manongi, and Hector Jalipa, "Gender Differences in Intention to Remain a Virgin until Marriage among School Pupils in Rural Northern Tanzania," *African Journal of AIDS Research* 8, no. 2 (2009): 157–66; Deborah Rubin, Cynthia P. Green, and Altrena Mukuria, *Addressing Early Marriage in Uganda* (Washington, DC: USAID, 2009); Getu D. Alene and Alemayehu Worku, "Differentials of Fertility in North and South Gondar Zones, Northwest Ethiopia: A Comparative Cross-Sectional Study," *BMC Public Health* 8, no. 1 (2008): 397.

11. Jennifer Cole and Lynn M. Thomas, eds., *Love in Africa* (Chicago: University of Chicago Press, 2009); Caroline H. Bledsoe and Gilles Pison, eds., *Nuptiality in Sub-Saharan Africa: Contemporary Anthropological and Demographic Perspectives,* International Studies in Demography (Oxford: Clarendon Press, 1994).

12. Dominique Meekers and Nadra Franklin, "Women's Perceptions of Polygyny among the Kaguru of Tanzania," *Ethnology* 34, no. 4 (1995): 315–29. But for an exception, see Stephen C. Lubkemann, "The Transformation of Transnationality among Mozambican Migrants in South Africa," *Canadian Journal of African Studies/La revue canadienne des études africaines* 34, no. 1 (2000): 41–63.

13. Blanc and Gage, "Men, Polygyny."

14. Bove and Valeggia, "Polygyny and Women's Health"; Alex C. Ezeh, Michka Seroussi, and Hendrik Raggers, *Men's Fertility, Contraceptive Use, and Reproductive Preferences,* Demographic and Health Surveys Comparative Studies 18 (Calverton, MD: Macro International, 1996); Hanan G. Jacoby, "The Economics of Polygyny in Sub-Saharan Africa: Female Productivity and the Demand for Wives in Côte d'Ivoire," *Journal of Political Economy* 103, no. 5 (1995): 938–71; Georges Reniers and Susan Watkins, "Polygyny and the Spread of HIV in Sub Saharan Africa: A Case of Benign Concurrency," *AIDS* 24, no. 2 (2010): 299.

15. Meekers and Franklin, "Women's Perceptions."

16. Leif C. W. Landberg, "Men of Kigombe: Ngalawa Fishermen of Northeastern Tanzania" (PhD diss., University of California, Davis, 1975); Pamela W. Landberg, "Widows and Divorced Women in Swahili Society," in *Widows in African Societies: Choices and Constraints,* ed. Betty Potash (Stanford: Stanford University Press, 1986), 107–31; P. Landberg, "Kinship and Community in a Tanzania Coastal Village" (PhD diss., University of California, Davis, 1977).

17. L. Landberg, "Men of Kigombe"; P. Landberg, "Kinship and Community."

18. Brad Weiss, *Street Dreams and Hip Hop Barbershops: Global Fantasy in Urban Tanzania,* Tracking Globalization (Bloomington: Indiana University Press, 2009), 9.

19. For a similar understanding in southern Tanzania, see Halley, "Sex and School," chap. 5, this volume. I also address this issue more extensively in "Women, Work, and (Re)Marriage: Entrepreneurship among Swahili Women in Coastal Tanzania," which will be forthcoming in a special issue of *Africa Today,* Objects, Money, and Meaning in Contemporary African Marriage.

20. P. Landberg, "Kinship and Community."

21. Pat Caplan, "Cognatic Descent Groups on Mafia Island, Tanzania," *Man* 4, no. 3 (1969): 419–31; Caplan, "Cognatic Descent, Islamic Law and Women's Property on the East African Coast," in *Women and Property—Women as Property,* ed. Renée Hirschon (London: Croom Helm, 1984); Roger Gomm, "Harlots and Bachelors: Marital Instability among the Coastal Digo of Kenya," *Man* 7, no. 1 (1972): 95–113; Susan F. Hirsch, *Pronouncing and Persevering: Gender and the Discourses of Disputing in an African Islamic Court,* Language and Legal Discourse (Chicago: University of Chicago Press, 1998); P. Landberg, "Widows and Divorced Women"; Middleton, *World of the Swahili;* Erin E. Stiles, *An Islamic Court in Context: An Ethnographic Study of Judicial Reasoning* (New York: Palgrave Macmillan, 2009); Erin E. Stiles, "'There Is No Stranger to Marriage Here!': Muslim Women and Divorce in Rural Zanzibar," *Africa: Journal of the International African Institute* 75, no. 4 (2005): 582–98; Stiles, this volume; Margaret Strobel, *Muslim Women in Mombasa, Kenya, 1890–1975* (New Haven: Yale University Press, 1979); Marc J. Swartz, *The Way the World Is: Cultural Processes and Social Relations among the Mombasa Swahili* (Berkeley: University of California Press, 1991).

22. Sue Keefe, "Romantic Desires and Polygynous Intentions: Islam, Gender, and Divorce in Coastal Tanzania" (PhD diss., Brown University, 2010).

23. See Wambui wa Karanja, "The Phenomenon of 'Outside Wives': Some Reflections on Its Possible Influence on Fertility," in *Nuptiality in Sub-Saharan Africa: Contemporary Anthropological and Demographic Perspectives,* ed. Caroline H. Bledsoe and Gilles Pison (Oxford: Clarendon Press, 1994), 194–214.

24. Keefe, "Romantic Desires."

25. See Masquelier, *Women and Islamic Revival.*

26. Pat Caplan, "Learning Gender: Fieldwork in a Tanzanian Coastal Village, 1965–85," in *Gendered Fields: Women, Men, and Ethnography,* ed. Diane Bell, Caplan, and Wazir-Jahan Karim (London: Routledge, 1993), 168–81; P. Landberg, "Widows and Divorced Women"; Middleton, *World of the Swahili.*

27. Middleton, *World of the Swahili.*

28. P. Landberg, "Kinship and Community," 130. See also Caplan, "Learning Gender"; P. Landberg, "Widows and Divorced Women"; Middleton, *The World of the Swahili.*

29. Christine J. Walley, *Rough Waters: Nature and Development in an East African Marine Park* (Princeton: Princeton University Press, 2010), 234.

30. Weiss, *Street Dreams.*

31. Keefe, "Romantic Desires."

32. Marc J. Swartz, "The Isolation of Men and the Happiness of Women: Sources and Use of Power in Swahili Marital Relationships," *Journal of Anthropological Research* 38, no. 1 (1982): 42.

33. See also Swartz, *Way the World Is.*

34. Swartz, "Isolation," 28.

35. Keefe, "Romantic Desires."

36. Ibid.

AFTERWORD

Understanding Gendered Lives through Intimate and Global Perspectives

SUSAN F. HIRSCH

AFRICAN SEXUALITIES, Sylvia Tamale's groundbreaking edited volume, includes an arresting short piece titled "A Night in Zanzibar" by the African feminist activist Jessica Horn. In an account brimming with vivid images and emotion, Horn describes an experience she had at an evening event for gender activists who were attending a conference in Zanzibar. The event was designed for the activists, primarily women, to relax together at a beachfront restaurant, as they enjoyed local food and entertainment. Horn recounts noticing several musicians setting up, while two *buibui*-clad women who had accompanied them stood by themselves and showed little interest in the expectant audience. To Horn's surprise, once the music began the women's demeanor changed immediately; they threw off their cloaks and danced with provocative energy. Motioning to Horn to stand up, one dancer engaged her in a sustained and intense encounter that began with them dancing together. After they danced long enough for Horn to feel more at ease rotating her hips, the dancer pushed her to the ground and straddled her. The ensuing mock lesson in sexual performance stunned Horn, although she remained a good sport throughout. Afterward she came to realize just how deeply affected she was by the power she felt during the encounter. In exquisitely honest writing she reflects on the striking difference between her initial assumptions about the seemingly detached buibui-clad woman and the physical sexuality of their power-laden mutual experience. Admitting an inability to narrate her own complex responses, Horn wrote a poem that pays "homage to the unceasing power of African women to subvert and reinterpret within, and well beyond, the veil of social norms."[1]

What Jessica Horn was challenged to express in prose—women's sexual agency in a majority-Muslim, geographically African context—is what the scholars in this volume accomplish in remarkable ways. In writing about marriage and sexuality along the western edge of the Indian Ocean, the authors excel in depicting gendered experiences that acknowledge the piety and faith commitments of both men and women at the same time as they reveal powerful individual agency to forge relationships, sexual and otherwise, through a diverse array of actions and discourses. In this volume gender, marriage, and sexuality appear in multiple forms and reflect many influences, including those of significant institutions (e.g., schools, madrasas, NGOs) and individuals (e.g., teachers, clerics, parents, politicians). Scholarship about Muslim communities along the coastal edge has taught successive generations of readers many lessons about the complex interweaving of Islam, power, and gender in Swahili society. Taken together, the chapters in this book address these interconnected realms more intentionally, and with analytic sophistication, while still rooting the analyses deeply in the history and culture of the region as portrayed in previous writing. Those of us who have contributed to and followed the anthropological and historical study of the Swahili coast find to our delight that these chapters take us further into marriage and other relationships than we had perhaps gone in the past and also toward new phenomena, such as balancing marriage with aspirations for school and work, interpreting contradictory sectarian perspectives on gender, coping with HIV/AIDS, or navigating the influence of media from across the Indian and other oceans. The book's vivid imagery and explicit language surprises (and perhaps shocks) some readers and reminds everyone that new understandings of the Swahili coast are emerging and are always possible.

Similar to prior scholarship, this volume treats coastal East African society as a site from which to build theories about gender relations, marriage, and sexuality that can be applied well beyond the region. Notwithstanding the many innovative topics explored in revealing and convincing detail, it is the emphasis—in multiple chapters—on sexuality as a grounding for women's agency that stands out as an especially fresh and intriguing aspect of the volume. Understanding women's sexuality as a facet of their gendered agency has been an important aim of feminist theory from its earliest days. At the same time, feminists and nonfeminists have voiced persistent concerns about overemphasizing women's sexuality, which can so readily be romanticized, misinterpreted, or misconstrued to serve sexist and misogynist ends. Such concerns are real; focusing on the power of women's sexuality presents a host of tricky challenges that scholars—including those who theorize gender—often prefer to sidestep.

This volume successfully confronts the challenges of writing about women's sexual agency by offering a wide array of well-contextualized examples. Moreover, the analysis accounts for why sexuality takes certain forms and how these forms are shaped by gender and other power dynamics. Among the palette of images that convey women's sexual agency are slaves who try to negotiate physical relationships with both owners and husbands, wives who go to court to plead for sexual satisfaction, elderly women who let loose profanity that triggers blushing, and many women and girls who project themselves as sexual beings through dance, attire, and everyday speech. Let me not overemphasize the liberating qualities of sexual agency. As the chapters reveal, these behaviors can risk contravening norms of gender and sexuality, and women's own roles in setting, enforcing, and resisting these norms defy simple analysis. Relatedly, the authors of these chapters do not shy away from depicting decidedly illiberal images, such as sexually abusive relationships, health-diminishing pregnancies, sex in loveless marriages, and limits on women's choices and actions in the name of honor, religion, or some other kind of duty. Yet the takeaway message that sexual agency is fundamental to living a full, satisfying, and religious life in these African, Islamic societies is surprising in its novelty. This perspective on women's sexuality provides a welcome complement to the pervasive emphasis on women's empowerment through neoliberal regimes of training, economic development, and schooling that rarely mention how sexuality and its potential power might play a role in the empowerment prescribed for women.

The depictions of sexual agency in the volume made me recall a scene I witnessed almost thirty years ago, when I was at the beginning of two decades of field research in coastal Kenya and Tanzania. Just one month into the research, I traveled with several unmarried Swahili women to Lamu for Maulidi, the celebration of the prophet's birthday for which the island is famous. Daily afternoon parades, all-night dancing, lots of visiting, and precious little supervision created an atmosphere of celebration and romantic intrigue. During the daytime I hung out with the young women on the flat rooftop of the large family home where we stayed. We cooked, planned the evening's attire and activities, and gossiped, while watching the foot traffic below. In the heat of midday we rested on and around a bed positioned under a small covered area in the corner of the roof. After dark the roof became the province of boys and men who flocked upstairs for the nighttime view, to chew *miraa* (khat), and to eat platters of rice and delicacies between their forays to see the dancing and pray at the mosque. One evening around midnight my friends and I had returned home briefly and were preparing to head out again. We were just in time to witness a male exodus from the roof. Men and boys charged down the stairs, through the large first-floor living room, and out the front door. Shortly after, as the house quieted, the latest son-in-law to marry into the family started to climb the steps to the rooftop holding the hand of his wife, who followed behind. The daughter-now-wife looked beautiful in her elaborate makeup and Maulidi finery. With head held high and a smile playing on her lips, she radiated confidence and expectation. Just as their feet disappeared from view, my Swahili friends erupted in giggles. Once it dawned on me that the young couple, having evicted everyone from the roof, planned to make good use of the rooftop bed, I felt embarrassed. By contrast, the reaction of the young women around me betrayed no shame but only their own aspirations for a sexually exciting married life. Who could blame the couple for kicking the boys out so that they could enjoy Maulidi fully?

My example of a woman's sexual agency is more subtle than Horn's and more intimately enacted in a family home. It no doubt resembles the thousands of observations of sexual agency made by the contributors to this book as they conducted their research. Some of the most significant evidence of women's sexual agency comes through lines of sight that require intimate contact with women, their families, and friends. Several of the authors comment on the depth of the relationships they forged during their research and beyond that afforded them such contact, and the scholarship they have produced on marriage, gender, and sexuality could not have been done as effectively without having gained such perspective. Analysis of the microlevel of intimacy benefits from being carried out in the microlevel of intimacy. Yet, similar to my point above about the tricky nature of writing about women's sexual agency, admitting as a scholar that one has forged intensive and intimate relationships—whether sexual or not—comes with a risk. Anthropologists have always valued deep connection with our interlocutors, yet questions are routinely raised about just how close such relationships should be and what consequence intimacy might have for scholarly findings. The contributors to this volume renew my conviction that research carried out at the microlevel of intimacy is especially insightful and welcome. Embracing this approach is one important way in which this volume breaks new ground.

The attention to men's perspectives on gender, masculinity, and male sexuality is another innovative aspect of the volume, which paves the way for additional scholarship on long-neglected topics, such as same-sex sexuality and the effects of masculinity on many aspects of social and familial life. The focus on African men is increasingly urgent, given the fears expressed—almost to the level of moral panic—about the "bulges" of young, jobless men across the continent. Attention to the variegated experiences and interests of African Muslim men can provide a corrective to assumptions that overreach or distort and can contribute to identifying causes and consequences of men's positioning in national, regional, and global political economies, as well as in families and relationships.

In this short afterword, I will not revisit the wide range of examples offered in the volume that, taken together, encourage us to rethink not only women's and men's sexual agency but gender relations and marriage broadly. The chapters insist on the role of state institutions, such as courts and schools, in shaping gender relations at the same time as rituals that celebrate marriage and mark religious holidays are highlighted for their vibrant influence. Examples are brought to life through the authors' attention to language and discourse. Through eloquent pleas, ritual cadences, teasing jokes, and explicit lyrics, readers experience the intensive interactions through which gender and gender norms are communicated and struggled over. The inclusion of actual speech creates the opportunity for alternative interpretations of the *Kiswahili cha ndani,* or insider meanings of Kiswahili, over which aficionados of the language can disagree, debate, and riff off of, at length.

In their introduction, Katrina Thompson and Erin Stiles mention the added value of attention to language as one of several innovative methodological contributions made through this volume, and they are also right to highlight the value of an interdisciplinary approach that includes anthropology, history, and discourse studies. In addition to breaking new ground through analysis at the microlevel of intimacy, the volume simultaneously pushes the field toward macrolevel analyses. Notably, the volume succeeds in reorienting the scholarly perspective on these communities by locating them at the western edge of the vibrant Indian Ocean. The shifting and broadening of perspective is a very welcome new position for a place that is often depicted as the marginalized or irreconcilably Other eastern edge of the African continent. An unbroken flow of people, goods, commerce, ideas, religious traditions, and entertainment around Indian Ocean venues has influenced gender, marriage, and sexuality in eastern Africa for centuries. The dhow trade may have waned, but the increasing intensity of global processes means that the nature and extent of regional influence should be much more prominent in future scholarship. This volume, particularly the introduction, sets out an agenda of thinking from this perspective that not only breaks new ground but should stimulate further research from an Indian Ocean perspective. The challenge that this volume poses to future authors is a steep one: to pursue research through broader and more innovative frames while still paying close attention to the microlevel of intimacy. Such scholarship, as this volume demonstrates, is both possible and necessary. Moreover, as also demonstrated by these authors, the result can surprise, convince, challenge, and delight us.

NOTE

1. Jessica Horn, "A Night in Zanzibar—Life Story and Poem," in *African Sexualities: A Reader*, ed. Sylvia Tamale (Oxford: Pambazuka Press, 2011), 185.

Glossary

All entries are Swahili terms unless otherwise noted.

adabu.	Manners (<Ar. *adab*).
aibu.	Shame.
arusi.	A wedding (also *harusi*).
bibi.	A term of address used with an adult (esp. married) woman.
bibiharusi.	A bride (often abbreviated as *bi arusi* or *bi harusi*).
bidaa.	Heretical religious innovation (<Ar. *bid'a*).
buibui.	An abaya; a long (usually black) robe that covers a woman's clothing as well as her arms past the wrists, and legs past the ankles.
bwanaharusi.	A groom (also *bwana harusi*).
dini.	Religion.
edda.	The three-month period a Muslim woman must wait after divorce before remarrying (<Ar. *'idda*).
fundi.	An expert tradesman; used (perhaps euphemistically) for traditional healers; specialists in spirit possession rituals.
haji.	The ritual pilgrimage to Mecca, one of the Five Pillars of Islam (English, *hajj*; <Ar. *hajj*).

harusi.	A wedding (also *arusi*).
haya.	Modesty, shyness.
heshima.	Respect, respectability.
hijabu.	A scarf or other fabric used by women to cover the hair, ears, and neck (English *hijab*; <Ar. *hijāb*).
jando.	A boys' puberty ritual.
jini.	Spirits, djinn.
joho.	A man's robe worn during weddings.
kadhi.	An Islamic judge, qadi (<Ar. *qadhi*).
kanga.	A colorful piece of fabric, usually with a Swahili saying on it; used by women to cover clothing or hair (or both), as well as for many household uses (sing. and pl.). See *leso*.
kanuni.	A regulation, code, canon, doctrine.
khuluu.	An Islamic divorce in which a woman financially compensates her husband for the divorce (<Ar. *khul'*).
kirumbizi.	A dance done by men during Lamu weddings.
Kiswahili.	The Swahili language.
kukata kiuno.	A sexualized dance performed by women (lit., to cut the waist).
kungwi.	A female ritual expert at some *unyago* and *singo*.
kutia ndani.	To seclude. Used for the bride after the legal wedding ceremony, and also for a girl after her first menstruation.
kutukana.	To insult one another; to use profanity with one another.
leso.	The Kenyan term for *kanga*.
madai.	A legal claim document (lit., claims).

madarasa.	Classes. When pronounced with Arabicized pronounciation as "madras," refers specifically to Qur'anic schools (<Ar. *madrasa*).
madhhab (Arabic).	A school of law (Swahili, *madhehebu*).
mahari.	Gift meant to be paid by the groom to the bride upon marriage as part of Islamic marriage contract (but often, in practice, to her family, or in some parts of the Coast, not at all) (<Ar. *mahr*).
malaya.	A prostitute.
mama.	Mother; when capitalized, a title of respect for a married woman old enough to be one's mother.
maneno.	Talk (lit., words).
matusi.	Profanity; insults, abusive language.
maulidi.	The ritual recitation of poems praising the life of the Prophet Muhammad. The proper noun *Maulidi* refers to the celebration of the the Prophet Muhammad's birthday (<Ar. *maulid*).
mganga.	A traditional healer; specialist in spirit possession rituals (pl., *waganga*; see *mwalimu*).
mgonjwa.	A sick person; used euphemistically to refer to an impotent man.
mila.	Tradition(s), custom(s).
Mji Mkongwe.	Stone Town (urban Zanzibar Town; lit., Old Town).
mke.	A wife (pl., *wake*).
mume.	A husband.
mwalimu.	A teacher, scholar; a title often given to educated male Muslims, including *waganga wa kitabu*.
mwanamke.	An adult (i.e. married) woman.

mwari.	A female initiate; a girl who has passed through puberty but is not yet married; virgin (in Lamu and Mafia, *mwali*).
mzee.	An old man; term of respect for an older man.
ndani.	Inside; private; see *kutia ndani.*
ndoa.	Marriage.
Ng'ambo.	The suburbs just beyond Stone Town, on the other side of Darajani Road (lit., the other side, abroad).
ngoma.	Dance; drum; drumming.
nikabu.	A piece of fabric (usually black) used to cover a woman's face except for her eyes (<Ar. *niqāb*).
nikaha.	An Islamic legal marriage ceremony.
nyakanga.	A female ritual expert at some *unyago*; ranked higher than *kungwi*.
pepo.	Spirit(s); wind
-pungwa.	Have an exorcism performed on one's behalf; be initiated into a spirit possession cult.
qibla (Arabic).	The direction of the Kaaba; used for Islamic prayer (English, *qibla*).
rubamba.	A type of Pemban spirit.
ruhani.	A type of spirit known to require piety from, and sometimes to have sexual intercourse with, those it possesses.
sawāhil (Arabic).	Coast; coastal.
shehia.	A semirural location; suburb. InZanzibar today, a small political district.
sheria.	Law; legal due; rights (<Ar. *sharī'a*).
singo.	A premarital ceremony where the bride is prepared for her wedding night; also called *unyago wa kusinga*.

somo.	A puberty or sex instructor.
talaka.	A divorce (<Ar. *talāq*).
talaka bure.	A "free" divorce (one initiated by the wife but without payment to the husband).
udhu.	Ritual purity.
uganga.	The work of an *mganga* (divination, curing, and magic).
uhuru.	Freedom.
ukungwi.	Premarital initiation rites, ranging from puberty rituals to marriage instruction.
unyago.	A puberty ritual for girls (sing. and pl.).
unyago wa kusinga.	See *singo*.
Uswahili.	Swahili culture.
utani.	A ritualized joking relationship.
uwezo.	Ability; used euphemistically about financial resources and sexual potency.
vishawishi.	Gifts and money offered by boys to girls they are pursuing as potential sexual partners (lit., temptations).
vyama.	See *chama*.
waganga.	See *mganga*.
waganga wa kitabu.	Healers who use traditional Middle Eastern Islamic methods
wali.	A government official (<Ar.).
walombo (Makonde).	Adult leaders of puberty rituals.
Waswahili.	Swahili people; coastal people; speakers of Swahili.
watu wa bidaa.	A term used in Zanzibar to refer to proponents of various Muslim groups and organizations in Zanzibar who demand the renunciation of what they call innovations to religious practice (lit., the innovation people).

wazalia.	People native to a particular place (lit., those born there); esp. slaves born in the islands (sing., *mzalia*).
zar.	A type of spirit possession ritual found in northeastern Africa, especially Northern Sudan. The term refers to the beliefs and practices as well as the spirits themselves.
zikiri.	Lit. recollection; meditative practice aimed at remembrance of the names of God (also *dhikiri* <Ar. *dhikr*).
zinaa.	Extramarital sex (<Ar. *zina*).

References

Alene, Getu D., and Alemayehu Worku. "Differentials of Fertility in North and South Gondar Zones, Northwest Ethiopia: A Comparative Cross-Sectional Study." *BMC Public Health* 8, no. 1 (2008): 397.

Alpers, Edward A. E. "'Ordinary Household Chores': Ritual and Power in a Nineteenth-Century Swahili Women's Spirit Possession Cult." *International Journal of African Historical Studies* 17, no. 4 (1984): 677–702.

———. "The Story of Swema: Female Vulnerability in Nineteenth-Century East Africa." In *Women and Slavery in Africa,* edited by Martin A. Klein and Claire C. Robertson, 185–219. Madison: University of Wisconsin Press, 1983.

Amory, Deborah P. "Mashoga, Mabasha, and Magai: 'Homosexuality' on the East African Coast." In *Boy-Wives and Female Husbands: Studies of African Homosexualities,* edited by Stephen O. Murray and Will Roscoe, 67–87. New York: St. Martin's, 1998.

Anderson, J. N. D. "Islamic Law in Africa." *Journal of African Law* 21, no. 2 (1977): 137–38.

———. *Islamic Law in Africa.* Oxford: Frank Cass, 2013.

Anderson-Fye, Eileen. "The Role of Subjective Motivation in Girls' Secondary Schooling: The Case of Avoidance of Abuse in Belize." *Harvard Educational Review* 80, no. 2 (2010): 174–203.

Appadurai, Arjun. *Modernity at Large: Cultural Dimensions of Globalization.* Public Worlds 1. Minneapolis: University of Minnesota Press, 1996.

Askew, Kelly M. "As Plato Duly Warned: Music, Politics, and Social Change in Coastal East Africa." *Anthropological Quarterly* 76, no. 4 (2003): 609–37.

———. *Performing the Nation: Swahili Music and Cultural Politics in Tanzania.* Chicago: University of Chicago Press, 2002.

Bang, Anne K. *Sufis and Scholars of the Sea: Family Networks in East Africa, 1860–1925.* London: RoutledgeCurzon, 2003.

Bangster, Maggie. "'Falling through the Cracks': Adolescent Girls in Tanzania: Insights from Mtwara." USAID Tanzania, 2010.

Barber, Karin. *I Could Speak until Tomorrow: Oriki, Women and the Past in a Yoruba Town.* International African Library 7. Edinburgh: Edinburgh University Press for the International African Institute, 1991.

Barwani, Ali Muhsin al-. *Conflicts and Harmony in Zanzibar: Memoirs.* Dubai: Ali Muhsin al-Barwani, 1997.

Baylies, Carolyn L., and Janet M. Bujra, eds. *AIDS, Sexuality and Gender in Africa: Collective Strategies and Struggles in Tanzania and Zambia.* Social Aspects of AIDS. London: Routledge, 2000.

Beck, Lois, and Nikki R Keddie, eds. *Women in the Muslim World.* Cambridge, MA: Harvard University Press, 1978.

Beck, Rose Marie. "Gender, Innovation and Ambiguity: Speech Prohibitions as a Resource for 'Space to Move.'" *Discourse and Society* 20, no. 5 (September 2009): 531–53.

———. "Texts on Textiles: Proverbiality as Characteristic of Equivocal Communication at the East African Coast (Swahili)." *Journal of African Cultural Studies* 17, no. 2 (December 2005): 131–60.

Beckerleg, Susan. "Medical Pluralism and Islam in Swahili Communities in Kenya." *Medical Anthropology Quarterly,* n.s., 8, no. 3 (September 1994): 299–313.

Beckmann, Nadine. "AIDS and the Power of God: Narratives of Decline and Coping Strategies in Zanzibar." In *AIDS and Religious Practice in Africa,* edited by Felicitas Becker and Wenzel Geissler, 119–54. Leiden : Brill, 2009.

———. "Pleasure and Danger: Muslim Views on Sex and Gender in Zanzibar." *Culture, Health and Sexuality* 12, no. 6 (August 2010): 619–32.

Beidelman, T. O. *The Cool Knife: Imagery of Gender, Sexuality, and Moral Education in Kaguru Initiation Ritual.* Washington, DC: Smithsonian Institution Press, 1997.

———. *Moral Imagination in Kaguru Modes of Thought.* African Systems of Thought. Bloomington: Indiana University Press, 1986.

Bell, Heather. "Midwifery Training and Female Circumcision in the Inter-war Anglo-Egyptian Sudan." *Journal of African History* 39, no. 2 (1998): 293–312.

Bernard, H. Russell. *Research Methods in Anthropology: Qualitative and Quantitative Approaches.* 4th ed. Walnut Creek, CA: AltaMira Press, 2005.

Biersteker, Ann. "Language, Poetry, and Power: A Reconsideration of 'Utendi wa Mwana Kupona.'" In *Faces of Islam in African Literature,* edited by Kenneth Harrow, 59–77. Portsmouth, NH: Heinemann, 1991.

Blanc, Ann K., and Anastasia J. Gage. "Men, Polygyny, and Fertility over the Life-Course in Sub-Saharan Africa." In *Fertility and the Male*

Life-Cycle in the Era of Fertility Decline, edited by Caroline H. Bledsoe, Jane I. Guyer, and Susana Lerner, 163. Oxford: Oxford University Press, 2000.

Bledsoe, Caroline H., and Gilles Pison, eds. *Nuptiality in Sub-Saharan Africa: Contemporary Anthropological and Demographic Perspectives.* International Studies in Demography. Oxford: Clarendon Press, 1994.

Boddy, Janice. *Wombs and Alien Spirits: Women, Men, and the Zar Cult in Northern Sudan.* Madison: University of Wisconsin Press, 1989.

Boellstorff, Tom. *A Coincidence of Desires: Anthropology, Queer Studies, Indonesia.* Durham: Duke University Press, 2007.

Boswell, Rosabelle. "Scents of Identity: Fragrance as Heritage in Zanzibar." *Journal of Contemporary African Studies* 26, no. 3 (2008): 295–311.

Bouhdiba, Abdelwahab. *Sexuality in Islam.* London: Routledge and Kegan Paul, 1985.

Bove, Riley, and Claudia Valeggia. "Polygyny and Women's Health in Sub-Saharan Africa." *Social Science and Medicine* 68, no. 1 (2009): 21–29.

Bowen, John Richard. *Muslims through Discourse: Religion and Ritual in Gayo Society.* Princeton: Princeton University Press, 1993.

Boxer, Diana, and Florencia Cortés-Conde. "From Bonding to Biting: Conversational Joking and Identity Display." *Journal of Pragmatics* 27, no. 3 (1997): 275–94.

Brennan, James R. *Taifa: Making Nation and Race in Urban Tanzania.* Athens: Ohio University Press, 2012.

Bromber, Katrin. "Mjakazi, Mpambe, Mjoli, Suria: Female Slaves in Swahili Sources." In *Women and Slavery: Africa, the Indian Ocean World, and the Medieval North Atlantic,* edited by Gwyn Campbell, Suzanne Miers, and Joseph Calder Miller, 111–26. Athens: Ohio University Press, 2007.

Brown, Penelope, and Stephen C. Levinson. "Universals in Language Usage: Politeness Phenomena." In *Questions and Politeness,* edited by Esther N. Goody, 256–89. Cambridge: Cambridge University Press, 1980.

Bruinhorst, Gerard van der. "Siku ya Arafa and the Idd el-Hajj: Knowledge, Ritual and Renewal in Tanzania." In Larsen, *Knowledge, Renewal,* 127–50.

Bujra, Janet. "Risk and Trust: Unsafe Sex, Gender and AIDS in Tanzania." In *Risk Revisited,* edited by Pat Caplan, 59–84. Anthropology, Culture, and Society. London: Pluto Press, 2000.

———. "Women and Fieldwork." In *Women Cross-Culturally: Change and Challenge,* edited by Ruby Rohrlich-Leavitt, 551–57. The Hague: Mouton, 1975.

Burgess, G. Thomas, and Andrew Burton. Introduction to *Generations Past: Youth in East African History,* edited by Burton and Hélène Charton-Bigot, 1–24. Athens: Ohio University Press, 2010.

Burgess, Thomas. "Cinema, Bell Bottoms, and Miniskirts: Struggles over Youth and Citizenship in Revolutionary Zanzibar." *International Journal of African Historical Studies* 35, nos. 2–3 (2002): 287–314.

Caldwell, John C. *Theory of Fertility Decline.* Population and Social Structure. London: Academic Press, 1982.

Campbell, Carol A. "An Introduction to the Music of Swahili Women." Seminar Paper no. 68, Institute of African Studies, University of Nairobi, 1976.

Campbell, Carol A., and Carol M. Eastman. "Ngoma: Swahili Adult Song Performance in Context." *Ethnomusicology* 28, no. 3 (1984): 467–93.

Campbell, Gwyn. "Islam in Indian Ocean Africa." In Simpson and Kresse, *Struggling with History,* 43–92.

Caplan, Pat. "Boys' Circumcision and Girls' Puberty Rites among the Swahili of Mafia Island, Tanzania." *Africa: Journal of the International African Institute* 46, no. 1 (1976): 21–33.

———. "'But the Coast, of Course, Is Quite Different': Academic and Local Ideas about the East African Littoral." *Journal of Eastern African Studies* 1, no. 2 (July 2007): 305–20.

———. *Choice and Constraint in a Swahili Community: Property, Hierarchy, and Cognatic Descent on the East African Coast.* London: Oxford University Press, 1975.

———. "Cognatic Descent Groups on Mafia Island, Tanzania." *Man* 4, no. 3 (1969): 419–31.

———. "Cognatic Descent, Islamic Law and Women's Property on the East African Coast." In *Women and Property—Women as Property,* edited by Renée Hirschon. London: Croom Helm, 1984.

———. "Gender, Ideology and Modes of Production on the Coast of East Africa." *Paideuma* 28 (1982): 29–43.

———. "'Law' and 'Custom': Marital Disputes on Northern Mafia Island, Tanzania." In *Understanding Disputes: The Politics of Argument,* edited by Caplan, 203–22. Oxford: Berg, 1995.

———. "Learning Gender: Fieldwork in a Tanzanian Coastal Village, 1965–85." In *Gendered Fields: Women, Men, and Ethnography,* edited by Diane Bell, Pat Caplan, and Wazir-Jahan Karim, 168–81. London: Routledge, 1993.

———. *Local Understandings of Modernity: Food and Food Security on Mafia Island, Tanzania.* Report presented to the Tanzania Commission for Science and Technology (COSTECH) on fieldwork carried out June–August 2002, Mafia Island, Tanzania. http://www.gold.ac.uk/anthropology/staff/pat-caplan/project-tanzania-global/.

———. "Monogamy, Polygyny or the Single State? Changes in Marriage Patterns in a Tanzanian Coastal Village, 1965–94." In *Gender, Family and Household in Tanzania,* edited by Colin Creighton and Cuthbert K. Omari. Aldershot, UK: Ashgate, 1999.

———. "Perceptions of Gender Stratification." *Africa: Journal of the International African Institute* 59, no. 2 (1989): 196–208.

———. "The Swahili of Chole Island, Tanzania." In *Face Values: Some Anthropological Themes,* edited by A. Sutherland and J. Boissevain. London: British Broadcasting Corporation, 1978.

———. "Where Have All the Young Girls Gone? Gender and Sex Ratios on Mafia Island, Tanzania." In *Agrarian Economy, State and Society in Contemporary Tanzania,* edited by Peter G. Forster and Sam Maghimbi. Aldershot: Avebury Press, 1999.

.———. "Women's Property, Islamic Law and Cognatic Descent." In *Women and Property, Women as Property,* edited by Renée Hirschon, 23–43. London: Croom Helm, 1983.

Chande, Abdin. "Radicalism and Reform in East Africa." In *History of Islam in Africa,* edited by Nehemia Levtzion and Randall L. Pouwels, 349–72. Athens: Ohio University Press, 2012.

Children's Dignity Forum. "Report on the Roundtable Discussion with Law Enforcers on the Application of Laws Preventing Pregnancies and Cases of Marriage of School Girls." Children's Dignity Forum, 2009. http://cdftz.org/reports.php?c=research%20report&p=.

Cleland, John, and Shireen Jejeebhoy. "Maternal Schooling and Fertility: Evidence from Consensus and Surveys." In *Girls' Schooling, Women's Autonomy, and Fertility Change in South Asia,* edited by Roger Jeffrey and Alaka Malwade Basu, 72–106. New Delhi: Sage, 1996.

Cochrane, Susan Hill. *Fertility and Education: What Do We Really Know?* World Bank Staff Occasional Papers 26. Baltimore: Johns Hopkins University Press for the World Bank, 1979.

Cole, Jennifer, and Lynn M. Thomas, eds. *Love in Africa.* Chicago: University of Chicago Press, 2009.

Comaroff, Jean. *Body of Power, Spirit of Resistance: The Culture and History of a South African People.* Chicago: University of Chicago Press, 1985.

Constantinides, Pamela. "Ill at Ease and Sick at Heart: Symbolic Behaviour in a Sudanese Healing Cult." In *Symbols and Sentiments: Cross-Cultural Studies in Symbolism,* edited by Ioan M. Lewis, 61–84. London: Academic Press, 1977.

Cooper, Frederick. *From Slaves to Squatters: Plantation Labor and Agriculture in Zanzibar and Coastal Kenya, 1890–1925.* New Haven: Yale University Press, 1980.

———. *Plantation Slavery on the East Coast of Africa.* Yale Historical Publications 113. New Haven: Yale University Press, 1977.

Cory [Koritschoner], Hans. "Jando: Part I: The Constitution and Organization of the Jando." *Journal of the Royal Anthropological Institute of Great Britain and Ireland* 77, no. 2 (1947): 159–68.

———. "Jando: Part II: The Ceremonies and Teachings of the Jando." *Journal of the Royal Anthropological Institute of Great Britain and Ireland* 78, nos. 1–2 (1948): 81–94.

Crapanzano, Vincent, and Vivian Garrison, eds. *Case Studies in Spirit Possession*. New York: Wiley, 1977

Cunningham, Hugh. *Children and Childhood in Western Society since 1500*. Harlow, UK: Pearson Longman, 2005.

———. *The Invention of Childhood*. London: BBC Books, 2006.

Curtin, Patricia Romero. "Weddings in Lamu, Kenya: An Example of Social and Economic Change (Mariages à Lamu [Kenya]: Un cas de changement économique et social)." *Cahiers d'études africaines* 24, no. 94 (1984): 131–55.

Decker, Corrie R. "Biology, Islam and the Science of Sex Education in Colonial Zanzibar." *Past and Present* 222, no. 1 (2014): 215–47.

———. "From Hygiene to Biology: Talking around Sex in Zanzibar's Colonial Girls' Schools." presented at the African Studies Association, San Francisco, November 19, 2010.

———. *Mobilizing Zanzibari Women: The Struggle for Respectability and Self-Reliance in Colonial East Africa*. New York: Palgrave Macmillan, 2014.

———. "Reading, Writing and Respectability: How Schoolgirls Developed Modern Literacies in Colonial Zanzibar." *International Journal of African Historical Studies* 43, no. 1 (2010): 89–114.

Declich, Francesca. "Contested Interpretations of Muslim Poetries, Legitimacy and Daily Life Politics." In Larsen, *Knowledge, Renewal*, 107–26.

Deeb, Lara. *An Enchanted Modern: Gender and Public Piety in Shi'i Lebanon*. Princeton: Princeton University Press, 2006.

Deutsch, Jan-Georg. *Emancipation without Abolition in German East Africa, c. 1884–1914*. Athens: Ohio University Press, 2006.

Dias, Jorge. "The Makonde People: Social Life." In *Portuguese Contribution to Cultural Anthropology*, 21–61. Johannesburg: Witwatersrand University Press, 1961.

Dilger, Hansjörg. *Leben mit Aids: Krankheit, Tod und soziale Beziehungen in Afrika: Eine Ethnographie*. Frankfurt: Campus Verlag, 2005.

———. "Sexuality, AIDS, and the Lures of Modernity: Reflexivity and Morality among Young People in Rural Tanzania." *Medical Anthropology* 22, no. 1 (2003): 23–52.

Douglas, Mary. *Purity and Danger: An Analysis of Concepts of Pollution and Taboo*. London: Routledge and Kegan Paul, 1976.

DuBois, John W. "Transcription Convention Updates." Appendix, July 28, 2006. http://www.linguistics.ucsb.edu/projects/transcription/Ao5updates.pdf.

DuBois, John W., Stephan Schuetze-Coburn, Susanna Cumming, and Danae Paolino. "Outline of Discourse Transcription." In *Talking Data: Transcription and Coding in Discourse Research,* edited by Jane Edwards and Martin D. Lampert, 45–89. Hillsdale, NJ: Lawrence Erlbaum Associates, 1993.

Eastman, Carol M. "Nyimbo za watoto: The Swahili Child's World View." *Ethos* 14, no. 2 (July 1986): 144–73.

———. "Women, Slaves, and Foreigners: African Cultural Influences and Group Processes in the Formation of Northern Swahili Coastal Society." *International Journal of African Historical Studies* 21, no. 1 (1988): 1–20.

Eile, Lena. *Jando: The Rite of Circumcision and Initiation in East African Islam.* Lund: Plus Ultra, 1990.

Esposito, John L.. *Women in Muslim Family Law.* With Natana J. DeLong-Bas. 2nd ed. Contemporary Issues in the Middle East. Syracuse: Syracuse University Press, 2001.

Ezeh, Alex C., Michka Seroussi, and Hendrik Raggers. *Men's Fertility, Contraceptive Use, and Reproductive Preferences.* Demographic and Health Surveys Comparative Studies 18. Calverton, MD: Macro International, 1996.

Fabian, Johannes. *Power and Performance: Ethnographic Explorations through Proverbial Wisdom and Theater in Shaba, Zaire.* Madison: University of Wisconsin Press, 1990.

Fader, Ayala. *Mitzvah Girls: Bringing Up the Next Generation of Hasidic Jews in Brooklyn.* Princeton: Princeton University Press, 2009.

Fair, Laura. "Identity, Difference, and Dance: Female Initiation in Zanzibar, 1890 to 1930." *Frontiers: A Journal of Women Studies* 17, no. 3 (1996): 146–72.

———. *Pastimes and Politics: Culture, Community, and Identity in Post-abolition Urban Zanzibar, 1890–1945.* Athens: Ohio University Press, 2001.

———. "Remaking Fashion in the Paris of the Indian Ocean: Dress, Performance, and the Cultural Construction of a Cosmopolitan Zanzibari Identity." In *Fashioning Africa: Power and the Politics of Dress,* edited by Jean Allman, 13–30. African Expressive Cultures. Bloomington: Indiana University Press, 2004.

Fawzy, Essam. "Muslim Personal Status Law in Egypt: The Current Situation and Possibilities of Reform through Internal Initiatives." In *Women's Rights and Islamic Family Law: Perspectives on Reform,* edited by Lynn Welchman, 14–91. London: Zed Books, 2004.

Ferguson, James. *Global Shadows: Africa in the Neoliberal World Order.* Durham: Duke University Press, 2006.

Fernandez, James W., and Mary Taylor Huber, eds. *Irony in Action: Anthropology, Practice, and the Moral Imagination.* Chicago: University of Chicago Press, 2001.

Fluehr-Lobban, Carolyn. *Islamic Law and Society in the Sudan.* London: Routledge, 1987.

Foucault, Michel. *The History of Sexuality.* New York: Vintage Books, 1990.

Frost, Mark. "'Wider Opportunities': Religious Revival, Nationalist Awakening and the Global Dimension in Colombo, 1870–1920." *Modern Asian Studies* 36, no. 4 (2002): 937–67.

Fry, Peter. "Male Homosexuality and Spirit Possession in Brazil." *Journal of Homosexuality* 11, nos. 3–4 (1986): 137–53; reprinted in *Anthropology and Homosexual Behavior,* edited by Evelyn Blackwood, 137–54 (New York: Haworth Press, 1986).

Fuglesang, Minou. "Lessons for Life—Past and Present Modes of Sexuality Education in Tanzanian Society." *Social Science and Medicine* 44, no. 8 (1997): 1245–54.

———. *Veils and Videos: Female Youth Culture on the Kenyan Coast.* Stockholm: Almqvist and Wiksell International, 1994.

Gaudio, Rudolf. *Allah Made Us: Sexual Outlaws in an Islamic African City.* Chichester, UK: Wiley-Blackwell, 2009.

Gearhart, Rebecca. "Seeing Life through the Eyes of Swahili Children of Lamu, Kenya: A Visual Anthropology Approach." *AnthropoChildren* 3, no. 3 (2013).

Gearhart, Rebecca, and Munib Abdulrehman. "Purity, Balance and Wellness among the Swahili of Lamu, Kenya." *Journal of Global Health* 2, no. 1 (2012): 42–44.

Geiger, Susan. "Women in Nationalist Struggle: TANU Activists in Dar es Salaam." *International Journal of African Historical Studies* 20, no. 1 (1987): 1–26.

George, Abosede A. *Making Modern Girls: A History of Girlhood, Labor, and Social Development in Colonial Lagos.* Athens: Ohio University Press, 2014.

Giles, Linda L. "Complexities of Identity in the East African Coastal Area." In *Contesting Identities: The Mijikenda and Their Neighbors in Kenyan Coastal Society,* edited by Rebecca Gearhart and Linda Giles. Trenton: Africa World Press, 2014.

———. "Societal Change and Swahili Spirit Possession." In Larsen, *Knowledge, Renewal,* 85–106.

———. "Sociocultural Change and Spirit Possession on the Swahili Coast of East Africa." *Anthropological Quarterly* 68, no. 2 (April 1995): 89–106.

———. "Spirit Possession and the Symbolic Construction of Swahili Society." In *Spirit Possession, Modernity, and Power in Africa,* edited by Heike Behrend and Ute Luig, 142–64. Madison: University of Wisconsin Press, 1999.

———. "Spirit Possession on the Swahili Coast: Peripheral Cults or Primary Texts?" PhD diss., University of Texas, Austin, 1989.

Gille, Halvor. "The World Fertility Survey: Policy Implications for Developing Countries." *International Family Planning Perspectives* 11, no. 1 (March 1985): 9–17.

Glassman, Jonathon. *Feasts and Riot: Revelry, Rebellion, and Popular Consciousness on the Swahili Coast, 1856–1888*. Portsmouth, NH: Heinemann, 1995.

———. "Sorting Out the Tribes: The Creation of Racial Identities in Colonial Zanzibar's Newspaper Wars." *Journal of African History* 41, no. 3 (2000): 395–428.

Gluckman, Max. "Les rites de passage." In *Essays on the Ritual of Social Relations,* edited by Gluckman. Manchester: Manchester University Press, 1963.

———. "Rituals of Rebellion in South-East Africa." In *Order and Rebellion in Tribal Africa,* edited by Gluckman. New York: Free Press of Glencoe, 1963.

Gomm, Roger. "Bargaining from Weakness: Spirit Possession on the South Kenya Coast." *Man* 10, no. 4 (December 1975): 530–43.

———. "Harlots and Bachelors: Marital Instability among the Coastal Digo of Kenya." *Man* 7, no. 1 (1972): 95–113.

Goodwin, Charles. "Action and Embodiment within Situated Human Interaction." *Journal of Pragmatics* 32, no. 10 (2000): 1489–1522.

———. "Practices of Seeing, Visual Analysis: An Ethnomethodological Approach." In *Handbook of Visual Analysis,* edited by Carey Jewitt and Theo Van Leeuwen, 157–82. London: Sage, 2000.

———. "Recording Human Interaction in Natural Settings." *Pragmatics* 3, no. 2 (1993): 181–209.

Gower, Rebecca, Steven Salm, and Toyin Falola. "Swahili Women since the Nineteenth Century: Theoretical and Empirical Considerations on Gender and Identity Construction." *Africa Today* 43, no. 3 (September 1996): 251–68.

Gregory, J. R. "The Myth of the Male Ethnographer and the Woman's World." *American Anthropologist* 86, no. 2 (1984): 316–27.

Gyimah, Stephen Obeng. "Polygynous Marital Structure and Child Survivorship in Sub-Saharan Africa: Some Empirical Evidence from Ghana." *Social Science and Medicine* 68, no. 2 (2009): 334–42.

Haleem, M. A. S. Abdel, trans. *The Qur'an*. Reissue. Oxford: Oxford University Press, 2008.

Hallaq, Wael B. *Sharīʿa: Theory, Practice, Transformations*. Cambridge: Cambridge University Press, 2009.

Halley, Meghan. "Negotiating Sexuality: Adolescent Initiation Rituals and Cultural Change in Rural Southern Tanzania." PhD diss., Case Western Reserve University, 2012.

Hammer, Annerose. *Aids und Tabu: Zur soziokulturellen Konstruktion von Aids bei den Luo in Westkenia*. Spektrum, vol. 54. Hamburg: LIT Verlag, 1999.

Haram, Liv. "'Prostitutes' or Modern Women? Negotiating Respectability in Northern Tanzania." In *Re-thinking Sexualities in Africa*, edited by Signe Arnfred, 195–213. Uppsala: Nordiska Afrikainstitutet, 2003.

———. "Tswana Medicine in Interaction with Biomedicine." *Social Science and Medicine* 33, no. 2 (1991): 167–75.

Harries, Lyndon. "The Initiation Rites of the Makonde Tribe." In *Communications of the Rhodes-Livingstone Institute*. Vol. 3. Lusaka: Rhodes-Livingstone Institute for Social Research, 1940.

Haugen, Einar. *The Ecology of Language*. Edited by Anwar S. Dil. Language Science and National Development. Stanford: Stanford University Press, 1972.

Hawley, John C. *India in Africa, Africa in India: Indian Ocean Cosmopolitanisms*. Bloomington: Indiana University Press, 2008.

Heald, Suzette. "The Power of Sex: Some Reflections on the Caldwells' 'African Sexuality' Thesis." *Africa* 65, no. 4 (1995): 489–505.

Helle-Valle, Jo. "Sexual Mores, Promiscuity and 'Prostitution' in Botswana." *Ethnos* 64, no. 3 (1999): 372–96.

Higgins, Christina. *English as a Local Language: Post-colonial Identities and Multilingual Practices*. Bristol, UK: Multilingual Matters, 2009.

Hinawy, Mbarak Ali. "Notes on Customs in Mombasa." *Swahili* 34, no. 1 (1964): 17–35.

Hirsch, Jennifer S., Sergio Meneses, Brenda Thompson, Mirka Negroni, Blanca Pelcastre, and Carlos Del Rio. "The Inevitability of Infidelity: Sexual Reputation, Social Geographies, and Marital HIV Risk in Rural Mexico." *American Journal of Public Health* 97, no. 6 (2007).

Hirsch, Susan F. *Pronouncing and Persevering: Gender and the Discourses of Disputing in an African Islamic Court*. Language and Legal Discourse. Chicago: University of Chicago Press, 1998.

Ho, Engseng. *The Graves of Tarim: Genealogy and Mobility across the Indian Ocean*. Berkeley: University of California Press, 2006.

Hoffman, Valerie J. "Islamic Perceptions on the Human Body: Legal, Spiritual and Social Considerations." In *Embodiment, Morality, and Medicine*, edited by Lisa Sowle Cahill and Margaret A. Farley, 37–55. Theology and Medicine 6. London: Kluwer Academic Publishers, 1995.

Hofmeyr, Isabel. "The Black Atlantic Meets the Indian Ocean: Forging New Paradigms of Transnationalism for the Global South—Literary and Cultural Perspectives." *Social Dynamics: A Journal of African Studies* 33, no. 2 (2007): 3–32.

Hofmeyr, Isabel, Preben Kaarsholm, and Bodil Folke Frederiksen. "Introduction: Print Cultures, Nationalisms and Publics of the Indian

Ocean." *Africa: The Journal of the International African Institute* 81, no. 1 (2011): 1–22.

Horn, Jessica. "A Night in Zanzibar—Life Story and Poem." In *African Sexualities: A Reader,* edited by Sylvia Tamale, 184–86. Oxford: Pambazuka Press, 2011.

Horne, Jackie C. *History and the Construction of the Child in Early British Children's Literature.* Farnham, UK: Ashgate Publishing, 2011.

Horton, Mark Chatwin, and John Middleton. *The Swahili: The Social Landscape of a Mercantile Society.* Oxford: Blackwell, 2000.

Hou, Ningqi, Dezheng Huo, and Olufunmilayo I. Olopade. "Protective Effect of Longstanding Lactation and Reproductive Factors: A Case-Control Study in North Tanzania." *Breast Cancer Research and Treatment* 134, no. 3 (2012): 1349–51.

Hunt, Jennifer. "The Development of Rapport through the Negotiation of Gender in Field Work among Police." *Human Organization* 43, no. 4 (December 1984): 283–96.

Hunter, Mark. *Love in the Time of AIDS: Inequality, Gender, and Rights in South Africa.* Bloomington: Indiana University Press, 2010.

———. "The Materiality of Everyday Sex: Thinking beyond 'Prostitution.'" *African Studies* 61, no. 1 (2002): 99–120.

Inda, Jonathan, and Renato Rosaldo, eds. *The Anthropology of Globalization: A Reader.* 2nd ed. Blackwell Readers in Athropology 1. Malden, MA: Blackwell, 2008.

Ingrams, William Harold. *Zanzibar: Its History and Its People.* London: H. F. and G. Witherby, 1931.

Ingstad, Benedicte. "The Cultural Construction of AIDS and Its Consequences for Prevention in Botswana." *Medical Anthropology Quarterly* 4, no. 1 (1990): 28–40.

Issa, Amina A. "From Stinkibar to Zanzibar: Disease, Medicine and Public Health in Colonial Urban Zanzibar, 1870–1963." University of KwaZulu-Natal, 2010.

———. "Wedding Ceremonies and Cultural Exchange in an Indian Ocean Port City: The Case of Zanzibar Town." *Social Dynamics* 38, no. 3 (2012): 467–78.

Jacoby, Hanan G. "The Economics of Polygyny in Sub-Saharan Africa: Female Productivity and the Demand for Wives in Côte d'Ivoire." *Journal of Political Economy* 103, no. 5 (1995): 938–71.

Juma, Khadija B. "Kiswahili cha asili cha kina mama wa visiwani Zanzibar." In *Utamaduni wa Mzanzibari,* edited by Juma, 24–39. Zanzibar: Baraza la Kiswahili la Zanzibar, 2008.

Kapferer, Bruce. *A Celebration of Demons: Exorcism and the Aesthetics of Healing in Sri Lanka.* Bloomington: Indiana University Press, 1983.

Karanja, Wambui wa. "The Phenomenon of 'Outside Wives': Some Reflections on Its Possible Influence on Fertility." In *Nuptiality in*

Sub-Saharan Africa: Contemporary Anthropological and Demographic Perspectives, edited by Caroline H. Bledsoe and Gilles Pison, 194–214. Oxford: Clarendon Press, 1994.

Karp, Ivan. "Laughter at Marriage: Subversion in Performance." In *Transformations of African Marriage,* edited by David J. Parkin and David Nyamwaya. International African Seminars 3. Manchester: Manchester University Press for the International African Institute, 1987.

Keefe, Sue. "Romantic Desires and Polygynous Intentions: Islam, Gender, and Divorce in Coastal Tanzania." PhD diss., Brown University, 2010.

Kennedy, John G. "Nubian Zar Ceremonies as Psychotherapy." *Human Organization* 26, no. 4 (1967): 185–94.

Kenya National Bureau of Statistics. *Kenya Integrated Household Budget Survey, 2005/6.* Nairobi: Kenya National Bureau of Statistics, 2006.

Keshodkar, Akbar. "Marriage as the Means to Preserve 'Asian-Ness': The Post-revolutionary Experience of the Asians of Zanzibar." *Journal of Asian and African Studies* 45, no. 2 (April 2010): 226–40.

Kessler, Clive S. "Conflict and Sovereignty in Kelantanese Malay Spirit Seances." In Crapanzano and Garrison, *Spirit Possession,* 295–331.

Kingsford, Kate. "Wider Worlds: The Indian Ocean and African Studies." *African Affairs* 111, no. 442 (2012): 145–51.

Koritschoner, Hans. "Ngoma ya Shetani." *Journal of the Royal Anthropological Institute* 66, no. 1 (1936): 209–19.

Kramsch, Claire J. "Introduction: 'How Can We Tell the Dancer from the Dance?'" In Krmsch, *Language Acquisition,* 1–30.

———, ed. *Language Acquisition and Language Socialization: Ecological Perspectives.* Advances in Applied Linguistics. London: Continuum, 2002.

Kresse, Kai. "Debating Maulidi: Ambiguities and Transformations of Muslim Identity along the Swahili Coast." In Loimeier and Seesemann, *Global Worlds of the Swahili,* 209–28.

———. *Philosophising in Mombasa.* Edinburgh: Edinburgh University Press, 2007.

———. "'Swahili Enlightenment'? East African Reformist Discourse at the Turning Point: The Example of Sheikh Muhammad Kasim Mazrui." *Journal of Religion in Africa* 33, no. 3 (2003): 279–309.

———. "The Uses of History: Rhetorics of Muslim Unity and Difference on the Kenyan Swahili Coast." Simpson and Kresse, *Struggling with History,* 223–60.

Lambek, Michael M. "Certain Knowledge, Contestable Authority: Power and Practice on the Islamic Periphery." *American Ethnologist* 17, no. 1 (1990): 23–40.

———. "Choking on the Qur'an and Other Consuming Parables from the Western Indian Ocean Front." In *The Pursuit of Certainty:*

Religious and Cultural Formulations, edited by Wendy James, 259–84. London: Routledge, 1995.

———. *Human Spirits: A Cultural Account of Trance in Mayotte.* Cambridge: Cambridge University Press, 1981.

———. *Knowledge and Practice in Mayotte: Local Discourses of Islam, Sorcery and Spirit Possession.* Toronto: University of Toronto Press, 1993.

———. "The Practice of Islamic Experts in a Village on Mayotte." *Journal of Religion in Africa* 20, no. 1 (1990): 20–40.

———. "Taboo as Cultural Practice among Malagasy Speakers." *Man* 27, no. 2 (1992): 245–66.

———. "Virgin Marriage and the Autonomy of Women in Mayotte." *Signs* 9, no. 2 (1983): 264–81.

Landberg, Leif C. W. "Men of Kigombe: Ngalawa Fishermen of Northeastern Tanzania." PhD diss., University of California, Davis, 1975.

Landberg, Pamela W. "Kinship and Community in a Tanzania Coastal Village." PhD diss., University of California, Davis, , 1977.

———. "Widows and Divorced Women in Swahili Society." In *Widows in African Societies: Choices and Constraints*, edited by Betty Potash, 107–31. Stanford: Stanford University Press, 1986.

Larsen, Kjersti. "Dialogues between Humans and Spirits: Ways of Negotiating Relationships and Moral Order in Zanzibar Town, Zanzibar." In *The Power of Discourse in Ritual Performance: Rhetoric, Poetics, Transformations*, edited by Ulrich Demmer and Martin Gaenszle. Performances 10. Berlin: LIT Verlag, 2007.

———. "Fastens materialitet: Ramadan som bemerkelsesverdig begivenhet på Zanzibar." *Norsk antropologisk tidsskrift* 3–4 (2011): 208–22.

———. "Gender Socialization: Sub-Saharan Africa: Swahili Societies." In *Encyclopedia of Women and Islamic Cultures: Family, Law, and Politics*, edited by Suad Joseph. Leiden: Brill, 2003.

———. Introduction to Larsen, *Knowledge, Renewal and Religion*, 11–37.

———. "Knowledge, Astrology and the Power of Healing in Zanzibar." *Journal des africanistes* 72, no. 2 (2002): 175–86.

———, ed. *Knowledge, Renewal and Religion: Repositioning and Changing Ideological and Material Circumstances among the Swahili on the East African Coast.* Uppsala: Nordiska Afrikainstitutet, 2009.

———. "Kunnskap, kjønnsidentitet og sosial endring: Ulike former for kunnskap i Zanzibar Town." *Norsk antropologisk tidsskrift,* 1993.

———. "Morality and the Rejection of Spirits: A Zanzibari Case." *Social Anthropology* 6, no. 1 (1998): 61–75.

———. "The Other Side of Nature: Expanding Tourism, Changing Landscapes and Problems of Privacy in Urban Zanzibar." In *Producing Nature and Poverty in Africa*, edited by Vigdis Broch-Due and Richard A. Schroeder. Uppsala: Nordiska Afrikainstitutet, 2000.

———. "Spirit Possession as Historical Narrative: The Production of Identity and Locality in Zanzibar Town." In *Locality and Belonging*, edited by Nadia Lovell, 125–46. London: Routledge, 1998.

———. *Unyago: Fra jente til kvinne.* Oslo Occasional Papers in Social Anthropology 22. Oslo: University of Oslo, 1990.

———. *Where Humans and Spirits Meet: The Politics of Rituals and Identified Spirits in Zanzibar.* Social Identities 5. New York: Berghahn Books, 2008.

LaViolette, Adria. "Swahili Cosmopolitanism in Africa and the Indian Ocean World, AD 600–1500." *Archaeologies* 4, no. 1 (2008): 24–49.

Le Guennec-Coppens, Françoise. "Social and Cultural Integration: A Case Study of the East African Hadramis." *Africa: Journal of the International African Institute* 59, no. 2 (January 1989): 185–95.

———. *Wedding Customs in Lamu.* Lamu Society, 1980.

Leiris, Michel. *La langue secrète des Dogons de Sanga (Soudan français).* Travaux et mémoires de l'Institut d'ethnologie 50. Paris: Institut d'ethnologie, 1948.

LeVine, Robert A., S. LeVine, A. Richman, F. Tapia Uribe, C. Sunderland Correa, and P. Miller. "Women's Schooling and Child Care in the Demographic Transition: A Mexican Case Study." *Population and Development Review* 17, no. 3 (September 1991): 459–96.

LeVine, Robert A., Sarah E. LeVine, and Beatrice Schnell. "'Improve the Women': Mass Schooling, Female Literacy, and Worldwide Social Change." *Harvard Educational Review* 71, no. 1 (2001): 1–51.

Lewis, Ioan M. *Ecstatic Religion: A Study of Shamanism and Spirit Possession.* London: Routledge, 1971.

———. *Religion in Context: Cults and Charisma.* Cambridge: Cambridge University Press, 1986.

———. "Spirit Possession and Deprivation Cults." *Man* 1, no. 3 (1966): 307–29.

Liebenow, J. Gus. *Colonial Rule and Political Development in Tanzania: The Case of the Makonde.* Chicago: Northwestern University Press, 1971.

Lienhardt, Peter. Introduction to *The Medicine Man: Swifa ya Nguvumali*, 1–80. London: Oxford University Press, 1968.

Limbert, Mandana E. *In the Time of Oil: Piety, Memory, and Social Life in an Omani Town.* Stanford: Stanford University Press, 2010.

Lodhi, A. Y. "Muslims in Eastern Africa—Their Past and Present." *Nordic Journal of African Studies* 3, no. 1 (1994): 88–98.

Loimeier, Roman. "Patterns and Peculiarities of Islamic Reform in Africa." *Journal of Religion in Africa* 33, no. 3 (2003): 237–62.

Loimeier, Roman, and Rüdiger Seesemann, eds. *The Global Worlds of the Swahili: Interfaces of Islam, Identity and Space in 19th and 20th-Century East Africa.* Beiträge zur Afrikaforschung 26. Berlin: LIT Verlag, 2006.

Lubkemann, Stephen C. "The Transformation of Transnationality among Mozambican Migrants in South Africa." *Canadian Journal of African Studies/La revue canadienne des études africaines* 34, no. 1 (2000): 41–63.

Mahmood, Saba. "Feminist Theory, Embodiment, and the Docile Agent: Some Reflections on the Egyptian Islamic Revival." *Cultural Anthropology* 16, no. 2 (2001): 202–36.

———. *Politics of Piety: The Islamic Revival and the Feminist Subject.* Princeton: Princeton University Press, 2005.

Malherbe, Vertrees C. "Illegitimacy and Family Formation in Colonial Cape Town, to c. 1850." *Journal of Social History* 39, no. 4 (2006): 1153–76.

Mamuya, S. J. *Jando na unyago.* Nairobi: East African Publishing House, 1972.

Marsden, Magnus, and Konstantinos Retsikas, eds. *Articulating Islam: Anthropological Approaches to Muslim Worlds.* Muslims in Global Societies 6. Dordrecht: Springer, 2012.

Marshall, W. A., and J. M. Tanner. "Variations in Pattern of Pubertal Changes in Girls." *Archives of Disease in Childhood* 44, no. 235 (June 1969): 291.

———. "Variations in the Pattern of Pubertal Changes in Boys." *Archives of Disease in Childhood* 45, no. 239 (February 1970): 13–23.

Marston, Milly, Emma Slaymaker, Ide Cremin, Sian Floyd, Nuala McGrath, Ivan Kasamba, Tom Lutalo, Makandwe Nyirenda, Anthony Ndyanabo, and Zivai Mupambireyi. "Trends in Marriage and Time Spent Single in Sub-Saharan Africa: A Comparative Analysis of Six Population-Based Cohort Studies and Nine Demographic and Health Surveys." *Sexually Transmitted Infections* 85, supplement 1 (2009): i64–i71.

Martin, Peter J. "The Zanzibar Clove Industry." *Economic Botany* 45, no. 4 (October 1991): 450–59.

Mashhour, Amira. "Islamic Law and Gender Equality: Could There Be a Common Ground? A Study of Divorce and Polygamy in Sharia Law and Contemporary Legislation in Tunisia and Egypt." *Human Rights Quarterly* 27, no. 2 (2005): 562–96.

Mason, John Edwin. "Fortunate Slaves and Artful Masters: Labor Relations in the Rural Cape Colony during the Era of Emancipation, ca. 1825 to 1838." In *Slavery in South Africa: Captive Labor on the Dutch Frontier,* edited by Elizabeth Eldredge and Fred Morton, 67. Boulder: Westview, 1994.

Masquelier, Adeline. *Women and Islamic Revival in a West African Town.* Bloomington: Indiana University Press, 2009.

Matory, James Lorand. *Sex and the Empire That Is No More: Gender and the Politics of Metaphor in Oyo Yoruba Religion.* Minneapolis: University of Minnesota Press, 1994.

Maulana, Aisha Omar, Anja Krumeich, and Bart van den Borne. "Emerging Discourse: Islamic Teaching in HIV Prevention in Kenya." *Culture, Health and Sexuality* 11, no. 5 (2009): 559–69.

Mayer, Ann Elizabeth. *Islam and Human Rights: Tradition and Politics.* 4th ed. Boulder: Westview, 2007.

McCurdy, Sheryl. "Fashioning Sexuality: Desire, Manyema Ethnicity, and the Creation of the 'Kanga,' ca. 1880–1900." *International Journal of African Historical Studies* 39, no. 3 (2006): 441–69.

McIntosh, Janet. "Reluctant Muslims: Embodied Hegemony and Moral Resistance in a Giriama Spirit Possession Complex." *Journal of the Royal Anthropological Institute* 10, no. 1 (March 2004): 91–112.

McMahon, Elisabeth. *Slavery and Emancipation in Islamic East Africa: From Honor to Respectability.* New York: Cambridge University Press, 2013.

McMahon, Elisabeth, and Corrie Decker. "Wives or Workers? Negotiating the Social Contract between Female Teachers and the Colonial State in Zanzibar." *Journal of Women's History* 21, no. 2 (2009): 39–61.

Mead, Margaret. *Coming of Age in Samoa: A Psychological Study of Primitive Youth for Western Civilization.* New York: Morrow, 1961.

Meekers, Dominique, and Nadra Franklin. "Women's Perceptions of Polygyny among the Kaguru of Tanzania." *Ethnology* 34, no. 4 (1995): 315–29.

Middleton, John. *The World of the Swahili: An African Mercantile Civilization.* New Haven: Yale University Press, 1992.

Mir-Hosseini, Ziba. *Marriage on Trial: A Study of Islamic Family Law: Iran and Morocco Compared.* Society and Culture in the Modern Middle East. London: I. B. Tauris, 1993.

Miran, Jonathan. "From Bondage to Freedom on the Red Sea Coast: Manumitted Slaves in Egyptian Massawa, 1873–1885." *Slavery and Abolition* 34, no. 1 (2013): 135–57.

Mirza, Sarah, and Margaret Strobel, eds. *Three Swahili Women: Life Histories from Mombasa, Kenya.* Translated by Mirza and Strobel. Bloomington: Indiana University Press, 1989.

Mlama, Penina O. "Digubi: A Tanzanian Indigenous Theatre Form." *Drama Review* 25, no. 4 (1981): 3–12.

Monfouga-Nicolas, Jacqueline. *Ambivalence et culte de possession: Contribution à l'étude du Bori Hausa.* Paris: Éditions Anthropos, 1972.

Moore, A. M., A. E. Biddlecom, and E. M. Zulu. "Prevalence and Meanings of Exchange of Money or Gifts for Sex in Unmarried Adolescent Sexual Relationships in Sub-Saharan Africa." *African Journal of Reproductive Health* 11, no. 3 (2007): 44.

Moreau, R. E. "Joking Relationships in Tanganyika." *Africa: Journal of the International African Institute* 14, no. 7 (July 1944): 386–400.

Morrow, Sean. "'No Girl Leaves the School Unmarried': Mabel Shaw and the Education of Girls at Mbereshi, Northern Rhodesia, 1915–1940." *International Journal of African Historical Studies* 19, no. 4 (1986): 601–35.

Mortimer, Jeylan, and Reed Larson, eds. *The Changing Adolescent Experience: Societal Trends and the Transition to Adulthood.* Cambridge: Cambridge University Press, 2002.

Mraja, Mohamed S. "The Reform Ideas of Shaykh 'Abdallāh Sālih al-Farsī and the Transformation of Marital Practices among Digo Muslims of Kenya." *Islamic Law and Society* 17, no. 2 (2010): 245–78.

Mtoro bin Mwinyi Bakari. *The Customs of the Swahili People: The Desturi za Waswahili of Mtoro bin Mwinyi Bakari and Other Swahili Persons.* Edited and translated by J. W. T. Allen. Berkeley: University of California Press, 1981.

———. *Desturi za Wasuaheli na khabari za desturi za sherī 'a za Wasuaheli.* Edited by C. Velten. Göttingen: Vandenhoeck and Ruprecht, 1903.

Mtwara Regional Administrative Officer. "Hali ya elimu mkoani Mtwara [The state of education in the Mtwara Region]," 2007. Unpublished internal report.

Newman, Henry Stanley. *Banani: The Transition from Slavery to Freedom in Zanzibar and Pemba.* New York: Negro Universities Press, 1969.

Ngubane, Harriet. "Some Notions of 'Purity' and 'Impurity' among the Zulu." *Africa* 46, no. 3 (1976): 274–84.

Nguyen, Vinh-Kim. "Viropolitics: How HIV Produces Therapeutic Globalization." In *HIV/AIDS: Global Frontiers in Prevention/Intervention,* edited by Cynthia Pope, Renée White, and Robert Malow, 539–50. New York: Routledge, 2009.

Niyibigira, E. I., V. Y. Lada, and Z. S. Abdullay. "Mango Production and Marketing in Zanzibar: Potential, Issues and Constraints." *XXVI International Horticultural Congress: Horticultural Science in Emerging Economies, Issues and Constraints* 621 (2002): 89–93.

Njau, Bernard, Sabina Mtweve, Rachel Manongi, and Hector Jalipa. "Gender Differences in Intention to Remain a Virgin until Marriage among School Pupils in Rural Northern Tanzania." *African Journal of AIDS Research* 8, no. 2 (2009): 157–66.

Nooter, Mary H. "Secrecy: African Art That Conceals and Reveals." *African Arts* 26, no. 1 (January 1993): 55–102.

Norrick, Neal R. *Conversational Joking: Humor in Everyday Talk.* Bloomington: Indiana University Press, 1993.

———. "Issues in Conversational Joking." *Journal of Pragmatics* 35, no. 9 (2003): 1333–59.

Norris, Sigrid. "The Implication of Visual Research for Discourse Analysis: Transcription beyond Language." *Visual Communication* 1, no. 1 (2002): 97–121.

Ntukula, Mary. "The Initiation Rite." In *Chelewa, Chelewa: The Dilemma of Teenage Girls,* edited by Zubeida Tumbo-Masabo and Rita Liljeström, 96–119. Uppsala: Nordiska Afrikainstitutet, 1994.

Nuotio, Hanni. "Zanzibari Women in the Maulidi Ritual." In Loimeier and Seesemann, *Global Worlds of the Swahili,* 187–208.

Nyanzi, Barbara, Stella Nyanzi, Brent Wolff, and James Whitworth. "Money, Men and Markets: Economic and Sexual Empowerment of Market Women in Southwestern Uganda." *Culture, Health and Sexuality* 7, no. 1 (January 2005): 13–26.

Ochs, Elinor. "Becoming a Speaker of Culture." In Kramsch, *Language Acquisition,* 99–120.

———. Introduction to *Language Socialization across Cultures,* edited by Bambi B. Schieffelin and Ochs. Cambridge University Press, 1986.

Ong, Aihwa, and Stephen Collier, eds. *Global Assemblages: Technology, Politics, and Ethics as Anthropological Problems.* Malden, MA: Blackwell, 2005.

Onwuejeogwu, Michael. "The Cult of the Bori Spirits among the Hausa." In *Man in Africa,* edited by Mary Douglas and Phyllis M. Kaberry, 279–305. London: Tavistock, 1969.

Oyèwùmí, Oyèrónké. *The Invention of Women: Making an African Sense of Western Gender Discourses.* Minneapolis: University of Minnesota Press, 1997.

Parent, Anne-Simone, Grete Teilmann, Anders Juul, Niels Skakkebaek, Jorma Toppari, and Jean-Pierre Bourguignon. "The Timing of Normal Puberty and the Age Limits of Sexual Precocity: Variations around the World, Secular Trends, and Changes after Migration." *Endocrine Review* 24, no. 5 (October 2003): 668–93.

Parkin, David J. *The Cultural Definition of Political Response: Lineal Destiny among the Luo.* Language, Thought, and Culture. London: Academic Press, 1978.

———. "Inside and Outside the Mosque: A Master Trope." In *Islamic Prayer across the Indian Ocean: Inside and Outside the Mosque,* edited by Parkin and Stephen C. Headley, 1–22. London: Routledge, 2000.

———. "Wafting on the Wind: Smell and the Cycle of Spirit and Matter." *Journal of the Royal Anthropological Institute* 13, no. 1 (2007): S39–S53.

Parkin, David, and François Constantin. "Some Key Dates in Swahili History." *Africa: Journal of the International African Institute* 59, no. 2 (1989): 144.

Peletz, Michael G. *Islamic Modern: Religious Courts and Cultural Politics in Malaysia.* Princeton Studies in Muslim Politics. Princeton: Princeton University Press, 2002.

Perry, Donna L. "Wolof Women, Economic Liberalization, and the Crisis of Masculinity in Rural Senegal." *Ethnology* 44, no. 3 (2005): 207–26.

Porter, Mary A. "Talking at the Margins: Kenyan Discourses on Homosexuality." In *Beyond the Lavender Lexicon: Authenticity, Imagination, and Appropriation in Lesbian and Gay Languages,* edited by William Leap, 133–53. New York: Gordon and Breach, 1995.

Poulin, Michelle. "Sex, Money, and Premarital Partnerships in Southern Malawi." *Social Science and Medicine* 65, no. 11 (2007): 2383–93.

Pouwels, Randall L. "Eastern Africa and the Indian Ocean to 1800: Reviewing Relations in Historical Perspective." *International Journal of African Historical Studies* 35, no. 203 (2002): 385–425.

Prestholdt, Jeremy. *Domesticating the World: African Consumerism and the Genealogies of Globalization.* Berkeley: University of California Press, 2008.

Prins, A. H. J. *The Swahili-Speaking Peoples of Zanzibar and the East African Coast (Arabs, Shirazi and Swahili).* London: International African Institute, 1967.

Purpura, Allyson. "Knowledge and Agency: The Social Relations of Islamic Expertise in Zanzibar Town." PhD diss., City University of New York, 1997.

Radcliffe-Brown, A. R. "On Joking Relationships." *Africa: Journal of the International African Institute* 13, no. 3 (1940): 195–210.

Ramsden, Peter. *Chole—A Woman's Place.* Part of the BBC series Other People's Lives. 16mm film. Royal Anthropological Institute, 1982.

———. *Chole—Circumcision.* Part of the BBC series Other People's Lives. 16mm film. Royal Anthropological Institute, 1982.

Ranger, Terrence O. *Dance and Society in Eastern Africa, 1890–1970: The Beni Ngoma.* London: Heinemann Educational, 1975.

Raum, Otto. "German East Africa: Changes in African Tribal Life under German Administration, 1892–1914." In *History of East Africa,* edited by Vincent Harlow, E. M. Chilver, and Alison Smith, 3 vols., 2:144–208. London: Oxford University Press, 1965.

Rebacz, Ewa. "Age at Menarche in Schoolgirls from Tanzania in Light of Socioeconomic and Sociodemographic Conditioning." *Collegium antropologicum* 33, no. 1 (March 2009): 23–29.

Reese, Scott S. "The 'Respectable Citizens' of Shaykh Uthman: Religious Discourse, Trans-Locality and the Construction of Local Contexts in Colonial Aden." In Simpson and Kresse, *Struggling with History,* 189–219.

Regional Committee on School Pregnancy. "Utoro na mimba mkoani Mtwara." Office of the District Executive Officer, Mtwara, Tanzania, 2007.

Reniers, Georges, and Susan Watkins. "Polygyny and the Spread of HIV in Sub-Saharan Africa: A Case of Benign Concurrency." *AIDS* 24, no. 2 (2010): 299.

Ribeiro, Fernando Rosa. "*Fornicatie* and *Hoerendom;* or, the Long Shadow of the Portuguese: Connected Histories, Languages and Gender in the Indian Ocean and Beyond." *Social Dynamics* 33, no. 2 (2007): 33–60.

Richards, A. I. *Chisungu: A Girls' Initiation Ceremony among the Bemba of Zambia.* London: Tavistock, 1982.

Rispler-Chaim, Vardit. *Disability in Islamic Law.* International Library of Ethics, Law, and the New Medicine 32. Dordrecht: Springer, 2006.

———. "Hasan Murad Manna, 'Childbearing and the Rights of a Wife.'" *Islamic Law and Society* 2, no. 1 (1995): 92–99.

Roberts, D. F., and R. E. S. Tanner. "A Demographic Study in an Area of Low Fertility in North-east Tanganyika." *Population Studies* 13, no. 1 (1959): 61–80.

Romero, Patricia W. "Does Being 'Sexy' Keep a Marriage Going in Lamu?" Paper presented at the African Studies Association annual meeting, 1992.

———. *Lamu: History, Society, and Family in an East African Port City.* Princeton: Markus Wiener, 1997.

———. "Mama Khadija: A Life History as Example of Family History." In *Life Histories of African Women,* edited by Romero, 140–58. London: Ashfield Press, 1988.

Rorty, Richard. *Philosophy and the Mirror of Nature.* Princeton: Princeton University Press, 1979. Royal Anthropological Institute. *Face Values.* Film series. Royal Anthropological Institute, 1978.

———. *Other People's Lives.* Information booklet to accompany the BBC Television series of ethnographic films Other People's Lives. Royal Anthropological Institute, 1981.

Rubin, Deborah, Cynthia P. Green, and Altrena Mukuria. *Addressing Early Marriage in Uganda.* Washington, DC: USAID, 2009.

Ruete, Emily. *Memoirs of an Arabian Princess from Zanzibar.* Zanzibar: Gallery Publications, 1998.

Russell, Joan. *Communicative Competence in a Minority Group: A Sociolinguistic Study of the Swahili-Speaking Community in the Old Town, Mombasa.* Leiden: Brill, 1981.

Saleh, Mohamed. "Les Comoriens de Zanzibar et le culte des esprits kibuki malgaches." In *Madagascar et l'Afrique—Entre identité insulaire et appartenances historiques,* edited by Didier Nativel and Faranirina V. Rajaonah, 425–37. Paris: Karthala, 2007.

Saunders, Lucie Wood. "Variants in Zar Experience in an Egyptian Village." In Crapanzano and Garrison, *Spirit Possession,* 177–91.

Schielke, Samuli. "Being a Nonbeliever in a Time of Islamic Revival: Trajectories of Doubt and Certainty in Contemporary Egypt." *International Journal of Middle East Studies* 44, no. 2 (2012): 301–20.

Scully, Pamela. *Liberating the Family? Gender and British Slave Emancipation in the Rural Western Cape, South Africa, 1823–1853.* Social History of Africa. Portsmouth, NH: Heinemann, 1997.

Seppälä, Pekka, and Bertha Koda, eds. *The Making of a Periphery: Economic Development and Cultural Encounters in Southern Tanzania.* Uppsala: Nordiska Afrikainstitutet, 1998.

Serjeant, Robert B. "Recent Marriage Legislation from al-Mukallā, with Notes on Marriage Customs." *Bulletin of the School of Oriental and African Studies* 25, no. 3 (1962): 472–98.

Shadle, Brett Lindsay. *Girl Cases: Marriage and Colonialism in Gusiland, Kenya, 1890–1970.* Portsmouth, NH: Heinemann, 2006.

Sharp, Lesley Alexandra. *The Possessed and the Dispossessed: Spirits, Identity, and Power in a Madagascar Migrant Town.* Comparative Studies of Health Systems and Medical Care 37. Berkeley: University of California Press, 1993.

Sheldon, Kathleen. "'I Studied with the Nuns, Learning to Make Blouses': Gender Ideology and Colonial Education in Mozambique." *International Journal of African Historical Studies* 31, no. 3 (1998): 595–625.

Shepherd, Gill. "Rank, Gender, and Homosexuality: Mombasa as a Key to Understanding Sexual Options." In *The Cultural Construction of Sexuality,* edited by Pat Caplan, 240–70. London: Tavistock, 1987; repr., London: Routledge, 2006.

Sheriff, Abdul. "Between Two Worlds: The Littoral Peoples of the Indian Ocean." In Loimeier and Seesemann, *Global Worlds of the Swahili,* 15–30.

———. *Dhow Cultures and the Indian Ocean: Cosmopolitanism, Commerce, and Islam.* New York: Columbia University Press, 2010.

———. "The Slave Trade and Its Fallout in the Persian Gulf." In *Abolition and Its Aftermath in Asia and the Indian Ocean World,* edited by Gwyn Campbell. New York: Routledge, 2005.

Shoaps, Robin. "'Moral Irony': Modal Particles, Moral Persons and Indirect Stance-Taking in Sakapultek Discourse." *Pragmatics* 17, no. 2 (2007).

———. "Morality in Grammar and Discourse: Stance-Taking and the Negotiation of Moral Personhood in Sakapultek (Mayan) Wedding Counsels." PhD diss., University of California, Santa Barbara, 2004.

———. "Ritual and (Im)moral Voices: Locating the Testament of Judas in Sakapultek Communicative Ecology." *American Ethnologist* 36, no. 3 (2009): 459–77.

Silberschmidt, Margrethe. "Disempowerment of Men in Rural and Urban East Africa: Implications for Male Identity and Sexual Behavior." *World Development* 29, no. 4 (2001): 657–71.

Silberschmidt, Margrethe, and Vibeke Rasch. "Adolescent Girls, Illegal Abortions and 'Sugar-Daddies' in Dar es Salaam: Vulnerable Victims and Active Social Agents." *Social Science and Medicine* 52, no. 12 (June 2001): 1815–26.

Simpson, Edward, and Kai Kresse. "Cosmopolitanism Contested: Anthropology and History in the Western Indian Ocean." In Simpson and Kresse, *Struggling with History*, 1–41.

———, eds. *Struggling with History: Islam and Cosmopolitanism in the Western Indian Ocean*. New York: Columbia University Press, 2008.

Skene, Richard. "Arab and Swahili Dances and Ceremonies." *Journal of the Anthropological Institute of Great Britain and Ireland* 47, no. 2 (1917): 413–34.

Spear, Thomas. "Early Swahili History Reconsidered." *International Journal of African Historical Studies* 33, no. 2 (2000): 257–90.

———. "Neo-traditionalism and the Limits of Invention in British Colonial Africa." *Journal of African History* 44, no. 1 (2003): 3–27.

Stambach, Amy. *Lessons from Mount Kilimanjaro: Schooling, Community, and Gender in East Africa*. New York: Routledge, 2000.

Stiles, Erin E. *An Islamic Court in Context: An Ethnographic Study of Judicial Reasoning*. New York: Palgrave Macmillan, 2009.

———. "'There Is No Stranger to Marriage Here!': Muslim Women and Divorce in Rural Zanzibar." *Africa: Journal of the International African Institute* 75, no. 4 (2005): 582–98.

———. "When Is a Divorce a Divorce? Determining Intention in Zanzibar's Islamic Courts." *Ethnology* 42, no. 4 (October 2003): 273–88.

Stockreiter, Elke. "Child Marriage and Domestic Violence: Colonial Discourses on Gender and Female Status in Zanzibar, 1900–1950s." In *Domestic Violence and the Law in Colonial and Postcolonial Africa*, edited by Emily S. Burrill, Richard L. Roberts, and Elizabeth Thornberry, 138–58. Athens: Ohio University Press, 2010.

———. "Tying and Untying the Knot: Kadhi's Courts and the Negotiation of Social Status in Zanzibar Town, 1900–1963." PhD diss., University of London, School of Oriental and African Studies, 2008.

Strauss, Anselm L. *Basics of Qualitative Research: Grounded Theory Procedures and Techniques*. Newbury Park, CA: Sage, 1990.

Strobel, Margaret. "Muslim Women in Mombasa, Kenya, 1890–1973." PhD diss., UCLA, 1975.

———. *Muslim Women in Mombasa, Kenya, 1890–1975*. New Haven: Yale University Press, 1979.

Sullivan, Noelle. "Mediating Abundance and Scarcity: Implementing an HIV/AIDS-Targeted Project within a Government Hospital in Tanzania." *Medical Anthropology* 30, no. 2 (2011): 202–21.

Summers, Carol. "'If You Can Educate the Native Woman . . . ': Debates over the Schooling and Education of Girls and Women in Southern

Rhodesia, 1900–1934." *History of Education Quarterly* 36, no. 4 (December 1996): 449–71.

Swartz, Marc J. "The Isolation of Men and the Happiness of Women: Sources and Use of Power in Swahili Marital Relationships." *Journal of Anthropological Research* 38, no. 1 (1982): 26–44.

———. "Shame, Culture, and Status among the Swahili of Mombasa." *Ethos* 16, no. 1 (March 1988): 21–51.

———. *The Way the World Is: Cultural Processes and Social Relations among the Mombasa Swahili.* Berkeley: University of California Press, 1991.

Tannen, Deborah. *Conversational Style: Analyzing Talk among Friends.* New York: Oxford University Press, 1984.

Tarlo, Emma. *Visibly Muslim: Fashion, Politics, Faith.* Oxford: Berg, 2010.

Thomas, Lynn M. "The Modern Girl and Racial Respectability in 1930s South Africa." *Journal of African History* 47, no. 3 (2006): 461–90.

———. *Politics of the Womb: Women, Reproduction, and the State in Kenya.* Berkeley: University of California Press, 2003.

Thompson, Katrina Daly. "Discreet Talk about Supernatural Sodomy, Transgressive Gender Performance, and Male Same-Sex Desire in Zanzibar Town." *GLQ: A Journal of Lesbian and Gay Studies* 21, forthcoming.

———. "How to Be a Good Muslim Wife: Women's Performance of Islamic Authority during Swahili Weddings." *Journal of Religion in Africa* 41, no. 4 (2011): 427–48.

———. "Strategies for Taming a Swahili Husband: Zanzibari Women's Talk about Love in Islamic Marriages." *Agenda* 27, no. 2 (2013): 65–75.

———. "Zanzibari Women's Discursive and Sexual Agency: Violating Gendered Speech Prohibitions through Talk about Supernatural Sex." *Discourse and Society* 22, no. 1 (January 2011): 3–20.

Tibenderana, Peter Kazenga. "The Beginnings of Girls' Education in the Native Administration Schools in Northern Nigeria, 1930–1945." *Journal of African History* 26, no. 1 (1985): 93–109.

Tomlinson, Thomas Symonds, and Gordon Kennet Knight-Bruce. *Law Reports Containing Cases Determined by the High Court for Zanzibar and on Appeal Therefrom by the Court of Appeal for Eastern Africa and by the Privy Council.* Vol. 3, 1923–27. London: Waterlow and Sons, 1928.

Topan, Farouk. "From Mwana Kupona to Mwavita: Representations of Female Status in Swahili Literature." In *Swahili Modernities: Culture, Politics, and Identity on the East Coast of Africa*, edited by Pat Caplan and Topan, 213–27. Trenton: Africa World Press, 2004.

———. "Vugo: A Virginity Celebration Ceremony among the Swahili of Mombasa." *African Languages and Cultures* 8, no. 1 (1995): 87–107.

Tsing, Anna Lowenhaupt. *Friction: An Ethnography of Global Connection.* Princeton: Princeton University Press, 2005.

Tucker, Judith E. "Muftīs and Matrimony: Islamic Law and Gender in Ottoman Syria and Palestine." *Islamic Law and Society* 1, no. 3 (1994): 265–300.

———. *Women, Family, and Gender in Islamic Law.* Themes in Islamic Law 3. Cambridge: Cambridge University Press, 2008.

Turner, Victor W. *The Forest of Symbols: Aspects of Ndembu Ritual.* Ithaca: Cornell University Press, 1967.

United Nations. Department of International Economic and Social Affairs. *Relationships between Fertility and Education: A Comparative Analysis of World Fertility Survey Data for Twenty-Two Developing Countries.* New York: United Nations, 1983.

———. Department for Economic and Social Information and Policy Analysis. *Women's Education and Fertility Behaviour: Recent Evidence from the Demographic and Health Surveys.* New York: United Nations, 1995.

———. UNICEF. "Basic Profile: Mtwara Rural District, Mtwara Region." Dar es Salaam: UNICEF Tanzania, 2008.

United Republic of Tanzania. National Bureau of Statistics. "Tanzania Demographic and Health Survey 2004." MEASURE DHS, ICF Macro, Calverton, MD, 2004.

———. "Tanzania Demographic and Health Survey 2010." MEASURE DHS, ICF Macro, Calverton, MD, 2010.

———. "Tanzania HIV/AIDS and Malaria Indicator Survey 2007–8." MEASURE DHS, ICF Macro, Calverton, MD, 2008.

———. "Tanzania Population and Housing Census 2002." MEASURE DHS, ICF Macro, Calverton, MD, 2002.

United Republic of Tanzania. National Bureau of Statistics and ORC Macro. *Tanzania Demographic and Health Survey 2004–5.* Dar es Salaam: National Bureau of Statistics, 2005.

United Republic of Tanzania. Ministry of Education and Vocational Training. "Basic Education Statistics, 2010 Regional." Ministry of Education and Vocational Training, 2010. http://dl.dropbox.com/u/4464339/TZ%20BEST%20regional%202010.xls.

Van Hoven, Ed. "Local Tradition or Islamic Precept? The Notion of Zakāt in Wuli (Eastern Senegal)." *Cahiers d'études africaines* 36, no. 144 (1996): 703–22.

Waller, Richard. "Rebellious Youth in Colonial Africa." *Journal of African History* 47, no. 1 (2006): 77–92.

Walley, Christine J. *Rough Waters: Nature and Development in an East African Marine Park.* Princeton: Princeton University Press, 2010.

Weiss, Brad. *Street Dreams and Hip Hop Barbershops: Global Fantasy in Urban Tanzania.* Tracking Globalization. Bloomington: Indiana University Press, 2009.

Werbner, Pnina. "The Virgin and the Clown: Ritual Elaboration in Pakistani Migrants' Weddings." *Man* 21, no. 2 (1986): 227–50.

Westermarck, Edward. "Marriage Ceremonies in Morocco." *Sociological Review* 5, no. 3 (July 1912): 187–201.

Weule, Karl. *Native Life in East Africa: The Results of an Ethnological Research Expedition.* Translated by Alice Werner. London: Sir Isaac Pitman and Sons, 1909.

Wolf, Angelika. "AIDS, Morality and Indigenous Concepts of Sexually Transmitted Diseases in Southern Africa." *Africa Spectrum* 36, no. 1 (2001): 97–107.

World Bank. "World Development Report 1980." New York: Oxford University Press for the World Bank, 1980.

———. "World Development Report 1993: Investing in Health." New York: Oxford University Press for the World Bank, 1993.

Wortham, Stanton E. F. "Socialization beyond the Speech Event." *Journal of Linguistic Anthropology* 15, no. 1 (2005): 95–112.

Wright, Marcia. *Strategies of Slaves and Women: Life-Stories from East/Central Africa.* New York: Lilian Barber Press, 1993.

Würth, Anna. "A Sana'a Court: The Family and the Ability to Negotiate." *Islamic Law and Society* 2, no. 3 (1995): 320–40.

Yahya-Othman, Saida. "If the Cap Fits: Kanga Names and Women's Voice in Swahili Society." *Swahili Forum* 4 (1997): 135–49.

Zein, Abdul Hamid M. el-. *The Sacred Meadows: A Structural Analysis of Religious Symbolism in an East African Town.* Evanston: Northwestern University Press, 1974.

Contributors

NADINE BECKMANN is a senior lecturer in social anthropology at the University of Roehampton. She previously carried out postdoctoral research at the Universities of Oxford and Bradford and was lecturer in International Development at the University of Leeds. Her research focuses on HIV/AIDS and Islam, sexuality and reproduction, biopolitics, and notions of morality and uncertainty in Zanzibar. Recent publications include *Strings Attached: AIDS and the Rise of Transnational Connections in Africa* (2014), coedited by Alessandro Gusman and Catrine Shroff; "'The Quest for Trust in the Face of Uncertainty'—Managing Pregnancy Outcomes in Zanzibar" (2014); and "Responding to Medical Crises: AIDS Treatment, Responsibilisation and the Logic of Choice." She has published numerous book chapters and journal articles, including in *Development and Change,* the *Journal of East African Studies, Anthropology and Medicine,* and *Afriche e Orienti.*

PAT CAPLAN is Emeritus Professor of Social Anthropology at Goldsmiths, University of London. She has been carrying out research on Mafia Island, Tanzania, since 1965 on topics including kinship, gender relations, political economy and development, personal narratives, food and health, spirit possession, and local perceptions of modernity. She has published numerous books and articles on these topics and her most recent book is the biography of a Tanzanian activist: *Mikidadi wa Mafia: Maisha ya mwnaharati na familia yake nchini Tanzania* (2014). An enlarged English version will shortly be appearing. She has also done research in Chennai, Madras, for many years and, in the last two decades, in South Wales.

CORRIE DECKER is an associate professor of history at the University of California, Davis. She researches the history of development, education, gender, sexuality, and childhood in twentieth-century eastern Africa. She is the author of *Mobilizing Zanzibari Women: The Struggle for Respectability and Self-Reliance in Colonial East Africa* (2014), and her work has appeared in *Past and Present,* the *Journal of Women's History,* and the *International Journal of African Historical Studies.*

REBECCA GEARHART, professor of anthropology, Illinois Wesleyan University, has spent over twenty-five years conducting ethnographic research in coastal Kenya. Recent publications include *Contesting Identities: The Mijikenda and Their Neighbors in Kenyan Coastal Society,* coedited by Linda Giles (2014); "Concepts of Illness among the Swahili of Lamu, Kenya," coauthored by Munib Said Abdulrehman (2014); and "Seeing Life through the Eyes of Swahili Children of Lamu, Kenya: A Visual Anthropology Approach" (2013).

LINDA L. GILES is an independent scholar and adjunct assistant professor at Illinois Wesleyan University. She received her PhD in anthropology from the University of Texas at Austin and taught in the Anthropology Program at Illinois State University until her retirement. Her research area is the East African coast, where she has conducted research primarily among the Swahili and Mijikenda peoples on spirit possession. Articles focusing on that research have been published in *Africa, Anthropological Quarterly, Mankind Quarterly,* and several edited volumes and encyclopedias. More recent research has focused on the theft, global trade in, and repatriation of Mijikenda ancestor memorial statues, conducted with John Mitsanze and Monica Udvardy and published in *Cultural Survival* (2004) and *American Anthropologist* (2003). She has also coedited, with Rebecca Gearhart, *Contesting Identities: The Mijikenda and Their Neighbors in Kenyan Coastal Society* (2014).

MEGHAN C. HALLEY, PhD, MPH, completed her BA in anthropology with a concentration in African studies in 2005 from the

University of Wisconsin–Madison. She completed her MPH with a concentration in adolescent health in 2009, and her PhD in medical anthropology in 2012, both at Case Western Reserve University. She is currently an assistant research anthropologist at the Palo Alto Medical Foundation Research Institute in Palo Alto, California. While her international research interests continue to include youth and cultural change in rural East Africa, her current domestic research focuses on issues of culture and health within the US healthcare system, particularly in the area of cancer screening and treatment.

SUSAN F. HIRSCH, a cultural anthropologist and professor in the School for Conflict Analysis and Resolution at George Mason University, has written widely on law, conflict, and gender in East Africa and the United States. She is the author of *In the Moment of Greatest Calamity: Terrorism, Grief, and a Victim's Quest for Justice* (2006); *Pronouncing and Persevering: Gender and the Discourses of Disputing in an African Islamic Court* (1998); *Contested States: Law, Hegemony, and Resistance* (1994); and articles about reflexive ethnography, transitional justice, and hate speech, among other topics. Her most recent book, coauthored with E. Franklin Dukes, is titled *Mountaintop Mining in Appalachia: Understanding Stakeholders and Change in Environmental Conflict* (2014), and appears in the book series Studies in Conflict, Justice, and Social Change, which she coedits. She is a past president of the Association for Political and Legal Anthropology and a former trustee of the Law and Society Association.

SUSI KREHBIEL KEEFE is visiting professor of anthropology at St. Olaf College in the Department of Anthropology and Sociology. She received her AM and PhD in anthropology from Brown University, where she was also a predoctoral trainee in anthropological demography in the Population Studies and Training Center. Based on over two years of ethnographic fieldwork in northern and coastal Tanzania, she has published articles and chapters on Islam and ethics, marriage and kinship, and modern love among Pare and Swahili women.

KJERSTI LARSEN holds a PhD in social anthropology from University of Oslo. She is a professor in the Department of Ethnography, Museum of Cultural History, University of Oslo, where she was head of department from 2003 to 2006. Larsen has been adjunct professor at the Department of Development Studies, Norwegian University of Life Sciences, and a visiting scholar at various institutions, including the Centre for Cross-Cultural Research on Women, University of Oxford; Centre d'Études Africaines, École des Hautes Études en Sciences Sociales; and the International Institute for the Study of Islam in the Modern World, Leiden University. She conducts research in Muslim societies in East Africa, both on the Swahili coast, particularly on Zanzibar (1984–present), and in Northern Sudan, mostly in the Bayoda desert (1997–2008). Her publications include the monograph *Where Humans and Spirits Meet* (2008) and the edited volume *Knowledge, Renewal and Religion* (2009). Her main interests include ritual and performance; religion, knowledge, and gender; everyday-life politics and social change; modernity, identity, and mobility in African societies and the Indian Ocean region; and Islam and Muslim practices.

ELISABETH MCMAHON is an associate professor of history at Tulane University. Her book *Slavery and Emancipation in Islamic East Africa: From Honor to Respectability* (2013) looks at the gendered social dynamics of the abolition of slavery for all strata of society living on Pemba Island, in Tanzania. She has published numerous book chapters and articles, including in the *Journal of Social History*, the *International Journal of African Historical Studies*, the *Journal of Women's History*, and the *Women's History Review*.

ERIN E. STILES is an associate professor of anthropology at the University of Nevada, Reno, where she also chairs the interdisciplinary minor program in religious studies. Her research focuses on the intersections of religion, law, and gender. She has conducted ethnographic research on marital disputing and Islamic law in Zanzibar and is currently developing a project on religion and marriage in Utah. She is the author of *An Islamic Court in*

Context: An Ethnographic Study of Judicial Reasoning (2009). She has published several book chapters and her work has also appeared in *Africa, Islamic Law and Society,* and *Ethnology.*

KATRINA DALY THOMPSON is an associate professor of African languages and literature at the University of Wisconsin, Madison, where she directs the African languages program and serves on the steering committees for African studies, religious studies, and the Lubar Institute for the Study of the Abrahamic Religions. Her research concerns power and identity in African discourse, mainly in Shona and Swahili, and her current project focuses on Swahili talk about sexuality within the context of Islamic taboos. She is the author of *Zimbabwe's Cinematic Arts: Language, Power, Identity* (2012), and her work has appeared in *Modern Language Journal, Critical Discourse Studies,* the *Journal of Religion in Africa, Discourse and Society, Language in Society,* and the *Journal of African Cultural Studies.*

Index

Tsing, Anna, 18, 143–45
Tucker, Judith, 249, 265
Tumbatu Island, 250
Turner, Victor, 233

udhu (ritual purity), 131, 133, 190
uganga, 210, 293, 294, 305, 312–14, 316, 318n
ukungwi, 17, 33–34, 53
Unguja, 4, 16, 24, 36, 60, 61, 118, 123, 201, 227, 245, 246, 249, 250, 251, 253, 266
United Arab Emirates, 3, 271
United States, 6, 8, 185, 200, 231, 334
Universities Mission to Central Africa, 78
unmarried girls and women, 51, 119, 121, 170, 172, 183, 187, 192, 201, 230, 252
unyago, 7, 14–15, 17, 21, 24, 34, 85, 92, 137, 148, 151, 153–55, 179–81, 210–14, 220–23, 226, 231–34, 236–37, 252, 301–2
unyago ya kutapisha, 212–13, 217, 218, 232
utani. See joking relationships
Utendi wa Mwana Kupona, 171

virginity, 122, 121, 131, 200, 223, 227, 281–82
virgins, 37, 88, 125, 126, 128, 194, 198, 211, 249, 251, 264–65, 280
vyombo, 173, 230, 233
vyou. See Qur'an schools

waganga. See mganga/waganga
wage earners, 271
wali, 62, 74, 75–77
Walley, Christine, 335
Wasini, 293, 304
Watumbatu (Mtumatu), 249, 268fn, 259
weddings: wedding ceremony, 169, 173, 302 (see also nikaha); wedding day, 129, 186, 278, 284; wedding dress, 8, 173; wedding feast, 282; wedding

guests, 122, 172, 179, ; wedding night, 122, 128, 252; wedding preparation, 19, 126, 168, 170, 172, 188, 226
Weiss, Brad, 355
Wete, 293
widowed, state of being, 61, 70, 72, 229, 230, 231, 332
wife, Muslim, 22, 169, 178, 179, 201, 203, 210, 226, 336
wifely behavior and duties, 179, 322
wives, outside, 332, 339
women, unmarried. See girls and women, unmarried
women's groups, 104–5
women's speech, 23, 174, 175–76, 182, 201–2
World War I, 7, 69
World War II, 37, 42, 44

Yemen, 5, 8, 11, 254, 278

Zanzibar, colonial, 15, 46, 154
Zanzibar, rural, 245
Zanzibar, urban, 17
Zanzibar Association for People with HIV/AIDS (ZAPHA+), 135
Zanzibar Education Advisory Committee, 45, 51
Zanzibar Government Girls School (ZGGS), 37, 49
Zanzibari Muslims, 17, 170, 177, 197, 200
Zanzibaris, 10, 37, 41, 117, 118, 120, 125, 137, 246
zar, 291, 319n
Zanzibar National Archives, 36
Zanzibar Town, 4, 17, 24, 51, 118, 121, 168–72, 178, 183, 188, 190, 201, 203, 209, 210, 212, 214, 222, 227, 228, 231, 232, 249, 292, 293, 295, 296, 298
el-Zein, Abdul Hamid, 285
zikiri, 137, 306, 307, 310, 314
zinaa, 119, 121, 131